Forest Society

Forest Society

A SOCIAL HISTORY OF PETEN, GUATEMALA

NORMAN B. SCHWARTZ

University of Pennsylvania Press   PHILADELPHIA

Library of Congress Cataloging-in-Publication Data

Schwartz, Norman B.
    Forest society: a social history of Petén, Guatemala / Norman B. Schwartz.
        p.   cm. — (University of Pennsylvania Press ethnohistory series)
    Includes bibliographical references and index.
    ISBN 0–8122–8248–5 (cloth). — ISBN 0–8122–1316–5 (pbk.)
    1. Indians of Central America—Guatemala—Petén (Dept.)—History.
    2. Mayas—History.   3. Ladino (Latin American people)—History.
    4. Ethnic relations—Guatemala—Petén (Dept.)   5. Chicle gum
    industry—Guatemala—Petén (Dept.)   6. Petén (Guatemala: Dept.)-
    -Economic conditions.   7. Petén (Guatemala: Dept.)—Social
    conditions.   I. Title.   II. Series: Ethnohistory series
    (Philadelphia, Pa.)
    F1465.1.P47S37   1990   90–41539
    972.81'2—dc20   CIP

Third paperback printing 1995

For Joseph H. Schwartz and
Bertha Goldberg Schwartz

Contents

Illustrations

Preface

This book is about the people of Petén, the northern lowlands of Guatemala, from the final Spanish conquest of the region in 1697 to modern times. The aim is to describe and to understand the history of social patterns and cultural standards in post-conquest Petén, in relation to the regional ecology and economy and also in relation to the broader national political economy. As will be seen, the cultural standards of the Peteneros include their own particular understanding of their history and the natural environment. Although the bulk of the material deals with the years between 1697 and the early 1970s, the period immediately preceding 1697 as well as the 1980s are discussed, in part to emphasize that the story begins and closes with the conquest of a distinctive Mesoamerican region.

The study combines historical reconstruction with ethnogaphy and with what is sometimes called ethnohistory. The historical account of Petén up to about the 1890s relies most heavily on the rich stores of colonial and post-colonial documents in the Archivo General de Centro América in Guatemala City and in the town halls, churches, and departmental capital of Petén. For the years roughly between the 1890s and 1960, archival research has been combined with lengthy, mostly open-ended interviews with older Peteneros. Several Peteneros, most notable among them the late don José María Soza, also have published histories of Petén or their own towns, and these, too, have been invaluable. Conventional ethnographic fieldwork and survey research was carried out on several occasions between 1960 and 1985 without neglecting the documentary records for those years, particularly documents housed in town halls and in the offices of FYDEP (Empresa Nacional de Fomento y Desarrollo Económico del Petén, National Enterprise for the Economic Development of the Petén), which effectively ruled Petén from 1960 to 1987. Field trips to Petén were made in 1960–1961 and 1974–1975 and the summers of 1970, 1978, 1980 and 1985. The author is most familiar with people and places in the central lake, great savanna, and northwestern sections of Petén, but over the years visits were made to all the other parts of Petén, except the far northeastern Aguas Turbias area and the far southwest corner, where the Usumacinta River runs into the Salinas River. Short trips also were made to the areas in western Belize and northern Alta Verapaz closest to Petén. Most of the ethnographic data on the so-called cooperatives strung beside the Pasión and Usumacinta Rivers were collected in the summers of 1975 and 1980. Most of the participant-observer data on chicle tree-tappers' forest camps in northwestern Petén were collected in late 1974 and early 1975.

Many of the anthropological studies of Guatemala concentrate on the more or less "traditional" Indian communities located in the central and western highlands of the republic. From these works, one learns that Ladinos (roughly, people of Indian or Spanish-Indian biological descent who are culturally and linguistically more Hispanic than Indian, and who are socially distinct from Indians) have oppressed Indians. A social history of lowland Petén reveals a somewhat different picture, one that shows Ladinos and Indians having a good deal in common—in domestic life, in everyday economic activities and, importantly, in relation to superordinate groups that would not identify themselves or be identified by others as either Indian or Ladino. To be sure, although many younger Peteneros do not consider ethnicity of much importance, it remains a delicate issue for older people, and it must be said that it is still correlated with variations in socioeconomic position. However, the point is that ethnic relations in Petén are different from those elsewhere in Guatemala, and over time they became better than those in other areas.

An attempt has been made to retain the flavor of Petén usage, for example, by writing San Pedrano instead of Sanpedrano. However, there is one exception. I decided to write "Petén," where many if not all Peteneros would prefer "El—the—Petén," because it seemed more natural to drop the "the" in a work written in English.

Finally, it will become clear shortly that the post-conquest history of the northern lowlands of Guatemala has been as neglected by scholars as the region itself has been neglected by southern Guatemalans. The intention here is to help overcome the scholarly neglect.

Acknowledgments

A study of this sort would not be possible without the help of many other people. Most of all, I am indebted to many Peteneros, too numerous to single out by name, for their courtesy and instruction. I must thank, too, chicleros not only from Petén but also from other parts of Guatemala, Belize, and Mexico, and settlers who have come to Petén since the 1960s. I have read somewhere that civilized behavior accompanied by humor and stoicism are the marks of a patrician. If so, there are patricians, poor and wealthy, in every corner of Petén. Participant-observation can be intrusive, but one would never know that from the way native Peteneros and more recent settlers behave. Wherever necessary pseudonyms were used to protect their privacy.

Among friends I may name, I am particularly indebted to Professor Ruben E. Reina, who in 1960 introduced me to Petén and guided my initial research work there. Since then, we have written together about the region and have shared our data. In this way I continue to benefit from Ben's insight into cultural processes and his knowledge of the history of Petén. Both of us were fortunate enough to meet and to talk at length on several occasions with don José María Soza. Professor Grant D. Jones and Dr. Lawrence H. Feldman also have generously shared their data with me. Larry provided me with documents he uncovered in Europe, and Grant read and helped shape Chapter Two of this study. Pierre Ventur helped me understand the role of the Kekchí of San Luis in Petén. Over the years, Professor Arthur J. Rubel patiently listened to a great deal of talk about Petén and helped me articulate my understanding of ethnic relations there. When I had problems deciphering and grasping the import of colonial documents, I counted on the expertise of Professor Juan A. Villamarin. For the organization of data used in many of the tables presented below, I relied on the competence and steady hand of David G. Schwartz Esq. Professor Karen Rosenberg did statistical analyses of data presented in Chapter Five. All the photographs in this book are mine, but Michael B. Schwartz's line drawings, several of which are reproduced here, reveal more than photographs can. Robert Schultz generously helped with the figures in Chapters Four and Five. Judith Villamarin and Professor James Sexton read the entire manuscript and made many editorial suggestions and stylistic corrections—very hard work, for which I am grateful. My thanks, too, to Professors James M. Taggart and Marshall J. Becker for needed moral support.

Lic. Luis Luján Muñoz and Lic. Francis Polo Sifontes, when they were serving their respective terms as Director of the Instituto de Antropología and Historia de Guatemala (IDAEH), and Dr. Flavio Rojas Lima, Secretary General of the Seminario de Integración Social de Guatemala helped me establish good working relationships with successive Promotors of FYDEP. A long list of middle level FYDEP staff, governors of Petén and their staffs, mayors and secretaries of the Petén *municipios*, and Catholic priests gave me free access to their archives and just as freely shared their observations and ideas about Petén. Since 1985, several Peteneros have been kind enough to maintain an active correspondence with me about matters of shared interest.

Over the years, the Latin American Studies Program and the Faculty Research Fund at the University of Delaware has supported my research. I also thank the University for giving me released time to work on the manuscript, most of which was completed in 1988. Acknowledgments are also made to Dean Helen P. Gouldner and Provost Richard B. Murray for their support and encouragement.

Delia T. Schwartz critically read the entire manuscript, with the belief that a decent respect for the complex experiences of others demands honesty and logic. Whatever is clear, reasonable, and compassionate in this study owes most to her sharp pen.

I know better than anyone that this book does not discharge my obligations to everyone in Petén and elsewhere who tried to improve the work. There are, as noted in several places in the text, lacunae in this study that others will fill. If their luck holds, they will be able to say thank you to as many friends as I am privileged to thank.

Introduction

This study is about the social history of Petén—the northernmost department of Guatemala—after the Spanish conquered it in 1697. It attempts to describe and account for post-conquest sociocultural changes and continuities in the region. This task involves, in part, explaining why despite many changes a Petenero magically transported forward from the early eighteenth century would feel reasonably at home in modern Petén, up to about 1970 at least.

Recently MacLeod has called for more regional histories of Guatemala, because although there are general histories of the republic, "monographic regional work on which such general studies perhaps should have been based has hardly begun" (1983:189). Such works are especially lacking for peripheral areas of Guatemala such as Petén—the tropical lowland zone between Yucatán to the north and the Guatemalan highlands to the south. In the case of Petén, scholars have been overwhelmingly more concerned with pre-Hispanic Maya than with post-conquest Peteneros, but there are exceptions. There are several essays by Reina and by the present writer, and Jones's (1989) book on Maya resistance to Spanish rule in southeastern Yucatán and Petén in the decades before 1697. Soza, a native Petenero, has written a more commemorative work (1970) which also contains much valuable historical information. In distinction to Jones, this study takes up events after the conquest, from 1697 to modern times. It also is more analytic and more anthropologically oriented than Soza's work.

To situate the study, it should be noted that in recent years Mesoamerican anthropologists have been shifting the focuses of their research. If they are not always looking at new events, they are examining them in new ways and in larger national and world contexts. There is, for example, less inclination to study the "little community" in structural-functional terms and more to see it as an outcome of mutually formative microsocial and macrosocial processes. There is less concern with reporting the survival of pre-Hispanic traditions among Indians and more with understanding how Indians have resisted domination and, in doing so, have created distinctive cultural patterns linked to local autonomy. More generally, greater attention is being given to relationships between ecology and society; between state power and the content of local community culture; between world economics, regional politics, and subregional sociocultural patterns; between capitalist development and the contradictions among social class, ethnicity, and community. There are a growing number of studies on the violent conflicts in which the state opposes its own society, and also on what may be the final, destructive conquest of tropical lowland forests. Along with this, historians and historically-minded anthropologists are more than ever examining subnational regions and uncovering the diverse outcomes of the processes and relationships mentioned above. (The literature is large and growing rapidly, but to illustrate, compare Adams 1957 with Adams 1970, or the first *Heritage of Conquest* — Tax 1952 — with the second one — Kendall, Hawkins, and Bossen 1983. See, too, MacLeod and Wasserstrom 1983a and Chambers and Young 1979.)

Although my major concern is the social history of one particular place, the study of that place has something to say about the broader concerns noted above. An appreciation of what has happened in Petén since 1697 can contribute to emerging generalizations about the factors that shape and that ameliorate or temper relations between conquerors and the conquered; interconnections among ethnicity, community, and social class; interdependencies among tropical ecology, enclaved economies, and social formation; and finally, contemporary colonization and so-called development of tropical lowlands.

Petén is a distinct geo-cultural region of Guatemala. In many ways, it has more in common with western Belize and southern Yucatán than with Guatemala. Nonetheless, it belongs to that troubled nation. Peteneros have had and still have to live with the problems that beset other Guatemalans, including ethnic conflict, contradictions between community and social class, poverty, legal injustice, political repression, dependent economic development, and most recently a horrible civil war. Since the 1970s, Peteneros also have felt the impact of colonization, economic growth, and deforestation that characterize so much of contemporary life throughout the tropical lowlands of Latin America. As will be seen, Peteneros have worked out their own solutions to these problems.

The post-conquest history of Petén may be roughly divided into several periods: early colonial 1697–1720s, and later colonial 1720s–1821; independence 1821–1890s; enclave economy 1890s–1970s; and modern colonization since the 1970s. Each period is treated in a separate chapter, except for that of the enclave economy, discussed in two chapters. For each period, local political and economic activities and their relations to larger systems are described. Social, economic, and political relationships between local lower and upper sectors, and relationships among different ethnic (status) groups, including those within the lower sectors, also are described. Throughout, I have tried to report what Peteneros have done as well as what was done to them. Most of the time, they have had to contend with natural and macrosocial circumstances beyond their control, but they also have been self-conscious actors who have qualified the meaning and impact of these circumstances in their lives. They have created a society and a culture which—like their tropical forest habitat—is both part of and different from the rest of Guatemala.

Reference to ethnic relations illustrates one of the things the last sentence means. Unlike most of the western highlands and southern coast of Guatemala, in Petén relations between the Creole descendants of the Spanish (hereafter simply called Creoles), Ladinos, and Indians are moderate, one reason Peteneros boast Petén is "democratic, not like the rest of Guatemala." What goes on elsewhere in the republic does not occur in Petén. Indians are not treated with open contempt (Manz 1988:141) or "brutality" (Smith 1988:231). Unlike Momostenango in the western highlands, in Petén the Ladinos do not run a "virtual fascist state," ruling the Indians "by an elaborate mix of terror and paternalism," and "virulent racism" (Carmack 1983:242, 244). Although through the centuries an undercurrent of mutual fear marked ethnic relations in Petén, these relations have gradually become less discriminatory. In this as in other ways, Petén stands apart from the larger society.

In explaining how what happened in Petén came about, and more broadly in recounting the social history of the Peteneros or of any people, there is inevitably an interplay between narration and theory. "Theory" is a bit grand in this context because the occasion is not used to present an extended argument about basic assumptions, from which flow a series of logically related propositions tested against experience, and so on. Rather, the hope is that the following brief discussion will make clear the "theoretical" approach favored by the author.

The argument is that relations between the material base of a society (productive processes applied to a given physical/natural environment; patterns of effective, that is, economic control over labor and resources; and demography) and the struggle of individuals and groups to control resources, which implies a struggle for political domination, account for much of the society's social history and the ideas its people have about their history. This position assumes that people first and foremost strive to maintain and, where possible, to improve their physical well-being and safety, working with the materials at hand, which often turn out to be scarce. This is not to say that the ideas people have about living well and about justice are merely rationalizations (although they may be that, too) for practical adaptations to the environment, *de facto* control of resources, or political maneuvers. As Cohen (1988:133) says, citing the favorite book of his childhood, the house you build "depends" not only "on where you live and what you have to build with" but also on what you think about where you live. The ideas people have about who they are and who they should be affect what they do, but in general what they in fact are doing today is, in my view, more consequential for what they can and will do tomorrow. This seems particularly true when long stretches of history are considered. What some call "values," self-referential ideation, and so forth, and what Cohen prefers to call "spiritual phenomena," are or seem to be critical for short-term decisions, but "independently determined material and economic" sequences (Cohen 1988:133), related (I would add) to ecological considerations, demography, and political struggles, are more important for long-run patterns in social history. The argument does not require any insistence that these sequences "determine" spiritual phenomena, although they probably exert a selective influence on which of them will endure. Rather, it is to say that spiritual phenomena lack causal primacy with respect to material sequences, and the social history based on them. None of these relationships are linear, there is some indeterminacy among them, and none is a fixed proscenium for the others. For example, a group of people may have "spiritually" derived ideas about human nature that promote gender equality, which in turn create demands that men and women be given equal access to, say, factory employment, and that might eventually happen. But the argument here is that this is morely likely to occur when demands for labor are high and men (for whatever reason) are away. If the situation persists long enough, it will give a selective advantage to ideas about gender equality, which may not have been popular before, and this in turn will affect ideas about human nature. That women now have an independent source of income may also more or less force men to acknowledge gender equality, even to argue that what in fact is should be. In other situations, managers may respond favorably to ideas about gender differences, perhaps for philosophical reasons, but it does not detract from their response that playing up gender differences may weaken labor unity. The examples are oversimplified and do not take into account the history of "material and economic" sequences that set the terms for relations between labor and management, but they do illustrate the type of argument made here. Nor does it invalidate the argument to grant that there are also aggressive and appetitive motives for behavior that the analytic terms used here cannot account for without remainder. It is, in other words, important to keep in mind that people can be the subjects as well as the objects of their own history. But, these and similar considerations qualify rather than defeat the contention that social history is largely—not entirely—the outcome of the interplay between the material base and group (or "class" if one prefers) conflict.

Although the argument is a soft form of cultural (rather than historical, strictly speaking) materialism, it rejects the counter-argument that the ideas people have about who they are and who they should be count *most* in social history and analyses of it. Kristol clearly voices an important implication of the counter-argument when he asserts that the "causes of economic prosperity" are

> cultural in the largest sense of that term, involving a sense of self, and of the relation between oneself and others, which in turn generates attitudes and practices that are favorable or inimical to economic growth . . . if India or Peru were inhabited by Swiss or Dutchmen, they would be fairly prosperous countries not poor ones (1983:174).

To dismiss Kristol by saying "if things were different they would be different" misses his point about which variables count most in an analysis of social history.

The argument in the present volume is different: If the Swiss had lived in Guatemala when the Spanish conquered the country in the sixteenth century, they would have become an impoverished, subordinate status or class group, with a distinct relation to plantation production. True, they might wear feathers in their hats to distinguish themselves from ethnic others, might yodel for the tourist trade, and might possess a truly profound philosophy, the surface of which might be seen in their accounting techniques, but that they would be prosperous is quite doubtful. Moreover, their ideas about self and society, whatever their source, would affect how willing or unwilling they were to make alliances with poor workers from some other ethnic group, but whether in fact they were in a position to make that choice would depend much more on economic conditions and the distribution of power that their ideas did not in the first instance create. A lot depends on what you think, but a lot of what you think *about* and what you do depends on where you live and what you have to work with.

In short, to describe and explain what Peteneros did and what they thought about it is necessary to trace the history of relations among the material base of the society, cooperative and contentious struggles to control natural and human resources, communal and ethnic groups, and the value-laden ideas Peteneros have had about society, as well as the larger context of the regional society. All of these factors and the relationships among them are quite complex, and the analysis must be complex as well to account for major recurrent patterns in the sprawl of historical experience. In the event, the theoretical perspective taken here is hardly novel. More interesting is how that perspective is used to discuss particular regional histories.

To use Farriss's (1983) terms, from the beginning of post-conquest times, what distinguished Petén within Mesoamerica was a small population combined with a lack of natural resources of interest to those outside the region. The colonial elite could not rely on Indian tribute as the basis of the economy. The colony depended on raising livestock (cattle, horses and mules) for Yucatecan markets, but crown and private ranches did not flourish. No one was very rich; the majority depended on subsistence swidden cultivation, the elite were forced to concentrate on small-scale commerce and trade, and the state neglected the backwater region, all of which set the stage for moderate though hardly democratic relations between status (ethnic) groups and social sectors.

During the early eighteenth century, as the new Peteneros adapted to material circumstances, and partly because of those circumstances, they also built a society in which community, ethnicity, and socioeconomic position became commutative, and in which there was a marked continuity of social status. Each community acquired a distinctive social reputation, a distinctive ethnic and social signature, partly based on its place in a trading network centering on Flores, the administrative headquarters of Petén and the home of the Creole elite. Although Creoles, Ladinos, and Indians learned from each other, the social composition of each status group remained distinct, and the ethnically stratified social system was relatively stable. In the sparsely settled frontier region, the new Peteneros created enduring social and cultural patterns.

After independence from Spain in 1821, the Creole elite in Flores could not develop large commercial plantations and, unlike their counterparts in the highlands, consequently had no incentives to control land and labor. Coffee production, which after 1870 had such a dramatic impact on all aspects of life in Guatemala, had no impact on Petén. Rather, because the Caste War in Yucatán (1847–1855) and the Carrera Revolution (1839) disrupted trade with Yucatán, the Flores elite strengthened commercial ties with British Honduras (Belize), despite which the already sluggish economy grew yet more stagnant. This helps explain why there were few differences between poor Ladino and poor Indian farmers in Petén. Nevertheless, despite many similarities between the Ladinos and the Indians, status differences between them persisted into the early part of the twentieth century.

Then, in the 1890s, Peteneros began to produce and to export chicle, a natural base for chewing gum, for North American manufacturers. Although Mexican and British Honduran companies had exported lumber from Petén before the 1890s, it was the chicle industry that integrated the economy of the region into world capitalist markets. From the 1890s until about 1970, chicle was the economic basis of the region. For years, Peteneros called chicle "white gold" (*oro blanco*).

The production of chicle sharpened social class distinctions in Petén, but without enfeebling ascriptive formations based on community and ethnicity. In the annual cycle of production, *oro blanco* alternately weakened and reinforced community as a principle of organization. Discrimination against Indians was eased by the chicle industry, and it was further lessened by the short-lived political reforms of 1944–1954. Unlike most other regions of Guatemala, in Petén ethnicity is no longer a primary criterion for making economic or (most of the time) political decisions, and outward cultural differences between Indians and Ladinos have largely disappeared. Nonetheless, Indians and Ladinos still tend to marry endogamously and Indians have not achieved parity with non-Indians. The lack of parity is affected partly by underdevelopment and partly by persistent relationships between family, ethnicity, community, and social class.

The technology and ecology of chicle production in combination with laws prohibiting private ownership of chicle trees largely determined relations between labor and management in the chicle industry. Management, usually called "contractors" in Petén, could not gain exclusive ownership of the means of production and could not directly supervise the necessarily widely dispersed mobile labor force. Chicle tree tappers (chicleros) were conscious of their common class position, but the technology and ecology of production as well as the political climate prevented them from acting as a unified group. Contractors, too, shared a common class position, but intense competition for chicleros often fragmented their unity, while contractors and chicleros maintained a mix of mutually suspicious, labile patron-client and impersonal economic relations with each other.

For all its importance, *oro blanco* did not generate development in Petén. Although foreign chewing gum companies repatriated most of the profit from chicle, the industry did increase the wealth of the traditional merchant elite in Flores. But for want of opportunities, the elite did not invest profits in new forms of domestic production, and the chicle industry did not spin off new productive activities within the department. Because of the connections between chicle production and commercial trade, the industry not only increased the economic gap between the elite and lower sector Indians and Ladinos but also reinforced preexisting exchange relations between them. The chicle industry had a profound affect on individual lives, but it did not change the structure of the host society.

What Peteneros call the "fall" (*caída*) of chicle began in the late 1960s and early 1970s and overlaps in time state-led efforts to colonize and develop the northern lowlands. Since about 1966, there has been a tremendous increase in population, farming, ranching, logging, oil exploration, and commerce in Petén. There also has been extensive deforestation, unequal land distribution, decreasing access to land, increasing economic inequality, and political unrest. Deforestation puts the thin tropical soils and the poor smallholders who depend on them at risk, thereby feeding the fires of revolution. The second conquest of Petén threatens to replicate in the lowlands many of the conditions found in the highlands, including extremes of wealth and poverty, land hunger, environmental degradation, brutal repression, and endemic political violence.

From about 1720, after the Spanish consolidated their military gains in Petén, to about 1970, life in the region was relatively settled. The regional sociocultural system persisted, not in spite of changes but to an important degree because of them and what Peteneros did with them. The society was never egalitarian, democratic, or irenic, but degrees of socioeconomic inequality, repression, and unrest were not extreme. For centuries, most Peteneros were poor and had to cope with many political and natural hardships, but care must be taken to present the more satisfying as well as the harsh aspects of their lives. Until the late 1970s, they had open access to land, the elite were more concerned with commerce—even during the heyday of *oro blanco*—than with dominion over land and labor, racism gradually waned, and life along the frontier was relatively peaceful and settled. Now, in the late twentieth century, frontier settlement has finally unsettled society in Petén.

The social history of this one particular subnational region contributes to understanding several of the large issues mentioned at the beginning of the Introduction. In particular, the discussion deals with the relationships among the material base of a society (production, ecology, economy, and demography), struggles to control resources, social organization, and social values. The major thesis of this study is that relationships between the material base of the local society and the struggle to control resources (which are affected by macrosocial processes) simultaneously gave Peteneros an opportunity and also compelled them to build a stable moderate society, marked by continuity of social status and commutative connections between ethnicity, community, and social class. Although this stresses the causative role of relations between material base and struggles over resources, it also concludes that the values attached to community and ethnicity cannot be reduced to them without remainder. In Petén, social and economic relations based on community and ethnicity co-exist with and are as basic as relations based on social class. Moreover, to paraphrase what Patch (1985:49) says of Yucatán, Peteneros, not just the wider society and economy, also were givers of the conditions of their lives. They have acted as well as been acted upon in history. Now, more than ever, Petén is an integral part of a deeply wounded society. Genuine relief is no more apparent there than in the rest of the republic. Exploring the history of Petén offers few if any answers about what to do in the present, but scholarship can provide one ingredient for an answer—reliable knowledge. The hope is that this has been done in combination with an appropriate appreciation of how one group of people have coped, and often admirably, with nature, society, and themselves.

Chapter One

Physical Environment and Population

"Although this is today one of the most difficult New World areas in which to live, it must have seemed an ideal environment to ancient Maya" (Morley and Brainerd 1956:13).

"The forest is rich and provides one with everything, but making a milpa [cultivated plot] in the forest is very chancey, *muy eventual*" (Petén farmer 1978).

Introduction

Up to about 1970 the physical environment of Petén remained substantially the same as it was in 1697 when the Spanish conquered Tayasal, the last independent Maya stronghold in the region. To untrained eyes, that is, to most of us, as late as 1970 Petén looked and felt like a tropical forest—much of it still does. The region is so densely forested that from an airplane most of it appears to be one vast, undifferentiated giant head of broccoli, though in fact the natural environment is quite heterogeneous. A person on the ground may have a sense of being in a humid lowland, well described by García Márquez in *One Hundred Years of Solitude* (1970). Scholarly descriptions of Petén's physical environment will qualify these sensations; however, it is helpful and faithful to experience, while reading them, to keep in the mind's eye an image of a tropical lowland frontier.

Since 1882, when boundary disputes with Mexico were settled, Petén has contained about 36,000 square kilometers of land, one-third of Guatemala's total land surface. As is commonly the case for Petén, official reports are not in complete agreement. Some authorities say Petén covers 35,854 square kilometers, and others say the figure is 37,000 (cf. Simmons, Tárano, and Pinto 1959:585; FAO/FYDEP 1970). Whatever the exact figure, the department—roughly equivalent to a province or state—of Petén is very large, twice the size of New Jersey in the United States and larger than all of the Netherlands.

Until the mid-1960s this vast region was sparsely populated. As late as 1964 there were but 25,207 people in the department, about 45 percent of

Table 1:1 Population of Petén, 1714–1986[a]

Year	Urban	Rural	Total	Year	Urban	Rural	Total
1714	—	—	3,027	1921	5,250	2,333	7,583
1778	—	—	2,555	1936	—	—	9,728
1839	—	—	6,327	1940	5,737	4,829	10,566
1845	—	—	5,203	1950	—	—	15,897
1858	—	—	6,407	1960	—	—	21,330
1869	—	—	8,817[b]	1964	11,285	13,922	25,207
1879	—	—	6,547	1973	21,148	42,978	64,126
1880	—	—	8,374	1978	32,409	88,365	120,774
1893	3,837	2,238	6,075	1981	—	—	186,488
1904	—	—	10,000	1986	—	—	300,000 (est.)

Sources: Aldana 1974; Berendt 1868:423; Feldman 1982:255; FYDEP 1977; Guerra 1871; Juarros 1823; Mejía 1904; Méndez Zetina 1985; Morley 1938 I:1; del Ollo 1870; Thompson 1970:65; Valenzuela 1879.

[a]"Urban" refers to township capital and "rural" to village and subvillage population. The figures must be treated with caution for several reasons: there are discrepancies among sources; colonial censuses often excluded children under seven years of age; and in the eighteenth and nineteenth centuries, Indians in western and northern Petén were undercounted or uncounted, as are Mexicans in northwestern Petén today. Data become more accurate from 1950 on. The pre-Columbian Classic Maya population in Petén may have been over one million. In 1697, there were at least 60,000–80,000 Indians in Petén (Morley 1938 I:68–73; Soza 1970:479).

[b]This excludes 1,500 so-called "nomads" (perhaps Lacandón or Cehach Indians in western and northwesten Petén) who were not regularly included in censuses.

them residing in twelve small towns and the rest living in still smaller rural villages. In the early 1960s the national government opened Petén to colonization and land distribution, and since then the population has increased tenfold. At least 50 percent of the growth is due to in-migration. By 1973 the rural village population was double that of town population, and by 1986 there were probably about 300,000 people in the department (Table 1:1). What had been an isolated, relatively peaceful hinterland was now an increasingly well-populated, turbulent new frontier attracting landless campesinos (countrymen) from crowded Guatemalan highlands and Pacific coastal regions, well-capitalized cattlemen, foreign and national logging companies, bureaucrats, revolutionaries, and foreign entrepreneurs eager to exploit forest resources, including oil.

Until about 1970, 70 to 80 percent of Petén was densely forested, but since then the rate at which farmers, ranchers, and loggers have been

Map 1: Petén and Adjacent Regions

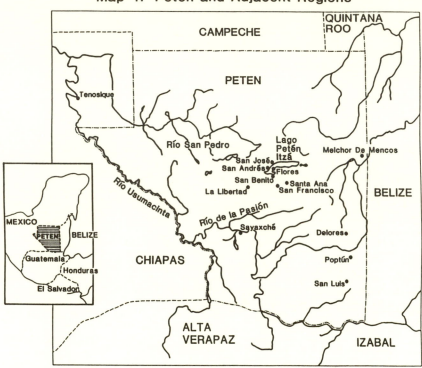

cutting back the forests has been increasing. Some 10 to 12 percent of the region was and is covered by highly acidic grasslands not well-suited to rain-fed agriculture. The remainder is taken up by lakes, swamps, and rivers (Simmons et al. 1959:571–82; Teracena de la Cerda 1974; Wiseman 1978). Between 1970 and 1986 small-scale farmers, cattlemen, lumbermen, and road builders were clearing the forests at such an accelerating rate that by 1985 some government officials claimed that 50 percent or more of Petén had been deforested (Field Notes 1985).

As for modern population centers, Flores, the capital of Petén since 1699, is located on an island, a *petén* in Maya, in Lake Petén Itzá (Map 1:1). For Peteneros this is *the* Lake and, appropriately enough, Flores, officially the only "city" in the department, is roughly at the geographic center of Petén. South of the Lake lie the great savannas of the region. Santa Ana, San

Table 1:2 Modern Land Distances, Petén, in Kilometers

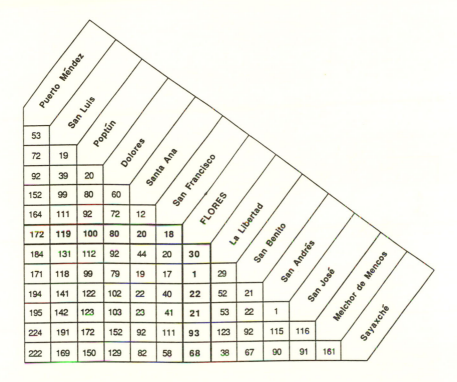

Puerto Méndez	San Luis	Poptún	Dolores	Santa Ana	San Francisco	FLORES	La Libertad	San Benito	San Andrés	San José	Melchor de Mencos	Sayaxché
53												
72	19											
92	39	20										
152	99	80	60									
164	111	92	72	12								
172	119	100	80	20	18							
184	131	112	92	44	20	30						
171	118	99	79	19	17	1	29					
194	141	122	102	22	40	22	52	21				
195	142	123	103	23	41	21	53	22	1			
224	191	172	152	92	111	93	123	92	115	116		
222	169	150	129	82	58	68	38	67	90	91	161	

Note: By water, the distance between Flores and San Andrés is 3 kilometers and between Flores and San José it is 3.5 kilometers.

Francisco, and La Libertad, capital towns (municipal centers or simply *pueblos*) of their respective like-named townships (*municipios*), are found on the plains, all within 30 kilometers of Flores (see modern land distances, Table 1:2; Map 2). Less noted in the scholarly literature is a much smaller but important savanna approximately 22 kilometers northwest of San Andrés, another town (*pueblo*). North of the Lake there are steeply inclined tree-covered ridges which eventually lower and thin out into the scrub and bush country of Yucatán, Mexico. North of the *pueblos* of San Andrés and San José the population is still relatively sparse. South of the grasslands there are forested ridges extending up to the mountains of Alta Verapaz,

Map 2: Petén, Guatemala

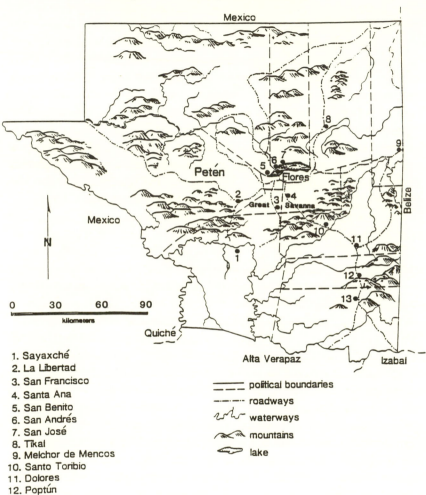

1. Sayaxché
2. La Libertad
3. San Francisco
4. Santa Ana
5. San Benito
6. San Andrés
7. San José
8. Tikal
9. Melchor de Mencos
10. Santo Toribio
11. Dolores
12. Poptún
13. San Luis

Guatemala. The hills and upland pastures of the southeast embrace the
pueblos of Dolores and Poptún. The highest elevations in Petén, 700 to
1,000 meters, are found in the rugged pine country of the far southeast,
near the *pueblo* San Luis. The Usumacinta River, "the father of Central
American rivers," forms Petén's western border with Mexico. The Chiapan

lowlands of Mexico are on the western side of the Usumacinta. The river *pueblo* of Sayaxché is located on the Pasión River, which flows west to join the Usumacinta. The Mopán River flows between Petén and Belize (formerly British Honduras) on the eastern side of the department. Melchor de Mencos, a border *pueblo*, sits alongside the Mopán. San Benito, a town on the mainland just opposite Flores, is adjacent to Santa Elena, officially a village subordinate to Flores. Together, Flores-San Benito-Santa Elena form a triangle, the largest urban concentration in the department.

Presumably in pre-Columbian times and certainly since 1697, the location of lakes, plains, forests, mountains, and rivers has had an important impact on the location and ethnic composition of the major population centers of Petén. The point will be discussed in Chapter 2, but first the physical environment is examined in somewhat greater detail.

Geography, Flora, and Fauna

The geology of Petén is marked by limestone folds and ridges running east to west. These form low, irregular surfaces, rising 100 to 300 meters above sea level in most of the department. The area north of Lake Petén Itzá, a geological continuation of the Yucatán Peninsula, contains many sinks, poljes, caverns, and underground streams, but relatively little surface water. Save for the plains, the region south of the Lake appears to have more surface water. The Maya Mountains of southern Belize, which reach into the far southeastern corner of Petén, are linked to the Antillean orogenic belt, "a region of geological thrusting and mountain building that sweeps east from the Guatemalan highlands into the lowlands" (Rice 1978:36). Here elevations rise to over 1,000 meters, very much higher than anywhere else in Petén. These mountains along with others form the boundary between Petén and Alta Verapaz, and those beyond Sayaxché box in the lowlands of Petén on the southeast, the south, and southwest (Lundell 1937:3).

The east-west ridges of the north and the south have formed a line of water-filled depressions on an "east-west fault fracture roughly coinciding with 17° north latitude" (Rice 1978:37). This is the interior drainage basin of central Petén, roughly 100 km long east-west and 30 km wide north-south. The string of lakes in the basin lacks a surface outflow to ocean waters. Lake Petén Itzá, some 34 km long and 5 km wide, is the largest lake in the basin.

There are numerous other lakes in the central basin. Going from east to west they are the Sacnab, Yaxhá, Champoxte, Macanché, Salpeten, Quexil, Petenxil, Petén Itzá, Picu, Sacpúy, and Zotz. Some very small lagunas and ponds also are located along the fault line. Several large lakes, for example, Laguna Perdida, are located west of and beyond the fault line. The lakes along the fault fracture rise and fall rather dramatically in roughly a forty year cycle.

The great plains begin some 12 km south of Flores and continue up to the Subín River. A range of low hills and bush separate the Lake from the irregularly shaped plains. These grasslands cover reddish acidic plasticine soils, contain many sinkholes (hollows in the limestone) and are low lying, varying from 10 to 80 meters above sea level (Lundell 1937:81–88). Many of the small hills on the plains are conical, resembling teats. Plains vegetation appears to be dominated by scrubby trees, particularly the fruit-bearing *nance (Byrsonima crassifolia)* and the *saha*. Although rainfall patterns vary from year to year, the grasslands are generally drier than other regions of Petén, and in some years drinking water is a scarce commodity during the dry season (roughly January to April), especially around La Libertad, which is at the heart of the plains and some 30 km from Flores. The southeastern hills begin their rise well outside the town of Dolores, and there is good grazing land around Dolores and Poptún.

The Ixcán and Azul Rivers drain northeast Petén, the latter flowing northeast and turning southeast to join the Hondo River in Belize and finally emptying its waters into Chetumal Bay. The Holmul River, rising in the extensive Bajo de Santa Fé, drains part of northeastern and eastern Petén. These rivers, like others of Petén, are very low during the dry season.

The Mopán River, a western branch of the Belize River, rises in the Maya Mountains. The Mopán drains east central Petén and then flows northeast to drain some of the eastern swamps. This river and two of its major streams, the Salsipuedes and the Dolores, were sites for mahogany cutting in the past. At times, even during the rainy season, their waters did not rise high enough to float the logs into the deeper Belize River (Morley 1938 II:187–88, 222–23). Generally, however, the Mopán flows fairly well, and some recent well-financed colonists, including military officers, have found its drainage area suitable for farming and ranching.

There are other rivers of note in southern Petén, for example, the Machaquilá and the Subín, and a good many streams in the far south. In general, southern Petén beyond the plains has better drainage and water flow than the northern regions beyond Lake Petén Itzá.

The Usumacinta River drains western Petén, taking this name at the junction of the Salinas and Pasión Rivers. The Pasión has its sources in the mountains, near San Luis, and flows across southern Petén, turns north, and then west to join the Usumacinta. The latter flows north by northwest, eventually disgorging its waters into the Gulf of Campeche, Mexico. "A considerable chain of low mountains, rising in the cordillera of central Chiapas, strikes east-northeast into Peten; through this chain the Usumacinta has cut a series of gorges" (Morley 1938 II:351). There are some nasty whirlpools (*anaites*) along the course of the Usumacinta, but the river becomes more placid after leaving Petén and moving toward the mangrove swamps of Tabasco, Mexico. In somewhat discontinuous patches, the alluvial soils of the Pasión and, to a greater degree, the Usumacinta are quite fertile (Millet 1974:99). At least until now, these have proven to be about the most productive soils in Petén.

The San Pedro, a tributary of the Usumacinta, drains much of the northwest. Throughout the northwest and in the northeast there are extensive wooded swamps (*bajos* or *akalches*). Many are "fringed" with logwood, *palo tinto* (*Haemotoxylon campechianum*), a natural dyestuff which in previous centuries commanded a significant market in Europe. Many of the swamps are seasonal, losing water through shallow holes. Indeed, during the dry season many of the streams and rivers of Petén lack running water, and the swamps may completely dry. Even the Usumacinta can run surprisingly low in the dry season, its water level dropping 9 to 10 meters, as it did in 1974. Although during the rainy season Peteneros have to cope with low lying areas that easily become waterlogged, they also have to contend with other conditions, which perhaps dispel the notion that tropical lowlands are perpetually wet.

Petén, located in the Northeast Trade Wind zone, has two seasons—dry as noted and wet. The climate is semitropical in the north and tropical in the south. Although temperatures can vary from 12 to 40° Celsius, they rarely drop below 18° C anywhere in Petén, and the yearly mean is 25 to 30° C (Table 1:3). Overall, the department has relatively uniform high temperatures (Deevey, Brenner, Flannery, and Habib 1980; Urrutia 1967).

Precipitation varies more than temperature. Although most of the rains, up to 90 percent in some years, fall between June and December, there is a fair amount of intraseasonal variability. Because seasonality is much more

Table 1:3 Temperature and Precipitation, Petén

Location		Temperature in ° Celsius	
	Mean	Range	Warmest/coldest month
Central area (Flores)	25.5	23.1–29.2	June — January
Southeast (Poptún)	24.3	20.3–26.7	April — January
Northeast (Uaxactún)	26.9	23.0–29.3	May — January
Southwest (Sayaxché)	26.4	23.6–28.8	May — January

Location	Mean precipitation in mm	
	Total	Monthly range
Central area (Flores)	2,007	45–362
Northeast (Poptún)	1,690	44–236
Northeast (Uaxactún)	1,198	28–216
Southwest (Sayaxché)	1,564	23–263

Source: Latinoconsult 1968. Some of these data require confirmation, particularly for south-eastern Petén where total precipitation may be a good deal more than shown.

marked north of Flores than south of it, the forest canopy is more open and there is more understory growth in the north. Everywhere in Petén and most intensely in the north and south-central zones, there is a very hot dry spell in the latter part of August, *canícula*, the dog days. The more tropical southern forests lack clearly defined wet and dry seasons. The far southeast, where precipitation can be 2,000 to 3,000 mm per year, exhibits the greatest extremes of temperature and rainfall in Petén. The west is wetter and more tropical than the east (Wadell 1938; Wiseman 1978).

This picture of climate is somewhat oversimplified. For one thing, much of the data comes from the Flores area; complete information for the other regions is lacking. In addition, winds and topography vary sufficiently within the department so that precipitation is often highly localized. For example, there may be tremendously intense downpours in Flores, while across the Lake in San Andrés and San José there is not a drop of rain during the same period. Similarly, in any given relatively low undulating area, the high ground is or seems subtropical, and the lower lying portions humid and tropical. This unevenness in precipitation is one reason milp-eros (maize farmers) say farming is *"muy eventual"* even within restricted areas.

There are several types of forest in Petén, the exact subdivisions of which have still to be classified in contemporary botanical terms. Here it is enough to note that semideciduous trees predominate in the north, tropical ever-greens in the south, and pines in the very far southeast (Lamb 1966). There are hundreds of different tree species in the Petén lowlands, but with the partial exception of the pines, none are densely clustered as tree species are in temperate forests. The trees of any single species are generally evenly spread but widely separated from each other. For example, although some stands of mahogany, *caoba* (*Swietenia macrophylla*) do occur in Petén, the norm is one mature *caoba* per 2.5 hectares of forest (Lamb 1966:152). Even the much more numerous chewing gum or chicle trees (*Achras zapota*) which dominate a large part of the northern woods of Petén rarely reach densities of 25 to 30 trees per hectare, although a maximum density of one hundred per hectare has been recorded (Holdridge, Lamb, and Mason 1950:47). Chicle tree tapping was the most important economic activity in the region from the 1890s to about 1970. Most of the chicle trees are found in the north, in the townships of San Andrés, Flores, and Melchor de Mencos, and in parts of San José and La Libertad. The south produces a less valuable type of chicle tree, locally called *chiquibul*. Since 1960 two other forest products have assumed commercial importance: allspice, *pi-mienta gorda* (*Pimenta officinalis*); and a dwarf palm, tiger fur, called *xate* or shate in Petén (*Chamaedorea* sp.). Allspice and shate are found almost everywhere in the forests, but they too seem more abundant in the north and northwest.

Commercial logging companies are primarily and sometimes exclusively interested in Petén's *caoba* and cedar trees. Because these trees are so widely scattered and so often snuggly surrounded by other trees, felling merely one of them may require cutting down 15 to 20 other trees. The govern-ment has had some limited success exporting native pine, found in the Poptún-San Luis area.

Unlike commercial loggers, Petén milperos cultivate, protect, and use dozens of tree species for nutritional, medicinal, and construction purposes and, of course, for firewood. Although most native Peteneros are now Ladinos, that is, of mixed Spanish-Indian cultural and/or biological heri-tage, and although many scholars tend to make sharp, almost dichotomous distinctions between Ladinos who, it is said, wish to dominate nature, and Indians who wish to live in harmony with it, at least in Petén both types of people treat trees in the same way, a way nearly identical to the arboricultural practices of the Lacandón Indians of Chiapas, Mexico (Nations and Nigh 1980). One can find Petén Ladinos and Indians who will talk about the trees in dissimilar ways, but this is unusual, and their actual management of trees is the same.

Faunal distributions in the department tend to follow the north-south division previously discussed in reference to precipitation and forests (Duellman 1963). Peteneros hunt a wide range of animals in the deep forests and at the maize fields, including brocket deer, peccary, agouti, rabbit, and many others. They fish in lakes and rivers, especially prizing a panfish (*Petenia splendida*) locally known as *blanco* (whitefish). Young boys, some very young indeed, are expert at using slingshots to hunt a wide variety of birds. Although adults are reluctant to discuss the matter, Peteneros do eat monkeys. Their shyness is due to the fact that monkeys "look like people." The taste of tapir is not much liked, but it too is consumed in Petén, although apparently not in neighboring Belize (Pohl 1977). Unlike the other animals mentioned above, monkey and tapir are rarely eaten in town, but appear regularly on the menus of forest camps. Since about 1965 to 1970, demographic growth, agricultural expansion, ranching, logging, and road construction have been responsible for an increasing scarcity of all game animals, including jaguars, which are hunted for their pelts. By the early 1980s, ordinary Peteneros as well as scientists had become anxious about the possible extinction of several species. A Petén hunter has remarked, "Now that we have more new [modern] things, there are fewer animals, but there are more snakes."

There is an uncomfortable number of poisonous snakes in Petén. The rattlers include the small *Crotalus cerastes* and the impressive, large—up to 2 meters—*C. terrificus*. Rattlers are more common on the plains and in the southwest than elsewhere. There are some fifty varieties of coral snakes, *Elapidae*. In the woods a jumping viper, probably *Bothrops nummifer*, is encountered. But the most feared snake, responsible for most fatal bites in Petén, is an aggressive beast called "yellow beard" (*barba amarilla*) in northern and central Petén, and *nahuyaca* in the southwest (Azurdia A. 1975). This pit viper, *Bothrops atrox*, is particularly numerous in the southern forests and on the great plains, where it can reach a length of 1.5 to 2 meters. Peteneros say that if *barba amarilla* is disturbed, and sometimes even if it is not, it will rear up and chase a person for long distances, and that its fearsome aspect is heightened because it has two heads. Of course, experienced woodsmen discount the idea of two heads, but they nod in agreement when the following story is told:

A farmer was weeding his maize field, near San Francisco, and maybe he was careless. Yellow beard bit him on the hand, because he was careless, or maybe it bit him just like that [*por sí*]. To avoid his death, he quickly cut off his hand [at the wrist] with his machete. Then he went back to the town and healed himself there. He was cured, but he kept thinking about his hand, and he wanted to see it, because it was his hand. Then one day he decided to look for his hand. He looked for it and he found it, right there where the snake had bitten him. The hand was bloated, swollen with the poison [even though, in some versions of this story, the farmer found the hand two weeks after the event]. He looked at the hand for it was his hand, and then picked up a stick and poked at it. The stick had a sharp end, and the pointed end of the stick pierced the flesh, broke the skin, and then the poison spurted up and hit the farmer in the eye. The poison was for him, and he went back to look for it. He was looking for his death. When it is one's time to die, one cannot avoid it (Field Notes 1974).

The story not only says something about the Petenero's fear of yellow beard but indicates a certain fatalism in the culture.

Another of the difficulties of living in Petén, as much a part of the environment as the trees and rivers, are the insects. Of insects there seems no end—gnats, ticks, hornets, wasps, ferocious ants, extremely annoying fleas, even more vexatious sandflies, impressively large, unpleasant spiders, still larger scorpions, and so on. Stand still for a moment and something is bound to bite. Insects both discomfort and endanger humans, animals, and crops. If some are as harmless or as beautiful as the many varieties of butterfly, or as useful as the stingless honeybee, an awesome number are harmful. Many are disease carriers; for example, the female blackfly (*Simuluim damnosum*) is the vector for Onchocerciasis, river blindness, which is apparently synergistic with other diseases. There are the so-called beef-worms, *colmoyotes* (*Dermatobia homins* and *D. cianiventrix*), vectors for leishmaniasis, which if untreated ulcerates skin tissue. Older chewing gum tree tappers (chicleros) bear with some pride the mark of the *colmoyote*—a partly chewed away nose or ear. The assassin bug (*Triatoma infestans*), probably not native to Petén, causes trypanosomiasis, Chagas's disease. The Asian tiger mosquito (*Aedes albopictus*), which transmits dengue fever with symptoms resembling those of a severe case of flu, is reported to have invaded Petén. It thrives in one of the signs of modernity, the standing water in discarded automobile tires. Although yellow fever has been practically nonexistent since about 1960, malaria, which had abated during 1950 to 1972, has surged in Petén since about 1976. Malaria has the highest incidence of all insect-borne diseases in the department.

Humans in Petén suffer from various health problems. They are affected with many debilitating intestinal parasites—roundworm and hookworm are endemic. Almost every child and adult has stomach worms, and a good many people think that this is a natural state of affairs. They maintain that people are as surely born with worms as they are with souls. Purgatives are taken not to eliminate worms, for this is not possible, but to control their numbers and to ameliorate the discomfort they cause. Tuberculosis too is common among native Peteneros, but no one wants others to know that he or she has it for fear of being shunned. Although medical personnel will not discuss the matter in public, some of them claim that venereal diseases affect a large number of recent migrants to the department. Shigella and amoebic dysentery are widespread, but the diarrhea-pneumonia complex is the most devastating illness among the young children (for discussion of disease in Petén, see Monzón López 1949; Saul 1973; Shimkin 1973).

In many ways, then, the natural and sociomedical environment of the region is not a forgiving one. At times even the plants and trees can be unsettling. To give but two examples, in low lying phryganous areas the bull's horn, which has long, nearly invisible iron-hard thorns, can cut deep and make movement a torture; and the sap of the *chechem* tree (the black poisonwood, *Metopium brownei*) will burn a nasty black scar on affected body parts.

In view of the myriad possibilities for illness, it is interesting that high blood pressure and severe anxiety attacks have recently become so prevalent among adults. In 1985 physicians did not agree whether this phenomenon is really so recent, but several report that at least 50 percent of their patients suffer anxiety attacks marked by sharp chest pains and difficulty in breathing.

Except for the anxiety attacks, Peteneros bear all of these illnesses, diseases, and biting insects with a kind of stoical good nature. I think they would appreciate Willey, Smith, Tourtellot, and Graham's wry comment about the insects: "Although the land they trod was relatively poor in physical resources, the [ancient] Maya [and modern Peteneros] had many living companions with which to share it" (1975:20).

Soils

However important trees, animals, and insects are, for the vast majority of Peteneros and the newly arrived colonists who are farmers at least part of the year, the soils and associated features of the Petén environment are of critical importance. Native classification of soils and their management are discussed elsewhere (Reina 1967), and here I will briefly outline scientific assessments of the soils of Petén. In doing so, I must enter a warning: a good deal has been written about the agricultural potential of Petén, but aside from limited soil studies carried out in restricted areas (notable examples include work by Cowgill 1962; Lundell 1937; Urrutia 1967), almost every recent discussion of the department as a whole is based on Simmons et al. 1959. Although the latter were able to identify twenty-six distinct soils in Petén, the scale of their work was too large to reveal microvariations in soils across all of the department. Thus it is difficult to discuss with confidence Petén's agricultural potential for modern populations dependent on slash-and-burn (swidden) techniques of cultivation. Certainly, scientific assessments of the potential differ greatly. For example, Manger-Cats (1966), following Simmons, believes that about 54 percent of the soils are suitable for rain-fed farming. Sanders (1977) argues that only about 40 percent are suitable, and an influential FAO study (FAO/FYDEP 1970) reports that no more than 31 percent of the soils are "good" or "moderately good," that is, suitable primarily for swidden cultivation (see also Latinoconsult 1974).

Policy recommendations about development and colonization of the department rest in part on which set of figures planners use. Some Guatemalan officials insist that given current swidden practices, Petén cannot support more than 150,000 people, that is, 25,000 to 30,000 farm families, aside from a minority who would not depend on farm income. Others argue that 500,000 people can be supported in Petén. Of course, political considerations having no direct relation to soils and ecology also affect which set of figures is chosen. Conservatives prefer the smaller and liberals the larger figures, but the point is that either can be justified by reference to the scientists (see Handy 1984:216–17; Millet 1974; Manger-Cats 1966). The political aspect of this situation will be discussed later.

Tropical and semitropical soils are often deficient in nutrients needed by crops. The structure and fertility of soil "depends largely on the quality and age of the rock from which it is formed" (Caufield 1984:65). Where the rock is old and weathered, as it is in much of the tropics, the soils may be of low fertility. The rich, dense appearance of a tropical forest is misleading, for most nutrients are held in the trees and plants and not in the soil. In some tropical forests, to take but a single example, most of the phosphorus is captured by trees; in contrast, in a temperate zone oak forest most of it is held tightly in the soil. Much the same may be said of nitrogen and magnesium. Most of Petén's soils are deficient in such critical elements as phosphorus, potassium, and nitrogen, and the soils of the plains are excessively acidic. Even the productive alluvial soils along the Usumacinta and Pasión Rivers are sufficiently deficient in nutrients to make Teracena de la Cerda (1974:30–31) pessimistic about their long term prospects.

Nor do difficulties end here. Sanders (1979) has usefully rearranged the twenty-six soils identified by Simmons et al. (1959) in terms of relationships among fertility, erodability, drainage, and friability. After noting that about 10 percent (354,394 hectares) of the soils are of the poor, highly acidic savanna type, Sanders observes that the other 90 percent of the soils (3,216,348 hectares) are found in forests. Many of these forest soils are fertile, but they are associated with drainage, erosion, and plasticity problems.

Thus, of the 3,216,348 hectares, 32.50 percent (1,178,257 hectares) have poor drainage. Another 46.36 percent (1,640,706 hectares) are well-drained if shallow soils, or soils on steep rocky slopes susceptible to erosion if cropped (unless, I would add, some sort of terracing is carried out). Only 10.98 percent (397,385 hectares) are deep soils with good drainage and limited susceptibility to erosion. (Shallow, well-drained fertile soils are associated with ancient Maya classic sites.) Sanders concludes that at best about 40 percent of the soils of Petén are well suited to cropping, and even so erosion may pose serious problems in many specific places.

Where fertility is high, drainage tends to be poor. Where there is limited potential for erosion, fertility tends to be low. Again, the soil is often highly fertile in low lying humid localities, but it is also compact and poorly drained. These patches are best suited to dry season cultivation. Once the rains begin, there is not only the danger that the cultigens will be flooded but also that the mosquitoes will (and usually do) turn the lowland into a torture chamber. That Peteneros can work in these places at the beginning of the rainy season is evidence of their need and strong will, but not of any special biological adaptation to the bites of mosquitoes.

Peteneros say that the best places to farm are on well-drained slopes with relatively loose, friable soils. The soils on these slopes (*laderas*) can be fertile. Unfortunately, although the *laderas* are often relatively easy to work and can produce well, they are easily eroded. Many of Petén's soils are naturally fertile, including the black calcareous lithosols that resemble redzinas and the brown calcaerous soils, but they are usually thin and, once denuded of trees, readily worn away by rain. Sanders's point bears repetition: in Petén high or good soil fertility all too often varies inversely with good soil texture, with good drainage and with minimum susceptibility to erosion.

The preceding general picture must be supplemented by a word about the extraordinary microenvironmental diversity in Petén. Similar soils, plants, and animals are found throughout the department, with some differences occurring north and south of the central basin, but it is important to note that these factors appear in nearly endless combinations. Microvariations in and relationships among topography, hydrography, parent rock and soil structure, vegetative cover and, of equal importance, histories of human intervention generate marked differences in soil fertility, friability, and erodability within quite narrow ecological bands (Blanton, Feinman, and Appel 1981:174–75; Rice and Rice 1984). As Rice (1978:38) has observed, "The significance of the existing soil variations cannot be overstated," and they have profound implications for "the food-production capabilities of aboriginal and contemporary populations."

Native Petén milperos share a common fund of agronomic knowledge, but they must adjust it to the particularities of differing microniches. The lowland forests appear "forbiddingly dense and difficult," but people can adapt to them by paying "close attention to the behavior of plants and animals and to the details of microenvironments" (Blanton et al. 1981:173). Rather than constantly repeat the same highly controlled methods, as do farmers in the Guatemalan highlands, lowlanders, close observers of nature, combine a willingness to fine-tune cropping techniques with a flexible readiness to change the details of cropping (Blanton et al. 1981). Milperos working in adjacent areas may and do operate in somewhat differing ways. As Peteneros would say, each milpero has his own "secrets," that is, his own private fund of knowledge about particular microniches. Peteneros contend that no one can ever truly "know what is in the heart of another." They tell stories, real and fancied, about what people *do*, but they rarely assign motives to the action. Without overstressing the point, one may note a certain parallel between their necessarily individualized adaptations (the secrets each one has) to microenvironmental variation and the stated belief that one cannot know the motives of another.

Deforestation

To say that no two people face exactly the same range of adaptive problems at any given moment is not to deny that some problems are shared by nearly everyone. A salient example is the current pace of deforestation in Petén. So long as small patches of forest-fringed land cleared of trees for cropping are given sufficient time "to rest," as milperos say, soil fertility appears to be maintained. If after one to three years of cropping the land is fallowed long enough, the forest will regrow sufficiently to protect the fragile soils from heavy rains, sun, and intrusive grasses. If the land is left treeless for too long, or permanently, then the ecological consequences can be devastating.

Milperos in Petén claim that the accelerating rate of deforestation has increased the length of the dry season over the past ten to fifteen years. As previously mentioned, the decrease in forest cover has decreased the availability of game animals that used to be an important source of animal protein for ordinary Peteneros. Above all, they fear the increasing aridity, and there is some scientific evidence, drawn mainly from studies in the Amazon Basin, to substantiate their claims and apprehensions about deforestation and climatic change.

In sum, there are several sources of deforestation in modern Petén: expanded ranching and commercial logging operations, a demographic explosion accompanied by a proportional increase in land-extensive swidden cropping, and a proportional increase in the number of trees cut down for fuelwood used primarily for cooking. Government officials have estimated that since about 1966, the rate of deforestation in Petén has been approximately 1.5 percent per year. Noting that by 1985 40 to 50 percent and by 1989 60 percent of Petén may have been deforested (*Prensa Libre* 13 May 1989:8) or degraded, the officials predict that in another fifteen to thirty-five years, by about 2000 to 2025, there may be no extensive forest areas in the region despite regulations designed to prevent their disappearance. The northern third of Petén is supposed to be closed to farmer colonization and subject to rules about controlled logging and reforestation, but government has lacked the personnel, and perhaps the will, to consistently or effectively enforce the rules.

In tropical forests a good deal of available moisture is collected by the trees and then by evapotranspiration returned to the air where it helps form rain clouds. If farmers shorten or eliminate fallow periods, or ranchers and loggers fell the trees, the climate will be adversely affected. That is, when wild or pasture grasses or other plants replace trees, there is a significant reduction in the amount of moisture recycled into the air, thereby reducing total precipitation, but not intensity of rainfall (Webster 1983). When the trees are permanently removed and their spongy rain-capturing capacity is lost, the heavy downpours so common in the lowlands can wash away thin fertile soil layers within a few short years. Then the exposed, weathered rock particles can harden and become lateritic, impermeable, and useless. Without the dense mass of vegetation supplied by trees, water runoff increases enough to cause flooding by raising stream and water levels, and so more fertile topsoils are washed away.

Both the early successional wild grasses that grow up in areas cleared of trees for crops and the pasture grasses planted for livestock tend to compact the soil, limiting water and rainfall infiltration, and without trees the soil is overexposed to the sun. Given proper crop to fallow ratios and provided that cleared areas are not too extensive, wild grasses will yield to returning trees, but that is not the case with pastures intentionally kept relatively treeless. (In Petén, cattlemen do not fell or burn cohune palms which, like the *nance* trees, are fire resistant). As the soil becomes compacted, new seeds become waterlogged. Soil nutrients, which are none too plentiful in the first instance, may be severely reduced. Nor is it certain that two of the most commonly planted pasture grasses in Petén and in much of Central America and Panamá—African star (*Cynodon plectostachyus*) and faragua (*Hyparrhenia rufa*)—are well suited to the environment (but for a more optimistic view of *H. rufa*, see Gudeman 1978:29; also see Sánchez 1981:392). As soils decline in fertility and, consequently, as pastures lose nutritional value, ranchers may try to improve matters by using chemical fertilizers, but once soil degradation begins it is far from certain that applications of chemical fertilizers can reverse the process. In any case, Petén ranchers prefer less costly methods. They expand into the forests or into farm lands. As land becomes scarce farmers in turn must dangerously shorten fallow periods or clear virgin forest, until the needs of ranchers once again intrude in what becomes a relentless and finally counterproductive cycle. By 1985 this process had not gone as far in Petén as it had elsewhere in Central America, although the 1989 reports are discouraging. As of 1985 the recent expansion of swidden cultivation appeared to be responsible for more forest degradation than did ranching. Nevertheless, if ranching continues to expand it may successfully compete with farming, as it has in many of the lowlands of Latin America (Partridge 1984). Eventually farming may become nearly impossible in an ecologically degraded region.

If, and it is a very big if, ancient Maya techniques of agricultural intensification could be reintroduced this might help to retard deforestation or help to provide alternatives to land-extensive swidden systems. For example, in addition to engaging in swidden farming, the ancient Maya intensified food production through irrigation systems and the use of raised fields in low lying places. Properly managed combinations of arboriculture and collection of marketable non-timber forest products, such as shate, and less extensive swidden cultivation might also help to preserve the forests. At present, however, modern populations in Petén rely primarily on swidden for subsistence and for a significant portion of their income. If, for whatever reason, they cannot let the land "rest" for adequate periods of time, the entire food production system may collapse.

There has not yet been sufficient scientific research in Petén to warrant definitively gloomy conclusions or statements of absolute confidence about the final consequence of the ongoing deforestation, but two additional observations can be made. First, even as influential and ordinary Peteneros and a wide range of officials have been calling on the central government to strengthen its efforts to protect the semitropical northern forests, successive regimes have opened the more tropical rain forests of southern Petén to uncontrolled farming and ranching. Research on other tropical lowlands suggests that it is precisely the south that is more threatened by the consequences of deforestation. Second, the sort of erosion evident in, for example, the Azueros Peninsula of Panamá now may be seen in a few places in southeastern Petén. Neither observation is reassuring. The Rices (1984:27–28), after noting that the ancient Maya developed a relatively "ecologically efficient regime that met increased demands for production," warn that this did not endure and should not "foster spurious—and dangerous—complacency toward future economic development" in Petén. In the Amazon Basin, deforestation "destroys the ecosystem nutrient cycle, and inevitably and rapidly leads to leaching, soil compaction, soil erosion and flooding"(Posey, Frechione, Eddins, and da Silva 1984:96). All this suggests that if the current rate of deforestation in Petén is maintained, the people who live there will have to cope with severely depleted natural resources in the near future. As Peteneros would say, it is all *muy eventual*.

The Other Side

Dry discussion of the physical features of Petén—the semitropical woods of the north dominated by chicle trees; the tropical forests of the south; the central lake district and the south-central plains; the rivers, swamps, and steeply inclined ridges; the many animals, snakes, and insects, the latter with names nearly as intimidating as the diseases they carry; the shallow soils whose fertility often varies inversely with their erodability and plasticity; the potential dangers of deforestation associated with demographic growth and expanded economic activities—is necessary to understand the history of the region, as the following chapters will show, but it omits other aspects of the environment that are significant for Peteneros.

In many ways, Peteneros find their habitat satisfying and beautiful, at the same time aware of its limitations and dangers. Both Ladinos and Indians say that if one treats the forests with respect and if one learns enough "secrets," the forests will provide what it needed to live. "Even if we get lost," a young Petenero assures us, "There is everything in the forest. This vine, see, has water to drink, and my father has taught me which [wild] grasses can be eaten, and there is fruit on the trees." Precisely because of the microniches, Peteneros find that there is always more to learn about the soils, the animals, the trees, and the weather signs. Their appreciation is as aesthetic as it is instrumental.

Although the atmosphere within the forests is hot and damp much of the year, it is comfortable beneath the protective shade of the trees. And there is much to see: bromeliads, orchids, and other epiphytes growing on trees, thick vines twisting upward from the base of trees and then hanging down from their heights; trees growing around other trees; an endless variety of shades of green; multicolored birds and flowers visible wherever the trees are cut back even a little; long lines of parasol ants passing in formation; giant termite mounds; huge weirdly shaped beetles—an endless array of fascinating flora and fauna. Lake Petén Itzá changes color and surface texture several times during the day. Now it is jade green, now blue and so smooth that the world turns upside down as the reflected clouds move across its surface. Then, with the turbulent white waves of late afternoon, the deep blue surface may appear to be the work of a pointillist. In the woods and on the grasslands, Peteneros can distinguish the sounds of birds, insects, and winds in a way no visitor can. Breezes moving through dense forest vegetation can produce an eery sound, strangely like a composed musical tune, and it is sometimes said that the goblins (*duendes*), dwarf spirit beings who own the forests, are whistling. Sometimes the forest is completely still—then there is total silence. Somehow, the slow, light speech of the Peteneros fits the environment, and not even the perplexities of modernity and the horrors of protracted civil war have been able to silence that most characteristic sound of Petén, soft laughter. Almost as noticeable are the pungent smells of beetles, decaying forest debris, freshly cut pimento, and, most pervasive of all wherever there are people, the smell of burning firewood. A remarkable number of Peteneros write poetry, which often speaks of these and other features that they find compelling and pleasing in their physical environment.[1]

If Petén is a "most difficult" place in which to live (Morley and Brainerd 1956:13), if it has a "deadly climate" (Munro 1918:17) and is "relatively poor in physical resources" (Willey et al. 1975:20), it is also fascinating. To be sure, all their lives Peteneros continue to learn the details of the environment primarily for practical reasons and they are perfectly aware of how difficult it is to live in Petén, but none of this detracts from the aesthetic or, more precisely, the palpably sensual pleasure they take from their habitat. Peteneros say there is security as well as danger, comfort as well as hardship in the forests. How their experiences in the colonial period contributed to this equivocality is discussed in Chapter 2.

Chapter Two

Conquest, Depopulation, and Colonization, 1697–1821

> "The conquest of the Maya by the Spanish was obviously a long and brutal process . . . In succeeding so well, of course, the conquest also marked the beginning of the modern Maya. But . . . that is another story" (Morley, Brainerd, and Sharer 1983:592).

> "Since the conquest, Tayasal has been a mere Spanish provincial village with nothing to distinguish it from a score of others" (Means 1917:185).

Introduction

In this chapter and the following one I recount the history of Petén from the period just before the Spanish conquest of Tayasal in 1697 to the years immediately preceding the beginning of chicle collecting in the department in the 1890s. While describing significant changes in Petén society, I will also give attention to important socioeconomic patterns laid down in the colonial period which still play an important role in the lives of Peteneros. Because there are gaps in our historical knowledge, these chapters are not definitive, but I believe enough is known to describe the major contours of Petén history from 1697 to the 1890s.

To address briefly the reasons for the gaps in our knowledge, two points may be noted. First, scholars have neglected the history of colonial Guatemala, particularly "the complicated period between 1690 and 1730" (MacLeod 1983:210), that is, precisely the period during which the Spanish conquered and established a colony in Petén. Even for those who have dealt with colonial Guatemala, Petén and the areas adjacent to it have been of marginal interest (Farriss 1983:4), and the same can be said of postcolonial Petén, as evidenced by Means's dismissal quoted at the beginning of this chapter.

Second, archeologists naturally enough have concentrated on preconquest Maya, leaving the "other story" to the ethnographers. The latter, however, have usually given their attention to the so-called traditional Indians of the central and western highlands of Guatemala and neglected the rural Ladinos and the ladinoized Indians who comprise the majority in areas such as eastern Guatemala and Petén.

One telling example of both points is that professional scholars have written much more about the exact location of Tayasal, the preconquest Itzá capital in Petén (for example, Chase 1976, 1985; Jones, Rice and Rice 1981; Reina 1962; Comparato 1983) than about the history of Flores, the capital of Petén ever since the Spanish conquest (Reina 1964 is an exception). Of course, the documentary record of the department is not as rich as that of other Guatemalan departments. For instance, an important 1821 census of Petén has apparently vanished. Recent publications by Jones, Hellmuth, and others cited below, however, are filling the gaps in our knowledge, and forthcoming research will continue to augment and correct what is now known of Petén's post-1697 history.

Without taking into account historical events of the region, modern patterns of behavior would be difficult to comprehend. There are apparent anomalies in contemporary behavior that can be explained with a historical accounting. There are two important examples, really cultural themes. First, both rich and poor Peteneros alike proudly point out that "here in Petén there is democracy [social equality], unlike the rest of Guatemala." The stress on social equality seems to contradict the obvious deference given social superiors, the social distance maintained between social strata, and so on. Second, native Petén authors celebrate "*la raza indoespañola*, our race" (Soza 1970:521), and certainly the marked racial discrimination against Indians elsewhere in Guatemala is simply unacceptable in modern Petén. Nevertheless, the descendants of the Indians and of the Spanish of eighteenth century Petén have retained their structural positions relative to each other up to today despite all sorts of political, economic, and cultural changes over the years. Historical continuities within Petén as well as unprecedented events, and the history of deliberate decisions made by Peteneros, with all their intended and unintended consequences, help explain these and other, sometimes paradoxical, modern patterns of behavior. Today's pattern of life is not only a response to current circumstances, some local and many beyond local control, and not only an expression of a particular regional culture, but is also related to what happened and to what people think happened in the past.

Conquest and Resistance, 1520s–1697

Although the history of the preconquest period is extremely complicated, there are some outstanding features of importance for our purposes. The areas to the west, northwest, and south of the Itzá of Tayasal in central Petén were progressively depopulated and disrupted by Spanish action in the sixteenth and seventeenth centuries; distinct Indian groups in Petén were increasingly mixed; and the Spanish were almost inevitably driven to crush the Itzá of Tayasal.

The Spanish conquered and established colonial rule over much of Yucatán between 1527 and 1546 and much of Guatemala south of Petén and Verapaz between 1524 and 1527, and Verapaz was pacified in the sixteenth to seventeenth centuries. To be sure, there was and still is continual Indian resistance to alien domination. Rebellions were frequent, and in a sense the Spanish conquest of Yucatán was not complete until 1901 (Farriss 1984:19), and active resistance continues today in Guatemala (see, for example, Brintnall 1979; Manz 1988). However, the Indians of Petén and much of Belize were genuinely independent long after Indians in adjacent areas were conquered by Spanish overlords or continued to rebel against them.

In Petén, at least since the fifteenth century, the Itzá at Tayasal (most probably present-day Flores) were the dominant, most highly organized military, political, and economic element. The Itzá were a Mayanized people of non-Maya origin who had migrated to and settled in Yucatán. Between 1200 and 1450 Itzá groups moved south from Yucatán to Petén, where they dominated previously established peoples.

Thompson (1977) has argued that the southern Maya lowlands was a distinct cultural and linguistic area. This, the Chan region, includes parts of lowland Chiapas, parts of southern Campeche in Yucatán, much of Belize, and all of Petén except for the mountainous corner south of modern San Luis. The various politically autonomous Chan groups—Yucatec speakers in the Lacandón area well west of Tayasal; Cehach in northwestern Petén; Chichanha and Chinamita in the northeast; Maya of western Belize and possibly Muzules around Tipú, Belize; Mopán Maya in south-central and southeastern Petén; primarily Itzá in the central sector—were closely related to the Yucatec Maya.

Chan groups, save for those at Chetumal and Tayasal, lacked supravillage, highly centralized polities (Thompson 1977:36). The Itzá themselves were divided into several ethnic-political units, often at odds with and sometimes engaged in wars against one another. The Chakán or Chatá(n) Itzá west of Lake Petén Itzá were semiautonomous subjects of the Tayasal Itzá, as were the Cobox a bit north northeast of the Lake. Other separate Itzá groups were located east of the Lake (Chase 1985).

Thompson probably exaggerated the cultural unity and identity of what he called the Chan area, and in any case it was not a static region. By the mid-to-late sixteenth century Yucatec Maya fleeing the Spanish were arriving in Petén and mingling with the population there; they continued the process well into the nineteenth century. In addition, even before the arrival of the Spanish, Kekchí may have been moving into southeastern Petén, then occupied by Mopán Maya and a non-Chan group, the Manché-Chol. There were also several Spanish *entradas* (incursions) into Petén between 1524 and 1696, and the Itzá rulers of Tayasal had sent emissaries to the Spanish at Mérida, Yucatán by the early seventeenth century.

Throughout the sixteenth and seventeenth centuries the Indians were devastated, and the areas around the Itzá were depopulated as a result of Spanish actions and European-introduced diseases against which the Indians had acquired no immunity. Although the details vary in each location, the general outcome was everywhere about the same (Farriss 1983:15).

At the beginning of the sixteenth century, western Petén was occupied by perhaps 30,000 Chol and Cholti speakers who between 1559 and 1721 were decimated by war, disease, and forced relocation. A motley group of refugees, including Yucatec speakers, Itzás, Cehaches, and Choles, apparently mingled all through this period and on into the nineteenth century. They have inherited the name "Lacandones," not to be confused with the aboriginal Cholti to whom the Spanish referred by the same name. These latter day Lacandones scattered into the forests, offering little direct resistance to the Spanish, and after the 1730s they were scarcely interfered with by the Spanish. By the middle of the seventeenth century, if not before, western Petén lost its economic importance for the Itzá as a result of the devastation there.[1]

The Cehach (a collective name for several probably politically independent groups), less numerous than other aboriginal western Petén groups, occupied the northwestern sector. By the beginning of the seventeenth century, people in the Cehach region were playing an intermediary role in trade between northern Yucatán and central Petén. This came about because in the 1570s the Spanish forcibly removed from the area just north of the Cehach a group known as the Putún Acalán, who had produced crops valued by the Itzá of central Petén and who had dominated trade between northern Yucatán and central Petén. But the Itzá apparently were not so interested in relations with the Cehach as they had been with the Putún Acalán. One reason was that the Cehach area did not produce in appreciable quantities valued agricultural trade goods, such as cacao. Another was that the Cehach could not obtain through trade sufficient quantities of these goods to compete with Belizean traders to the east of the Itzá (Jones 1982, 1983). Itzá interest in the Cehach may also have been lessened because the Cehach were subject to "intensive missionary activity" (Jones 1982:283) and, in my view, because there apparently was a massive demographic reduction among Cehach caused by European-introduced diseases (the area is full of swamps hospitable to disease vectors of European origin). Cehach remnants, and Yucatecan refugees among them, were probably absorbed by Lacandón area groups (Jones 1982, 1983), and some may have fled south to join the Itzá.[2] (Colonial and postcolonial authorities continued to refer to unconquered Indians in the northwest as "Cehach," but it is not clear that those people were directly descended from the indigenous Cehach.)

The Mopán and the Manché-Chol sector similarly lost economic value, from the Itzá perspective, during the sixteenth and seventeenth centuries. Missionizing efforts began in southeastern Petén by 1596, and the Itzá feared that Christianized Manché would conduce the Spanish to Tayasal (Bricker 1981:37; Jones 1982:283). The Manché, "perhaps goaded on by the Itza . . . rose up during Lent in 1633" (Bricker 1981:37). In fact, all through the seventeenth century the Dominican missionaries encountered difficulties with the Manché and finally decided to remove them from Petén.[3] Thus, what may have been a population of 10,000 Indians was cut down by war and disease, and the remnant forcibly resettled in Rabinal, Baja Verapaz. After 1700 the Manché-Chol had no role to play in Petén history (Bolland 1977:18; Bricker 1981:37–38; Mazzarelli 1976a:169; Andrews 1983:67).

The Mopán, perhaps 10,000–20,000 people (Morley 1938 I:37, 71; cf. Comparato 1983:177), fared little better. In 1692 the Council of the Indies ordered that a strong effort be made to conquer them (and the Manché) "once and for all" (Bricker 1981:38). The Mopán population, suffering the trauma of war and disease as other Indians did, was reduced by the Spanish. The remaining small population was settled in southeastern villages founded by the Spanish, and soon after again relocated elsewhere in Petén.[4]

With most of the zones around the Itzás losing population and significance for trade (except in salt; Andrews 1983) and becoming Christianized, ties with the Maya of Belize perforce grew in importance. The Itzá, for mutually reinforcing reasons of trade, ideology, and knowledge of Spanish abuses elsewhere, intended to retain their political independence and to encourage others to resist the Spanish. In this effort, the Maya of Tipú, Belize, played a crucial role.[5] Indeed, they "may have borne the major responsibility for having drawn out the long process of Itza conquest" (Jones 1982:283).

To abbreviate a long, complex history: The Spanish set up a mission at Tipú between 1544 and 1567, but their control over the region was weak from 1567 to 1608. They reestablished control in 1608, but the Tipuans, to protect their profitable role in Yucatán-Petén trade and probably urged on by the Itzá, rose up and expelled the Spanish civil and religious authorities in 1638. They were able to hold off the Spanish until 1695–96, hence the final Itzá conquest "was pursued not through the hostile territory of Tipú, but rather through the thoroughly weakened, Christianized Cehach region" (Jones 1982:288). By 1707 the Spanish had resettled the Tipuans in Petén, mostly around the Lake (Graham, Jones, and Kautz 1985). Lesser known Muzul Indians were settled in San Luis, Dolores, Santa Ana, and San José (Soza 1970:203).

Aside from their experiences with the barbed buffer role played by Tipú, the Spanish could not have been cheered by the prospect of conquering the Itzá. Not only were the distant forests inhospitable and lacking the allure of precious metals, but previous attempts to penetrate Petén had failed (Morley 1938:I). Besides, the Spanish consistently exaggerated Itzá power. Even so, several considerations drove the Spaniards forward. The Itzá were a source of anti-Christian influence on Tipuan, Yucatecan, and other Indians, and Petén was a vast refuge zone for Yucatán Maya. Longstanding crown desires for an inland route from northwestern Yucatán across Petén to highland Guatemala (for example, see a 1639 Royal Council of the Indies report, in Stone 1932) were intensified by increasingly intrusive English activity in Belize and in the Caribbean Sea.[6] The Spanish, coping with a depression in Guatemala that began in 1630, also may have been seeking additional sources of labor and food production in Petén and Chiapas and a way to gain control of the northern achiote trade (Comparato 1983:97, 125). Finally, there were mythic-historical reasons for the conquest of Tayasal. The Spanish, like the Yucatecan Maya, regarded the Itzá as an integral part of Yucatán history. "Thus, as long as they remained independent, the conquest of Yucatán was not complete" (Bricker 1981:23). So it was a series of practical and ideological reasons that compelled the Spanish to crush the Itzá.

A three pronged attack was mounted, with forces coming from Yucatán and Guatemala. In what comes close to being a premonitory situation, the actual conquest of the Itzá fell to the Yucatecan command, the Guatemalan forces perhaps finally less intensely interested or less able to reach Tayasal for the battle (Comparato 1983:238–39). The story of the campaign and the destruction of Tayasal has been retold many times, the accounts resting primarily on Villagutierre's book (now available in a magnificent English translation by Wood, edited and with notes by Comparato, 1983), and need not be repeated here. It is enough to say that in a single day—13 March 1697—Martín de Ursúa y Arizmendi, leading a force of 235 Spanish soldiers and 120 Indian road workers and muleteers, broke the power of Tayasal. Rey Canek and other Tayasal dignitaries were ultimately sent out of Petén and placed under house arrest in Santiago, Guatemala. When the Itzá sent emissaries to Mérida early in the seventeenth century, they prophesied that on 27 July 1697 they would "accept" Christianity. They were not far off, but perhaps not even Itzá seers could have foretold the pain and ravage which would accompany the (forced) conversion.

Ursúa, urging gentle treatment of the broken Itzá but not forsaking destruction of their icons and holy places, renamed Tayasal "Our Lady of Refuge and Saint Paul of the Itzás" (*Nuestra Señora de los Remedios y San Pablo de los Itzaex*). By 1700 a frontier garrison (*presidio*) was established here, and Remedios became and remained the capital of Petén, except for a brief interlude between 1880 and 1882. A prison was also built to house political exiles and criminals sent from the highlands to what became something of a "devil's island." In 1831 Remedios (also referred to as Petén and El Presidio in colonial documents) was renamed Flores in honor of Cirilo Flores, an acting head (*jefe*) of the Guatemalan state who was killed by an anti-Liberal mob in Quetzaltenango in 1826. Shortly after the conquest, Petén was placed under the civil rule of the Audience of Guatemala and under the religious rule of the Franciscans in Yucatán, which lasted until 1860 when religious control passed to the church in Guatemala.

The period of military consolidation (1697–1710) following the fall of Tayasal must have been utterly calamitous for the Itzá. They lost their freedom, were forced to convert, and saw the destruction of trade and their basic food production systems. If, to deny food to the isolated garrison, they burned their fields, as did the Indians around Sacpúy located about twenty kilometers northwest of Remedios, the Spanish retaliated by burning fields to prevent the Indians from fleeing to the woods. Although most of the Indians who died were killed by European-introduced diseases, their susceptibility to these diseases must have been intensified by humiliation in defeat, economic dislocation, and hunger.

A word more about the demographic impact of the diseases is needed. Throughout Mesoamerica native populations declined greatly after the arrival of the Spanish in 1519, the nadir reached in 1650. Population decreases primarily caused by diseases were drastic even where Spanish entry into a region was delayed, as in Petén. European-introduced diseases were transmitted to unconquered Indians by other Indians in contact with them and by the Spanish (Thompson 1966:31). Hence, Chan people probably suffered marked demographic losses prior to the 1690s. After 1697, the Itzá of the Lake, at least some 25,000 people (Hellmuth 1977) and perhaps as many as 40,000 (Comparato 1983:6), and other Chan groups experienced further population reduction. One indication of this may be seen in a 1714 census which included Indians and non-Indians under Spanish control and reported a scant 3,027 people for Petén (Feldman 1982:225).[7] Of course, other areas were similarly devastated, and there were uncounted "wild" Indians in the forests beyond the reach of the colonial authorities, but Petén remained sparsely populated for some 270 years after Tayasal fell (Chapter 1, Table 1:1).

Colonial Rule and Frontier Economy

Having at last conquered Petén, the Spanish set about building a colony there. Several important related tasks were carried out at the same time, including road work, initiation of livestock ranches, congregation (reduction) of Indians into villages and parishes, and so on. However, for the sake of clarity each significant event is treated separately below.

Between 1697 and 1699, for reasons of health and defense, the Spanish built a fort on the island of Remedios, now reserved primarily for Spanish and mestizo settlers, soldiers, and convicts[8] (Soza 1957:311; Comparato 1983:63). The new capital of Petén was in place by 1700, the same year Bourbon Felipe V ascended to the throne of Spain.

Colonial Context

The Bourbons intended to reform colonial administration by rationalizing and centralizing authority, modernizing society, and expanding colonial trade. By 1720 they ended the *encomienda* system, grants which entitled grantees to tribute from Indian communities, including labor, in return for which they rendered military service to the state and "civilized" the Indians (Wortman 1982:101). (In some marginal areas such as Yucatán and Paraguary *encomenderos* also could extract labor from Indians without paying them wages.) Apparently no such grants were awarded in Petén. In theory, the Bourbons also ended the *repartimiento* system, a state controlled labor service to which Spaniards applied for workers from Indian communities, and which was failing in many areas for want of laborers (Helms 1975:151–52). The rules were not uniformly implemented, and as late as the 1790s requests for *repartimiento* labor were being made in Petén (see, for example AGCA A3.a, 4150,227, 1793), but the system does not seem to have been used much there. Obligatory labor drafts (*téquios*, from the Nahuatl *tequitl*) of Indians for government and church projects were more common. Between 1746 and 1776, healthy male Indians 18 to 50 years old became obliged to pay a head tax of two pesos per year in cash rather than in goods, for example, maize, to subsidize defense, state, and church expenses, and remittances to Spain. Because crop failures did not excuse them from making tribute payments, many Indians were forced into debt peonage (MacLeod 1985:495–98; Wortman 1982:157–75). In one way or another, the state assured Spanish colonists of continued access to and control of Indian labor.

Petén was a remote colony, far from major centers of government and trade. Few Spaniards were attracted to the lowlands which lacked precious metals, were not a source of indigo, the major item of Guatemalan economy between 1700 and 1798 (Wortman 1982:157–75), and had a sparse Indian population. Moreover, Petén was surrounded by marginal areas, a hinterland within hinterlands.

Western Petén and lowland Chiapas were underpopulated; the scattered Indian remnants living there avoided contact with the Spanish. Verapaz to the south was a small isolated province controlled by Dominicans who did not encourage economic activity. Few non-Indians moved there (MacLeod 1983:203). Contributions squeezed from the Indians by mendicant religious orders in the sixteenth to eighteenth centuries "pressed most Indians to the brink of survival," and this led to widespread abandonment of towns in Verapaz and Petén (Richards 1985:92). Potential trade with Belize to the east was curtailed by Belize's coastal orientation, small population, and hostile relations with the Spanish. For example, there were rumors of a Zambo-Mosquito invasion of Petén from Belize in 1710, anxiety about Petén's vulnerability to Belizean attack in 1765, and so on. Sometimes rumor became reality and violence did occur, as in 1733 and again in 1754 when 1,500 Spanish soldiers coming from Petén tried without success to recapture Belize from the English.[9] Although there are hints in colonial documents that the Indians around San Luis were trading between southern Belize and Verapaz, during most of the colonial period there was no significant trade between Petén and Belize. That was to come later. In the colonial period (and early independence period) Petén's major trading partner was Yucatán, itself a "colonial backwater" (Farriss 1984:30). While demographic growth in Yucatán and new markets for its livestock products stimulated the economy after 1750 (Patch 1985), the great takeoff did not occur until the late nineteenth century when henequen became important in world trade. Moreover, vital as Yucatán was for Petén's commerce, the distance from the hub of the region in Remedios to southern Campeche was one hundred hard leagues. If colonial Yucatán was a backwater, Petén was even more remote.

Inadequate roads, another contextual factor, both reflected and reinforced the isolation. Contemporary Peteneros use pretty much the same words their colonial predecessors did to describe the roads and their consequences for the region. The roads were "bad," difficult to travel, not passable at the height of the wet season; the crown failed to invest in road improvement; as a result Petén was abandoned, isolated, and underdeveloped.[10]

The Royal Audience in Guatemala, acting through the governor of Petén, maintained the *camino real* (royal highway) there by relying primarily on corvée, *téquio* (in fact, corvée was used in Petén until 1944). The state also tried, with only partial success, to establish villages and poststations every 22 to 44 kilometers along the highway. There were two major branches of the road, one running north from San Andrés to Campeche, the other going from the southern shore of the Lake to Verapaz.

From San Andrés the *camino real* ran almost directly north through a string of villages to San Felipe, Campeche, turning northwest at Nohbecan, at about latitude 19°, to reach the town of Campeche. The trek from San Andrés to Nohbecan apparently took 9 to 15 days in the dry season.

The road was barely passable during the rainy season, but at all times it was less difficult and isolated than the southeastern route.

From the southern shore of the Lake the highway went southeast across the grasslands, then curved southwest around Poptún, crossing rugged mountains beyond Poptún to reach Cahabón, Verapaz. The distance from Remedios to San Luis, 40 leagues, and from San Luis to Cahabón, another 50 leagues, usually took 14 to 16 days to travel.[11] From early colonial times to about 1840 Petén's major commercial activity was the sale of livestock to Yucatán. Although most of what may have been private (Comparato 1983:10–11) and all crown ranches were located in the savannas and in the Dolores-Poptún area, it was simply not feasible to drive livestock over the high, broken terrain around San Luis to markets in highland Guatemala. For as long as livestock remained the major commodity, topography as much as anything else directed trade northward to Yucatán. This also contributed to keeping San Luis marginal to the main currents of life in Petén until well into the twentieth century.

Colonial governments had no interest in the other, lesser trails in Petén. There may have been a path from the western shore of the Lake through La Libertad to the Pasión and Usumacinta Rivers, and from there to Tabasco, but this was of little importance until the 1860s. There also were trails from Dolores and San Luis to Belize. By 1813 a trail running just south of the Lake and then going almost directly east to Belize began to increase in importance, though for most of the nineteenth century it was in poor condition (Pendergast 1967:160; González 1867). With the introduction of rubber tree tapping in the 1870s and then chicle tree tapping in the 1890s, traffic along this route and from the Río San Pedro to Tenosique, Mexico, was to become very important. From about 1826 to about 1944 the state tried, with uneven success, to keep open a road from Flores to Cobán via Chinajá, Alta Verapaz, but in 1960 Peteneros then in their sixties recalled that in their youth it was easier to reach Mérida via the old northern branch of the *camino real* (even though it had fallen into comparative disuse between 1838 and 1846) than it was to reach Cobán, and it was even easier to get to Belize.[12]

To anticipate much later developments, I will round off this discussion by adding that the one asphalted road in Petén, from Santa Elena on the northern shore of the Lake just opposite Flores to the ancient Maya site of Tikal, 62 kilometers, was completed in 1982. In 1970, at long last, a state agency opened an "all weather, third class" compacted dirt road which goes from Flores to San Luis and then struggles on to Izabal, beyond which there are paved roads to Guatemala City, 525 kilometers (326 miles) from Flores. For most of its length between Flores and San Luis, the road runs over the old *camino real*. Today this is the major commercial and passenger route within the department, and between it and the rest of the republic. Every year heavy rains wash out large portions of this and other roads. When this happens, except for those who can afford airplane travel, Petén is nearly as remote as it was in colonial times.[13]

Colonial Government

In comparison with those of other regions, the colonial government of Petén was not elaborate. Petén did not produce sufficient public revenues (see below) to support anything more than an elementary bureaucracy. Throughout this period, 1700 to 1821, Petén was a frontier military district and a penal colony ruled by a garrison commander resident in Remedios. The commandant, also titled the castellan, governor, and mayor, had extensive military, executive, managerial, and judicial authority over the district. His responsibilities included defense, custodial care of convicts, extraction of labor and goods from Indian communities and Indian confraternities, congregation of so-called wild Indians in pacified and nucleated Christianized villages, tax collection, supervision of public works (most of which had to do with the fort and the church in Remedios), road maintenance, management of the royal estates, dispute settlement, and transmission of yearly reports to higher authority. As might be expected in a place as remote as Petén, the commandant's power often exceeded his authority, and the only countervailing power within Petén was that of the church.[14]

The commandant exercised authority directly through his professional soldiers who not only bore arms but also served, for example, as managers of the crown livestock ranches, as farm inspectors, and so on. Over the years, their number varied from 60 to 80 men, and while the commandants considered this inadequate for defense against possible attack by the English in Belize or for extensive patrol, they rarely requested more than 6 to 8 additional soldiers at any one time. In dealing with Indians inclined toward rebellion, a commandant could also enlist the support of Ladinos, who resided in several Indian communities as well as in Remedios. "Pacified" Indians, too, could be armed to assist in the capture of runaway compatriots or "wild" Indians. In addition, the commandant indirectly ruled the Indians through native "governors" (*gobernadores*), that is, *caciques*, appointed upon his recommendation to manage Indian affairs within their respective villages. Finally, he relied heavily on the clergy for many record keeping and data collecting chores. Save for the vicar stationed in Remedios, priests lived in the Indian settlements where they exerted social, economic, and religious influence over their charges. Whatever the tensions between clergy and military, they shared a common concern—to control and dominate the Indians.

In fact, for most of the eighteenth century the military ruled a small population of about 3,000 people with, by the middle of that century, a ratio of Indians to non-Indians of roughly three to one. If this small number meant there were few natives from whom to extract an economic surplus, it also must have eased the burdens of control. In the seventeenth, eighteenth, and nineteenth centuries the authorities consistently overestimated the number and bellicosity of "wild" Indians, and they generally exaggerated their potential influence over pacified Indians. In Bricker's (1981) structuralist interpretation of Spanish history this sort of overestimation is called the "myth of pacification." There were, then, claims of thousands of "unpacified, barbarian" Indians in the forests, but the available evidence indicates nothing of the kind. Governor Bustamante in 1712, for example, reported that he had reduced (settled in Spanish-controlled nucleated villages) 585 Indians, but that 20,000 Indians remained unpacified. Governor or Commandant Hurtado in 1725 also spoke of numerous "dangerous" Indians in the woods and lamented that there were only 600 Indian families in the "reduction." Similar reports were made in 1754, 1757, 1765, and as late as 1880. Interestingly enough, a century later, in 1978, a group of tourists positively reported sighting "hundreds of Lacandón Indians" in the woods near Sayaxché, an exaggeration in the numbers of what may have been some long-haired guerrillas, but hardly "hundreds." After the consolidation of the 1697 conquest and the establishment of villages and parishes not later than 1710, few "wild" Indians were ever captured. For example, in 1757 Commandant Amate reported that after five incursions a body of Spanish soldiers and "*indios domésticos*" scoured the woods and captured and baptized ten Indians. The expedition cost seventy pesos—a sum that could have sustained ten soldiers in Remedios for nearly a month—and was considered relatively successful. In the far west there were small numbers of "Lacandones", and in the northwest there were so-called "Cehaches," who may have been or may have included Indian refugees from Yucatán, but the Spanish showed little interest in these areas. The priests, also prone to exaggerating the number of "wild" Indians, suspected that the military were less than diligent in mounting their dry season marches. If there really were numerous "wild" Indians in the forests (and there seem not to have been), they lived quietly, well beyond the zone of Spanish settlement. Nor did crown officials in Guatemala take enough interest in remote Petén to invest in extensive campaigns against them. After 1710 or perhaps somewhat later, there seem to have been few unconquered Indians left in Petén, and of those that were left the most numerous were the "Lacandones" and "Cehaches" far from Remedios.[15]

Most of the population under Spanish control was concentrated in five to seven villages located around Lake Petén Itzá, the plains nearest Remedios, and along the southern branch of the *camino real*, between Remedios and San Luis. The entire zone west of modern La Libertad, including the northwest and the southwest, and much of the northeast were beyond Spanish control. The authorities lacked the manpower to patrol these regions and saw little profit in doing so. The situation remained largely unchanged until the 1860s-1870s.[16]

The commandant had several sources of income to cover government expenses. The royal ranches produced about 1,500 pesos per year, which were used to maintain and improve the garrison, the church in Remedios, churches in villages, and so on. The commandery also received a *situado* (fixed income) of 1,200 pesos annually, this relatively small sum drawn by the government of Guatemala from highland tributary communities for the specific purpose of supporting frontier garrisons. The commandant may also have obtained direct access to village treasuries (*cajas*) after 1777, but more research is needed to clarify the matter. Although tribute payments, in the strict sense, seem not to have been common in Petén, income in kind was extracted from Indian farmers. Moreover, the Indians were obliged to perform *téquio* one day a week for the government. The governor also could draw on convict labor for various purposes. Nonetheless, commandants and clergy often complained about labor shortages which, in turn, led to grain shortages and difficulties in road construction and maintenance. At times a governor (for example, Hurtado in 1725) attributed labor scarcities to the excessive *téquios* imposed on the Indians by the priests, but the perceived scarcity must also be viewed in terms of the small population in colonial Petén.[17]

The Spanish soldiers were paid by the government in Guatemala which, from 1699 on, was slow to send supplies and salaries to Petén. The soldiers earned about 108 pesos a year in cash and in kind, from which they fed and clothed themselves. Although this was substantially more than the yearly wage of 12 pesos paid the ordinary Indian cowboys, it took a Spaniard about 48 pesos, at least until the 1760s, simply to feed himself properly, that is, in terms of his cultural norms. Funds were so slow to reach the garrison that to avoid dressing "in rags," soldiers had to borrow money from *vecinos* (non-Indians) and convicts. *Vecinos* overcharged the soldiers for loans, at an interest rate of 100 percent. At times the situation was so bad that secular and religious authorities recommended the soldiers be paid more in kind to ease want and exploitation. One wonders if the reported inability of the soldiers to bar *vecinos* from selling contraband liquor to Indians implies that they also eased their situation by accepting bribes from *vecinos*. Isolation, financial constraints, economic hardships, and food shortages made this kind of life unattractive to the soldiers. Few took up permanent residence in Petén, but of those who did many eventually prospered.[18]

Although the commandery, the soldiers, and the *vecinos* had to deal with many difficulties, they did establish a social, economic, and political system based in the first instance on ethnic stratification and backed by military power. Whatever the differences of rank among themselves, non-Indians were set above Indians. Ethnicity also became associated with community. Most non-Indians lived in Remedios, just as most of the elite later lived in Flores. Indians were found in villages, just as *poblanos* ("humble" people of rustic or *pujado* speech) later resided in the towns outside Flores. Soldiers, *vecinos*, and even convicts who remained in Petén and whose children became Peteneros gained enduring advantages from their initial headstart. The establishment of such families is discussed below, but here one case will illustrate the point. Agustín Pinelo, a Creole (Spaniard born in the Americas) born in Valladolid, Mexico, came to Petén as a soldier with Ursúa in 1697 and, in 1757 was eventually involved in ranching. A lineal descendant, apparently his grandson, Manuel Pinelo (1801–1867) held high political and bureaucratic offices in Petén and owned cattle ranches near modern San Francisco. During the 1830s, as the result of political differences with Commandant Segura, the family lost some property and never regained its former economic prominence, although it remained comfortable. Manuel's son, J. M. Pinelo (1833–1922), became a priest after his wife's death in 1873, and one of the department's most highly respected figures. One of his granddaughters married an affluent Flores merchant and rancher who has held important government posts in Petén. In turn, one of their daughters is married to a member of one of the wealthiest, most politically powerful families in the region. The family has close ties to high-ranking government officials in the national capital. Other contemporary members of the Pinelo family are prominent in departmental commerce, education, and government, and most of them reside in Flores or in nearby Santa Elena or San Benito. In 1839 Caddy referred to the Pinelos as "white creoles," but today at least some members of the family reject ethnic labels. Nevertheless, whether for reasons of class, education, residence, and/or ethnicity, Pinelos have not married Indians, or to use a more modern term, those descended from Indians.[19] This example is not meant to imply that the descendants of the first Spanish settlers in Petén invariably prospered, for some did not. Furthermore, the offspring of bureaucrats and merchants who came aprroximately between the 1720s and the 1750s often became wealthier and more powerful than the scions of the very earliest non-Indian families. Rather, the point is that the Pinelos and other non-Indians who settled in Petén during the colonial period, particularly those who did so in the first half of the eighteenth century, had advantages derived from their ethnic status as well as from family origins. Their ethnic identity gave them privileged access to bureaucratic posts, to commercial opportunities, to privately owned ranches, and, one may infer, self-confidence, which often derives from membership in a dominant group. By and large, the descendants of the early non-Indian settlers have maintained their superior political, economic, and social position.

The Church

The first churches in Petén were constructed no later than 1718. Juan Gómez de Pareda, 21st Bishop of Yucatán (1715–1728), consecrated the church bells, inscribed with the date 1718, in several of the oldest postconquest communities in Petén: Remedios, San Andrés, San José, Dolores, and Santo Toribio (Morley 1938 I:74; Soza 1957:203–6). The earliest surviving parish records, from Dolores and Santo Toribio, date from 1707–1709 (Parochial Archives, Flores). At first sight the changing number of villages within parish boundaries is bewildering, but in fact a relatively clear outline is present. Parish centers were established in Remedios, San Andrés, Dolores, San Luis, and San Martín (located on the *camino real* north of San Andrés; see Table 2:1). Although there was a priest resident off and on in San Martín until about the middle of the eighteenth century,

Table 2:1 Parishes in Petén, 1737–1819

1737[a]	1765[b]	1819[c]
Flores: S. Miguel, Concepción, S. Bernabe; Sta. Ana)	*Flores*: S. Bernabe	*Flores*
San Andrés: S. José, S. Jerónimo	*San Andrés*: S. José, S. Martín, Sta. Rita, S. Jerónimo, 10 ranches	*San Andrés*
Dolores: Sto. Toribio, S. Pedro	*Dolores*: Sto. Toribio, S. Felipe ranches	*Dolores*: Sto. Toribio, S. Felipe
San Luis: S. Francisco Javier	*San Luis*: Poptún	*San Luis*
San Martín: Sta. Rita	*Santa Ana*: S. Juan de Dios, S. Francisco, twelve ranches	*Santa Ana* (?): S. Juan de Dios, La Libertad
—	—	*San Benito*
—	—	*San Antonio*

Sources: For 1737 (Valdavida 1975), 1765 (AGI Guat. 859), 1819 (AGCA A1.17.1, Vicar Fajardo). Italicized settlements were parish headquarters. Where possible, settlements annexed to the parish are listed. Modern names for settlements are used, but note that La Libertad used to be called Sacluk, San Francisco was Chachaclun and San José was San Joseph, an eighteenth-century affectation. Between 1708–1718 if not earlier, churches were built in Flores, San Andrés, San José, Dolores, Santo Toribio, San Luis and possibly Santa Ana.

[a]This Concepción is not the hamlet of the same name located on the *camino real*, north of San Andrés. San Martín and Sta. Rita also were located on the royal road, north of San Andrés. Sometime between 1737–1750, Santa Ana became a separate parish apart from Flores. It may have been established by Mercedarians. San Martín's priests left Petén for Yucatán around 1763, or earlier.

[b]This San Francisco, located where the modern *pueblo* of the same name is (see Map, Chapter 1) should not be confused with San Francisco Javier, near San Luis, or with other San Francisco—most of them in southeast Petén—which appear and disappear in the historical records. In 1795, the Vicar of Petén mentioned five parishes in the district, apparently the same as existed in 1765.

[c]Vicar Fajardo noted that Dolores and San Luis lacked resident priests, at least at the time of his report. San Antonio seems not to have a priest for many years. Even in the 1980s, priests were in short supply, for example, in 1985 one priest, resident in San Benito, served not only that *pueblo* and its hamlets, but also the *pueblos* and several villages in San Andrés and San José.

sometime during the 1740s this and several other northern hamlets became subordinate to the San Andrés parish, and Santa Ana became the parish headquarters for the central plains zone. The Sayaxché parish, in the southwest, was not established until the twentieth century, and in 1985 northwestern and northeastern Petén lacked their own parishes (Table 2:1).[20] In short, parish boundaries generally coincided with the major centers of population.

Except during 1699, when there were nine priests in Petén, the church was usually short-handed in the colonial period and for a long time thereafter. Most of the time there were resident priests in Remedios, San Andrés, Santa Ana, Dolores, and San Luis. A provincial vicar and, at most, four parish priests were not considered sufficient for Petén. As early as 1709, royal officials remarked that three secular clergy (the number then in Petén) were too few,[21] but the situation really never did change. It was worse from 1821 until 1956, when there usually were two or sometimes three priests in the department.

The Franciscan ecclesiastic authorities in Yucatán "must have imposed themselves religiously" on Petén "from the very beginning" of the colony, despite objections from the Dominicans who had earlier been active among the Mopán (Valdavida 1975). From 1696 to 1860, the Franciscans sent vicars, parish priests, and pastoral inspectors to the Petén (Mercedarians did missionary work in the central savannas around the middle of the eighteenth century). In the villages Indians filled various subordinate positions as choirmasters, sextons, and so on. Just how much control the clergy had over the Indian *cofradías* (parish or community confraternities devoted to the care of one or more saints) is not clear. The *cofradías* were supposed to help support church workers, help pay the salaries of the cowboys who worked on church ranches, and provide various personal services to priests resident in their communities, for example, supplying them with fuelwood and tending their horses. However, toward the end of the colonial period, from 1795 on, the vicars complained of Indian "resistance" and the vexing reluctance of secular authority to do anything about it. The *cofradías* apparently were none too productive. They, like the *vecinos*, lacked the wealth to help the church to the extent the vicars would have preferred.[22]

Whether they resisted or not, the church demanded and extracted a good deal from the Indians. Although some were exempt from contributions and alms payments to the church and all were free from baptismal and burial fees (but not from the three pesos marriage fee), they were subject to many other impositions. Men of 18 to 50 years of age were tithed in kind, and each family had to provide its parish church with 300 pounds of maize each year. There were, besides, *téquio* and *cofradía* obligations. At the direction of the priests, at least until 1725, Indian men collected dyes and grew cotton, and the women were kept busy spinning it. The Indians may have been forced to purchase the end product, as well as other goods, at prices set by the clergy. (All this made the priests willing farm and trade inspectors.) Unfortunately, I do not know how the *vecino* merchants regarded what the priests were doing, but some commandants, for several reasons, did not like it. The women were kept so busy they could not accompany their husbands to the farm or to seek medical help in Remedios. The Indians were so occupied in meeting the demands of the clergy that they were unable to produce enough maize for the colony, and this led to price fluctuations (varying for most of the colonial period from two to six reales per *carga*, which may have weighed 84 pounds). Knowing of the excessive *téquios* and other demands, unpacified Indians who might otherwise have settled in reduced villages chose to remain in the woods. Despite these objections and aside from obvious material interests, ideological factors may also have prompted the priests to require so much of the Indians. They, and audiencia officials, considered the Indians inherently lazy (*perezoso*) and unorganized. If, as reported in 1765, the Indians were barely able to provide enough maize to sustain their own households, the priests could argue that the Indians' innate slothfulness was the cause, not the demands of the clergy for their labor.[23]

The priests had material and ideological means by which to squeeze the Indians. The clergy generally, but not always, had the backing of the military. They had goods and food to distribute in hard times. Indians who derived their own status from the clergy (for example, sextons) would have been a source of support, helping the clergy impose on Indian compatriots. Priests at times also shielded Indians from heavy-handed secular authorities. Finally, on the ideological side, Indians feared excommunication, and it is possible that at least some of them genuinely accepted the legitimacy of clerical demands and authority.

In addition to material support from Indians, income from religious fees and their own ranch, subsidies from the royal estate in Petén for church structures and ornaments, and travel subsidies from the crown, the clergy also received a salary from the crown sent through Guatemala. (In Petén, the clergy did not receive cash from tithes.) Early in the eighteenth century the vicar's salary was 400 pesos per year, and the priests' 200 pesos. By 1782 the vicar's annual salary was 480 pesos, his sacristan's 96 pesos, and the parish clergy's 360 pesos. In contrast, cowboys never received more than 12 pesos a year. Some indication of the purchasing power of these incomes is gained by noting relatively standard (though subject to short-term fluctuations) eighteenth century prices for several important commodities.

Maize cost 2 to 6 reales per *carga* (37.8 kg or 84 pounds, shelled); salt cost 3 reales for 4.5 kg; cloth cost 2 reales per *vara* (0.85 meter or 2.8 feet); a cow or bull cost 3 pesos, a horse 10 pesos, and a mule 20 pesos (one peso was worth 8 reales). The clergy were not poor, but they felt their incomes were not sufficient to sustain them properly nor enough to attract other priests to Petén. By the standards of Yucatán or highland Guatemala, they were probably correct.[24]

In short, if the church in colonial Petén possessed ideological authority and, certainly compared to Indians, relative economic power, it also had some tough problems. There were conflicts with secular authority, problems with *vecinos* at least over the sale of liquor to Indians, concerns about limited manpower and finances, doubts about the religious faith of the Indians and in this connection concerns about their readiness to rebel. The 1765 document (AGI Guatemala 859) provides an excellent example of clerical anxiety about the last problem. In it, the priests recall that in the past the Indians of San Luis had killed friars; that in 1734 Indians in a village near Dolores would have burned down the village church had not *vecinos* intervened (and Indians did burn parish records in Santo Toribio in 1738); that in 1762 an Indian surnamed Covoh (now spelled Cohouj) tried to stir a revolt in San Bernabe, a village near Remedios; and that despite two hundred years of domination, Maya in Yucatán rose up in 1760–1762, some fleeing to San Andrés where they found shelter and an audience. The priests warn that Indians in Dolores and Santa Ana can hear the guns of "Walis" (Belize) and may be roused by them. Indians, they say, also flee to the woods at the slightest hint of peril (or, as Cacique Zib more sympathetically put it in 1763, they have a "natural love" of hills and forests). Commandants might attribute flight to overbearing clergy, but the priests relate it to a lack of piety: "As recent [this in 1765] converts they are not firm in the Faith." Even if Christian, their faith is shallow, their habits bad. They "do not abandon some of the vices of infidelity" (AGI Guatemala 859, 1765). The authorities continued to be concerned with problems of flight and faith up to modern times.

Vecinos

After Tayasal fell, the Spanish command left 72 to 80 soldiers and several Maya-speaking mestizo families from Yucatán and Guatemala at Remedios. Shortly after 1700 they were reinforced by several military families from Campeche and Yucatán and some fourteen Spanish families with

Indian servants from Verapaz or more likely Guatemala (Soza 1957:88–89; 1970:117; Comparato 1983:398). Ursúa tried, with little success, to persuade more Yucatecans to move to Petén. Lack of economic opportunity, an insalubrious climate, food shortages, and other difficulties discouraged migration to distant Petén. In desperation, Ursúa appealed to mestizos (people of mixed Euro-Indian ancestry), Pardos (of Afro-European or Afro-Indian ancestry), Indians, and Spaniards of "no social status," "the unemployed and poorly occupied" (Comparato 1983:348, 362), but few responded. Migrants from the Guatemalan highlands were paid twenty-four pesos to settle in Petén, but most soon departed (G. Jones, personal communication). Nor had the situation changed in 1754 when Commandant Monzaval lamented that Spaniards did not want to live in Petén. Of the few migrants, apparently most came from Campeche, for which reason, or so Soza (1970:117) argues, their surnames—Aldana, Ayala, Burgos, Gongóra, Manzanero, Monterro, Penados, Pinelo, and so forth—are uncommon in Guatemala save for Petén. Soza exaggerates somewhat, for example, although Manzanero is specific to Petén, a surname like Aldana was common in Izabal in colonial times. It is true, however, that most of the old established families in the department do claim Campechano origins. Some of the early settlers were Ladinos, that is, Spanish-speaking Indians and/or Hispanicized Indians, and by the eighteenth century Ladinos commonly were the acculturated offspring of mixed Spanish-Indian unions. Whatever may have been their status elsewhere, in colonial Petén at least some and perhaps most of the Ladinos were regarded as *vecinos*, albeit lower in social status than the Spaniards and Creoles.

The earliest census data of which I know that yield some idea of the colony's ethnic composition are dated 1765 and 1778. Although these are late dates, Petén had so few settlers that the reports probably represent pre-1760s trends.[25] The 1765 report (AGI Guat. 859) said little about children, did not make fine ethnic distinctions, and was not a complete population count, but it did make clear that there were at least 1,168 Indians and 419 non-Indians (including 60 soldiers, 63 convicts, and 9 political exiles) in the reduction (Table 2:2). The 1778 census was more complete and more attentive to ethnic categories (Table 2:3). Spaniards, mestizos, Pardos, and some Indians lived in Remedios, that is, the Presidio. There were Ladinos in San Andrés, Santo Toribio, and Dolores, but the majority were Indians. Santa Ana, San José, and San Luis were exclusively Indian settlements.

From 1699 on, non-Indians lived in Remedios, and from the 1730s on

Table 2:2 Population of Petén by Parish, 1765

Parish	Indian	Non-Indian
1. Remedios*	—	312
San Bernabe	19 or 27	—
2. San Andrés*	256	69
San Joseph	110	—
San Geronimo	21	—
Haciendas (6)	78(?)	—
3. Santa Ana*	156	—
4. Dolores*	356	23
Santo Toribio	109	15
5. San Luis*	63	—
Total	1,168	419

Source: AGI Guat. 859, 1765.
*Parish headquarters. At this time there were four priests and a vicar in Petén. The data are obviously incomplete and undercount the population, but they do display the relative proportions of Indians to non-Indians and the respective locations of each group. Note that the priests report thirteen rural neighborhoods and/or ranches in Santa Ana (cf. Table 2:1), and two of the four crown ranches were located in Santo Toribio.

in San Andrés, Santo Toribio, and Dolores. For example, by the latter date there were, among others, Zetinas and Aldanas in San Andrés; Aldanas, Guzmáns, Heredias, and Hoils in Dolores; Contrerases in Santo Toribio (Parochial Archives, Flores). Although these people, except perhaps for the Aldanas, may have been Ladinos rather than Spaniards, the colonial documents on Guatemala, including Petén, do not consistently distinguish members of these ethnic status categories from each other (Valdavida 1975; Wortman 1982:290). What is clear is that people with Spanish surnames do not appear in San José or San Luis until well into the nineteenth century and then usually as officials in temporary residence. Even when permanent residents bearing Spanish surnames do appear in these two communities, they are identified as Indians. (Indeed, today, Peteneros regard San José and San Luis as "Indian" towns.)

I believe that the location of the non-Indians is related to the salience of livestock raising in colonial Petén, although defense was also an important contributing factor, as it most clearly was in the case of Remedios. Spaniards were the chief administrators of the royal ranches found just east of Santo Toribio and Dolores, but closer to the former, and their families may

Table 2:3 Population of Petén, 1778

Settlement	Spanish M	F	Mestizo M	F	Pardo M	F	Ladino M	F	Indian M	F	Total
Presidio	27	18	26	31	147	130	—	—	31	21	431
Santa Ana	—	—	—	—	—	—	—	—	117	84	201
San Andrés	—	—	—	—	—	—	21	15	133	142	311
San Josep	—	—	—	—	—	—	—	—	65	76	141
Santo Toribio	—	—	—	—	—	—	14	11	60	53	138
Dolores	—	—	—	—	—	—	3	3	143	136	285
San Luis	—	—	—	—	—	—	—	—	59	38	97
Total	27	18	26	31	147	130	38	29	608	550	1604

Source: Derived from an AGI document discovered by Dr. L. Feldman. (M = Male, F = Female.)

The document omits children ("parbulos"), presumably under 7 years of age, which may account for the discrepancy with Juarros's (1832) oft-cited figure of 2,555 for the population in Petén in 1778. Both reports seem to omit people living alongside the *camino real* north of San Andrés, not to mention the "wild" Indians in far western and northwestern Petén. The number of Pardos seem high, and I suspect they are lumped with Ladinos and even with Spaniards in other documents (in Petén, if a Spanish male married a Pardo woman, their children might well have been counted as Spaniards or Creoles). After 1821, census reports either make no ethnic distinction or refer to "Indians" and "non-Indians," and the terms Spanish, mestizo and Pardo drop out of official reports.

have resided in these villages. Non-Indians also established, perhaps as much for cultural as for economic reasons (Farriss 1984:33), cattle ranches wherever access to the *camino real* and the terrain made it possible, although the legal status of these ranches is unclear. Thus, as early as 1710 to 1720, apparently there were private ranches on the small savanna 24 to 30 kilometers northwest of San Andrés and around Santa Ana, that is, in that part of the great central plains nearest Remedios; and by the 1730s, around present-day San Francisco and La Libertad (Martínez Uck 1971; Valdavida 1975). Santa Ana is so close and accessible to Remedios that there would have been no need for owners to reside there, contrary to the situation in San Andrés where Spaniards and Ladinos had to live in order to manage their ranches north of the town and to patrol the region north of the Lake. Non-Indians also seem to have owned private ranches in the area between Dolores and Poptún. Stock raising was the major commercial agrarian activity in Petén until the early independence period. Although it was an important, perhaps the most important, source of nonfarm work for Indians, in absolute terms it did not require much in the way of permanent labor. On the royal ranches and, I assume, on private estates, the animals roamed largely unattended, except during yearly roundups for branding and counting. Given the sparse population in Petén and the competition among clergy, government, and *vecinos* for native labor, perhaps this was the only way to manage the herds. Unfortunately, I have not found any private account records, but if those of the royal estates are any indication, important as ranching was, it was not highly profitable. Apparently, cultural considerations played an important role in keeping the settlers engaged in ranching.

The *vecinos*, however, were not only ranchers and crown officials. They were also merchants who sold cloth, soap, wax, candles, sweets, and tobacco to the garrison; made profitable loans to the soldiers, acted as cattle dealers, and sold contraband sugarcane liquor (*aguardiente*) to the Indians from whom they purchased the cane. Although bureaucrats and merchants who came to Petén after about 1725 often acquired more wealth and power than the pioneer settlers, no one was very wealthy (Vicar Ponce de León AGCA A3.1, Leg. 590, Exp. 11700, 1795). Vicar Fajardo (AGCA A1.2233, Leg. 15510, Exp. 2160, 1812) made this point in his sarcastic complaint about the high-handed rule of Commandant Villar. Villar, he said, used the pretext of controlling contraband trade to fix rigid schedules for canoe travel on the Lake, but, in fact, with Tabasco and Yucatán so far away, no one could engage in smuggling. Besides, "no one [in Petén] has even five hundred pesos in cash" to finance this or any other economic activity.

In addition to a lack of wealth, and not to mention shortages of ammunition at the garrison, settlers often wanted for basic food staples. For the Spanish, daily portions of beef, maize, and beans were essential in an adequate diet. Some felt the need for a ration of one to two pounds of beef daily. Even convicts were entitled to beef every day. Yet, despite several sources of supply—*cofradía*, crown and perhaps private ranches—people in Petén had to cope with shortages. The distance of the ranches from the Presidio, poor road conditions, and careless drovers who resented this form of *téquio* made it difficult to provision Remedios with beef. To make things worse, maize and bean harvests were often poor, try though the Spanish might to get the Indians to produce more. At times the Spanish and the rest of the population were "forced" (as the documents put it) to eat such foods as *ramón* (breadnut, a famine substitute for maize) and even that cost one and a half reales per carga for transport, *camote* (sweet potato), *yuca* (manioc), *ñame* and *macal* (yams), green plantains, and mamey and sapote fruit. Although this list may indicate that the Indians persisted in producing a diversity of crops other than grains despite the Spanish attempt to get them to concentrate on maize and beans, and although it may also suggest that a healthy range of foodstuffs was available, the Spanish had culturally defined nutritional standards that hardly made these considerations good news. From their perspective, life in Petén was hard.[26]

The slowness with which the Audience in Guatemala sent supplies to Petén, the lack of opportunity to become rich, the sparse population, the poor roads, and the remoteness of Petén may have encouraged self-reliance among the ethnically diverse post-1697 Peteneros (Reina 1965; Comparato 1983:325). With so few Indians to command and with an Indian to non-Indian ratio of slightly less than three to one (Tables 2:2 and 2:3), the colonists may well have had to do for themselves things that were done elsewhere by Indian servants and field hands. In many aspects of daily life, non-Indians, other than the handful of Spaniards in Remedios, were probably similar to Indians. Even in Yucatán where absolute and relative numbers of Indians were much greater, mestizos and Pardos "were indistinct in many ways from their Maya neighbors;" for example, they all practiced the same type of swidden cultivation. And some *vecinos* were "non-Indian in little more than name" (Farriss 1983:18). All these factors also promoted intermarriage across ethnic lines. The documentary record is not clear, but Petén family traditions and genealogies indicate that some Spaniards married Ladinos and perhaps Pardos, although they almost never married Indians or people with Indian surnames, and the highest ranked Spanish families practiced ethnic or caste endogamy. Ladinos, mestizos, and Pardos in turn married people with Indian surnames, thereby lifting some Indians to the ranks of the non-Indians. Yet, without minimizing the extent of ethnic intermarriage or of some blurring of ethnic-cultural boundaries fostered by a need for self-reliance, it must be emphasized that the Indians were a subordinated group not only during colonial times, but for many years after Guatemala became a republic.

If the non-Indians (*vecinos*, priests, soldiers, and bureaucrats) were not wealthy, they had more economic resources than Indians. They also enjoyed superior political privileges and superior social status. Even though ethnic boundaries were breached, Spaniards, Pardos, and Ladinos, taken together, were set above the Indians, who comprised about 72–75 percent of the colonial population in Petén.

The Royal Hacienda

Before discussing the Indians specifically, a crown *hacienda* (estate) in Petén will be described, for it was of great concern to the Spanish authorities and important for all groups regardless of rank or caste. The *hacienda* was initiated during the tenure of Commandant Ruiz y Bustamante (1708–1718), who also sponsored the establishment of private and *cofradía* ranches (Soza 1970:611–14). Collectively referred to as "San Felipe," the royal ranches, situated in valleys just east of Santo Toribio, between 60 to 80 kilometers from Remedios, consisted of four separate spreads: San Felipe, Santa Cruz, Santa Gertrudis, and San Ignacio. Although as late as 1771 crown auditors bemoaned the paucity of documents on the estate, sufficient material is available to depict its operations.[27] What stands out vividly in the documents is that San Felipe was a centerpiece of colonial society and economy, was an important source of wage labor for Indians, and yet finally was not very profitable. Referring to the lack of interest in Petén of the Royal Audience in Guatemala, Comparato says the colony was a "poor relation" (1983:363). The guardians of San Felipe, the oldest child of this poor relation, eventually tried to disown it.

Income and produce from San Felipe helped subsidize the Presidio and the church. The estate supplied meat for convicts and helped pay for a wide range of equipment for the Presidio (hourglasses, flagpoles, cartridges, and so on). San Felipe also financed housing for soldiers; in 1769 it paid 32 pesos for their new thatch barracks. The estate also helped the church with such things as construction costs, purchase of ornaments, wages for artisans, and canoes for priests. In 1741 San Felipe paid 227 pesos for church ornaments and 103 pesos, 4 reales for the silversmith's wages and expenses. To take but one more example, in 1797 15 pesos from the estate were used to hire Indian artisans, masons, carpenters, and unskilled laborers to build a large canoe for the priest in San Andrés and 32 pesos were used for three thatch houses for the churches in San Andrés and in San José. Thus, although village parishes were aided somewhat by the estate, the main beneficiaries of its operation were the garrison, church, and population in Remedios.

San Felipe also provided full- and part-time employment to a fair number of Indian cowboys, although livestock enterprises did not make heavy demands on labor (Patch 1985:41–43). The estate manager, who reported directly to the commandant, was always a Spaniard, and Spanish soldiers worked as long distance drovers, but ranch foremen and cowboys were

Indians. Despite some lack of clarity in the records, it can be safely estimated that San Felipe had a permanent staff of about twenty-five men in most of the eighteenth century. In absolute terms, this is not a great number, but, for example, in the 1770s it constituted about 4 percent of the adult male Indian population. Furthermore, during the annual roundup at least an additional sixty Indians were hired for two weeks to help brand and count animals, repair corrals, and so on. Thus, at least once during the year, something like 10 percent of the adult male Indians worked at San Felipe, which does not include the Indians who were paid from estate income to work on Presidio and church projects. (An uncounted number of Indians, including at least fifty from San Andrés, also worked on private and *cofradía* ranches.)

Wages at San Felipe were relatively constant throughout the colonial period. Owing to the scarcity of labor in Petén, San Felipe had to pay the cowboys 12 pesos per year (and ranch work did not prevent the men from also making milpas, swidden plots primarily for maize and beans). Subforemen and foremen earned between 14 and 18 pesos per year; early in the eighteenth century the estate manager received 20 pesos, and 48 pesos toward the end of the century. Masons and unskilled laborers (*peónes*) hired by the Presidio for short-term projects were paid respectively 3 reales and 2 reales per day, which compares well with the highest wages—3 reales per day—paid *peónes* in colonial Mexico (Gibson 1964:252), but in Petén, Indians could not find wage work year-round. As mentioned above, throughout the eighteenth century maize cost 2 to 6 reales per *carga*, and (at least in 1765) 1 to 2 reales daily were needed to sustain an adult who had no farm. A complete harness set cost about 3 pesos, a horse 10 pesos, and a good pack mule 20 pesos. Scaled against these prices the cowboys' wages, though supplemented by some free portions of estate beef, were modest (and see Gibson 1964:333); however, scaled against wages for Indians in general, they were generous. In fact, their wages were equal to those of foremen on medium-sized ranches in Yucatán (Farriss 1984:184).

It is indicative of the economic situation that San Felipe, the most important royal enterprise in Petén, owned far smaller herds than comparable operations elsewhere in the Spanish colonies. The estate had about 2,000 cattle in 1725 and never more than 4,300 cattle (in 1808). Throughout most of the colonial period the annual cattle herd size varied from 2,500 to 3,500 head, and the annual horse and mule herd varied from about 70–140 (droughts and "lions" regularly killed 5–7 percent of the herds each year).

In contrast, even a small private ranch in eighteenth-century Yucatán might run 250 head of cattle (Chardon 1961:22), while Dominican estates in Chiapas and Verapaz had respectively 23,000 and 50,000 cattle in the 1760s (Wortman 1982:55, 137).

The estate sold livestock, tallow, cheese, butter, and milk to the local population and livestock to buyers from Yucatán. Highland Guatemalans, like Yucatecans, valued the hard-hooved Petén horses, but the evidence indicates that the highlanders did not buy cattle from Petén. Most of the trade was with Yucatecans who came in the dry season to buy livestock and to sell items such as sugar, cacao, axes, and machetes.

Income from the royal estate was as limited as its herds. From about 1775 to 1821, annual estate income varied from 1,350 to 2,120 pesos. Income for 1795 to 1797 was 4,789 pesos, not much more than the annual salary of the governor of Yucatán, yet Commandant Gálvez (AGCA A1.6, Leg.2159, Exp. 15492, 1797) could boast that this "copious" sum "had never been produced in all the years your Majesty owned" the *hacienda*. San Felipe paid its permanent labor force between 300 and 500 pesos per year (plus meat subsidies), thus on average it had roughly 1,000 to 1,500 to turn over to the Presidio. Since the annual expenses of the Presidio ran to 7,000 to 8,000 or more pesos, San Felipe never brought in enough to pay for more than a small portion of Presidio operating costs. (Equipment too was limited at San Felipe; for example, in 1797 it had four corrals, three pens, and eighteen packsaddles, up from sixteen packsaddles in 1784.) Estate income was derived equally, about 33 percent each, from the sale of cheese, cattle, and horses or mules. The price for an old cow was generally 2 pesos, and a young bull could sell for 8 pesos, but on average during the colonial period the price for a cow or bull was 3 to 5 pesos, that is, somewhat lower than the average price, 5 to 7 pesos, in Yucatán (Farriss 1984:485; Patch 1985). Conversely, prices for horses and mules were higher in Petén than in Yucatán, but San Felipe had few of these animals to sell.[28]

Commandants and clergy attributed the relatively low prices for Petén cattle to bad roads and to the region's isolation during the rainy season. The operation of the royal *hacienda* was also troubled by droughts, over-grazing, and administrative shortcomings connected, the authorities felt, with the distance between San Felipe and Remedios. All these problems and the limited financial returns from the estate led commandants and clergy, from the 1760s on, to recommend to the crown that San Felipe be sold at public auction. The crown did not act on the repeated advice, and

San Felipe endured until shortly after the colonial period ended. Even though the *hacienda* was probably the largest single agrarian commercial entity in colonial Petén and had many more animals than the *cofradías*, it was not a success. This indicates, as well as anything can, that the district was indeed a poor relation.

The Indians

As the preceding sections make plain, almost every dimension of colonial life involved the Indians, but here I will discuss several aspects of their situation more specifically. To establish a setting for this discussion I will return for a moment to the beginning of the eighteenth century to review some previously mentioned factors.

After suffering military defeat and an enormous loss of population, the surviving Indians were congregated into nucleated villages by the Spanish. It is well known that the Spanish carried out these reductions to facilitate political and economic control of the Indians and to effect their Christianization. The first few years of postconquest military consolidation and reduction were particularly harsh, Indians and Spanish practicing scorched earth policies, and some Indians fleeing however they could from the Spanish. The worst days passed when the relatively gentle Ruiz y Bustamante was appointed commandant in 1708, by which date the major villages of the colony had been founded and (by 1718) churches built in them. There were no further important reductions after 1720, although allegedly there were many "infidel" Indians roaming the forests well into the nineteenth century.[29] Most of the resettlement villages were set astride the *camino real*, and to some (presumably unintentional) extent colonial parish lines roughly overlay preexisting native political boundaries.

The conquest, military-religious consolidation, and subsequent normalized conditions of colonial life destroyed not only the native polities of Petén, but also much of the preconquest productive, commercial, social, and cultural system. Through warfare, disease, dislocation and then reassembly in new "reduced" villages, the Itzá were nearly eliminated as a distinct ethnic entity in the region. Hellmuth (1977) argues that in fact they did not survive as a recognizable group, but Reina (1962) believes that they did, in San José. This particular issue aside, the point here is that despite some blurring of lines, ethnicity was now the basis of socioeconomic and political status. Production was largely based on social and military relations by which surpluses were extracted from Indians (Weeks 1986). Spanish secular and clerical authorities alternately removed Indians from assigned villages to meet labor needs elsewhere, and if each side also took turns charging the other for this and other abuses, the Indians themselves were a subject people. The Indians did rebel at times. However, that they also believed spirit beings would retaliate for injuries they suffered at the hands of the Spanish, that they resorted to duplicity in dealing with non-Indians, or took flight to the woods (and if caught were fined, whipped, or sent to mines far from Petén) are all the marks of a defeated people (Wortman 1982:98; Comparato 1983:393). After 1697 non-Indians largely set the terms of life for Indians in Petén.

The Spanish settled most of the new villages with diverse groups. Spanish administrators grouped together in the same villages Indians of differing ethnopolitical backgrounds, and they dispersed into different villages Indians (for example, the Muzules or Tipuans) of like background. Perhaps this was done because there were relatively few surviving (or available, for some survivors fled to deep forests) native Petén Chan Indians and/or because the Spanish were indifferent to intra-Indian ethnopolitical differences. In addition, some numbers of Ladinos, mestizos, and Indians from Yucatán and Guatemala also settled in the new villages. Thus most villages were, at least initially, heterogeneous with respect to cultural backgrounds.

The history of San Andrés, located on the northern shore of Lake Petén Itzá, illustrates the process of village formation. But first, recall that the principal colonial settlements were Remedios, San Andrés, San José, Santa Ana, Santo Toribio, Dolores, and San Luis. In the nineteenth and early twentieth centuries other major settlements were added, beginning as ranching (San Francisco, La Libertad, Poptún), logging (Sayaxché) or border trading (Melchor de Mencos) centers. San Benito is a special case, discussed below. Although Santo Toribio eventually lost importance, and although minor settlements appear, disappear, and sometimes reappear in a somewhat bewildering fashion all through Petén's post-1697 history, the major villages have endured up to today.[30]

"New" San Andrés may have been the site of an old Cobox, Cohouj, or Chaken village.[31] If so, then during the intense violence of 1697–1700 the original population apparently deserted the place. The Spanish established or reestablished a new village here shortly after 1700 and appointed an Indian "governor" to supervise its strictly Indian affairs. The first Indian governor I have been able to identify, don Bernardo Chatha (Chatá), having served the Spanish loyally since 1708, was appointed in 1713, but he may have had a predecessor.[32] Later, other Chatás were to serve in the same capacity, but there is no evidence that the Indian governors of San Andrés or any other settlement in Petén were recruited from any preconquest Indian aristocracy. Although, as mentioned earlier, it is known that shortly after the conquest Rey Canek and other dignitaries from Tayasal were sent to the highlands, the available documents are mute about what happened to Indian leaders in other communities. In the absence of any mention of them in the documents and in family traditions, one may speculate that they fled with their subordinates to the forests, but unless new information is discovered this must remain a speculation. A church was erected in San Andrés by 1718, and soon afterward private livestock ranches were set up northwest of the village. The first postconquest inhabitants probably included some Cohouj Indians (perhaps even some who had lived here prior to the conquest) related to those of San José and some Chatá Indians (Hellmuth 1971:18; Valdavida 1975; see also Morelet 1871:219–20; Soza 1957:181). In 1707 Tipuans were resettled in central Petén, and some may have been placed in San Andrés. Between 1700 and 1713 several Cehach from the northwestern San Pedro River region and several Muzules, originally transferred from Belize to southeastern Petén, were sent to San Andrés and San José (Valdavida 1975). Somewhat later more Muzul Indians seem to have been added to the population (see Commandant García 1754, cited in footnote 15). But the majority of the founding population came from Yucatán, specifically from Campeche, according to oral tradition in San Andrés. Soza (1970:466–68) says that the implacable refusal of Itzá people to remain in reduced villages compelled the Spanish to settle San Andrés, and other new villages, with Maya Indians and Ladinos from Yucatán. In addition, at least one Spanish military-bureaucratic family, the Aldanas, were posted to San Andrés, and there may have been others.[33] Whereas in other predominantly Indian settlements some form of Petén Maya was spoken (Berendt 1868), in San Andrés Yucatec Maya may have become the common language, although more research is needed to settle the point (Schumann 1971). Maya was used by many San Andreños until the 1920s, but today only a handful of elderly people speak Maya; Petén Maya is still common in San José as is Kekchí in and around San Luis.

Maya Indians, Ladinos, mestizos, and Spaniards from Yucatán continued to pass through and, in some cases, remain in San Andrés, their arrival usually linked to oppression (Farriss 1984:72, 86) and political upheaval in Yucatán, for example, the Jacinto Canek revolt of 1761 and, after the colonial period, the War of the Castes from 1846 to 1870, border dispute disturbances from 1880 to 1883, and the Mexican Revolution from 1910 to 1917 and 1920 to 1926. Thus the first inhabitants of postconquest San Andrés were a mixture of Chan peoples, Indians from Belize, and Indians and non-Indians from Yucatán.[34]

The available evidence suggests that throughout the eighteenth century and indeed the nineteenth, there was some attrition of early Indian surnames in San Andrés. The same may be observed in several other Petén villages, again perhaps excepting San José. The reasons for this are not altogether clear, but it is reasonable to suppose that the disadvantaged position of the Indians is part of the story (see, for example, Vicar Fajardo AGCA A1.17.1, Leg. 188, Exp. 3843, 1819).

The Spanish regulated, and disrupted, native cultivation practices in various ways. They forced the Indians to concentrate on grain crops (maize, beans) for these were "easily weighed, controlled, stored and transported," as a consequence of which root and tree crops were neglected (Hellmuth 1977:436). As I have indicated elsewhere, the Indians may have persisted in growing a wider range of crops than Hellmuth would concede, although the Spanish were so focused on grains and beef that they considered it a hardship to consume these additional foods. As in Yucatán, the Spanish authorities ordered each married Indian to cultivate 60 *mecates* (about 2.64 hectares) to sustain his family (Farriss 1984:127), but compliance was far from complete. For example, in 1765 Indians in Santa Ana barely planted 30 to 40 *mecates* each, and even in San Andrés, which was something of a maize basket for central Petén from early colonial times until 1965–1970, they cropped no more than 50 to 60 *mecates* (AGI Guat. 859, 1765). Recurrent epidemics worsened the situation (Reina 1967). Moreover, aside from the possibility or probability that the Indians were reluctant to stress grains to the extent the Spanish desired, and aside from the chance that they hid part of the harvest from inspectors, the Indians were also diverted from giving full attention to farming by forced labor and by wage labor opportunities in ranching and sugarcane cultivation. Labor was scarce in Petén and livestock were important, and *vecino* merchants wanted sugarcane to make *aguardiente* to sell to Indians, illegal though this was. The Spanish, then, placed contradictory demands on Indian labor and contributed to the very situation they lamented. Despite repeated official orders to stimulate grain production, there often were shortfalls in Petén (Reina 1967, 1968).

As discussed in the sections on the church and the state, the Indians were also subject to a wide range of forced labor drafts (*téquios*). They had to provide church and state with one day of labor per week (and were only in 1808 relieved of the obligation to provide food rations to the priests), had to work on roads, to carry mail, to provide hospitality for travelers, to contribute to their own community treasury chests (*cajas*), and so on. They could not be merchants, and whatever the law, they were shunted about to meet labor demands. Even if, as seems highly unlikely, there were no illegal abuses imposed on them, the Indians were controlled by their own governors, by the clergy and by the state. Subordination, obviously, was part of what it meant to be an Indian.

No doubt the severity of domination varied from time to time and from official to official, but domination it was. Penalties for insubordination could be harsh, not only during the first few violent years of the colony, but also at its end. For example, in 1803 several Indian men and women from San Andrés fled to Sacpúy, twenty-four kilometers away by land, there, according to the charge, to "live in the woods, as apostates." A Spanish judge sent Indian soldiers under Sergeant Moo from San José to bring them back. In court the Indians argued through a translator (a Pinelo) that they never intended to quit San Andrés permanently, but left because they were short of maize and unable to pay their tax debts, and because a smallpox epidemic in the village hindered farm work. Nor did they wish to borrow from the community chest, because interest rates were high. Their explanation was to no avail; the men were sentenced to "one hundred lashes of the whip," and the women sentenced to eight days in jail. In 1805 higher authority decided that since the accused had already served time in jail, they were not to be whipped, but for two years the threat of the lash was held over them. In 1812 Vicar Mendoza complained that Commandant Abella, contrary to law, had imprisoned one of his Indian servants for one month without giving reasons for the action. In 1819 Vicar Fajardo denounced a commandant for mistreating Indian church singers (*cantores*) and punishing one with fifty lashes. Lest it seem that the church was a disinterested protector of Indians, it should be added that Mendoza was upset because priests had difficulties securing personal services in Petén and mistreatment of Indians added to their problems. Fajardo was concerned that by abusing Indians and preventing them from leaving their assigned villages to work on ranches, secular authority would harm not only Indian welfare, but also church interests.[35] Both secular and clerical authorities protected Indians, insofar as they did, from each other's abuses much as one might guard any scarce resource. Of course, this did not change the subordinate status of the Indians.

Yet the Indians were not entirely objects of alien rule. To begin with, the Spanish permitted Indian governors and their staffs authority to manage local village administration, public order, and some aspects of economy (Farriss 1984:263). In Petén, a *cacique* (or governor) usually had two *alcaldes* (mayors), four councilmen, a scribe, and messengers on his staff. Indians managed their own *cofradías* and served as church deacons and singers. By the eighteenth century the secular clergy lacked the pious rigor of their predecessors, and if this made them less protective of Indians, it also made them less zealous in combating "pagan" customs. The paucity of clergy in Petén, the absence of non-Indians in some villages, and the low ratio of non-Indians to Indians in others (Table 2:3) also may have allowed, as in Yucatán (Farriss 1984:45; also see Edmonson 1982), Indians to retain certain customs, such as those related to swidden cultivation, ritual, and language. The ethnic complexity of most villages, however, may well have diluted expression of these customs (Foster 1960). At a minimum, the Indians retained some few rituals (Schwartz 1971, 1983) and the use of native languages well into the twentieth century, not to mention ongoing use of preconquest swidden techniques. The documents cited in previous sections make it clear that Indians had some freedom in maize sales, in buying *aguardiente* from *vecinos* in San Andrés and Remedios (for example, see AGI Guat. 859, 1765; Gálvez 1813), and in trading with "wild" Indians (for example, see Amate 1757).[36] Nor were the Indians completely confined to assigned villages; they left home to work on private and royal ranches and to serve as soldiers. That the Spanish could not get them to produce more grains may testify in part to problems of tropical agriculture, but also in part to incomplete domination. The charges that religious and secular authorities hurled at each other concerning the movements of the Indians also imply a certain degree of (Indian) freedom. In short, Indians did have a certain amount of room for independent action.

Particularly in their villages, Indians enjoyed a margin of autonomy and security. Indian governors and *cofradías* partly insulated Indians from Spaniards (Farriss 1984:262–68), and to some extent villages were communities. Although priests and Indian governors, backed by Spanish authority, could squeeze funds from the *cofradía* and the community *caja*, these also were foci of community formation (MacLeod 1983:207). Reina (1966) attributes the strong sense of community in Petén to Spanish cultural influences, and

Farriss adds that the pre-Columbian "territorially-based community of a pueblo and its dependencies . . . with or without extended kinship ties that may have originally co-existed as a basis for social integration" was compatible with Iberian devotion to community (1983:19). Yet in colonial times assignment to a village was not volitional. Some members of a village might be governed by native authorities who were not of their own ethnic group, and Indian *caciques* at times were as ready to force unpaid labor from and to mistreat Indians under their rule as the Spanish, as did, for example, *cacique* don Pedro Cohouj of San Andrés in 1802. Living in a village community obliged an Indian to render various services to the village, the *cacique*, the clergy, and the Spanish secular authorities. Community life was part of an ethnically stratified system of direct and indirect rule imposed on Indians by foreign conquerors. Probably in colonial times and certainly in postcolonial times, as later chapters will show, "community" had an equivocal meaning in Petén.

The isolation and vastness of Petén provided Indians with an alternative to submission (village life) or to open defiance. They could flee to the forests.[37] Veridical or not, Spanish perceptions that there were countless so-called wild and dangerous Cehach and Lacandón Indians in the woods where, if the clergy are to be believed, the Spanish were not eager to penetrate, meant that there were zones of refuge for Indians unwilling to accept alien rule. Farriss (1984:72) notes that because the Maya of Yucatán could escape to Petén if they felt unduly oppressed by the Spanish, they came to see themselves and to be seen by others as a peaceful people, in spite of their numerous armed rebellions. Peteneros have the same image of themselves, most likely for the same reason. In colonial (and postcolonial) times, free forest Indians were said to cause continual unrest (*continua intranquilidad*) in the region. Townspeople regarded the deep forests as dangerous places, and for this reason the woods could provide shelter — safe cover — for those Indians who would not submit to cacical or Spanish rule (Soza 1970:468). In Petén, "forest" like "community" came to carry a certain ambiguous significance.

Blacks in Petén

Peteneros whose first (father's) patronym is, for example, Escalera are said to be descended from runaway black slaves from British Honduras (now Belize). Their forebears eventually married Spaniards, Ladinos, and Indians in Petén, and today they are phenotypically indistinguishable from other Peteneros. But, as is the case for other Peteneros, they are identified with a specific community, San Benito de Palermo (a black saint), and with a distinct behavioral style. Among Peteneros, San Benito has a reputation for disorder and the "Negroes" often are or were charged with moral laxity. Modern circumstances may reinforce the stereotype, for example the only brothels in central Petén are located in San Benito, but the image derives from colonial times.

Black fugitives may have entered Petén as early as the 1720s. In 1727 the Spanish found several blacks and white Irish Catholics in the Maya Mountains in southeast Petén, brought them to Remedios, and then may have sent them to the Guatemalan highlands. At other times, for example in 1729, 1737, 1757, 1767, 1774, 1795, and 1813, blacks, sometimes with infants, fled to Petén, were baptized as Catholics, and settled around the Lake. At least by 1795 they were numerous enough to cause Indian officials in San Andrés and San José to call for their expulsion from these villages. Don Raymundo Chatá, *cacique* of San Andrés, representing both his own *pueblo* and San José, petitioned the commandant to remove the "Mulatos" because of their "moral corruption and lawlessness." "We also ask that you free us from rendering *repartamientos* to the Mulatos." (Incidentally, in the same petition, Chatá reminds the authorities that the Indian officials were ready to "continue the conquest of the Carib Indians" located along the road leading to Tabasco.) The Spanish too were concerned about how to handle the blacks. As the commandant was not considered a disinterested party, nor too quick to comply with orders from distant superiors, the Guatemalan Audience sought the more impartial advice of Verapazan officials. In deciding whether to allow the blacks to remain in the Indian villages, to transfer them to Remedios or to Guatemala, or to settle them somewhere else, the authorities weighed several matters: that the "ageless customs" of the blacks might disturb the Indians; that blacks resist authority, do not practice forms of collective labor, are of "little use"; that because the soils near Remedios are suitable for livestock but not for agriculture, blacks might work on ranches and/or as artisans serving Remedios; and so forth. Finally, in 1800, five years after *cacique* Chatá addressed his plea to the commandant, blacks were assigned to the insalubrious, marshy mainland shore immediately opposite Remedios.[38] Their situation was precarious for many years. Despite court orders to the contrary, from at least 1789 to 1825 several notables in Remedios, who off and on held high bureaucratic posts or had kinsmen who did, would invite or lure blacks to Petén and then sell them back to the British. (With independence in 1821, all forms of slavery were ended in Guatemala, but slavery was not outlawed in British Honduras until 1838.) It is, then, not surprising that the San Beniteños avoided unnecessary social contact with non-blacks until the end of the nineteenth century when conditions brought about by the growth of commerce, logging, and especially chicle extraction led to increased commingling and intermarriage among Peteneros.[39]

Stereotypes about the blacks clearly served Indian and Spanish interests. Insofar as one may judge from their modern descendants, blacks too more or less accepted the stereotypes. Although they may have internalized negative images of themselves, it is equally or even more probable that by going along with these views, blacks found a way to help maintain some distance from non-blacks. The (modern) implication of the belief that San Beniteños of black descent are immoral and lawless is that they can also be dangerous. Prudence dictates that one treat them with caution. This notwithstanding, powerful people in Remedios (later Flores) had the better of the relationship. With little good farm land at their disposal, the blacks often had to work for people in Remedios. In effect, they were a source of cheap wage labor. During the colonial period and really up to modern times, notables in Remedios/Flores were able to dominate and exploit people in San Benito.[40]

Ethnicity and Status Continuity

Ethnicity was a major determinant of status in the Spanish colonies, and ethnic endogamy was the rule. Nevertheless, ethnic boundaries were not completely impermeable. For one thing, the "significant inequalities of privileges and obligations attached to various caste identities created a strong incentive for upward percolation" (Farriss 1984:108). For another, in places like Yucatán and Petén, isolation, sparse population, relatively limited economic stratification, and the presence of non-Indians in Indian villages all relaxed constraints on ethnic intermarriage and passing. In any event, some mestizos, Ladinos, and apparently Pardos, "became incorporated," to use Farriss's words (1984:108), "into the Spanish caste," and some Indians entered the mixed groups. Downward "percolation" was also possible, at least in San Andrés where some Ladinos who married Indians and at the same time suffered economic misfortune eventually became identified as Indians. If an Indian entered the *vecino* group, he was released from certain labor obligations but gained little else. He was still excluded from top positions in colonial society. The social and legal system was such that aside from the role of village governor, all important positions in the bureaucracy, in the military, and in commerce were reserved for and held by Spaniards and a handful of people of mixed heritage who were eventually admitted to their ranks. No one identified as an Indian, and certainly no one with an Indian surname, ever attained or was granted high status in colonial Petén.

With very few exceptions the Spanish elite resided in Remedios. For example, Pinelos were posted off and on to San Andrés, but their permanent address was Remedios. There were also Aldanas in San Andrés, and interestingly enough one of them wed a Chatá, but the Aldanas more usually married people from Remedios. Remedios (Flores) has remained the elite center in Petén.

Similarly, there has been a continuity of family and ethnic status in the department. The children of the Creoles (people of actual or putative Spanish descent born in the Americas) who attained significant positions in the colony—military officer, bureaucrat, merchant, for instance—have retained high status up to today. To be sure, over the years some once important families have lost wealth and power, others have risen in the system, and some Creole families who came to Petén after the mid-eighteenth century have overtaken those who were present at the founding of the colony. However, this amounts to the circulation, the rising and falling, of privileged families within a dominant group. Taken as a group or socioethnic stratum, these families still possess disproportionate wealth, power, and prestige in Petén, and most of them still reside in or very near Flores. Those who are descended from Indian and from some Ladino families are still in subordinate positions. Still today exceptions are few, and even so they have not become part of the elite stratum in Petén. Modern Peteneros often use circumlocutions and code words for those who in colonial times would have been identified as Indians, Ladinos, Creoles, or Negroes, by discussing them in terms of community membership, for example, rather than ethnicity, but they know who is who and relate to each other accordingly. Genealogies indicate that what once would have been "caste" lines are still roughly in place, particularly for elite and middle sector families. No doubt genealogies can be and are manipulated to rationalize changes in family status (Schwartz 1969), but that people care to do this in the first place suggests that lineage and a sense of history are important. Family (which in Petén implies ethnic identity) position in social, political, and economic hierarchies has been relatively constant in postconquest Petén.[41]

Earlier, the Pinelos were used as a specific example of this continuity. Here the example may be broadened. In the 1750s, when a Pinelo served in the bureaucracy, a Zetina was a scribe on the commandant's staff. Then, and later, members of the Ayala, Baldizón, Berges, Castellanos, Cetina, and Pinelo families were chief administrators of San Felipe. Military officers and bureaucrats were recruited from the Aldana, Guerra, Gutiérrez, Ozaeta, and Rodríguez families. Most people had diverse careers, for example, the Baldizónes, Castellanos and Pinelos were also merchants and/or private ranch owners. The list is not complete, and some of the above may have had Ladino rather than Creole origins, but it is enough to make the point. Some of these families have suffered declines in fortune and position, others have become very wealthy and powerful over the years, but as a group their lineal and collateral descendants still dominate Petén society. Whether one records the names of the owners of most luxury hotels or very large commercial establishments in Petén; the leadership of Petén's agronomists' association (*Prensa Libre* 28 June 1984), or of FEDOCOPETEN—La Federación Integral de Cooperativas de Petén— (*Prensa Libre* 4 December 1984); Soza's roster of "notables" (1970:229–334); or departmental beauty contest winners from 1937–1986, the same names recur: Baldizón, Castellanos, Cetina, Ozaeta, and so on. New names may appear, old ones drop out, but these and other colonial families comprise the majority on these lists. Indeed, those charged with challenging authority or engaging in contraband activity in the nineteenth century (AGCA *Ramo Criminal* 1822–1899) simply link the register of eighteenth- and twentieth-century notables. As mentioned several times, people of Indian descent are either absent or overwhelmingly underrepresented on any one of these lists. Even when, for example, a Yama (pseudonym) works in government or in education, that individual is almost always subordinate to a member of one of the old colonial elite families, although he or she is culturally indistinguishable from them. In the 1980s, when several Yamas were school teachers, members of the Castellanos family were departmental supervisors of education. (For further documentation of status continuity, see the Appendix.)

There is what may be called a structural replication of Remedios/Flores in the villages (now towns) of Petén. The role played by the Baldizónes, Castellanos, Ozaetas, and so on at the departmental level has been played by Aldanas, Canos, and Manzaneros, among others, in San Andrés and by Betancurtes and Trujillos in the great savanna. Most major towns have their own local elites with colonial roots, except for San Luis and perhaps San José. (In the mid-twentieth century a Ladino family dominated otherwise all-Indian San Luis.) In San Martín (pseudonym) for example, as in Flores, although some families lost status while others improved their position, the overall picture shows the type of continuity described above. A major difference is that in the mid-twentieth century a family of Indian heritage became relatively wealthy and powerful, primarily because of their work in the chicle business. In 1982 a Ladino asked a member of that family to sponsor his child's baptism, the first time in the history of San Martín that a Ladino had so honored an Indian. In this context some Ladinos do not use the word "Indian," but rather a code phrase, such as, "Their grandparents were humble people, *humildes.*" It says a good deal about Petén society and culture that this Indian family makes clear it has a genealogical connection through concubinage with an old colonial Spanish family. To some extent Peteneros align even exceptions with the rules.

The phenomenon of an interconnected set of families maintaining superior position, in part based on ethnic stratification, is not, of course, peculiar to Petén. "Notable family networks" are common in Latin America (Balmori, Voss, and Wortman 1984). As in Petén, the networks have been united by common interests, residential propinquity, and ties of consanguinity and affinity. Their internal ranking is reminiscent of the status differences within Flores and between Flores and town elites. Notable families protected their patrimony by following diverse political, economic, and professional careers and through marriage alliances. In the absence of strong central government and "rationally" organized economic institutions, notable family networks dominated regional and national social systems. Balmori, Voss, and Wortman (1984:50–51) point out that in most of Guatemala these networks were particularly important between 1821 and 1930, but in some places, usually remote ones such as Petén, they have continued to perpetuate their dominance.

In Petén notable families maintain elite status not simply because of initial advantage and the traditional respect accorded them. In addition, they accept talented newcomers, usually assimilating them through marriage alliances. They also respond relatively flexibly, as subsequent chapters will show, to new economic and educational opportunities. The more successful individuals and families have not been sentimental about economic matters. For example, land ownership as such is not given any special cultural value, this perhaps distinguishing Peteneros from other Guatemalans (Adams 1970:40). Choosing between investment in ranch land, automotive outlet stores, beer distributorships, and so forth is based primarily on considerations of profit, rather than prestige or tradition. Perhaps the low level of economic development for most of the eighteenth and nineteenth centuries left Peteneros with few alternatives. Finally, people of Spanish, Ladino, Indian, and black descent may also have internalized their respective roles, to the advantage of the Spanish and some Ladinos, but this is difficult enough to judge from observed behavior let alone read out of colonial documents. For now it suffices to record the relative continuity of status in the department.

Patterns of ethnic endogamy help maintain ethnic stratification, but they do not preclude one group from acculturating to the standards of another. I have said little about acculturation in colonial Petén and the available documents are of limited help, but the issue has been touched upon in various sections of this chapter.

It is important here to note some contextual considerations. In the Spanish colonies generally, Indians who became part of a permanent estate labor force usually were also relatively soon ladinoized (MacLeod 1983:194), but even the largest estate in colonial Petén—San Felipe—did not have a large permanent staff. Moreoever, although the Spanish directed many aspects of production, they had no economic incentive to occupy Indian land. The Indians had effective control of their milpas, which for the most part they farmed as they had in the past. These factors tended to slow the pace of acculturation (Farriss 1983). At the same time, most of the reduced Indians lived close to Remedios, and even in more distant villages, such as Dolores and Santo Toribio (but not San Luis), there were resident Creoles and Ladinos, a situation which favored ladinoization. In this balance of forces, some favoring and some retarding acculturation, it is not surprising that over time Indians in a village such as, for example, San Andrés became ladinoized far earlier than those in, for example, San Luis.

With respect to the practical arts, the Spanish apparently learned about swidden cultivation from the Indians in Yucatán and/or Petén. The Indians were forced to concentrate on grain and sugarcane production, but they did continue to produce a large variety of preconquest foodstuffs. Indeed, modern Petén cultigens are nearly identical to pre-Columbian ones, and many crops, trees, and animals are still referred to by their Maya names. Indians learned how to handle livestock and to build Spanish-style structures, and the Spanish learned to live in Maya-style houses. The Indians were introduced to beef and to *aguardiente*, using the latter to excess, according to the Spanish sources.[42] (Unfortunately, the documents do not reveal what the Indians thought about this charge). Although Spaniards and Indians learned from each other, it is, of course, important to recall that most forms of production and their associated social relations were imposed upon the Indians by the Spanish.

In regard to religious matters, Indians were instructed in the routines of the Catholic faith. To judge from their petitions to place priests in their villages, although this involved material as well as spiritual interests, Indians did identify themselves as Catholic, and they also were inducted into the Catholic system of ritual kinship (*compadrazgo*). Yet the clergy found their conversion to Catholicism lacking in depth and piety, and even in modern times forms of worship in Petén include preconquest as well as Catholic elements (Schwartz 1983). Concerning other spiritual elements of the belief system, it is difficult and often impossible to say whether the Iberian or native American contribution is greater. To take one important example, goblins in Petén have some of the characteristics of ancient Maya *balam* deities, but wear European dress. They may be called *duendes* (Spanish) or *alux* (Maya), but all in all resemble the goblins of Chan Kom, Yucatán (Redfield and Villa Rojas 1962:119–21). Again, the Santa Cruz ceremony practiced in San Andrés until the 1920s may be related to pre-Columbian deer rituals, but instead of deer, pigs—introduced to the New World by the Spanish—were used (on the ritual, see Redfield and Villa Rojas 1962:157; Schwartz 1971:295; Thompson 1930:112–13). Although Indians rather than Ladinos participated in the Santa Cruz ritual, almost everyone in Petén, regardless of ethnic identification, claims to accept the reality of the goblins. A more elusive example, and here I anticipate matters discussed further on, is that many aspects of existence in Petén are given ambiguous meaning, a certain dual quality which is more reminiscent of pre-Columbian equivocality (Thompson 1970) than, say, European gnosticism. Many social forms in Petén, most importantly including community as a principle of organization, are compatible with both Spanish and Maya heritages, although forms of kinship owe much more to the former than to the latter (Farriss 1983:19). In short, social and ideological systems precipitated from colonial experience were matters of mutual acculturation. The colonial political and economic systems, on the other hand, were Spanish creations and under Spanish control.

More firmly than anything else, the Indians did retain their native languages. Insofar as symbolic meanings are implicated in language, many of these too must have persisted. Several reasons can be suggested for this situation. To begin, Indian villages were partly insulated from the Spanish by the *caciques* and their staff. The general tendency toward ethnic endogamy and the influx of Indians from other places seeking refuge in Petén may have reinforced use of Indian languages. The absence of Spaniards and even Ladinos in some communities, San José and San Luis for example, also must have played a role in this process. Moreover, even if an Indian did learn Spanish, he or she could not advance very far in the social system. At most, that Indian could become a *cacique*, no small matter for an Indian, but knowledge of Spanish was not required for the post. Conversely, the Spanish may not have been strongly motivated to insist that Indians learn Spanish, that is, to share with them the language of trade, law, and power. Rather, people like the Pinelos and Zetinas, who appear as translators in legal documents cited above, learned Maya. Whatever the exact combination of reasons, outside of Remedios native languages were in general use and many Indians were monolingual until the early twentieth century (Berendt 1868; González 1867; Mejía 1904). Even in the ethnically mixed town of San Andrés, many people spoke Maya until the 1920s, and Petén Maya and Kekchí are still commonly used at home in San José and San Luis respectively. Despite defeat, subordination, and enforced acculturation, Indians continued to use native languages, with all this implies for enculturation.

Concluding Discussion

By 1697 another story was begun in Petén. Unlike that of a novelist, this one is not very neatly plotted and some desired information is unavailable. Although there are gaps in knowledge and exceptions to general patterns, the major contours of the tale can be traced.

From 1697 until the 1960s, Petén was sparsely populated and isolated from major centers of trade, government, and social life. Depopulation, begun before 1697, was accelerated by the Spanish conquest and the fierce

Itzá resistance to it. Settlers were not attracted to Petén, because it had few natural resources to exploit, lacked a large Indian population to rule, and was a remote place with an uninviting tropical climate. Although a road was built through Petén to link Yucatán and highland Guatemala, its condition and maintenance were not good. Internal trade was limited and directed mostly toward Remedios, which began as a military-administrative outpost and soon became the center of regional commerce, but was hardly a large urban market center. Most people lived in relatively self-sufficient villages strung along the *camino real*. The major item of export was livestock destined for Yucatán, itself not a very economically dynamic place. Indeed, because all of Central America was of "limited economic importance to the Spanish crown," little was invested in roads and administrative infrastructure, which in turn led to the devolution of state power to provincial towns (Weeks 1986:33). Limited population, isolation, bad roads, little internal and external trade, slow economic growth (manifested in part by price stability and comparatively low prices for grains in Petén during the colonial period), a larger context of "limited economic importance"—these factors reinforced each other. Postconquest Petén was a frontier hinterland.

Production for trade and for support of district government and church was based largely on social-military relations. Although Indians were paid wages on the royal estate and, presumably, on private *vecino* ranches, and for craft labor, they were subject to a wide range of corvée. As for the Spanish, their wealth (what there was of it) rested as much, if not more, on social and political relations than on ownership of productive resources.

In Petén, as in Yucatán, the Spanish ruled indirectly through *caciques* governing reduced Indians. Villages were settled—resettled in some instances—with Indians of differing ethnic and political backgrounds, but for the Spanish what counted was that they were Indians rather than that they were Itzá, Muzul, or Mopán. There were also other ethnic groups in Petén: Spanish, Ladino, Pardo, black. Perhaps because the population was so small and generally poor, and perhaps too because Indians who achieved non-Indian status were exempted from certain *téquios*, ethnic lines blurred at the edges. Nevertheless, ethnic endogamy was the general rule. Ethnicity was a major principle of social, political, and economic organization.

Community was also an important principle of social organization, in connection not only with native Indian proclivities but also with the way the Spanish ran the colonies. Community was important to both native and Iberian cultural patterns, and a sluggish economy may have further reinforced parochialism. In addition, the caciqual system afforded Indians a measure of security and freedom, insulation from non-Indians, in their own organized communities. The Indian communities apparently were not as closed as many of their counterparts elsewhere in the colonies because *vecinos*, lacking economic incentives, did not encroach much on their land. Over time each community came to be identified with a particular set of families (Soza 1970:468) and with a particular ethnic signature, which perhaps helped to unify villagers of diverse origin.

Although secular and clerical authorities regarded Indians in general as lazy, given to excessive use of *aguardiente*, and religiously fickle, each Petén community eventually acquired a more specific social reputation. For example, Spanish Remedios was (and still is) thought of as urbane or selfish, black San Benito as festive or wicked, Indian San Luis as stable or backward, and so on, the positive or negative valence given depending on whether people were (or are) describing their own or someone else's community. For the moment, the details are less important than the observation that in Petén community and ethnicity became to some extent interchangeable terms, and the pattern has colonial roots.

No one in colonial Petén was outstandingly wealthy. Commandants and vicars often speak of poverty within the district. But there were also family economic inequalities which were relatively congruent with ethnic, political, and social inequalities. Families might improve or lose their position, but status differences between groups largely defined in terms of ethnicity endured. People of actual or putative Spanish descent and those Ladinos and Pardos who came to be identified with them, usually through a marriage bond, remained superordinate to people of Indian, black, and, in some instances, Ladino descent. Notable families, most of them resident in Remedios, worked actively to maintain their position. Slow economic growth, remoteness, and lack of appreciable numbers of newcomers, contributed to the continuity of status.

Despite defeat, forced labor, economic, residential, and other dislocations, Indians did hold onto some aspects of native culture. Non-Indians may have learned as much from Indians as Indians did from them. So long as it is kept in mind that this occurred in a society dominated by Spanish conquerors, it may be said acculturation went both ways.

Peteneros have their own understanding of colonial history, much of it compatible with the preceding description. They emphasize isolation, gov-

ernment neglect, descent from Campechanos, formation of a "new In-
dohispanic race," and, once the conquest was complete, tranquility. This
history, one is told, generated a specific Petén social personality, modified
in one way or another by community type. Peteneros are self-reliant,
affable, and egalitarian. "We are all equal here, democratic, not like the rest
of Guatemala" is almost a refrain. Part of this description is accurate, for
example, the theme of neglect; and part of it is clearly exaggerated, for
example, the talk of equality. Some statements reflect ongoing possibilities.
For instance, when violence occurred, people could retreat into the deep
forests, and in this sense Petén was tranquil. In general, Peteneros, especially those from Flores, draw on their history to support their view that
Petén has a separate cultural and psychosocial identity within Guatemala.

By the 1720s the Spanish had consolidated their military gains, set up
private ranches (albeit most of them seem to have failed) and crown
ranches, and settled Indians in assigned villages where priests could oversee
their Christianization. Life in Petén settled down. There were disturbing
periodic crop failures, epidemics, and injustices particular to a system based
on conquest, ethnic inequality, and forced labor. There also were occasional armed incursions by outsiders and internal Indian resistance, although after 1710 the scale of resistance never approached that of the
periodic Indian rebellions in Yucatán. More constant were concerns about
possible incursions by Belizeños, rebellious Maya from Yucatán, and so-
called Cehach and Lacandones in northwestern and western Petén, and
vicars worried about uprisings in the reduced villages. Yet life did become
normalized. In terms of trade and politics, villages were tied to Remedios
rather than to each other. Relatively stable, hierarchical patterns of relationship emerged among families, ethnic strata, and communities. The
remote society was settled. Then, in 1820–1821, the Central American colonies broke away from Spain and became independent nations.

Chapter Three

Social Continuity and Economic Stagnation, 1821–1890s

> "Guatemala[n] . . . severance in 1823 from the southern states of Mexico . . . accounts for the extraordinary isolation of El Peten" (Calvert 1985:149).

> Flores: "The houses are but mean thatched huts . . . the Church . . . half-dilapidated . . . In a Catholic community if the church is neglected, the inhabitants must be poor indeed" (Caddy 1840, in Pendergast 1967:76–77, 94).

Introduction

The separation in 1821 of Mexico and Central America from Spain had relatively little impact on social relations in Petén, and the same may be said for most of Central America. But Guatemalan independence, the Conservative rise to power in 1838, and the War of the Castes in Yucatán beginning in 1847 had the combined effect of increasing Petén's isolation. Although trade with British Honduras (Belize) and Mexican involvement in the logging industry became important, they did not vitalize Petén's economy and did not really commercialize agroforest production in the region. Rather, this was accomplished in the late nineteenth century by North American demands for natural latex bases for commercially produced chewing gum. To obtain the latex, chicle trees in Yucatán, Belize, and Petén were tapped, and with that Petén was brought into the modern world market system. Several distinguishing features of what Peteneros call *la chiclería* had profound consequences not only for the economy of the region, but also for its society and culture. *La chiclería* completely dominated life in Petén for some eighty years, from the 1890s to about 1970. To appreciate just what did change because of *la chiclería*, and what did not, the period between independence in 1821 and the beginning of chicle tree tapping in Petén in the 1890s is described here.

National and Regional Contexts

The Central Americans declared themselves independent of Spain in 1821, and of association with Mexico in 1823. Their attempts between 1824 and 1839 to form a Central American Federation failed. The period was marked by internal dissension, endless military contests, political instability, and fiscal crisis (Karnes 1961:94). Guatemala formally became an independent republic in 1847, although functioning as such prior to this date. Guatemalan Liberals, led by Mariano Gálvez, were overthrown in 1838 by the Conservative Rafael Carrera, whose autocratic rule endured from 1839 until his death in 1865. There followed several years of violent struggle for power, which ended when the Liberals, led by Justo Rufino Barrios, took control of Guatemala in 1871. Barrios promoted Liberal policies such as separation of church and state and economic modernization, but he was no less autocratic than Carrera. After Barrios's death in 1885 and another period of political instability, his nephew, José Reyna Barrios, became president (1892–1898). Reyna Barrios was succeeded by the dictator Estrada Cabrera, whose tenure, 1898–1920, roughly coincided with the heyday of *la chiclería* in Petén.

Throughout the period from 1821 to 1895 national regimes neglected Petén. Gálvez did foment a scheme to colonize Petén and Verapaz with Europeans, but he barely considered the people or the natural conditions of the northern lowlands in his plans. For several reasons, including a completely inadequate system of roads and the "chronic penury of the state," which persisted well into the 1850s, the venture failed miserably (Griffith 1965:15). We are given some indication of Petén's image in Guatemala by the fact that Gálvez sought foreign settlers because, among other things, he had no hope that highland Guatemalans would venture that far north.[1] Yet Guatemalan officials were aware that the north was not "integrated" (to use a word much favored by officials in this context) with the rest of the republic, and the dream of colonizing Petén endured, as often as not among bureaucrats and intellectuals who knew next to nothing about the northern lowlands.

Independence did not bring radical changes in society or government, except that now Creoles rather than crown officials ruled. Thus Gálvez tried to cope with the national fiscal crisis by relying on measures carried over from the colonial period (Karnes 1961:59). These included state monopolies on liquor and tobacco, for which tax collection was not very effective outside of the Guatemala City-Antigua area. One reason for this was that Guatemalans had become expert at contraband. In addition, officials in the interior regions of the country were hardly immune to malfeasance (Wortman 1982:238–54).[2]

Several mutually reinforcing events brought Carrera to power. These include Ladino discontent with continuing white Creole preeminence, Liberal reform laws designed to promote legal equality but which in effect tended to reduce the autonomy of the local community (a matter of great importance to Indians), clerical opposition to Liberal reforms (civil marriage, for example), decisive clerical influence among the Indians, and destabilizing rumors about the causes of a cholera epidemic that began in British Honduras in 1836 and then spread to Guatemala. Once in charge, Carrera restored the church to its former position of privilege, although he could not fill its coffers. He also conferred political power on Ladinos, which was a break from the colonial past. At the same time he had to form an alliance with the white Creole economic elite—the Guatemala City merchants and the highland cochineal traders—and this softened the impact of the change in Ladino fortunes. (Cochineal superseded indigo as Guatemala's major export commodity from about 1750 to 1850.) That Carrera and his appointed provincial governors perpetuated forced labor systems which affected Indians more than others did not diminish Indian loyalty to his regime. As matters turned out, methods of labor control were to become far more repressive after 1871 when the Liberals returned to power (McCreery 1986; Weeks 1986; Woodward 1985:113; Wortman 1982:247–70).

Liberal policies of economic modernization and growing world demand for coffee tied Guatemala much more closely to international commerce than ever before. Coffee was grown primarily in Alta Verapaz and in the Pacific piedmont region (Helms 1975:249). The western highlands, the more ladinoized eastern highlands and northeastern region, and Petén were not exploited for coffee. Coffee production began a rise to preeminence in the 1840s, was certainly the premier crop in Guatemala by the 1870s, and is still of signal importance. For example, in 1982 coffee exports accounted for 32 percent of the dollar value of *all* Guatemalan exports (*Worldmark Encyclopedia* 1984). The Liberals, desiring to modernize the national economy but lacking the means and perhaps the will to diversify agricultural production, relied on income derived from coffee exports to underwrite their programs. In reciprocal relations with coffee producers the state grew more centralized and much stronger. In this situation the government served the interests of coffee producers. "Once large-scale coffee production began . . . the primary function of government became facilitating the planting, harvesting, and exporting of coffee" (Weeks 1986:37). Coffee production has always required a good deal of hand labor, especially during the harvest season, and the state undertook to make sure that the coffee plantations would have a large supply of cheap labor. For this reason, as well as for more abstract ideological reasons, in 1877 the Liberals eliminated communal land ownership, an act which particularly affected rural Indians living in coffee-producing areas by pushing them onto marginal lands and thereby forcing them to seek seasonal plantation employment. In 1879 the government also codified debt peonage laws, which were not abrogated until 1934. "Private debt contracts," a form of forced labor, grew to "unprecedented levels" between 1870 and 1920 (Mc-Creery 1986:99).[3] These developments reinforced "the power of landed property" (Weeks 1986:41). Coffee brought Guatemala into modern international trade, but the "social basis of coffee production" was precapitalist and coercive (Weeks 1986:39). Although foreign-owned banana companies entering Guatemala in the 1890s did not use forced labor, their interests were served by that system. Wages on coffee plantations were so low that labor was attracted to banana plantations where wages were higher. Because the commercialization of agricultural production for world markets was supported by a coercive labor control system, the state, although stronger than before, was deprived of mass popular support. This made it possible, indeed relatively easy, for foreign interests, beginning with the banana companies, to "support" and to dominate successive regimes. As for peasants, particularly Indian peasants, they may have been better off under late colonial regimes.

The Liberals also modernized (the word is proper despite the labor control system) other aspects of Guatemalan society. Church and state were separated. Early under the first Barrios, an infrastructure of "railways, telegraphs, highways, schools, and hospitals" was built "in an astonishingly brief period of time" (Karnes 1961:163). Yet, as in most matters, for Peten "brief" must be qualified. Besides having limited resources, the state was too greatly concerned with coffee production and its labor requirements to take much interest in underpopulated Petén. For example, there was no hospital in Petén (that is, Flores) until 1883 (Martínez Uck 1971:9), telegraph service to Flores was not inaugurated until 1894, and the highways remained undeveloped until about 1965–1970.[4]

The highlands of Alta Verapaz, immediately south of Petén, became more closely integrated into the rest of the republic when European immigrants, most of them German, began commercial coffee production there in the 1860s. Unused to "forced labor for individual growers," the Kekchí Indians around San Pedro Carchá staged an unsuccessful rebellion in 1864 (King 1974:29). Kekchí had been moving north since the sixteenth century, but now ever increasing numbers of them fled to Petén to escape repression and poverty. In view of recent developments from 1978 on, it is more appropriate to regard the 1864 uprising as an unfinished revolution.

Petén was affected by many of the events summarized above, but it was also in good measure peripheral to them. For one thing, many of the soils in the northern tropical lowlands are not especially well suited to coffee cultivation. Even though bananas flourish in Petén, Petén's population could not have satisfied labor demands in either coffee or banana production. Furthermore, road construction and maintenance here have always been and remain very costly. From the perspective of nineteenth-century investors Petén was uninteresting, and the state simply had no pressing need to look that far north. So long as state and elite economic interests concentrated on commercial agroexport crops such as cochineal, and then coffee and bananas, Petén almost inevitably was bound to remain a remote frontier.

Events of the nineteenth century in Yucatán and British Honduras had more direct effects on Petén. Largely owing to the disruptions brought about by the War of the Castes in Yucatán and Carrera's revolution, trade and communication between Yucatán and Petén declined. As a result, livestock raising became somewhat less important in Petén. The War of the Castes and several other events recounted below turned the old *camino real* region north of San Andrés into something of a no-man's land, so far as most Peteneros were concerned. Refugees from the War of the Castes fled to Petén, some to take up permanent residence there and others to move further south. Some Yucatecans who settled in the great savanna south of Flores went into cattle ranching and commerce and became part of Petén's middle and elite social sectors. One savanna community favored by the Yucatecans, Sacluk (today, La Libertad), benefited from their presence and grew in importance after the 1860s, when commercial logging in western Petén became relatively important.

As for British Honduras, from the 1820s to at least the 1860s it dominated Guatemala's foreign trade (Bolland 1977:176; Woodward 1966:69, 116). But the major route from Guatemala to Belize ran down the Motagua River

Valley to Izabal, located on the south side of the Golfo Dulce, and then went into Belize. In a word, the route skirted Petén (Griffith 1965:11; Thompson 1829:417–22). Nevertheless, in view of all other surrounding areas, it is hardly surprising that Petén-British Honduran trade increased from the 1840s on. Peteneros believed north-central Petén was dangerous; western Petén was largely unexplored; and to the south, in the highlands, people were engaged in commercial activities which excluded Petén. Thus Peteneros increasingly looked east to Belize, with which they eventually established the sort of economic relations they had had with Yucatán. To a lesser extent they also increased contact with Tabasco, Mexico, via Tenosique. *La chiclería* would strenghten both sets of ties, but particularly those with Belize.

One further word is needed to set the context: In 1824 the estimated population of Guatemala was 660,580. At that time Petén's population was about 5,000. In 1893, about when *la chiclería* began in Petén, the population of Guatemala was 1,364,678 and that of Petén 6,075.[5] As Karnes (1961:15) says, "To question the accuracy of these figures would be reasonable but fruitless," and they are accurate enough for the point made here. While national population more or less doubled in the seventy-two years since independence from Spain, Petén's population, despite short-term fluctuations, remained relatively constant, which underscores the continuing remoteness of the region.

Government and Politics in Petén

Independence did not fundamentally change the structure of provincial government. The governor, appointed by the national executive instead of the crown, remained the supreme political and military authority in the district (Petén was not made a department until 1860).[6] Locally elected mayors were subordinate to him and sometimes, contrary to law, appointed by him. Most governors served for one to two years, but they could hold the post more than once, for instance, Clodoveo Berges did so four times between 1892 and 1918.[7] The Judge of First Instance, intermediate between local judges and the national judiciary, never seemed to have had the political power possessed by the governor. (Off and on in the nineteenth century the judge for Verapaz also served Petén, in which case he operated out of and lived in Cobán, Alta Verapaz.) From 1826 to 1898 about half of the governors were neither native to nor permanent residents

Table 3:1 Mayors of San Andrés, 1829–1986

| Ethnic background | 1829–1926 | | 1937–1986 |
	First Mayor	Second Mayor	Mayor
Creole descent	3	—	—
Creole and/or Ladino descent	4	—	8
Ladino descent	6	1?	8
Indian descent	1?ᵃ	9	5
Total	14	10	21

Source: Archivo Municipal, San Andrés.

The two-mayor system apparently ended in Petén sometime between 1927 and 1933. The identities of the intendents (1933–1944) are not germane to this table. Because second mayors did not sign documents as often as first mayors, their names appear less frequently in the documents. Because of gaps in the documentary record for the years 1830–1844, and several other years, the record is not complete, until 1944 and from then on it is complete. It may be added that old style local military commanders (sometimes also called *gobernadores* or *corregidores*) were always of Creole and/or Ladino descent.

ᵃIn 1829, a man who had been second mayor signed several documents over the title of first mayor, so his exact administrative position is not clear.

of Petén. But the other half and almost all lesser functionaries were because, Soza (1970:287) says, Petén was too remote to attract outsiders. Of the governors who were native Peteneros, almost all were born in Flores and could trace their roots back to important colonial period families (see Soza 1970:657–59).

In the Petén towns that had had mixed ethnic populations (Creole, Ladino, Indian) prior to 1821, non-Indians took formal command of local government. The office of *cacique* was abolished and the positions of chief mayor (*alcalde primero*) and subordinate mayor (*alcalde segundo*) were created. (In some parts of Guatemala, however, the two mayors may have had equal authority.) Township councils consisted of the two mayors, a syndic (*síndico*, legal representative), and normally four councilmen or aldermen (*regidores*). Flores often had six councilmen. Members of council were elected by literate males eighteen years of age and over, and in the nineteenth century this alone would have assured non-Indians control of local government except in San José, San Luis, and some lesser places where there rarely were any resident non-Indians. The two-mayor system seems to have lasted until the late 1920s or the early 1930s. In San Andrés the chief mayor, syndic, and at least two *regidores* were invariably Creoles or Ladi-

Table 3:2 Election Returns, San Andrés, 1891–1916

Year	Position	Votes	Winning candidate
1891	First Mayor	30	Non-Indian
1896	" "	31	Non-Indian
1916	" "	23	Non-Indian
1891	Second Mayor	30	Non-Indian ?
1896	" "	38	Maya
1916	" "	29	Maya
1891	Syndic	26	Non-Indian
1896	"	34	Non-Indian
1916	"	25	Non-Indian
1891	First Alderman	30	Non-Indian
1896	" "	38	Maya
1916	" "	31	Non-Indian
1891	Second Alderman	31	Maya
1896	" "	27	Pardo ?
1916	" "	20	Maya
1891	Third Alderman	32	Pardo ?
1896	" "	30	Maya ?
1916	" "	15	Maya
1891	Fourth Alderman	27	Non-Indian[a]
1896	" "	22	Not determined
1916	" "	24	Maya

Source: Archivo Municipal, San Andrés.
[a]Also appointed *alcalde auxiliar* of the *aldea* San Juan.

nos, and the second mayor and at least one, but more usually two, *regidores* were almost as unexceptionally Indian. (In that the second mayor was an Indian, one may see in the *alcalde segundo* an attenuated continuation of the colonial *cacique*.) This pattern, quite fixed in San Andrés (Tables 3:1 and 3:2), was generally the same in Dolores, Santo Toribio, San Francisco, and Sacluk; in Flores, both mayors were non-Indian. The most important appointed official in a township was, and is, the scribe (secretary). If the nineteenth-century system was anything like that in the twentieth century, the secretary often must have dominated the mayor. With noticeably few exceptions, most of them in San José, secretaries were Creoles or Ladinos. Quite commonly they were from Flores and returned there upon leaving office.

Just how many townships there were at any given moment in the nineteenth century is not altogether clear. Before trying to explain why this is so, I should say something about the organization of government in Guatemala, which is in most respects similar to those of other Spanish American republics.

The government is republican rather than federal, hence all subdivisions below the national level are creations of central government. The head of central government is an elected president. In Guatemala, no matter what a particular constitution may call for, the president is more powerful than the congress or any court. The national capital is the largest, most populous city in the nation, as well as its center of commerce, industry, communications, and so on. For administrative purposes, the national territory is divided into departments, of which there are twenty-two in Guatemala. The national executive appoints and dismisses each chief departmental officer, the governor. Governors are primarily administrators responsible for carrying out policies originating in the national capital, although a clever one can acquire more power than allowed for by law. For instance, he can apply national policy with various degrees of stringency, and he often has influence or "pull" (*cuello*) with the powerful national executive. The capital of the department is typically the largest, most urbanized, most economically important settlement in the department.

Departments are divided into *municipios*, the smallest unit of government, administration, and territory with any local autonomy (Adams 1957:342). The center or capital of a *municipio* is usually the largest town in the township. "A majority of the 325 *municipios* in the country [Guatemala] have the demography of a rural New England township but the government of an incorporated city. Scholars who emphasize the demographic situation have chosen 'township' as the English gloss, while those who emphasize governmental structure have chosen 'municipality'" (Tedlock 1987:47). "County" is also used at times.

More important yet, the system of government is unitary and "rational." The constitutional chain of command (president, governor, mayor), territorial-administrative units (nation, department, township), and—to a remarkable degree—population densities and economic power (at these three levels: national, departmental, and township capital) coincide with each other.

The Spanish-American institution of township was derived from the Roman *municipium*, an urban place with its surrounding rural territory.

The medieval Spanish descendant of the *municipium* "enjoyed a large measure of autonomy in the management of local affairs" (Cardenas 1963:4). In the sixteenth century the Spanish brought to the New World an idealized, thoroughly planned version of Romano-Iberian township. The concept is now embodied in the *municipio*. In some places the *municipio* is more than the basic unit of local government; it is also a unit of cultural tradition, ethnic identification, and shared patrimony (Cámara 1952:145–46; also see Tax 1952).

The *municipio*, a corporate entity in law, normally consists of a capital town (central *pueblo*) plus a defined territory along with whatever subordinate villages (*aldeas*) and small rural hamlets or neighborhoods (*caseríos*) are in the territory. The township mayor appoints an auxiliary mayor to represent him in the *aldeas*. Commonly, both capital town and township have the same name. Each capital town is traditionally protected by a (Catholic) patron saint who may also protect the entire county, but each major village also has its own saint. The largest municipal *pueblo* in a department usually doubles as the capital of the department, in which instance it is for legal purposes a "city," whatever its size.

With this brief explanation, I return to the problem of identifying townships in nineteenth-century Petén. Officials then were not always consistent or precise in their use of "*pueblo*," sometimes using the word to refer to a *pueblo*, and sometimes to refer to some other entity such as an *aldea*. They might continue to label a place a *pueblo* long after it had lost that status and been made subordinate to some other town, as happened to Santo Toribio when it lost population and importance and became an *aldea* of Dolores. Some of the minor settlements north of San Andrés were also called *pueblos* when they were no such thing. Furthermore, some of these and other small communities were not continuously inhabited. Economic, political, and/or health conditions often forced people to abandon a particular site, to which they might or might not return. In any event, the names of the sites pop in and out of the censuses in somewhat irregular fashion. The names of settlements also changed over time, and several places had the same name. Furthermore, the authorities in Petén were neither in control of nor intimately familiar with the entire department, hence they did not consistently carry out census counts or visit every settlement in the region. In short, the exact number, location, and legal status of all the settlements mentioned in nineteenth century documents are not completely known.

Table 3:3 Prominent Petén Settlements, 1700–1985[a]

	1700–1708	1740s	1845	1879	1904	1985
1 Flores (Remedios) [1814]	x	x	x	x	x	x
2 San Benito [1873]	—	—	x	x	x	x
3 San Andrés [1820]	x	x	x	x	x	x
4 San José (Sn. Joseph) [1851]	x	x	x	x	x	x
5 San Francisco (Chachaclun) [1828]	?	x	x	x	x	x
6 Santa Ana [1840]	x	x	x	x	x	x
7 La Libertad (Sacluk) [1828]	?	x	x	x	x	x
8 Dolores [1828]	x	x	x	x	x	x
9 Poptún [1966]	—	x	x	x	x	x
10 San Luis [1828]	x	x	x	x	x	x
11 Melchor de Mencos (Fallabón; Plancha de Piedra) [1962]	—	—	?	x	x	x
12 Sayaxché [1929]	—	—	—	?	x	x
13 Santo Toribio	x	x	x	x	x	x
14 Nohbecan (Nojbecan; Nokbekan)	x	?	x	x	—	—
15 San Antonio	—	x	x	x	—	—
16 San Juan de Dios	—	—	x	x	x	x
17 Thubucil (Tubucil)	—	—	x	x	—	—
18 San Rafael	—	—	—	x	—	—
19 St. Barbara (Machaquilá)	—	—	—	x	x	x
20 Concepción	—	x	—	x	—	—

Sources: AGCA censuses, González 1867, et al. (see note 8 this chapter for other sources and explanatory comments).

Key: x = mentioned in documents for year indicated.

Alternate names of a settlement are given in parentheses. The date in which a settlement was granted *municipio* status is given in brackets.

[a]The table oversimplifies a much more complex, dynamic situation, and only a few lesser settlements are mentioned, for illustrative purposes. The point is that although minor settlements came and went, the major ones endured.

It is important to note, however, that the major settlements and the core families respectively associated with each did continue from early or mid-colonial times up to the present. Flores, San Andrés, San José, Santa Ana, Dolores, and San Luis endured. Even Santo Toribio, one of the earliest colonial towns, but much reduced in significance by the mid-nineteenth century, still exists, and older Peteneros continue to identify certain families (the Contreras, for example) with the place. Table 3:3, a reasonably complete summary of Petén settlements in the eighteenth to the twentieth century, demonstrates the persistence of the major *pueblos* in Petén.[8]

Nineteenth-century Petén governors operated with very limited financial resources. Central government had little to spare for any interior department, and Petén was furthest from Guatemala City. Until 1874 public employees in Flores were largely sustained by the *situado*, the old subsidy carried over from colonial times but now reduced to a mere hundred pesos per year (Soza 1970:281–82), although communal milpas and judicial fines may have helped support some officials. But as late as 1855, Leyland (1972:256) found, there was no doctor in Flores (nor was Petén a "devil's island" any longer). San Felipe, the former crown ranch which had helped subsidize government in Petén, was allowed to deteriorate and was finally abandoned. This was one reason that dairy products became, as Morelet (1871:224–25) says, "great luxuries" by the 1840s. For want of funds, schools were often shut down (Mejía 1904). In 1802 the first Petén primary school was opened in Remedios. *Vecinos* and *presidio* personnel paid one to one and a half reales (and one real in other towns) per academic month to pay for educational supplies brought in from Mexico, for the rental of a schoolhouse, and for the teacher's salary. In 1840 the parents of the students were still paying the monthly one real fee, and a public fund in Flores contributed six reales per pupil per year to the school. In 1871 the Liberals began promoting public education throughout Guatemala, but for many years teachers' salaries were slow to reach Petén (Soza 1970:290–91) just as soldiers' wages were in earlier years.

By 1874 an office of *Rentas y Aduanas* (Internal Trade and Customs) was established in Flores. *Rentas* helped support departmental government, and the old *situado* was ended. *Rentas* collected duties on goods imported from British Honduras (primarily to Flores), on rubber extracted from Petén's forests for overseas markets and on mahogany trees cut in Petén by British Honduran and—in greater quantity—by Tabascan (Mexico) firms. But there were problems in *Rentas*, sufficient to prevent Flores officials from receiving their monthly salaries on a regular basis. In what reads exactly like a contemporary report, Valenzuela (1879) charged that Tabascan loggers defrauded *Rentas* and that Flores officials were lax about the matter. In 1878 *Rentas* collected about $3,000 (by now the dollar sign may be used for the peso) from the mahogany cutters and about $1,000 from Petén-Belize trade, but Valenzuela was sure much more could have and should have been obtained. Indeed, he felt tax rates could be raised. Then, as they do now, loggers responded that any increase would lead them to abandon their operations, but Valenzuela most probably correctly dismissed this as a mere tactic. To improve *Rentas's* performance, he recommended that a non-Petenero be appointed to head the office.[9]

Although *Rentas*, with all its shortcomings, eventually became the major source of income for the department, governors could also draw on other resources. Wealthier Peteneros paid fines to have themselves and/or their workers exempted from corvée (*téquios, faenas*). In the 1890s and presumably earlier, the minimum fine per day of *téquio* missed was two reales (Archivo Municipal, San Andrés, Session 28 January 1895). There were other judicial fines, and the department may have received a portion of income derived from state monopolies on liquor and tobacco. The governor also directed *téquios* for road work, mail and carrier service, militia duty, and so on. The governor apparently also could require that mayors select townsmen who would render him personal service on a monthly rotational basis; the burden seems to have fallen mostly on San Andrés and San José. Nevertheless, the departmental government was hardly affluent.

Municipal corporations were even poorer. For example, in 1889 the patrimony of Santa Ana consisted of but 2 hoes, 2 shovels, and 2 carts for road work. Santa Ana also owned 24 plates, 6 glasses, 2 cups, a crystal, a tablecloth, a table, 6 chairs, an oil lamp, a coat of arms, and a flag. The capital town had 54 *cargas* of maize on hand (its *aldea*, Juntecholol, had 35). The school in the *pueblo* had 2 tables, 10 chairs, 3 benches, 2 corner pieces, a clock, a water jar, and some books. The governor raffled off a cow to help the township repay a debt of some $8. At the end of the year Santa Ana had $56 in the *caja*, $36 of which was set aside for the cemetery fund. Measured against costs, Santa Ana's funds were decidedly meager. Thus, a window and two doors for the school in Juntecholol cost $4 and $7 respectively, and a horse could cost $23 (Memoria de Obras Públicas de Santa Ana, 31 December 1889; also see Governor Vidaurre's judicial inspection trip or *visita*, AGCA Visitas Judiciales 1862). Some *pueblos* fared better than others, but none were prosperous. Rather, by all contemporary domestic (for example, González 1867; Valenzuela 1879) and foreign (for example, Morelet 1871) accounts, township governments were economically hard-pressed.

That townships had their own sources of income and labor does not alter the picture. Proceeds from communal milpas went to the *caja* (and from 1898 to 1920 were used to pay mayors' salaries). Each man from 18 to 50 years of age had to provide the community with 100 pounds (45.4 kg) of maize each year. Men also had to work for the *pueblo* at least one day every two weeks, or pay a 2 real fine. After 1874 townships received some tax income from rubber extracted from within their jurisdiction, but tax collection was imperfect. At various times the central government ordered that communal (but not necessarily collectively worked) coffee, tobacco, henequen, and cotton fields be planted. For example, in 1864 each man had to plant 4 *mecates* (about 0.18 hectares) of cotton. That year 6.9 hectares were planted in San Andrés and 4.6 in San José, but of this amount two men alone planted 5.3 hectares, that is, not everyone complied with the order. Often the mandated crops did not do well because, people claimed, seeds were delivered too late, or labor was scarce because of illness, and so on. But even if everything had gone well, an absence of local markets, lack of road access to major nonlocal markets, and inadequate labor supplies would have limited the income derived from these crops. In fact, things often went badly, not only with cash crops, but also with basic subsistence ones. Maize, the staple food, was often in short supply and the government often had to order that emergency milpas be made. Nothing seemed to produce much wealth for the *municipios*.[10]

Moreover, government produced hardships for people. The various unpaid labor drafts, unpaid militia duties, and taxes all played a part in causing people to flee Petén. No doubt crop failures (Reina 1967), epidemics (Jones 1977), political injustice, and beckoning economic opportunities in British Honduras (Mazzarelli 1976a) also encouraged emigration. Periods of political instability and concerns about rebel Indians (see below) also contributed. Of all these, forced labor and taxation seem to have been most burdensome, and they fell more heavily on Indians than non-Indians. Thus it is clear from San Andrés genealogies, which can be securely traced back to the 1830s, that more Indians than Ladinos left to take up residence elsewhere, primarily in Benque Viejo and Soccotz, western British Honduras. There is also the well-known case of the San Luis Mopán Indians who fled in 1883 to southern British Honduras to avoid corvée and taxes, returning only briefly in 1886 to snatch their church bells and saints. In 1891 another group of Mopán Indians from San Luis joined them. As late as the 1930s Mopán and Kekchí from this area moved to British Honduras to evade forced road labor (Howard 1977). Farm failures and epidemics could make life very hard in Petén, and on occasion government could make it intolerable.[11]

Politics, at least among the elite in Flores, were highly personal and based on ties of kinship and *compadrazgo*. For more ordinary people, politics, it seems, centered on attempts to obtain official favors and, perhaps even more, to stay clear of authority. Unfortunately, available documents, such as reports of *visitas* and correspondence between mayors and governors, reveal little about the give and take of politics, but they can be supplemented by records of criminal cases (AGCA *Ramo Criminal* 1822–1899), which are in some ways more revealing.[12] During the *visitas* people did have an opportunity to speak out about local government, but they rarely took it. Rather, they petitioned officials for assistance, explained why some mandated crop had failed, and so forth. This does suggest how poor the *pueblos* were, but it says little (except in the null sense) about political maneuvers. However, this information and the criminal cases lead me to suspect that for Indians and poor Ladinos politics was largely a matter of evading or softening autocratic impositions—less gaining of power and more keeping on the good side of and staying clear of the powerful. This picture is reinforced by the available travel accounts. Thus, Morelet, who found Peteneros "gentle in manner," also reported that the Indians of San Luis were fearful of "Spanish" authorities and more relaxed when out of their sight (1871:216, 283). National level autocracy was replicated at the local level. Caddy remarked that Governor Ozaeta appointed his sister's husband mayor of San Andrés, "I believe contrary to the wishes of the greater part of the inhabitants who had the right of election" (in Pendergast 1967:90–92), and this was comparatively mild behavior (see below). Repeated observations about the good nature of Peteneros (Maler 1910:159; Morelet 1871:215), their docile demeanor (Valenzuela 1879), their mannerly submission to superiors (González 1867:92), and so on, in part imply harsh government. Of course, people are on best behavior with important visitors such as those just cited, and Peteneros do have a tradition of civility, but docility can also be a prudent response to and a symptom of the presence of autocracy. In the nineteenth century, when government was autocratic, ordinary people found good-natured docility to be a wise policy.

When there were important changes in national regimes, local politics could turn violent. In 1838, during the Carrera revolution, Petén Governor Segura jailed members of the faction, led by a Baldizón and an Ozaeta from Flores, declaring for Carrera. Ozaeta then led some two hundred men toward Flores. Segura ordered a military commander in San Andrés to intercept him, but Ozaeta captured the officer. Upon entering Flores Ozaeta freed his faction and roughly treated and jailed some Flores notables in the opposition. Several wealthy Floreños quickly purchased their freedom with two horses or fifty pesos and then fled to Mexico and British Honduras. They were joined by frightened Indians who, by abandoning their milpas, forced people who bought their crops to survive on *ramón* (breadnut, a famine food in Petén), palm hearts, and so forth. Ozaeta sealed off Petén and ruled in so despotic a fashion that when complaints reached Carrera, he ordered Ozaeta's removal from office and his capture. Enroute to prison, Ozaeta and the officer in charge of his escort fought a duel in which Ozaeta was killed.[13]

In 1871 somewhat similar events occurred when the Liberals took power. Governor Matus refused to relinquish his post, instead raising a troop from San Andrés and menacing Flores. Liberal Governor Trujillo defeated Matus, who fled to British Honduras, but litigation about his actions dragged on in the courts for several years.[14] One of Matus's descendants now living in Petén laments that the family was unable to recoup its fortunes after the incident, and others say, in effect, that the Matuses had it coming. True or not, this claim and counterclaim, as well as other similar stories, indicate that Peteneros have long political memories. The documentary evidence suggests that as disturbing as the Ozaeta and Matus interludes were, they did not occasion the sort of bloodshed which attended such events in the Guatemalan highlands. Of equal interest is that the leading actors in these and like dramas were almost always from Flores. High politics in nineteenth-century Petén, as Caddy felt (in Pendergast 1967:167), were usually a matter of intra-Flores dispute.

One further comment is necessary. Despite autocratic government and instances of harsh injustice, repression seems not to have been as heavy-handed in Petén as elsewhere. This may have been related to the limited economic development of the region, and so to decreased needs to impose severe controls on labor, and to the Peteneros' possibility of flight to unexplored forests. In Guatemala, state-sponsored coercion of labor, large-scale commercial agriculture, and concentrated private landholding were interrelated (and still are), but agriculture was not commercialized in nineteenth-century Petén, and there was no private land tenure, and—with so few people—no pressure on the land. With independence, Petén became a state *finca* (estate). Presidents Estrada Cabrera (1898–1920) and Ubico (1931–1944) did award private land titles to fifty-four Petén notables, over 90 percent of them from Flores, but their holdings came to a scant 1.5

to 2.0 percent of Petén's total land surface (Latinoconsult 1974). I do not mean to make light of the *téquio* system, official demands for increased milpa production which disrupted fallowing schedules (Reina 1968), debt peonage, autocracy, injustice, or ethnic discrimination, all of which were harsh enough to force some Peteneros to emigrate. Nonetheless, although it was cold comfort for Peteneros, until the 1890s political conditions were even worse in other parts of Guatemala. With the rising importance of *la chiclería*, certain (but not all) aspects of the of the political situation in Petén would deteriorate.

"Wild" Indians, Rebel Indians

Until 1837 officials felt that Lacandón Indians menaced western Petén, for which reason there was a military post in Sacluk. In the 1830s there may have been as many as 3,000 Lacandón in the western forests, although it is not clear how the authorities reached this conclusion (Soza 1970:470). Nor is the identity of the 1,500 "nomads" mentioned in, for example, the 1869 and 1870 censuses clear, but they may have been Lacandón Indians. For a longer time "unbaptized" or "wild" Indians, sometimes called *Huites*, from far northern Petén threatened towns and villages on the north side of Lake Petén Itzá.[15] To protect these places a military *gobernador* and soldiers were stationed in San Andrés (Soza 1970:256–57). Sometimes threat became reality. Thus in 1852 raiders variously identified as Santa Cruz, Santa Rita, or Cehach Indians burned several houses in San Andrés, caused the death of a resident, and spread fear throughout northern and central Petén (Soza 1957:292; 1970:250). The "bandits" who burned milpas around San José in 1867 (Reina 1967:15) may have been Huites or perhaps Santa Cruz Maya (cf. Berendt 1868). About that time, some five men coming from Yucatán via British Honduras were said to be planning an invasion of Petén (AGCA *Ramo Criminal* 1858), and in 1881, according to don Leandro Cano, soldiers from San Andrés were sent north to deal with "rebellious" Indians. The authorities, for example, Governor Vidaurre in 1861, also were concerned, needlessly as it turned out, that Maya refugees from the War of the Castes (1847–1901) might rouse the Indians of San Andrés (Thompson 1977:22; also see AGCA *Ramo Criminal* Leg.1, 1853, involving Peteneros in seditious communication with "rebel" Indians in Yucatán).

As a result of rebel Maya reversals in the War of the Castes, in which Indians tried to end white domination, one group of Indians called the

Santa Cruz withdrew to southeastern Yucatán, northern Belize, and northeastern Petén, set up a small state, and maintained their autonomy from 1847 to between 1893 and 1900. Until 1883 they and the British were more or less allies. The Anglo-Mexican Treaty of Belize, ratified in 1897, defined the northern border of British Honduras and led to the suppression of the Santa Cruz.

Before this, however, the Santa Cruz group put great pressure on less well organized Maya, pushing them into western British Honduras and eastern Petén. In the 1860s one such group, the San Pedro Maya, established several villages (the Holmul cluster) in eastern Petén (Jones 1977). The Holmul cluster, subordinate to but semiindependent of San Pedro in British Honduras, included Yaxhá, located some seventy kilometers east of Flores and Holmul, as well as some very small hamlets on the Río Bravo, about a hundred kilometers east by northeast of Flores. The authorities in Flores made limited contact with the Holmul cluster, but through such poorly chosen intermediaries that one may conclude they knew little about conditions in the east. In 1867 another group of San Pedranos fled to Santa Rita which, I believe, is located somewhat north of San Andrés, Petén; most of them returned home to Belize a few years later. In the 1860s the movements of San Pedranos and especially of Santa Cruzanos frightened Peteneros enough that they temporarily cut all links with British Honduras (Berendt 1868:422–24).[16] In the 1880s the Holmul cluster people returned to British Honduras, perhaps because of an epidemic then raging in Petén, and by 1904 there were only three families left at Yaxhá, the rest having moved to British Honduras. (The few people remaining in Macanché, a nearby village, also had gone or were preparing to go to British Honduras; Maler 1908b:61, 126–27.)

Although incidents of violence (for example, in 1852 and 1867) were unsettling, the perceived danger from "wild" and rebel Indians seems to have been exaggerated. There were several disturbing but quite futile attempts, in 1851, 1868, and 1873, by seditious Ladinos or Creoles to rouse Indians against the authorities in Flores. In other cases, Indians apparently acted alone, and the response of the authorities was disproportionate to the danger. For example, in 1873 Governor García Salas sent a force against what may have been Santa Cruz Indians discovered in northeastern Petén. Despite news that the Indians planned an attack and were well-armed, no battles were joined and no men lost, although the troops did capture one Indian. Several years later Valenzuela (1879) reported that the Indians in the north were peaceful and would have welcomed more contact with the Petén polity. But in 1880 once more there were rumors that Santa Cruzanos (or Cehach, according to oral tradition in San Andrés) were poised to strike at central Petén. In some fright, the governor moved the departmental capital south to Sacluk (La Libertad) for two years (1880–1882) and asked Guatemala City for military assistance. The government sent Salamatecan troops (perhaps joined by some men from San Andrés) who did not meet hostile Indians or fight any battles; rather, their commander discovered that Mexican soldiers had been moving about the north, probably to pressure Guatemala to conclude a border treaty with Mexico. (By that treaty, signed in 1883, Guatemala ceded to Mexico a triangle of land 10,400 km^2 thrusting north by northwest from Petén into Campeche. Supposedly 4,000 or more people lived there, but few of them were included in censuses of Petén.) For his error, the governor was removed from office and jailed, and the capital was returned to Flores.[17]

These rumors about dangerous Indians "out there" in the woods recall colonial times. In any case, the Santa Cruz seem not to have been a major threat to Peteneros; in fact, a small number of them apparently quietly became part of the Indian population of San Andrés, San José, and San Luis. Yucatecan refugees were also relatively rapidly assimilated into Petén society with which, after all, they had always had contact. Nonetheless, these movements did help to depopulate northern Petén, an "uninhabited wilderness" in the 1890s (Maler 1908b:138; Maudslay and Maudslay 1899:230). Yet the decline in livestock trading with Yucatán (brought about by the War of the Castes) and, later, new economic developments in Petén appear to have done more to depopulate the north than the "wild" and the rebel Indians. Certainly the Indians inspired fear, which at times was soundly justified, but the loss of the Yucatecan market had the greater impact. Thus while readily granting the need for some qualification, what Morelet said in 1847 could have been repeated, generally speaking, in 1895: "The sound of arms has been but seldom heard in the peaceful district of Peten, since the time of Don Martin de Ursua" (1871:215). Or, if arms were heard, little blood was shed.

Had they faced determined enemies, it is doubtful the Petén military could have coped with them. In 1840 Caddy was quite unimpressed with the army of two to three hundred "Mestizos and Indians." His reaction to meeting Ozaeta and his staff—the "most motley group of fellows I ever saw . . . dressed in any way most suitable to themselves"—was similar (in

Pendergast 1967:73). Lest this be thought foreign prejudice, I will add that the Guatemalan González also found the soldiers lacking in military bearing and discipline (1867:89). Nor do they seem to have been better equipped in 1867 than in 1765 (see AGI Guat. 859). But governors had sufficient arms to enforce the will of the state upon the local population, even if they could not deal effectively with Huites and supposed invaders.

One need not belittle the fear occasioned by violent incidents such as the 1852 raid on San Andrés, to suggest that finally Peteneros had more reason to fear their own government than "wild" or rebellious Indians. Settled Indians seem to have feared their social and political superiors. For the Creole ruling class and Ladino elements allied with them, the belief that rebelliousness might prove contagious could justify strong rule. It also revealed latent fears about how well-anchored their rule really was. Furthermore, I believe relations between autocratic but penurious rulers and "good-natured" subjects, recurrent epidemics, periodic crop failures, and poverty all generated persistent tensions which account for what appear as overwrought responses to "unbaptized" Indians.

Economy and Society to About 1895

Making a Living

In the nineteenth century, the preponderant majority of Peteneros were subsistence farmers—milperos. Internal and external trade did generate some wage labor opportunities and cottage industries, but they occupied relatively few people. For this reason, I have decided to discuss making a living first, beginning with agriculture, and then to speak of trade patterns. This will involve some repetition, but beginning with trade would too, and I prefer to begin by talking about what most people did to support themselves. Census records, official reports, and travelers' accounts all make plain that the majority made a living by small-scale rainfed agriculture. The major crop, as always, was maize, supplemented by other cultigens, primarily beans.

In the absence of account books, it is difficult to say precisely what quantity of maize and how much income farms generated, but some broad suggestions are possible, particularly for the last quarter of the nineteenth century. In 1960–1961, it was possible to interview several elderly people born in the 1890s (and two other men, one born in 1887 and one in 1865) who had vivid recollections of what they experienced or what their parents told them about the last decades of the nineteenth century. In dealing with milpa, I have relied heavily on these interviews which, it should be said, are consistent with available documentary records and with modern studies of Petén agriculture.[18] To set a context for what follows, I will also note that modern Petén farmers can produce three maize crops a year: (1) in the major wet season plot (planting-harvesting period from about May to November) called *milpa de cosecha* or *de quema* (milpa of harvest or fire); (2) in a smaller wet season plot (November to February) called Yaxkin (name of the seventh of the nineteen Maya months), *segunda* (second), or sometimes the "emergency" milpa; and (3) in a dry season low-lying plot (March to May) called *payapak*, or San José (because it is traditionally seeded on 19 March, St. Joseph's day). A man who devotes all or most of his working days to farming and who has the assistance of one or two unmarried sons (in Petén, women do not customarily work *in* the milpa) can handle 5 to 6 hectares a year. If everything goes well, the farmer can produce about 115 to 138 *quintales* (a quintal equals 100 pounds or 45 kilograms) of shelled maize, of which some 37 *quintales* will be used to feed his household (the average modern household size equals six people).[19] Thus, under *favorable* conditions, a farm family can produce enough maize to sustain itself and two additional families. If the farm family keeps yard animals such as chickens and pigs, it will be able to provide for itself and one other family. There is little or no doubt that modern milpa techniques are the same as those used in the eighteenth and nineteenth centuries—and in preconquest times too, except that then metal tools were not available—but twentieth century social and economic conditions are not the same.

In the last century Petén farmers apparently made smaller milpas than they do today, cropping perhaps 2.2 to 3.7 hectares. The major wet season milpas in particular seem to have been smaller, although government ordered men to make 10 *mecates* or *cuerdas*, about 0.44 hectares, that is, close to the modern average *segunda* plot. Government also ordered men between twenty-five and fifty years of age to crop at least 30 *mecates*, about 1.3 hectares, or pay a two peso fine). Several reasons may be advanced for the *milpa de cosecha* difference. To begin, a man had to perform *téquio* service at least two days a month, which did not include time spent traveling to and from the place where he worked, or time spent working on government-mandated crops such as tobacco, coffee, henequen and cotton. Second, household size was smaller and available labor thus less abun-

Table 3:4   Distribution of Population by Household, San Andrés, 1845

Number of persons in household	Number of households	Total population
One (widow)[a]	15	15
One (widower)	4	4
One (bachelor)	2	2
One (identity unclear)	1	1
Two	30	60
Three	40	120
Four	32	128
Five	13	65
Six	5	30
Seven	4	28
Eight	4	32
Nine	2	18
Total	152	503

(Mean household size = 3.3)

Source: AGCA 1845 ("Padrón General de los Habitantes del Pueblo de San Andrés"), a household census. Another 1845 document ("Senso General de la Poblac" del Distrito del Petén") which gives global not household data reports 161 households and 601 people in San Andrés, in which case mean household size = 3.7. I believe the discrepancy has to do with an *aldea* excluded from the *padrón* but included in the census (*aldeanos* tended to have large households).

[a] Total number of widows (those living alone + those living with others) = 49. The total number of widowers = 5. Thus, about 9.7 percent of the population consisted of widows!

dant than it is today. For example, in 1845 the average household size was about 4 persons. Even in Flores, the most prosperous town in Petén, average household size was 4.4 persons in 1845 and 4.2 in 1861. In San Andrés, a more rural place and one that produced more maize than most communities, the average was 3.7 in 1845 and 3.3 in 1863. A more realistic picture of the manpower situation emerges when one considers that in 1845 in a town such as San Andrés, 67.5 percent of the households had 4 or fewer people in them, and that there were an appalling number of widows, 9.7 percent of the population, in the community (Table 3:4). To be sure, the census data are not exact, for example, the 1845 household-by-household *padrón* census of San Andrés does not tally with the less detailed 1845 general census of the Petén district, and some men may have avoided being counted to evade *téquio*, including militia duty. Yet the number of widows was equally great in Flores, where the *padrón* counts were carefully done, are generally consistent with other census data, and are reasonably accurate. Households were undoubtedly smaller in the last century, as were milpas. Of course, with small households, subsistence needs were correspondingly less, but someone had to provide food for all those widows. (Although the matter is not entirely clear, most widows seem to have been supported by their sons.) That is, milpa plots were smaller in part because of the corvée system and in part because there was less available manpower. In addition, health conditions, hardly good in modern Petén, were worse in the nineteenth century when epidemics were far more common. This too could have had a negative effect on farm production.

Finally, there were several economic deterrents to production. The internal market for milpa products was small, primarily in Flores and in the savanna communities close to the departmental capital. Road and transport systems were not sufficiently developed to stimulate production for more distant markets even if more labor could have been invested in farming. Government, moreover, imprudently interfered with cropping cycles (Reina 1968). To some extent, the disincentives would have been partly balanced by household needs for cash and by very high prices for maize in times of scarcity (González 1867:84). Whatever the precise combination of reasons, milpas were smaller in the nineteenth than in the twentieth century, and, without doubt, maize was often in short supply, as indicated by the previously mentioned government orders concerning milpa production. People often had great difficulty provisioning themselves, let alone producing a large surplus.

Nineteenth-century milpas were closer in size to those of the eighteenth century (Chapter 2) than to the twentieth. Even in San Andrés, the maize basket for central Petén, I doubt that a farm household produced more than 50 to 84 *quintales* a year (based on the 2.2 to 3.7 hectare figure given above). Most of the time the San Andrés farmer had to feed an average of 3 to 4 people and all too often had to contribute to the support of a widowed parent. He also had to contribute one *quintal* a year to the community fund and to work on a community milpa. Assuming that people consumed no more maize then than they do today, that is, about 0.77 kilograms (1.7 pounds) a day, an amount which constitutes some 75 to 85 percent of daily caloric intake, a farmer would have needed about 26 *quintales* of maize for his household and the community fund. If he kept yard animals, the amount could easily have been 30 *quintales*, leaving him with 20 to 54 *quintales* for sale. However, constant documentary and informant references to nineteenth-century maize shortages suggest the lower figure is closer to reality. González (1867:84) observed that in Petén a *fanega* of maize (probably 0.6 to 0.7 *quintales*, and thus smaller than the Mexican *fanega*) cost 2 reales in normal times, although it could climb to 24 reales in times of scarcity. In an unexceptional year, then, a San Andrés milpero might have earned from maize sales 7 to 23 pesos, plus additional income from bean sales and occasional wage labor work. Data on wages are quite scant, but there are some hints that a field hand could earn $6 to $8 a month in cash or in kind (between 1845 and 1874). Going a step further and averaging $7 and $23 from maize sales, plus perhaps another 5 to 10 pesos from beans and other crops, and perhaps $10 from wage labor, for an average annual income of 30 to 35 pesos, while recalling that a man officially identified as an Indian (as most men in San Andrés were) had to pay a $2 head tax, the conclusion would be that the nineteenth-century San Andrés milpero's income was perhaps somewhat better, but not by much, than an eighteenth-century San Felipe cowboy's was (Chapter 2). If he did not work off-farm, he earned about what the eighteenth-century cowboy did. These figures may be compared with the price of horses, $12 to $23 (1829, 1860, 1863, 1866); bulls, $5 to $12 (1852, 1860); apparently fine shoes, $12 (1863); a fine comb, $5 (1868); and "medical" treatment, $3 to $6 (1863, 1871) during the 19th century (AGCA *Ramo Criminal* 1822–1899, for the years indicated in parentheses). Although most of the time the San Andrés milpero could feed himself and his household, he was, in a word, quite poor, as all those who visited Petén observed.[20]

There were, of course, nonfarm or urban occupations, and there also were some wage labor opportunities in ranching, logging, and tree tapping.

A small proportion of Peteneros were engaged in nonrural lines of work. By far the greatest number of these people lived in Flores, and a certain number lived in Sacluk. Travelers often missed or underestimated the occupational diversity in Flores. For instance, not only does Morelet (1871:209) speak of a "most perfect equality," but a more astute observer, Berendt (1868:424), too, saw "little division of labor" there. Perhaps they were misled by the relative uniformity of housing in Flores and the generalized poverty in the department. However, they were not entirely wrong. Even in Flores, the most urban place in nineteenth-century Petén, the majority were farmers. The Flores census data in 1861, for example,

Table 3:5 Occupation, Flores, 1881

Occupation	Male head of household	Other male
Hacendado[a]	7	0
Physician	1	0
Clergyman (vicar and priest)	2	0
Teacher	0	1
Artisan: Moccasin maker	33	15
Carpenter	4	3
Mason	2	0
Tailor	2	0
Blacksmith	1	3
Silversmith	1	4
Coachmaker	0	1
Drummer	0	1
Disabled and unemployed	7	1
Farmer	111	73
Not determined	2	1
Total	173	104

Source: AGCA 1861 ("Padrón . . . de Flores"). There were, in addition to these 173 households, another 80 listing a widow as head of household, 12 listing a spinster as head of household (of whom 10 had children) and 1 in which a husbandless "married" woman is listed as head. The total is 266 households and 1,122 people. The total number of widows (including 80 heads of household) is 97, or 8.6 percent of total population. All but 7 male heads of household have Spanish surnames; these 7 were farmers.

[a]The seven "*hacendados*" include a merchant, the governor, a judge, a colonel, a shoemaker and two farmers. Most of the important people in Flores were involved in commerce and trade, without being listed as "merchants" probably because of the high taxes imposed on merchants (see note 2).

show that of 173 male heads of household, 35.8 percent were nonfarmers, and 64.2 percent were farmers. Of other men (and the Flores *padrón* is very unusual in that it does list occupation for males other than heads of household), 29.8 percent were nonfarmers, and 70.2 percent were farmers (Table 3:5). At this time in Guadalupe Sacluk (formerly Sacluk), 25.9 percent of male heads of household were neither milperos, cowboys, nor field hands (Table 3:6). Elsewhere, almost everyone was a subsistence farmer. Thus, although there were cowboy-farmers in Santa Ana and San Francisco, and part-time loggers along with some cowboys in Dolores and Poptún, most of the men in the first three communities were milperos. In San José and San Luis, for all practical purposes, everyone was a milpero.

Table 3:6 Occupation, Guadalupe Sacluk (La Libertad), 1861

| Occupation | Male head of household by surname | |
	Spanish	Indian
Hacendado	2	0
Merchant	1	0
Military officer	3	0
Military commissionaire	3	0
Government storekeeper	2	1
Moccasin maker	6	0
Carpenter	0	2
Musician	0	1
Sacristan	2	3
Cowboy	7	7
Farmer	25	26
Servant (or field hand?)	11	10
Not determined	1	3
Total	63	53

Source: AGCA 1861 ("Padrón . . . Guadalupe Sacluk").
"Guadalupe" was added to "Sacluk" by post-1848 Yucatecans who settled here. In 1880, the town was renamed "La Libertad." Unlisted above are seven female heads of households, 3 with Spanish surnames, who owned ranches (*hacendadas*), and 4 who operated government stores (1 with a Spanish surname, 2 with an Indian surname, and 1 undetermined). The government stores, called *estancos*, sold liquor and tobacco.

In 1861 in San Benito of 54 male heads of household, 52 men (96.4 percent of the total) were farmers, and only 2 men (a carpenter and a painter, 3.7 percent of the total) were not. The percentages for San Andrés were about the same. For example, in 1848 (Table 3:7) of 116 male heads of household, 89.7 percent were milperos and 10.3 percent were not; in 1863 (Table 3:8), of 186 male heads of household 94.1 percent were milperos and 5.9 percent were not. Even if some men obscured their occupations to avoid taxes, it is clear that Flores was the one urbanized town in the entire department, with Guadalupe Sacluk a distant second.

Flores was urban in its ratio of nonfarmers to farmers and in the types of occupation there. The governor, the Judge of First Instance (when in Petén), a physician (now and then), the vicar, several types of artisans and even a coachmaker lived and worked there. Military officers posted to San Andrés and Guadalupe Sacluk as well as several township secretaries con-

Table 3:7 Office, Occupation, and Ethnicity, San Andrés, 1848

Office			Occupation		
	Non-Indian	Indian		Non-Indian	Indian
Commandant	1	0	Proprietor	1	0
First Mayor	1	0	Storekeeper	1	0
Second Mayor	0	1	Carpenter	1	0
Deputy Mayor	0	1	Sugarcane grower	6	1
Syndic	1	0	Horse/mule owner[a]	5	3
Alderman	2	2	Farmer	25	71
			Servant	0	2
Total	5	3	Total	39	77

Source: AGCA 1848 ("Padrón . . . del Pueblo de San Andrés").

Excluded are households headed by widows. The total population was 620 people, excluding 83 "Yucatecos" who the *padrón* lists apart from the San Andreños. Most of the Yucatecos eventually moved to the great savanna or to highland Guatemala. Some people listed as "Non-Indians" may have been Creoles and some Ladinos, but for purposes of this table they are grouped together. The (military) commandant was at times called the *gobernador* or *corregidor*). *Regidor* (alderman) may also be called councilman.

[a]The *padrón* lists horse/mule owners as farmers (*labradores*), but for analytic purposes they are listed separately. Two sugarcane fields owners also owned horses/mules.

Table 3:8 Office, Occupation, and Ethnicity, San Andrés, 1863

Office			Occupation		
	Non-Indian	Indian		Non-Indian	Indian
Military Cm.	1	0	Cattle purveyor	1	0
First Mayor	1	0	Rancher	2	0
Second Mayor	0	1	Gov't. storekeeper	2	0
Syndic	1	0	Carpenter	2	0
Alderman	2	2	Mason	1	0
Sacristan	0	1	Medic (or curer?)	1	0
Choir master	1	0	Sugarcane processor	0	1
			Charcoal maker	1	0
Total	6	4	Total	10	1

Source: AGCA 1863 ("Padrón General . . . del Pueblo de San Andrés").

Occupation for nine of the officials was given as "farmers," one of whom (the first mayor) was a cattle purveyor. "Military Cm." was the Military Commissionaire. In addition to the 21 men listed above another 175 were listed as farmers.

sidered Flores home, the address to which they returned even if resident elsewhere much of the time. There were carpenters, masons, and smiths in the departmental capital. But, as Table 3:5 shows, the single most important nonrural occupation, in terms of numbers, was that of moccasin maker. At some point, apparently in the 1850s, Flores artisans began to make moccasins for export to British Honduras. By 1861, 17.3 percent of Flores men were making moccasins; this was a genuine cottage industry. In fact, the census data do not reveal the entire range of urban income producing activities in Flores. From the 1860s on, loggers who worked in western Petén came to the departmental capital to make purchases, particularly for clothing which Floreños imported from British Honduras (Valenzuela 1879). By the 1880s, and probably earlier, contraband in spirits, tobacco, and cattle was a common activity in Flores, one harking back to colonial times. Successful smuggling, of course, leaves few tracks in the documentary record, but it may have been very important. This activity was engaged in by some of the most prominent and powerful families in the city (AGCA *Ramo Criminal* 1822–1899).

There were far fewer urban occupations in Guadalupe Sacluk. Thus in 1861 there were several professional military officers there, a merchant, three storekeepers, and nine artisans, of whom six were moccasin makers. There also were five big ranch owners, three of them widows. A place such as San Andrés was, by comparison, almost entirely rural in occupational composition. For example, in 1863, of the nonmilperos, one man was a cattle purveyor, two were ranchers, two were storekeepers, two were carpenters, and one was a mason (there was also some sort of medic or possibly a curer in the town at this time).

It may be added here that Flores was also the most populous settlement in Petén until about 1880 (Tables 3:9 and 3:10). Thus, in 1845 when the population of the district (or more precisely, the towns and hamlets under government control) was 5,203, a large number of people—1,025, or 19.7 percent of the total—lived in Flores. Even under very conservative assumptions, for example, those used for 1869 (Table 3:11), when the *settled* population (that is, excluding what the census calls 1,500 "nomads," probably in far western Petén) was 8,817, there were 1,177 people in Flores (13.3 percent of the total). In 1870, when the settled population dropped to 7,524 —probably because of movements among the Holmul and similar groups—the population of Flores was 1,222 (16.2 percent of the total). In 1880 La Libertad (formerly Guadalupe Sacluk) and Flores had about the

Table 3:9 Population of Petén, 1845

Settlements	Number of Households and Number of People by Age								
	HH	Men 15–50	Boys 1–14	Women 12–40	Girls 1–11	Men 50+	Women 50+	Total	Mean HH size
Flores	233	282	192	306	141	19	85	1025	4.4
San Benito	47	35	41	55	77	8	17	233	5.0
Dolores	164	130	142	164	82	27	33	578	3.5
G. Sacluk	105	99	63	129	43	9	26	369	3.5
San Andrés	161	141	139	155	124	13	29	601	3.7
San José	139	157	105	130	105	17	23	537	3.9
Santa Ana	60	67	33	69	30	7	10	216	3.6
S. Juan de Dios	56	56	50	61	34	5	5	211	3.8
San Luis	153	148	162	151	115	20	21	617	4.0
San Antonio	30	71	33	50	17	11	2	184	6.1
Thubucil	28	54	15	34	11	0	1	115	4.1
Nohvecan	8	27	2	11	4	1	0	45	5.6
Chachaclun	72	63	61	87	36	13	15	275	3.8
Sto. Toribio	51	50	41	53	36	5	12	197	3.9
Total	1307	1380	1079	1455	855	155	279	5203	4.0

Source: AGCA 1845 (a loose page found, as were several other censuses, in among more carefully labeled documents). HH = household; the column on the far right is derived from the census. Figures are rounded to nearest tenth.

A partly legible note on the water-stained document says "Faltando del pueblo de Concepcion por no hab___ilido." Here as in other censuses, Poptún was included with Dolores.

same population—1,431 and 1,420 respectively. This came about because Yucatecans migrating to Petén favored La Libertad and also because the panic about rebel Indians in 1880 led government officials and others to flee to the savanna. Since the departmental capital was returned to Flores in 1882, a better indication of Flores's share of Petén population comes from the 1893 census (Table 3:11) in which 6,705 people were counted. Of this number, 1,671 lived in Flores (24.9 percent of the total) and 1,901 in La Libertad (28.4 percent). Even in 1904, when the population of the department was roughly estimated to be 10,000, there were some 1,000 or 10 percent of the total in the island capital. Because of its population size and relatively urbanized character, Flores was the major market in central Petén for farm products. (That Flores's own farmers, approximately two-thirds of its inhabitants, were unable to supply Flores with all of its food needs

Table 3:10 Population Growth, Petén, 1845–1977

Township	1845	1859	1880	1893	1921	1940	1950	1964	1973	1977
Flores	1025	1199	1420	1671	1801	2559	3303	4104	8774	12203
S. Benito	233	247	656	318	623	957	1411	3036	4682	2802
S. Andrés	601	715	511	634	895	1229	1808	1851	2372	4104
S. José	537	486	805	298	355	622	935	564	567	799
S. F^{co}	275	390	600	630	610	909	900	1100	1400	1680
Sta. Ana	216	244	620	458	187	149	244	312	1276	5108
Libertad	369	520	1431	1901	1610	878	1204	1182	3576	8938
Melchor	—	—	—	—	—	—	—	2391	4693	8680
Dolores	578	467	940	300	422	538	801	1176	6563	20611
Poptún	—	—	—	—	—	—	—	—	9484	10515
San Luis	617	770	1190	319	1310	2758	4282	9250	15468	20784
Sayaxché	—	—	201	176	89	876	807	1341	5001	11918
Other[a]	752	1509	—	—	—	—	—	—	—	—
Total	5203	6547	8374	6705	7902	11475	15695	26307	63856	108142

Sources: AGCA 1845–1859 (*Padrón* and census documents); FYDEP 1977 (for 1881–1977). In 1977, FYDEP projected 3.0 percent/year population growth for Petén, i.e., it projected 213,573 people there by the year 2000. They were considerably off the mark! For example, FYDEP projected that La Libertad township would have 18,164 people in the year 2000, but by 1980 the figure was at least 14,000. Note that until 1960, Melchor de Mencos was usually counted with and not distinguished from Flores, although it was mentioned separately at least once, in 1869 (as Plancha de Piedra, population 56). Until 1966, Poptún was usually subordinate to and counted with Dolores; until 1929, Sayaxché was an *aldea* in the township of La Libertad. Totals for any given year are approximate because census takers often omitted people outside the established zones of settlement, e.g., people moving in and out of the Holmul group, Indians more or less hidden in the deep forests, etc. In addition, some censuses include an unidentified "nomadic" population (said to number 1,500), but most do not. None used here mention "nomads;" those for 1869 and 1870 do.

[a]"Others" refers to *aldeas*, rural neighborhood clusters and ranches which were either in the far west or northwest or were difficult to identify with any given township. Many were not permanent, e.g., between 1845–1881, of 35 settlements mentioned in censuses, 19 appear only once (and others which do not appear in censuses are mentioned in criminal court records). Some small settlements were relatively permanent, but their names were not, e.g., owing to the habit of placing a Spanish name in front of a Maya one, a settlement may appear under three different names, e.g., San Pedro Yaxhá is sometimes listed as "San Pedro," or simply as "Yaxhá."

not only suggests that milpas were small in the nineteenth century, but also that some Floreños who were listed in census reports as farmers may have been engaged full- or part-time in some other line of work, for example, contraband.) Cowboys, particularly in the vicinity of Santa Ana and perhaps San Francisco, worked for Flores livestock owners. (Gonzáles [1867]

Table 3:11 Areal Distribution of Population, Petén, 1845–1977

Area	Percent of total population by year									
	1845	1869	1880	1893	1921	1940	1950	1964	1973	1977
Flores	19.7	13.3	17.0	24.9	22.8	22.7	21.0	15.6	13.7	11.3
Lake	46.1	39.2	40.5	43.6	46.5	46.8	47.5	36.3	25.7	18.4
Savanna	16.5	21.0	31.7	44.6	30.5	16.9	15.0	9.9	9.8	14.5
Southeast	23.0	21.0	25.4	9.2	21.9	28.7	32.4	39.6	49.4	48.0
Other areas	14.4	18.8	—	—	—	—	—	—	—	—
East	—	—	—	—	—	—	—	9.1	7.3	8.0
West	—	—	2.4	2.6	1.1	7.7	5.1	5.1	7.8	11.1
Total	100.0	100.0	100.0	100.0	100.0	100.0	100.0	100.0	100.0	100.0

Sources: See Tables 3:9–3:10. "Lake" = *pueblos* of Flores, S. Benito, S. Andrés and S. José, and near-by *aldeas*. "Savanna" = S. Fran*co*, Sta. Ana and La Libertad. "Southeast" = Dolores, Poptún and S. Luis. Until 1869, "Other" = far west and northwest. From 1964, "East" = township of Melchor de Mencos. "West" = Sayaxché.

Note: Even if the data were absolutely accurate, and they are not, the table would be approximate, simply because several townships sprawl across several areas, e.g., Flores covers part of central and northern Petén, etc. But approximate does not mean wrong or misleading. Until about 1964, most Peteneros lived in *pueblos*, not in *aldeas*; even today most large *aldeas* are near *pueblos*. Data for 1869 are included as a "worst" case test in that almost all *aldeas* and hamlets were put in "Other" (and in 1869, there were either an unusually large number of Yucatecan refugees in Petén or an unusually large number of them were counted; most of them lived in the far north). Excluded are the elusive "1,500 nomads."

found that some from Santa Ana worked as cowboys for "affluent people," *personas acomodadas*, in Flores, and Petén oral history suggests that some San Franciscans also did.) That is, most of the nonrural workers in Petén lived in Flores, and to earn cash, many of Petén's farmers and cowboys had to sell to or work for people in Flores.

Just how many full-time cowboys there were in the nineteenth century is not entirely clear. For example, the Guadalupe Sacluk *padrón* for 1861 (Table 3:6) reported 14 cowboys, or about 12 percent of the town's male head of household labor force. Even if some farmers tended herds part of the time, this is a small number of men, considering that this was the largest cattle ranching community in Petén. Six years later, in 1867, González reported that there were ten large ranches (*haciendas*) and suggested that there were as many as 12,000 head of cattle here. (In the 1890s, however, there seem to have been only about 1,000 cattle.) There were another 2,000 head around Santa Ana, 1,300 head plus 320 horses around Flores, and several herds in the Dolores-Poptún area, where the largest owner was a Floreño (cf. Soza 1970:614; Valenzuela 1879). González believed that there were more cattle in Petén at the beginning of the nineteenth century than in the 1860s. The herds were not increasing in size (Soza and Valenzuela concur), many *haciendas* had deteriorated, and Dolores, which once had had many cattle and had been prosperous, was now a poor place (as Morelet found it in 1847, twenty years earlier). Even if González's 12,000 figure is exaggerated, the number of cattle apparently was relatively impressive, and Soza (1957:127) says that until about 1900 there still were big cattle and horse ranches in Petén. But this does not necessarily imply a large number of cowboys. Since colonial days herds in Petén have been allowed to graze unattended much of the year. Modern ranchers say that a single cowboy with occasional assistance from a second man can look after as many as 500 head of cattle. Thus, despite the size of the herds given above (and assuming the figures are roughly accurate), the number of cowboys given in the Guadalupe Sacluk *padrón* appears reasonable. Ranching probably was not a major source of *full-time* wage employment.

After the 1840s far fewer herds went north to Yucatán. Rather, aside from hides used by moccasin makers and whatever beef was sold to loggers around Dolores and in western Petén, I believe that most of the cattle were smuggled to and sold in British Honduras. Peteneros did sell cattle to Yucatecans, however, at least as late as the 1870s. Soza (1970:614), who says that most of them went northwest from Flores to Tabasco, would disagree, but González (1867:89) found sizable herds being driven east to British Honduras, yet to judge from AGCA *Ramo Criminal* records (for example, in 1852 and 1860), this may mean herds of about 15 head of cattle.[21] In any case, the more crucial point is that although ranching continued to be of some importance for a long time, after the disruptions occasioned by Carrera's revolution and the War of the Castes, it became less important than it had been. Crown ranches no longer provided work; *cofradía* ranches declined, and by the end of the nineteenth century they had disappeared.[22] Despite the contraband trade, private ranching too began a secular decline, and, by 1900, was of relatively little economic significance. The industry was not revived until about the 1960s–1970s.

Loggers and Tappers

These two ways of making a living merit special notice. Logging has a very long history in the tropical lowlands of Mexico and Central America. The British engaged in cutting logwood and mahogany (*caoba*) from 1630 on, and *caoba* trade became the mainstay of British Honduran economy from the 1770s until the 1860s. After 1870 sugarcane replaced mahogany in importance (Bolland 1977). In Petén, although commercial *caoba* cutting apparently can be traced back to the early 1820s, it became much more economically significant in the 1860s and 1870s (Mazzarelli 1970b:20–21; Reina 1964:267; Valenzuela 1879). Even though *caoba* was losing value for British Hondurans, they did continue to export it, concentrating their Petén operations in the southeast, around Dolores. Firms from Tabasco, Mexico, and later the United States, focused on the western riverine regions of the department. The Guatemalan government began logging operations on the Usumacinta in 1874, but conceded the business to the Hamet (or Jamet) and Sastre Company in 1880. The concession then passed to the American-owned Guatemalan and Mexican Mahogany and Export Company, which placed its field headquarters in La Libertad (although Jamet apparently continued to cut wood in and around Sayaxché until the early part of the twentieth century; Maler 1908a:11; Soza 1970:93). Some of the British Honduran crews were quite large, up to forty or more men at a time. They were a diverse lot—Jamaicans, Yucatec Mayas, Honduran Ladinos, and so on (González 1867:10). In the southeast, there do not seem to have been many native Peteneros directly engaged in woodcutting. In the west, crews were equally diverse: trees were felled by Lacandón Indians, blacks, men from Guadalupe Sacluk (many of them originally from Tabasco, Campeche, and Yucatán), and other places.

Since Englishmen, Mexicans, and Americans financed the logging operations, it is most probable that they captured most of the profit from the work (a point the level-headed Valenzuela [1879] makes about the Mexicans). But within Petén merchants and liquor dealers from Flores and Guadalupe Sacluk (La Libertad) also were well rewarded. Because of its location La Libertad became, as noted, the Petén headquarters for the Tabascan and North American firms. Later, between 1890 and 1900, a family from Cayo, British Honduras, of Lebanese Catholic origin began a logging operation here. Imported goods from British Honduras destined for western Petén passed through middlemen in La Libertad, as well as Flores. The loggers made purchases and sought relaxation in the savanna town, although it might not have seemed like much to an educated outsider: "A woodcutter is indeed to be pitied who has to seek recreation in such a hot, dull, dreary place as Sacluk [La Libertad]; the condition of the water alone would justify his preference for aguardiente" (Maudslay and Maudslay 1899:231). Dreary perhaps, but *padrón* data indicate that La Libertad was more complexly organized, more town-like ("more urban" would not be quite appropriate) than other Petén *pueblos* save, of course, Flores. As mentioned, loggers bought goods, particularly clothing, in Flores, and Flores merchants supplied their counterparts in La Libertad with other goods and perhaps food staples (for toward the end of the century, agriculture had declined in La Liberated [Maler 1911]) for resale to the woodcutters.

Growing international demand for natural rubber also affected Petén. In 1866 the Guatemalan Ministry of Government, Justice and Church Affairs granted an English company a concession to extract rubber (*hule*) from the forests of Petén. Thereafter, Mexican and British Honduran businessmen (some of Lebanese extraction) extended credit to Flores merchants and to some other Peteneros from La Libertad and San Andrés who, in turn, organized work crews to tap the trees. In some cases, the foreign businessmen worked with Petén labor contractors they knew from logging operations. Contractors offered tappers (*huleros*) cash advances (*enganches*, lit. "hooks") for a stipulated amount of rubber. If a tapper did not fulfill his contract and repay the *enganche*, he might be obliged to work off the debt at wages and labor determined by the contractor. The *huleros*, like the loggers, spent weeks on end in the forest, and upon returning to a *pueblo* apparently drank heavily. (But, then, logging if not *hule* tapping was marked by all sorts of misconduct, as Valenzuela [1879] observed.) The Petén labor contractors who obtained *hule* licenses were usually Creoles or Ladinos (although by this time there was no legal basis for this ethnic distinction) and whereas the tappers were usually Indians, some were Ladino. Contractors also paid *téquio* exemption fines for their workers (see for example, Municipal Archives, San Andrés, 1887 and 1894). In Guatemala, rubber exploitation peaked between 1899 and 1901. It became quite insignificant after 1913 (Sierra Franco 1941), although it was revived in the 1950s outside Petén on the south coast. Thus this extractive economy had a short history (from about 1870 to 1900) and never a truly vital one in Petén. Yet rubber tapping, like logging, prefigured many of the conditions found in chicle collecting: foreign businessmen advancing credit to Petén merchants who then acted as local managers and labor contractors, *enganches*, debt peonage, men leaving home for long periods to work in the forests, a pervasive tone of immorality in the entire operation, negative images of labor, and so on.[23] In the 1890s British Honduran businessmen who had been involved with *hule* used their contacts in Petén to initiate the far more important chicle extraction economy.

Patterns of Trade

Much of what may be said about trade is implied in the previous section. I will now examine commerce in Petén in the nineteenth century more directly. With the preponderant majority of the population engaged in subsistence agriculture, it is no surprise that the travelers cited throughout this chapter commented on Petén's limited commerce. After the 1840s Petén traded primarily with British Honduras and secondarily with Tabasco, Mexico, although in neither case was trade really extensive until the 1890s. Thus, in 1840 Caddy remarked that Petén-British Honduran trade was of "small extent" (Pendergast 1967:73). In 1847, Morelet noticed but "slight relations . . . between Peten and Tabasco" (1871:168), an observation echoed by Mejía at the end of the century: there are "few commercial relations with Belice and Tabasco" (1904:25). Yet with the increase in logging after the 1860s, later the *hule* economy, and so forth, the momentum of trade with British Honduras to the east and with Tabasco to the northwest did pick up. At the same time, and in part because of this increase as well as changes in the ranching sector, southeastern Petén (Santo Toribio, Dolores, Poptún, and San Luis) declined in economic importance. San Luis in particular became increasingly peripheral to Petén's major commercial interests, which may help explain why the authorities in Flores showed so little interest in the place. Given their reaction to corvée and taxation, the Indians of San Luis doubtless would have been content with even less attention. Perhaps, too, San Luis's economically marginal position may help explain why it was for so long the most Indian of Petén's communities, although the constant arrival of other Kekchí from Alta Verapaz also helped. Even today, because of many factors—dispersed settlement pattern, social institutions (for instance, *cofradías*), language, and so forth—San Luis seems more like a so-called traditional Indian community in highland Guatemala than one of the ladinoized settlements of lowland Petén. If this was what San Luiseños wanted, until very recently their marginality to the economy of Petén enabled them to express their will.

During the nineteenth and for much of the twentieth century, Petén's internal and external trade centered on the Lake and savanna regions, with

Flores at the hub. Interactive factors account for Flores's position: geographic location (literally, the center of the department), concentration of political power, initial advantage as the address for most Petén notables, and population density. Given population distribution in Petén, and links between demography and economy, not to mention a privileged head start, perhaps it could not have been otherwise (Tables 3:9 and 3:10). Until the 1950s, the Lake region (Flores, San Benito, San Andrés, San José) usually held roughly 39 to 47 percent of Petén's *settled* population, with Flores the largest settlement in this region. The savanna region (San Francisco, Santa Ana, La Libertad) fluctuated more, varying usually from about 16 to 30 percent of the population. The southeast, save for the 1890s low point, contained roughly another 22 to 29 percent (Table 3:11). All of this was to change dramatically in the 1960s, as will be noted in Chapter 6. But until then, the Lake and the plains together were the demographic center of Petén. The plains towns were 18 to 30 kilometers from Flores, that is, 5 to 8 hours by foot. The southeastern settlements were 60 to 119 kilometers away (San Luis being the most distant), from 2 to 5 days of travel because of the distance and the steeper terrain in the far southeast.

Tables 3:9 to 3:11 do not pretend to present a completely accurate demographic picture. For example, they do not reveal the fact that because San Luiseños lived in dispersed rural neighborhoods, their county capital was one of the smallest in Petén until the later 1960s. Moreover, because censuses do not always list central *pueblos* and *aldeas* separately (for example, Melchor was often included with Flores in the census until 1966), the picture of town size can be distorted. Also, as mentioned previously, people such as the so-called nomads living west of La Libertad and those in *aldeas* and *caseríos* north of San Andrés were not regularly counted. As for refugees from the War of the Castes in Yucatán, for example, those who resided at Tubucil (also spelled Thubucil) sometimes were and sometimes were not included in the censuses, perhaps because not all of them remained in Petén or because the authorities in Flores had less than full information on them. Even today there are uncounted Mexicans living in northwestern Petén. Finally, even counts for the same year but from different sources are not always consistent with each other (cf. Tables 1:1 and 3:9–3:10). Rather than try to smooth out the differences, I have let them stand to reflect the sort of discrepancies found in source material. Yet, with all these caveats, two things may be said with some confidence. First, for many decades a majority of Peteneros lived in the Lake and savanna regions. Second, demographic growth in Petén was negligible in the nineteenth century (from 5,203 people in 1845 to 6,705 in 1893). The lack of growth is one factor that suggests a relatively flat, nonvital economy.

Tables 3:12 and 3:13 summarize what has been said above and in the preceding section. Although the tables and their appended notes[24] are, I believe, self-explanatory, there is one final point to make. Peteneros say that each town (that is, *pueblo*) in the department has a distinct "nature." People derive their character, and thus their mode of interacting with others, from their natal community. For instance, Floreños tend to regard San Andreños as fickle, capricious, and at times combative. San Joseños, they say, are more humble, closer to nature and the forest. For San Andreños and San Joseños, Floreños are not only urbane, politically well connected and often well educated (*buenas plumas*; "good writers"), but also overbearing and (San Andreños especially will add) selfish. Of course, members of a community, when speaking of themselves, make the above traits positive. For instance, San Andreños do not say that they are combative, but rather that although they are peaceful they do know how to defend themselves. Whether negatively or positively described, these characteristics are said to derive from the ethnic-cultural origins of a town's population. Thus, the mix of Creoles, Ladinos, and Indians in San Andrés makes its people capricious; the putative Itzá origin of San Joseños gives them an edge in the forest; and the Spanish background of Floreños is a major reason why they are "civilized" and *buenas plumas*. Further dilation on these intercommunity stereotypes aside, the point is that they seem to reflect traditional patterns of trade in Petén. San Andrés has traditionally supplied Flores with food staples, trying to hold back in times of plenty and sell at inflated prices in times of scarcity. Floreños have used their political and economic power to counter these moves, and San Andreños have tried to resist such impositions. In this sense, "capriciousness" can characterize the way San Andreños prefer to sell maize and beans to Floreños, and "selfishness" sums up the San Andrés impression of Flores buyers. Similarly, San José's soils may not be as fertile as those of San Andrés (Reina 1967), and so rather than food staples, the town has sold craft items, firewood, and so on to Flores (Table 3:12), "humble" things if one wishes, but also things that Floreños could have postponed buying or, if pressed, obtained in San Benito. Almost by definition, trade between San José and Flores was bound to be more placid than between San Andrés and Flores. Natural variations in harvests and farmers' desires to realize profits

Table 3:12 Petén Trade Patterns: Overview, 1840s–1890s

Community	Major products and services	Primary destination
San Benito	1. Rice, pigs	1. Flores
	2. Brooms, palm oil, and similar household items	2. Flores
	3. Firewood	3. Flores
	4. Cured hides	4. Flores (?)
	5. Craft and field labor	5. Flores
San Andrés	1. Basic grains: maize, beans	1. Flores and savanna towns
	2. Lime (for stucco)	2. Flores (and savanna towns?)
	3. *Aguardiente*; crude brown sugar	3. Flores and San José
	4. Muleteers; female servants	4. Flores
	5. *Hule* (rubber) after 1860s[a]	5. Overseas markets
San José	1. *Tinajas* (water jugs) and similar items	1. Flores and nearby towns
	2. Firewood and thatch for roofing	2. Flores
	3. Mail carriers[b]	3. Flores-Chinajá-Cobán
Santa Ana	1. Cowboys	1. Flores ranch owners
S. Francisco[c]	1. Citrus fruits (?)	1. Flores (?)
	2. Minor production of cacao, cotton, and coffee	2. Unclear
	3. Rush hats, made by Yucatán refugees	3. Yucatán
	4. Beef and probably hides for moccasins	4. Unclear; probably British Honduras
Guadalupe Sacluk (La Libertad)[d]	1. Cattle (and perhaps some horses)	1. British Honduras and Yucatán
	2. Distribution center linking Flores and western Petén, i.e., sending salt, forest products, etc. from the west to Flores and selling manufactured goods (e.g., machetes, cloth) to Lacandón, clothes to loggers, etc. (Most salt probably from Tabasco via Tenosique)	2. Serving loggers in the west (esp. after 1860); trading with Lacandón Indians at least from 1840s on; redistributing products from Flores to western Petén

Table 3:12 (Continued)   Petén Trade Patterns: Overview, 1840s–1890s

Community	Major products and services	Primary destination
	3. *Hule* (rubber) after 1860s (probably from western part of township)	3. Overseas markets
Lacandón in western Petén[e]	1. Honey, wax, tree gums, cacao, tobacco (bartered) 2. May have transmitted salt 3. Loggers (?)	1. La Libertad (and from here probably to Flores) 2. La Libertad 3. Tabasco, Mexico
Sayaxché and other river settlements in far west[f]	1. Loggers	1. Tabasco, Mexico
Dolores[g]	1. Cacao; cotton of some importance 2. Some beef 3. Some coffee 4. Loggers 5. Religious services	1. Flores and perhaps Cahabón 2. British Honduras and loggers in vicinity 3. Unclear 4. British Honduras 5. Southeastern Petén
San Luis[h]	1. Some tobacco and cacao 2. *Junco* (rush) for hats, etc.	1. Cahabón and Cobán; Flores 2. Yucatán (for hats) and Cahabón (for roofing)

Sources: AGCA censuses, Andrews et al. 1983 (see note 24 this chapter for other sources and comments under superscripts).

assured that the supply would be less than stable, but people cannot do without food. From Flores's perspective, synonyms for San Andrés might well have been "capricious" and "nettlesome". Yet, durable as these stereotypes are, they do yield to change. For example, after the 1960s, San Andrés played a less important role in supplying Flores with food staples. With that, San Andreños began to look somewhat less capricious or fickle to Floreños. This is to say, community-character stereotypes are linked to community economic role. Once in place, the stereotypes may become

Table 3:13 Flores Trade Patterns, 1840s–1890s

Major services and products	Primary market
1 Services: Administrative, medical and religious[a]	1 Towns and major villages, especially those under government control
2 Trade: Clothes, spirits, manufactured goods, etc.	2 Central Petén; western Petén via La Libertad
3 Cattle and horses (as owners and purveyors)	3 British Honduras (less so to Yucatán)
4 Moccasins	4 British Honduras
5 *Hule* after late 1860s	5 Overseas markets
6 Minor production of rush hats	6 Yucatán?
7 In general, major redistribution center for goods entering Petén	

Major imports	Primary source of supply
1 Clothes, spirits, manufactured goods, e.g., metal tools	1 British Honduras
2 Salt	2 British Honduras; Tabasco, Mexico
3 School supplies	3 Yucatán
4 Foodstuffs, brooms, firewood, hides, etc. and labor	4 San Benito
5 Grains, sugarcane, lime, muleteers	5 San Andrés
6 Craft goods, firewood, thatch	6 San José
7 Labor, especially cowboys	7 Santa Ana
8 Fruits	8 San Francisco
9 Forest products	9 Western Petén, via La Libertad
10 Cacao, cotton, tobacco	10 Dolores; San Luis
11 Rush	11 San Luis?

Sources: Derived from Table 3:12 and (especially for 1890s) interviews with don Pedro Castellanos, Flores.
[a] For much of the century and certainly from the 1860s–1870s on, there were few priests in Petén—sometimes only a vicar and priest residing in Flores and making circuits of major settlements. In this sense, Flores was also a religious service center.

internalized and affect behavior, but they rest on a more material base, the economic side of which is summarized for the nineteenth century in Tables 3:12 and 3:13.

Economic Strata, Political Power

Those visiting Petén for scholarly or official reasons, from Caddy in 1840 to Mejía in 1904, were inevitably struck by the poverty of the population, their humble homes, meager possessions, simple clothing, dilapidated churches, and limited commerce. Yet they also observed differences in wealth and rank.

A small minority of Peteneros, if not grandly rich, were relatively affluent. They could afford, for example, to pay *téquio* exemption fines for themselves and their workers, to ransom themselves from jail for $50 (in 1839), and speak of $6,000 loans (in the 1860s; González 1867:89–91). If in the 1840s Floreños lived in "mean thatched huts" (Caddy in Pendergast 1967:76–77), by the 1870s some of them could afford tin roofs and one even had a two story house (Valenzuela 1879). In 1872 there was a terrible fire in Flores, which some people suspected was started by seditionists. The fire destroyed 109 houses, 85 (detached) kitchens, and merchandise (purchased on credit from British Hondurans). Total losses were estimated at $50,000 (AGCA *Ramo Criminal* Leg. 3, 1872). Although the calculation is necessarily quite rough, this means that each establishment (house, kitchen, goods) was worth on average $459, more than the equivalent value of many milperos' establishments outside Flores in the 1960s. Again, if most of the time people dressed in plain "cotton drawers," sumptuary differences were apparent on festive days in, for example, Flores, La Libertad, and San Andrés (González 1867:88). Those listed in *padrón* censuses as proprietors, *hacendados*, and merchants were paying $20 in taxes (see note 2), probably not much less than some milperos earned in a year. The more important sugarcane growers, too, must have been relatively prosperous. Their crop was valuable. Manufacture and sale of *aguardiente*, in theory under strict government control, was an important industry in Petén until the 1930s when President Ubico prohibited its production (Soza 1970:619). In the last half of the nineteenth century, six *mecates* (about 0.25 hectares) of sugarcane were worth $30 (see, for example, AGCA *Ramo Criminal* Leg.2, 1868), not much less than the value of some coffee lands in highland Guatemala (Boddam-Whetham 1877:75–82), although the scale of production in Petén was immeasurably smaller than in the highlands. It is easier to note that economic differences existed than to establish clear-cut economic strata and to calculate the number of people in a given stratum. However, *padrón* data, legal records, and, for the last two decades of the nineteenth century, oral history make possible a global assessment.

The economic elite were the big proprietors, big ranchers, and merchants. These men or their relatives were also important bureaucrats and military officers. They may have constituted (this is a rough calculation based on census data) 3 to 5 percent of the population. For example, in Dolores, at least from the 1820s to 1850s, there were four important ranchers and merchants, about 3 percent of the local population. In Flores, La Libertad, and San Andrés between the 1840s and 1860s, the percentage of those listed as proprietors, big ranchers, and merchants is about the same, 2 to 4 percent (Tables 3:5 to 3:8). Although San José, San Luis, and possibly Santa Ana may have lacked big ranchers and merchants, in each of the other *pueblos* there were several relatively prosperous families, the local economic elite.

As might be expected, there were some differences between Flores and the other towns. Not only did the wealthiest people live here, but in addition a disproportionate number of affluent Floreños were engaged in contraband. Members of what might be called the middle class or sector— artisans, storekeepers, and spirit sellers—were more numerous in Flores than in the other communities. In most towns the middle sector comprised approximately 3 to 11 percent of the population, but in Flores the figure was closer to 25 to 30 percent. Even if outside Flores there were some successful farmers in the middle sector, the group was not very large. In any given settlement other than Flores, 85 to 95 percent of the men may have been milperos and/or cowboys, with the cowboys a small proportion of this number.

Before inquiring further about the social identity of the elite and the middle sector, it is important to glimpse part of the meaning of poverty. Perhaps the best way to do so is to refer back to the *téquio* system. In 1894 a military officer, don Estanislao Aldana (1849–1909) of San Andrés, himself not subject to corvée, paid $18 ($6 per man) to the township to have his *sirvientes*, Juan Cohouj, Anecleto Pantí, and Ignacio Pantí, exempted from *téquio* for a year.[25] Six pesos may not seem a grand sum—after all, merchants had to pay an annual tax of 20 pesos—but few milperos could afford to buy themselves out of *téquio*. There can be little doubt that had they been able to do so, they would have. Although the elderly informant quoted below was describing conditions in San Andrés in the early 1900s, his remarks surely also would be valid for the nineteenth century. The informant, a bilingual Maya and Spanish speaker, was discussing with two bilingual friends and the present writer "the time of the sticks."

The mailman was not paid. One (man) was drafted each month, and only those who lived above [*arriba*, lit. above; the northern part of town, but in San Andrés "those who lived above" also used to be a euphemism for "Indian"] were drafted, the more humble and brutish people. Now we are all equal [at which the two men giggle, appear embarrassed, but nod in agreement]. But [now speaking with great intensity] life was *triste* [sad, boring]. In the making of the milpa, both those who lived below [*abajo*, southern part of town, but in times past a euphemism for "Ladino"] and those who lived above were all on the same footing. The army was Indians and Ladinos, but the mails was solely Indians. It was terrible. If one did not go, he was beaten with sticks; the governor [*jefe político*] would beat him . . . They (the mail carriers) went on foot, and before they used to carry (sacks of) coffee to Chinajá, then mail and other things (Field Notes 1960).

He went on to add that because of this "imposition," the father of one of his guests fled to Soccotz, British Honduras (see below) and

men went away, so their poor wives and children gave one pity. They had nothing, and a lot of them had to work for the *buenas plumas* in Flores and here. That is why the children from *arriba* do not read. They had to work at the milpa and could not come to the second grade school here.

In the informant's view, this explains differences in educational attainments between "those who thought they owned the earth and the humble people."

One of the guests later related:

My parents spoke Maya. My father had a milpa and was Catholic. He was in the Hermanos de la Cruz [an Indian ceremonial and credit sodality in San Andrés which lasted until the 1920s]. Three months before I was born [in 1905], my father went to Soccotz, to live, as he had a lot of relatives there. It was the *téquio*. My father had to carry the mail from San Andrés to Verapaz, but once when he got to San Benito he started to drink, and then he lost the mailbag. He became frightened and did not want to tell the authorities [in Flores], so he left Petén. My mother was a poor woman and could not support the family. She went to the large milpa of don Fulano, the milpa at San Jerónimo. My mother had to go to work there to pay a fine for my father and to support the children. I grew up at the milpa. Because of this, I grew up without going to school and without any shoes. I grew up barefooted. A good man is one who gets along with everyone, talks, is social. A man must be a man. His first obligation is to support his family, buy [them] shoes, harvest maize, be hardworking [*guapo*, lit. handsome, but slang for "hardworking" or "readiness to work hard"] (Field Notes 1961).

This sort of statement could be repeated many times over, and the point would be the same. If milperos, some of whom fled Petén in part because of *téquio*, had the means, they would have bought their way out of forced labor. Few ever did.

Unlike poor milperos, the wealthy had multiple careers in ranching, commerce, the military, government, and contraband. To a lesser extent, those in the middle economic sector also had multiple careers in cottage industries, government, and, particularly later in the twentieth century, education. (The affluent could educate sons in Yucatán and British Honduras, and some of the children entered the professions, such as medicine and law.) Those in both the wealthy and the middle sector also became labor contractors in the *hule* and later in the chicle economy. For instance, members of the Baldizón family of Flores, who had been merchants and tavern keepers in the eighteenth century, were merchants, ranchers, labor contractors, high-ranking military officers, and department governors in the nineteenth century (also physicians in the twentieth). To take an example from San Andrés, don Estanislao Aldana, referred to above, was an army officer, a "proprietor" who regularly paid *téquio* exemption fees for his workers and *sirvientes*, a *hule* labor contractor, and first or head mayor of his *pueblo*. Don Carlos Manzanero (1872–1957) was the San Andrés secretary for many years, a military officer, and labor contractor. Men like don Estanislao, born outside Flores, often moved to the island capital. Even if they did not, they tended to marry into Flores families, that is, the economic elite and the middle sector did intermarry and were more or less endogamous. Many, though not all of these people were also born to privilege.

Many affluent Peteneros of the nineteenth century were descendants of the privileged colonial Creole caste. Of course, some Ladinos, who might later claim or suggest they were of Creole descent, were also well-off. Whatever their exact origins, they often had a head start on others, for example, through access to political office and a command of Spanish. Because they controlled important political positions at the local and departmental levels (Tables 3:1 and 3:2; Soza 1970:657–59), they had the authority to assign *téquio* chores to others, to impose or to fail to impose *rentas* on merchants, to enforce collection of *hule* taxes or not, and so on. In short, caste privilege and political power could improve the economic position of friends and relatives and undermine the position of rivals. Conversely, the wealthy could "help" the authorities; wealth could be translated into political power. Of course, the rich and the powerful often or usually were the same people, or members of the same family. In Flores, wealth, power, and prestige were tightly interconnected, one reinforcing or leading to the others. The situation was replicated in most of the *pueblos*, even if local elites did not have the money, power, or social status of their Flores counterparts.

Smith argues that "the economic health of a Guatemalan community depends as much on its place in (and the condition of) the regional marketing system as on access to certain factors of production such as land" (1988:212). In nineteenth-century Petén, the economic strength of a group was (and is today too, in many ways) in part a function of the community's location in the regional trade system as well as the group's access to scarce resources. In Guatemala, a—perhaps *the*—critical resource for families outside the national capital usually was productive land rather than commerce (Balmori et al. 1984:70). But in Petén land was not scarce nor, in the absence of large commercial plantations and despite the existence of several fairly large ranches and sugarcane fields, of primary importance. Of equal or perhaps greater importance was control of trade and access to credit, for without access to credit one could not become a labor contractor. Economic position depended at least as much on one's place in the exchange system as on access to the means of production, or on control of land. Because of mutually dependent and reinforcing relationships between trade, politics, and social status, and because they worked at it, Creole families in Flores retained their initial advantages.

It cannot be denied, however, that social mobility, up or down, was possible. Even so, upward economic mobility was limited by the absence of new significant economic opportunities in nineteenth-century Petén. For this reason, several old Creole families in Flores became moccasin makers, a respectable but not an elite occupation. Also, as mentioned previously in the Matus case, the wrong political choice could have lasting negative economic as well as political consequences for a family. That the Baldizóns sided with Carrera certainly did not hurt their favored position in Petén. In San Martín, don Fidel Rojas, the self-taught son of a poor milpero, became, in part by utilizing his position as municipal secretary, the dominant political and economic figure in the municipality. He also enjoyed the respect of Floreños and had enormous prestige in San Martín. Some of the children of his favorite relative, his brother's son and his closest political-economic associate, married into Flores families. That don Fidel's own sons are neither rich nor powerful simply indicates that downward mobility also is, and was, possible. Nevertheless, they do retain some (diminished) prestige which has helped them out of several scrapes. In the history of any particular family, privileged birth and political power led to prosperity (just as prosperity can lead to respect and power), but for political and other reasons the family may see its fortunes diminish. It must be repeated, however, that there was, after all, a relatively enduring congruity between social, political, and economic position.

Ethnicity

After 1821, the censuses do not refer to "Spanish," "Pardo," and so forth. Rather, in census and other official documents, people are referred to as Indians or Ladinos. Adams has pointed out that in Guatemala "there is a great deal of common understanding with respect to the characteristics which mark a person as being Indian or Ladino. . . . Basically, the distinctions between the groups are social and cultural" rather than "racial" (1957:267). But there are important variations in the system. For example, "An upper class Guatemalan of Spanish biological descent, and Spanish cultural heritage disclaims being a Ladino; to him, Ladino is the same as mestizo," although Ladinos and Indians might refer to him as a Ladino (Adams 1957:269). In some regions ethnic identity depends more on social group membership than on cultural patterns (Schwartz 1971).

Adams's comment about upper class Guatemalans is significant, as most Floreños do not define themselves as Ladinos. For them, a more critical distinction is that between Floreños (or urbanites) and *poblanos* (lit. "townsmen," "villagers," but here closer to "rustic," "one who does not speak 'educated' Spanish"). *Poblanos* may be Indians, Ladinos, "Cobaneros" (Kekchí Indians), or others. *Poblano* also implies economic role. If a Floreño says Fulano de Tal is a *poblano*, one may be reasonably sure that Fulano is a poor milpero or unskilled laborer who was born in and/or resides in a *pueblo* other than Flores (although there also are some *poblanos* in Flores too). If, in addition, the speaker says Fulano is *humilde* (humble, timid), that would imply he is an Indian or of Indian descent, just as the adjectives "capricious, aggressive," and so on, would usually imply that Fulano is a Ladino. Townspeople, who by no means appreciate the word *poblano*, may identify ethnic others as Indians, Ladinos, Cobaneros, or Beliceños (blacks), or use a circumlocution. For instance, a Ladino may refer to "more capable" (Ladinos) or "humble" (Indians) people, as an Indian may speak of "those who thought they owned the earth" (Ladinos) or "poor, honest" people (Indians). Townspeople have no particular ethnic term for Floreños, but to refer to "those of Flores" (*los de Flores*) usually implies middle or elite sector status. Today young Peteneros claim they attach no importance to ethnic identification. For them, for example, "Cobanero" refers to place of birth, not ethnicity. In effect, they give greater weight to social class (or social sector, as some scholars would prefer) membership than to ethnic status. Yet, as we shall see, ethnicity continues to play a role in the social and political arenas.

Two additional points should be made. First, to avoid cumbersome circumlocutions, for example, "Ladinos, or those of Ladino descent, real or presumed," and so on, I shall use "Ladino" when appropriate. The context will make clear whether "Ladino" refers to non-Indians in towns (*pueblos*) outside the city (*ciudad*) of Flores, or also includes Floreños. Similarly, I shall use the word "Indian," rather than a circumlocution. Unless otherwise stated, "Floreño" will refer to people of real or putative Spanish descent and to those without such descent who have married into Flores families, that is, whose children have become Floreños. In Petén, in the case of heterogamous unions, a child takes the father's ethnic identity. In the instance of an illegitimate child, ethnic identity is taken from the mother, unless the father socially and/or legally acknowledges the child as his own. Second, I will use San Andrés as a "type site" in what follows, although recognizing that Petén communities did and do differ from each other in various ways. Thus it is accurate to say that ethnically homogamous marriages outnumbered heterogamous ones in the nineteenth century, but the frequency varied from one *pueblo* to the next, in part because the ratio of Indians to Ladinos varied across settlements.

Ethnicity, Class, and Power

During the nineteenth century, as in colonial times, Indians had low social status and suffered from a range of discriminatory practices, although after 1871 not all of these were legal. Until the 1870s at least some Indians in Petén may not have been allowed to enter commerce without special permission, but the issue is not entirely clear because of the paucity of AGCA documents concerning it.[26] Nevertheless, *padrón* data, municipal archives, and *Ramo Criminal* records clearly indicate that commerce was almost invariably in the hands of Floreños and Ladinos. There is no question that the big proprietors, merchants, and ranchers were Floreños and/or Ladinos, and most members of the middle sector also were drawn from these status groups. In 1840 the "Croesis" ("white man, a Creole") of San Andrés whom Caddy met (Pendergast 1967:92) was probably an Aldana or

Pulido. In 1868 Berendt (1868:424) reported that "the *ladinos* or so-called whites, (though with a good deal of mixed blood), form a kind of patriarchal aristocracy" in Petén, holding Indian and black "field hands" in debt peonage. (Blacks from British Honduras continued to flee to Petén all through the nineteenth century.)[27] In the late nineteenth century, *hule* contractors were overwhelmingly non-Indian, but *sirvientes* usually were Indians. In a word, the economic elite were Floreños and Ladinos. The ethnic composition of the middle sector was largely the same, but there were some Indians and blacks (or people of Indian and black descent) among them. The poorest sector was made up of Ladinos, blacks, and Indians, the latter in the majority.

In politics too, as observed earlier, non-Indians predominated. Floreños controlled the departmental government, and Ladinos controlled local government (see, for example, Tables 3:2 and 3:3) except in San José and San Luis. Even so, in some matters, San Joseños came under the authority of the Ladinos in San Andrés; for example, in the militia most of the time they served under officers from San Andrés. Again, at least in the 1890s, the schoolmaster and secretary in San José was Rómulo Aldana, a nephew of don Estanislao (see above). Wealthier Ladinos, as mayors, made *téquio* assignments or exempted favorites from them, and the affluent could of course buy their way out. Ladinos (and, of course, Creoles) not Indians, were high-ranking military officers. Although poor Ladinos and Indians shared many *téquio* and militia duties, the carrier chores, such as taking mail to and from Chinajá, were imposed almost exclusively on Indians. That is, even in their shared poverty, Indians suffered more disabilities than Ladinos. Presumably, blacks in San Benito fared little better than Indians or poorer Ladinos (Berendt 1868; Valenzuela 1879).

The inferior status of Indians was manifested in other ways. For instance, both Ladinos and Indians were raised as *crianzas* (nonadopted children), a disadvantaged position, in Ladino and Indian households. The difference is that it was rare for a Ladino to be a *crianza* in an Indian household but the reverse was common enough. In what might be called the darker side of politics and commerce, non-Indians were also predominant. Serious crimes were and are adjudicated in the Court of First Instance located in Flores, and about the period from 1822 to 1899 two observations may be made. First, it appears that Creoles (including Floreños) and Ladinos had the confidence to strike out at authority, but Indians and Beliceños rarely did. Crimes against the authority of local and central government included charges of contempt, threat, rebellion, and sedition. Granted that court records are not always clear about ethnic status nor always complete, it appears that of twenty-three or twenty-four crimes against authority, sixteen were committed by Creoles or Ladinos acting alone or leading others, another four or five were committed by Indians, and three by an ethnic motley. The figures are impressive, considering that the majority of the population were Indian. Moreover, members of elite families in Flores figure prominently in the most serious cases (AGCA *Ramo Criminal* 1822–1899).

Second, the way in which legal experts defended Indians and Indians defended themselves in court underscores the inferior status of Indians as well as the tensions between Ladinos and Creoles. For example, in 1860 an Indian from Santo Toribio was accused of selling a horse, probably in foal, for $23 to a visitor from Belize and then stealing it back. In his defense, the Indian asked for consideration because "the Indians are always victims of the Ladinos." The court found the Indian guilty but because of mitigating circumstances and because of his "class" (ethnic identity) freed him. In 1863 an Indian living at Ixpayac (a savanna ranch) was accused of killing his *compadre*, another Indian, in a drunken brawl. M. Trujillo, speaking for the defense, argued that the law prescribes special consideration for Indians charged with crimes, as it does for children, and that Indians live "in darkness," ignorant of Christianity, yet have the deepest regard for the bonds of ritual kinship. Moreover, he said, his client was provoked into fighting and the outcome was unpremeditated. Because of the legal circumstances described by Trujillo, because it was not clear that the brawl directly led to the deceased's death, and because the accused had already served time in jail pending the outcome of the case, the court acquitted and freed him. In mitigation of crimes Indians were accused of committing, Creoles pointed to the childlike innocence of the "unfortunate Indian race," and Indians themselves spoke of their "inequality of blood and condition," although some Indian authorities were quick enough to defend their rights. Note, for example, don Hilario Cohouj, mentioned next. When local Ladino and Indian authorities quarreled, as in the case of Pulido versus don Hilario in San Andrés in 1860, the Creole governor from Flores interceded, and noting the tension between Ladinos and Indians, tried to patch things up. In general, Ladinos felt that high-ranking Creole authorities shielded Indians and prejudiced the interests of Ladinos (AGCA *Ramo Criminal* 1860, 1863, 1868, and 1871).[28]

In summary, those charged with serious crimes were more often Creoles and Ladinos than Indians and blacks. In addition, those with authority and those who were quickest to defy authority were drawn from the same small circle of affluent (and related) families. Since power and authority circulated within this group, the opportunities to avenge slights and injuries must have been plentiful. Finally, the law and high ranking (Creole) authority helped maintain ethnic distinctions, that is, helped maintain a stress on status over class differences. Although in many ways Ladinos had the edge over Indians, most members of both groups were in the lower sector. The main beneficiaries of a system that divided the lower sector into unequal status groups were, as might be expected, the Creoles.

Acculturation and Assimilation

Despite their disadvantaged social status (with some subtle legal advantages), Indians in the nineteenth century as in the eighteenth century seem not to have had strong incentives nor perhaps strong encouragement to ladinoize. *Padrón* records and observations of travelers indicate that Indians' material circumstances were about on a par with those of poorer Ladinos. In any event, Indians maintained certain aspects of their culture, of course within a context of non-Indian domination. Mopán Maya continued to be spoken in southeastern Petén, and Petén Maya in the savannas and the Lake region (Berendt 1868). Some Indians spoke no Spanish, forcing the courts in dealing with them to rely on translators, such as Sr. Pulido (AGCA *Ramo Criminal* Leg.5, 1878). Even in San Andrés, where about one third of the population was Ladino, Yucatec and Petén Maya were commonly used by Indians until the 1920s, although by this date most of them were bilingual. Morelet (1871:230) observed that although "There [were] schools in every village in the district . . . the Indians obstinately refuse[d] to permit their children to attend them." Aside from labor demands and discriminatory practices inhibiting school attendance, Indians (and poor Ladinos) may have had little material reason to insist their children go to school.

In the latter part of the nineteenth century there were cultural differences other than language between Indians and Ladinos. For example, in several towns, Indians (and some Ladinos) dressed in Mayan style, which was apparently quite similar to the Indian dress of Yucatán, although the departmental authorities tried to modernize dress. The Indians had interior kitchens (as diagnostic of Indian identity as anything else in Guatemala) and, in San Andrés for example, practiced at least one important ritual exclusive to themselves—the pig ceremony.

A Brotherhood of the Cross (*Hermanos de la Cruz*) sponsored a "pig" or "Santa Cruz" ceremony which closely resembled the pig ceremony of the Maya of Soccotz, British Honduras, described by Thompson (1930) and which, as noted in Chapter 2, may be related to pre-Columbian deer rituals. I do not know whether this ceremony had any connection with the rebel Santa Cruz discussed above, but the Brotherhood's membership was exclusively Indian, with an exception to be noted below. The ceremony was organized by a *prioste* (owner or manager), a position of prestige that circulated among Indian males. Prior to the ceremony the *prioste* and several others prayed for several days, and they along with others contributed to decorate a house owned by the Brotherhood with ribbons, fruits, milpa products, and strings of reales. On 1 May or 3 May, the head and shoulders of a cooked pig were placed on a small table decorated with ribbons and food, and a piece of bread was placed in the pig's mouth. One man carried the table about town, a rope about his waist being pulled by a second man who "beat the pig" and threw maize behind him to "call the pigs." The men danced in a burlesque manner and sang songs in Maya. A procession followed them through town. The dancers stopped before each saloon (owned by Ladinos and Creoles) and were served drinks to "revive" them so they could continue. No one before whose house or saloon they paused could refuse them a drink. The dancers finally became exceedingly drunk and apparently at times had to be replaced by other dancers. The ceremony lasted three days, and at the end the pig may have been shared by the Indians. On the morning of the fourth day, the *prioste* and other leaders of the Brotherhood went to the town hall and, while the mayor watched, distributed the money which had been used as decoration among Indians who had contributed to the ceremony. Ladinos did not participate beyond serving drinks to the dancers and viewing the event with amused condescension. One reason given for the abandonment of the ceremony is that the last *prioste* stole the Brotherhood's funds. Although raised by an Indian family, he was of Ladino descent, and some people say he was the only Ladino member of the Brotherhood. Whether this account of the abandonment is veridical really is less important than the idea that just as the Brotherhood ritual expressed ethnic distinctions, so did its abandonment.

The church, especially under the Liberals, could do little to curtail practices such as that just described. Indeed, there were some governors who were quite actively hostile to the clergy, including even the much admired José María Pinelo (1833–1922), the third native Petenero to be ordained (Soza 1970:282–83). Ecclesiastic control over Petén passed from Mérida, Yucatán to Guatemala City in 1866, an act which, if anything, deepened the straitened material circumstances of the clergy in Petén. At times there were, as in the days of the colony, five priests, including the vicar, in the department; at other times there were no more than two. When the clergy numbered two, they tended to reside in Flores, rarely visited distant places such as San Luis (Morelet 1871:272), and perhaps because being so few that they could not continuously minister to their flock, did not always enjoy the esteem of townspeople. Some elderly Peteneros used to say, "Look, the priests existed to charge. They charged for a mass, a wedding, everything. They were wolves, *lobos*, but now it is different" (Field Notes 1960–1961). Flores always was and still is the headquarters of the church in Petén; native Petén priests have come from Flores and are descended from Creole stock. Therefore, disparaging remarks about clerical *lobos* may also reflect tensions between the towns and Flores, between socioeconomic sectors, and/or ethnic status groups. In any case, the clergy did not have an opportunity to play the strong social and religious role among the Indians (or the Ladinos) of Petén that they had elsewhere in Guatemala (cf. Wortman 1982:272–73).

In addition to rituals such as those of the Brotherhood, there were other patterns of social distance among ethnic groups. As noted, Valenzuela (1879) observed little social contact between Floreños and San Beniteños. Ladinos did not ask Indians to serve as the baptismal sponsors (godparents) of their children, but the reverse was common. Floreños, Ladinos, and Indians apparently had separate social events, and some towns were largely ethnically homogeneous. In a more ethnically mixed community such as San Andrés, Indians were concentrated in the northern section of town and Ladinos in the southern part, advantageously near the shore line. Legal and consensual unions were largely homogamous with respect to ethnicity (Table 3:14).[29] In short, to some extent Indians had a life and language apart from Ladinos.

Although this division must be recognized, the degree of cultural and social separation must not be exaggerated. Whatever their (syncretic) practices, the Indians were Catholic. They had been forced to acculturate to certain Hispanic standards—bilateral descent, monogamy, neolocality, and

Table 3:14 Homogamous and Heterogamous Unions, San Andrés, 1863–1961

Type of union	1863		1880–1905		1961	
	Number	Percent	Number	Percent	Number	Percent
Homogamous intensive			20	71.4	114	62.6
	124	76.1				
Homogamous extensive			3	10.7	33	18.1
Heterogamous intensive			3	10.7	17	9.3
	39	23.9				
Heterogamous extensive			2	7.1	18	9.9
Total	163	100.0	28	99.9	182	99.9

Sources: AGCA *padrón* for 1863; marriage records, Archivo Municipal, San Andrés for 1880–1905; Field Notes for 1961. The 1863 *padrón* does not give place of birth. (Error in percentages due to rounding.)

Key: Union = Legal marriages and consensual unions; homogamous = Partners of like ethnic identity; heterogamous = Partners of unlike ethnic identity; intensive = Partners native to San Andrés; extensive = At least one partner not native to San Andrés; until the early 1970s it was quite rare for both partners to be non-native to the *pueblo*.

Note: Interestingly, in a large, prominent family of Ladino descent, from 1830 to 1960, 95.1 percent of marriages were homogamous and 4.9 percent heterogamous; for a large family of Maya descent, from 1830–1960, the percentages were 90.7 homogamous and 9.3 heterogamous. A difference is that for the first family, 67.2 percent of the marriages were intensive, for the second 81.4 percent were.

so on. Moreover, if roughly some 80 percent of marriages were homogamous with respect to ethnicity, 20 percent were not. And whatever their initial identity, people who moved from a town to Flores sooner or later became identified as Ladinos or Floreños. For example, in the middle of the nineteenth century the Yamas (pseudonym), an Indian family from San Andrés moved to Flores and eventually became part of the middle sector of the city. As a group Indians did not achieve socioeconomic parity with non-Indians, but acculturation did occur, and for some individuals assimilation into superordinate groups was also possible.

It is important to add here that the outcome of the operation of one organizational principle tended to reinforce the outcome of other organizational principles. For example, San Benito, a sort of small trade-item and labor preserve for Flores, was ethnically homogeneous in part because the blacks there and the people in Flores used ethnicity as a criterion for selecting marriage partners, but also because their unequal socioeconomic class status (and differences in community membership) restricted and reduced the chances for intermarriage. Major organizational principles displayed a certain congruence. To use San José as an example, the *pueblo* was an organized community with a distinctive role in the central Petén trade network, and its inhabitants were Indians, the vast majority of them poor milperos. Ethnicity, community, and socieconomic status were not completely coincident, but they were correlated with one another.

Little has been said about Belizean or more broadly Caribbean cultural influences on Peteneros, and the documents are almost entirely mute about the matter. Yet, at least after the 1840s, Peteneros had increasingly frequent contacts with the ethnically diverse population of British Honduras, particularly in connection with contraband trade and, later, rubber and chicle tapping. Moreover, toward the end of the century, several Floreños educated their sons in Belize City. To judge from what older Peteneros say and from certain modern practices (although one must be extremely cautious about reading the past from the present), Peteneros apparently picked up some specific traits, for instance, some curing techniques and a number of English and Creole English words from the Beliceños. However, Beliceños who came to live in Petén acculturated to their hosts' standards, much more than the other way around. For example, matrifocal households are rarely found in Petén, where the more standard Hispanoamerican nuclear family household based on the conjugal bond is prevalent. That the cultural influence of Belize on Petén was limited was due to the fact that most of their contacts were narrowly economic and that Beliceños who became Peteneros were a minority, most of them confined to San Benito and *monterías* (logging camps) located on the edges of the department. Their descendants eventually intermarried with Peteneros and became culturally indistinguishable from them, although until relatively recently they did maintain a separate *social* identity, based in part on community.

Community and Social Character

Community

If for no other reason than that the administrative structure of the government made it so, community was a basic element of social life. People were recruited for *téquio* service on the basis of community membership, although there was also an ethnic component to recruitment. Thus, as mentioned, a disproportionate number of Ladinos served as officers, and Indians as soldiers in the militia, but Ladinos were not sent to Chinajá with the mail. Whatever benefits government conferred, such as the right to draw on communal funds of maize in times of need and access to farmland, was based on community membership. One (if literate) voted for a township mayor, not a departmental governor, because representative government existed only at the community level. Communities were largely endogamous. Each one had a distinctive reputation and its own unifying symbols. In San José, three skulls, still kept in the church sanctuary to the dismay of priests, are said to be those of ancient *priostes*. The skulls are the cynosure of All Souls' and Saints' ceremonies in San José and express the "laws" and Mayaness of the community. In San Andrés, veneration of St. Andrew and a special yearly mass held on 18 February express the unity and distinctiveness of the community. The 18 February mass, which was initiated by the bishop of Yucatán in 1816 at the request of San Andreños to combat a plague, protects all growing things born within the community—plants, animals, children—regardless of ethnicity or religion (Catholic or Protestant), *sic passim*. In La Libertad, a huge ceiba tree, among other things, somehow gives the community a special identity. For each of the older settlements in Petén there is an identifying symbol. To be sure, local town elites, particularly from San Andrés, San Francisco, La Libertad, and Dolores, were much more likely than milpero townspeople to marry Floreños and/or relocate in Flores. Floreños as much as or possibly more than their fellow townspeople were their reference group. Local town elites were members of the the middle sector, branches of a tree whose roots and thickest limbs were in Flores. Nevertheless, for them as for others, the local community was (and is) an important, valued principle of social organization.

Social Character

Stringing together references to crop failures, epidemics, repression, and so on may paint a picture of unrelieved misery, yet there was more than this to life in nineteenth-century Petén. Most of the time people could feed themselves, there was no pressure on the land, festivals seem to have been occasions for genuine pleasure, and even harsh institutions were somewhat softened in practice some of the time. Maudslay and Maudslay, after condemning debt peonage, remarked that

> . . . the system does not seem to work so badly after all; for if the patrones are too harsh, which did not seem to be the case, the frontiers of Mexico and British Honduras are not far distant, and a man could always take a few days' walk through the forest and leave his debts behind him . . . Naturally such a mixed community as that which inhabits the isolated province of Peten would be likely sometimes to give trouble to the officials . . . the last Jefe Politico had paid with his life for some effort to enforce the orders of the Central Government, a customs-house officer had been murdered shortly before my arrival . . . although the Peteneros resent too much interference on the part of Government officials . . . I don't think they can be called a disorderly people, and I have never heard of them causing any annoyance to travelers (1899:231).

One might say that debt peons could readily evade servitude, and officials were slain by courteous people.

Travelers found Peteneros easygoing, "idle" (Caddy in Pendergast 1967:98; also see González 1867:82), "sensual" (Berendt 1868:424; also see Mejía 1904), and (outside of Flores) not too eager to learn. Floreños had, they say, a great love of dancing and festivities, and for Indians drink was "their ruling passion" (Morelet 1871:220, speaking of San Andrés and San José; also see Berendt 1868; González 1867; Valenzuela 1879). Except for Maler (1908b:127) who found the "Indians" of San Andrés and San José (but not the people of Flores) "taciturn," the others agree that Peteneros were good-natured but not necessarily pacific. If Caddy (Pendergast 1967:167) found that "murders, especially arising from jealousy, are of frequent occurrence," Morelet (1871:216) felt that "assaults on life and property are unknown," or as Berendt said of "rare occurrence." Peteneros, Berendt felt, were "not much given to fighting" (1868:425); quick to anger, but not violent (González 1867). Peteneros led *"una vida tranquila"* (a peaceful life; Mejía 1904:25). In fact, theft does seem to have been rare and land disputes almost nonexistent (for economic reasons discussed previously), but for the rest, the truth fell between the extremes of Caddy and Morelet. Although it is difficult to be precise, because several political murders may not have reached the court and because in several cases Creole authorities may have prevented homicide charges from being brought against cronies and kinsmen, it is possible to document 35 to 38 killings through court records between 1822 and 1899 (AGCA *Ramo Criminal*). Although Petén had a small population, the rate does not seem high in the context of an isolated frontier zone where, moreover, for want of medical attention injuries that might otherwise have been healed ended in death. Even if all the killings are counted as murders, and 6 to 9 of them seem not to have been, the homicide rate was at most about 0.5 persons per year, or (using a figure of 6,000 for the Petén population) roughly a rate of 8 per 100,000, making nineteenth-century Petén safer than, for example, the twentieth-century southern United States (11 homicides per 100,000 population in 1988). Whatever one makes of this, visitors, from Caddy in 1840 to Mejía in 1904 and others ever since, have always found Peteneros hospitable, courteous, and affable.

Although I have argued that the civility of the Peteneros may have been a cover, a prudent response to autocratic rulers, it is important to add that courtesy per se could also have been positively valued. Peteneros *are* friendly, courtly, and gentle in manner, and have little taste for violence. To walk about town armed is, they say, "brutal" and "uncivilized." "Real men," one can hear teenagers ready to square off against one another assert, "fight with fists, not with knives and guns." Similarly, the "idleness" reported by travelers reflects, in my view, the very limited commercial and economic opportunities available in nineteenth-century Petén, and also that (some) surplus production was appropriated by the authorities. Yet today, when they are anything but idle, Peteneros still find time to talk, visit, and laugh easily. In the nineteenth century, too, there must have been genial as well as harsh aspects to their lives.

Concluding Discussion

As in the instance of several other places on or near the Caribbean side of Central America, for long decades the state did not maintain a strong presence in Petén, and most contacts with other regions were narrowly economic (see Helms 1975:313–18). The sparse population combined subsistence agriculture with wage labor in ranching and (especially after the 1860s) in extractive economies. In Petén, as elsewhere, the extractive economies dictated that men be away from home for long periods. In other places somewhat similar conditions contributed to the formation of matrifocal households, but not in Petén, perhaps in part because women had few ways to earn an independent living. Economic conditions, including the absence of population pressure on the land, also contributed to relatively open community organization. As for the cultural influence of non-Hispanic lowland littoral Caribbean groups on Petén, they must not be exaggerated. For instance, patterns of ethnic interaction in Petén had much more to do with the particularities of Petén's history and economy than with any possible Caribbean cultural influences. Immigrants, mostly black, acculturated to Petén standards, and, to repeat, most of the external contacts were economic. In addition, they were filtered through and thus thinned out by intermediate populations, for example, Maya in western Belize. Much stronger was the Spanish colonial imprint left on local government, ethnic relations, and community organization. Although external contacts with Yucatán decreased over the course of the century, refugees kept coming from there, but their cultural patterns were for the most part consistent with the Petén way of life, and, of course, many Peteneros had orginally come from Yucatán.

Guatemalan independence from Spain did not decrease the isolation of Petén. The state, preoccupied with commercial coffee production in the highlands and often in fiscal crisis, neglected the northern lowlands. Inadequate systems of communication and transportation kept the region functionally distant from the highlands. The economic changes—a decline in ranching, redirection of trade from Yucatán to Belize, an increase in commercial woodcutting, and so on—which occurred in Petén between the late 1830s and the early 1890s did not stimulate economic or demographic growth. In fact, for political and health reasons as well as economic ones, there was some reduction in population toward the end of the century. If anything, the region became more of a hinterland than it had been in the colonial period.

At the same time, because Petén was an economic backwater and because it included no large commercial agrarian enterprises, there was apparently less political repression, or at least less need in Petén to coerce labor on a comprehensive scale, than elsewhere in the republic (such as the coffee growing regions), and farmers in Petén were not dispossessed of their land. Of course, this does not mean that Peteneros were free from autocratic state impositions, corvée, or communal constraints, but when people felt too greatly oppressed they could and did flee to Mexico, to British Honduras, and to the forests of Petén. Flight to the forests was possible because the authorities did not control all the territory within their jurisdiction and because they had little economic incentive to enter forests distant from population centers. In addition, in Petén, as elsewhere in the Maya lowlands (see Bricker 1981), postcolonial officials as much as crown officers eschewed incursions into isolated forests because of the exaggerated threat from "wild" and rebel Indians.

Flores, as always, was the center of government, trade, wealth, and society. In Petén, and presumably elsewhere in Guatemala, the links between "caste" privilege, bureaucratic power and position, and wealth were so close that it would be as reasonable to conclude that prestige and power led to economic prosperity as to conclude the reverse. In addition to whatever else occupied the elite and some of the middle sector, they were merchants and traders. Although the documentary evidence is admittedly slim, what there is suggests that the affluent did not maintain stable patron-client relations with the poor. Some scholars argue that in peasant societies, subsistence farmers (or peasants) build many-stranded, enduring reciprocal relationships with kinsmen, fellow villagers, patrons, and, to a lesser extent, with the state to minimize the impact of hardships such as crop failure. With patrons they exchange servile loyalty for political and economic support. Patron-client reciprocities become the basis for morality in these societies (Scott and Kerkvliet 1973). But in the absence of commercial plantations or any other relatively large, labor intensive enterprise, the elite had no need for an appreciable number of client laborers. The economy of Petén did not generate the sort of patron-client system Scott and Kerkvliet describe. Petén farmers did petition government officials (and, hence, affluent Floreños who occupied important bureaucratic positions) for material assistance, and some poor Peteneros were "servants" and debt peons, but patronage as such does not seem to have been a universal feature of the regional society. Rather, local (town) Ladino elites often had marriage and kinship ties as well as political and economic ones with middle-and upper-sector Floreños. Thus there were vertical and patronage ties between local and regional (*pueblo* and Flores) elites, but apparently a good many ordinary milperos operated without durable patronage relationships. They relied instead more on kinsmen and *compadres* in their own and other communities.[30] Even so, there were not many horizontal cross-community relationships. Patterns of trade linked the *pueblos* to Flores, rather than to each other.

Ethnicity and community reputation tended to coincide, perhaps primarily as a consequence of the fact that each community had a somewhat distinctive position in the internal trade network of Petén, with Flores at its center, and secondarily because ethnicity was a basis for economic position. (However, if ethnicity remained an important principle of social organization, it is worth recalling that most Ladinos, blacks, and Indians also shared a common life as milperos.) Related to this, hierarchies of prestige, wealth, and power tended to be congruent. Yet *economic* differences, as opposed to status and political differences, between Floreños and people in the *pueblos* should not be overstated. The elite, especially in Flores, were certainly better off than the milperos, but by all accounts they were not rich in any grand sense. Sociopolitical inequalities may well have been as great as or even greater than economic ones.

In more ways than one, a visitor from eighteenth-century Petén would have been at home there in the late nineteenth century. Settlements, ethnic groups, socioeconomic hierarchies, and even government would have been familiar. The visitor would have noticed some differences—ranching was declining, the Flores church was not so richly appointed, after midcentury there were more refugees from Yucatán in Petén than before, some new inventions had appeared, and so forth—but these were not radical departures from the past.

Chapter Four

La Chiclería: An Extractive Economy

"Unfortunately the exploitation of *chicle* hastens the downfall of the population of Peten, ruins agriculture and increases the demoralization of the lower classes, naturally inclined as they are to all vices" (Maler 1908b:74).

"El chiclero no pide vuelto" (a chiclero does not ask for change; Petén saying.)

Peteneros are "a ramshackle, undefinable lot" (Halle 1941:28).

Introduction

From the 1890s to about 1970, *la chiclería*, the commercial production of chicle, a natural resin base for chewing gum, for export dominated the political economy of Petén and the imagination of Peteneros. What rubber was to Amazonia, chicle was to Petén.

In the late 1890s, foreign capital, principally North American, began to penetrate Guatemala. From then on and all through the twentieth century, Guatemala experienced a growing dependence on American investment and commodity markets. During these years the state grew increasingly centralized and, save for a revolutionary interlude between 1945 and 1954, increasingly repressive. After 1954 the military exercised ever-growing and more direct control over the state and the society, although they did permit a freely elected civilian government to assume office in 1985. In Guatemala there is a connection between capitalist penetration and repression (Lovell 1988). Dependency theorists in particular have stressed "the role that the external forces of the world economy have played in stimulating the production and export of raw materials and primary products" in so-called Third World countries such as Guatemala, "thereby providing the basis" for class relations within these countries and between them and developed capitalist countries. The "dependent" export economies are based on "gross exploitation" of labor (Patch 1985:47–48), marked by elite and state investment in mechanisms of repression, rather than socioeconomic development.

Whatever one's theoretical perspective, the "bottom line for any economic venture organized for profit is to secure a regular supply of labor and expropriate its surplus" (Weinstein 1983:29). Normally, the capitalist's ownership or control of the means of production permits him or her to secure and control labor. But in extractive economies such as Amazonian rubber and *la chiclería*, workers could own the means of production. More important, for ecological reasons, workers were spatially dispersed and could not be closely supervised. In neither case could capitalists organize "factories in the field" which, by congregating workers in one place, facilitate labor control. In Amazonia labor was organized and its surplus captured, not by ownership of the means of production or control over the productive process, but rather by control over the exchange system (Weinstein op.cit.). To an important degree, this was also true in Petén's extractive economy.

La chiclería generated few "linkages," that is, investments stimulated by the production of a given commodity. In general, the extractive economy gave rise to more consumption than production or fiscal linkages. The extractive economy also alternately heightened and lowered the value of community membership, contributed to ladinoization of the population, and increased preexisting socioeconomic differences within the department.

It will be recalled that in the 1890s, when *la chiclería* began in Petén, the department was underpopulated and its economy sluggish. Most Peteneros were subsistence agriculturists, some of whom worked part time as loggers, *huleros*, and cowboys. Logging was largely confined to the western rivers, Guatemalan rubber was not in demand, and there was a distinctly weak market for Petén's large but untended cattle herds. The dynamic sectors of the national economy were found outside the region, in coffee and banana production areas. Even in the 1920s, when chicle was Guatemala's third most important export, it did not come close to matching the value of the other two commodities. There was no imperative for the state to take an active interest in Petén, and, until the 1930s, it did not.[1]

The economy of Petén tempered the action of local government, but even so it could not be called benign. Peteneros were subject to unpaid militia service, road levees, and other "abuses," as Peteneros would say, such as Governor Berges's (1890s) practice, under vagrancy laws, of sending men convicted of public inebriation to work as underpaid or unpaid loggers in western Petén. As always, Peteneros also suffered from periodic and severe maize shortages, as in 1901, and epidemics (the worldwide influenza epidemic of 1918–1919 seems to have hit Flores with great force). Forced labor, grain shortages, epidemics, and a lack of economic opportunities led people to emigrate, mainly to British Honduras. The departmental government lacked the power and, probably, the will to stem this movement.

After *la chiclería* came to Petén, military activity also contributed to emigration. The Mexican Revolution of 1910 to 1917 unsettled people living in northern Petén, many of whom retreated to the central part of the department. In 1916 Guatemalan anti-Cabrera forces invaded Petén from Tabasco and, before they were defeated, destroyed the Arthes and Sons logging and chicle property on the Río San Pedro and advanced to within forty kilometers of Flores. About the same time, a force of foreign chicleros, unhappy with the Guatemalan government's treatment of them, tried to invade Plancha de Piedra (now Melchor de Mencos) from British Honduras. In 1926 people from Dolores, upset by revolutionary turbulence originating in Yucatán and fed up with Guatemalan government impositions, fled to the forests.[2] Additionally, during the first two decades of this century, *la chiclería* allegedly occasioned a good deal of violence. This claim will be examined below.

A good many things, then, kept population low in Petén: a backwater economy, undeveloped road systems, poor health conditions, violence, and so on. Indeed, small as it was, the population apparently declined between 1880 and 1918.[3]

This brief summary slides over many nuances of late nineteenth-century Petén history, but it does point up the fact that right before the advent of the chicle extractive economy, the department was, as always, a remote hinterland. The history of chicle in Petén and its impact on the isolated region is the subject of this chapter and the next.

La Chiclería: History, Ecology, Technology

American Connections

In 1848 John Curtis of Maine produced the first commercial chewing gum from spruce tree resin. Because loggers rapidly depleted the supply of New

England spruce, substitutes were needed. By the 1870s chicle became the favorite, although after 1924 other resins (East Indian jeluton, guttas, and so on) were mixed with it. Chicle remained the main base for chewing gum until about 1944–1945, when it was replaced by petroleum derived synthetics. There were several reasons for the substitution: depletion of chicle trees beginning in the 1920s, shipping and related problems during World War II, Guatemalan government plans right after the war to increase export taxes on chicle, perhaps the quality of Petén chicle and formation of a tappers' (chicleros') union, and the comparative cost advantage of synthetics.[4]

In 1866 United States manufacturers began to finance chicle tree tapping in Veracruz, Mexico, and by 1871 the first commercial chewing gum with a chicle base was produced. Shortly thereafter the first flavored gum was put on the market, its brand name, Yucatán, indicating its provenience. World War I was a watershed for the industry. Wrigley initiated mass media advertising techniques to convince the public that masticating gum was an excellent way to reduce tension, even in battle, so American doughboys carried a supply in their kitbags. The "American habit," as it was once called, was "a relief for nervous tension, an aid to digestion, and, in the absence of water fit to drink, a mitigation of thirst" (Hoar 1924:1). United States companies, which for many years monopolized production, now began to sell chewing gum worldwide. By 1930 these companies were importing 15,000,000 pounds of chicle per year. In World War II, heavy USA military demands for chewing gum also contributed to the search for synthetics.[5] In 1914 the chewing gum industry began to report statistics, and by 1919 total output at factory values was $53.4 million. By the 1970s chewing gum sales were about $1 billion per year worldwide. Although the Wrigley company was the leader (with sales of $370 million in 1976 and $400 million in 1978), and American Chicle a near second, the Mitsui Company of Japan began to manufacture chewing gum in the 1960s. By 1976 Mitsui became and has remained the single most important buyer of Petén chicle. The American connection has been replaced by commercial ties to Japan.[6]

The Chicle Tree

In the social sciences, ecological factors are sometimes treated as a proscenium within which the main action takes place. But in *la chiclería*, ecology is an active element, directly affecting not only the technology of chicle production but also the sociology of the extractive economy.

The chicle tree (*Achras zapota*, but some authorities now prefer *Manikara sapota*) is a broadleaf evergreen of the Sapotaceae family, of which there are 35 genera and some 600 species.[7] Although chicle has been tapped for commercial purposes in several Latin American countries—Panamá during 1900–1925 (Joly 1981), Honduras, Colombia, and Venezuela during 1900–1930 (Konrad 1981)—the primary areas of exploitation have always been Yucatán, Mexico, Belize, and Petén. Within Petén, the area north of parallel 17° 10′ is richest in chicle. South by southeast from Lake Petén Itzá to Izabal and Alta Verapaz an inferior type of chicle, *chiquibul*, is common.[8]

For commercial purposes, an area must normally contain seven to ten large chicle trees per hectare. Although in northern Petén the concentration can reach fifty or more trees per hectare, the average is about twelve to twenty-four. Today, after decades of tapping, averages of productive trees in some places are less. As early as the 1930s, in "the more accessible areas where exploitation has been continued longest, very few sapodillas remain. In like areas, as along the San Pedro de Martir River in Northern Petén, the mahogany trees have been cut also, thus leaving culled forest in which neither of the two species is prominent" (Lundell 1937:15).

There have been reports that a previously untapped mature chicle tree can yield about 14 kilograms of latex, and may be productively tapped two to three years in succession, depending on the age of the tree, region of production, and degree of damage done by the initial tapping. Perhaps this was so in the early days of *la chiclería*, but for many years now figures of this sort would be extraordinary. (In what follows, pounds are used because Peteneros record chicle production in pounds, not kilos.) A tree usually yields from 1.0 to 5.0 pounds of latex, the average being 2.5 to 4.0 pounds. Further, chicleros say that a tree should not be tapped two years in succession, but rather after initial tapping should be allowed to "rest" for four to five years (some say up to fifteen years) before it is retapped.[9]

For complex reasons related to the nature of Petén's tropical forests, all efforts to cultivate chicle trees in plantation stands have failed. This is important because on average some five to fifteen percent of tapped trees are killed during each tapping season. Chicle latex is drained from ducts on the inner bark of the tree, and the latex is not renewed until new ducts have formed on the inner bark. Because the outer bark is so tough, tubes cannot be inserted into the tree as is done in rubber tapping. Rather, the bark must be cut with a machete. As tappers cut through the hard outer bark, even the most skillful of them will make some slices through the cambium layer. When the cambium is cut and the cortex dried, the wood is exposed before callus has time to cover it (Lundell 1937:15), and thus the tree is vulnerable to decay organisms and wood-boring insects, which may kill it. Young trees are much more likely to be killed by tapping than mature ones, for which reason the law prohibits tapping trees less than 30.4 cm in diameter. But because depletion rates are so high, the regulation is not always honored. For example, with a chicle tree death rate of 5 percent per annum, if in 1900 an area had fifty chicle trees per hectare, it would be reduced to six commercially useful trees by 1941 and completely depleted by 1977. If the death rate was 15 percent, the area would be depleted by 1934. Young chicle trees do not grow rapidly enough to replenish a depleted area for commercial purposes. An exhausted area largely loses its practical value for *la chiclería* for many years. No wonder that Lundell found depleted areas in the 1930s and that in Petén today a chiclero may walk several kilometers to find a "good" tree. Between 1900 and 1920 a chiclero could collect as much as 300 pounds or 3 *quintales* (nonmetric quintal) per month, about 18 to 24 quintals per season, but today he collects on average 5 to 10 quintals per season. Konrad (1981) reports a similar situation in Yucatán: between 1900 and 1930, chicleros collected on average 22 quintals of latex per season, but by the 1970s the average was 11 quintals. With fewer mature trees in any given area, chicleros must tap younger ones, thereby accelerating the depletion process. Thus today in Petén, to collect 10 quintals, a chiclero may have to tap four hundred or more trees. The depletion rate led, in part, to the search for synthetics, and the use of synthetics in turn helped reduce international market demand for chicle(see below).[10] The importance of this development for Petén economy and society is discussed further on.

Tapping Technology

During the tapping season (roughly July/August to January), tappers set up forest camps composed of from six to twenty-five men, plus a female cook (prior to the 1940s, camps of forty and more men were common). The foreman (*capataz*) is responsible for selecting a campsite, the two most important criteria for his choice being access to water (ponds, rills, or other sources) and the number of chicle trees within walking distance of camp. He also tries to assess how many of the trees are "good." In the case of previously tapped trees, he notes the color of machete scars left on them. A chiclero says that "The scars are red one year after the extraction of milk [latex] and turn black by the third or fourth year. If the scars are black, he [the foreman] cuts the trees again to see if the milk will flow."[11] In general, once chicleros have to walk more than two hours (roughly 8 km) from camp to find trees worth tapping, the *capataz* will relocate the camp. Thus camps are normally moved about every six to eight weeks, roughly three to five times during the collecting season.

Chicleros normally work seven days a week during the tapping season. They arise between 3:00 and 5:00 A.M., some eating food prepared by the cook whose wages they pay, others preferring to prepare their own food. They then set off with their gear (Table 4:1) in search of trees, returning to camp around 4:00 to 5:00 P.M. To have help in case of injury or disorientation in dense forest, most go off in pairs and stay within visual or whistling range of their companion. The actual tapping, however, is an individual chore.

In selecting trees to tap, a chiclero takes several things into account. On the one hand, he wants to find productive trees—tall, thick ones (*A. zapota* commonly grows to 12 to 16 meters, and some reach 30 meters, with diameters of about 1 meter, although some are as thick as 2 meters)—which tend to be widely scattered. On the other hand, he would also prefer trees that are relatively easy to climb (that is, relatively thin) and not too distant from each other. A veteran chiclero says, "If the trees are thin [and concentrated], a good chiclero may tap as many as twenty a day," but ten is closer to the norm. If the trees are tall, mature, and dispersed, he may not be able to tap more than five to eight a day. To find an optimal area, the chiclero wanders several kilometers from camp. If he finds a particularly rich area, he usually keeps the information to himself or shares it with his buddy, because no one can claim untapped trees even if he discovers their location.

To tap, the chiclero makes a V-shaped channel with his machete at the base of the tree, putting a small canvas or rubber bag (*anulada, bolsa*) at the joint of the V. Next, he puts on metal spurs, like those of telephone repairmen but heavier, ties a long *mecate* (rope) about his waist ("the *mecate* is the life of a chiclero"), and, ascending the tree, makes V-shaped cuts in the bark, leaning away from it against the rope with each swing of the machete. He may also cut into thick branches, in which case he is almost parallel to the ground. The cut must be sharp and clean (but not deep enough to damage the tree) to allow the white, milky latex to flow smoothly down the herringbone pattern of cuts into the *anulada*. Rate of flow depends on the age of the tree, whether and when it was last tapped, the time of the day when it is tapped, and the rain. The heavier the rainfall, the swifter the flow. Unfortunately, very heavy precipitation makes the bark of a tree slippery and the ascent that much more difficult. Too little rain, and the latex will not flow; too much, and there can be a wasteful overflow from the *anulada* onto the ground. A tree drains normally in about twelve hours, that is, a worker taps one day and collects the latex the next day. The contents of the *anuladas* are poured into a larger bag (*depósito*) at the camp.

To remove excess moisture from the latex, it is cooked in a large iron pot. On Sundays the chicleros cook the sticky mass, as well as do laundry, chop firewood for the coming week, and so forth. Although the foreman supervises the cooking and the men do assist each other, each man is responsible for the proper processing of his own chicle. If the fire is "strong," properly banked and fed, some 200 pounds of latex can be cooked in about two hours. The men take turns stirring the heavy gum with large wooden paddles, all the while observing its color, aroma, and texture. When the boiling bubbles of latex "look like glass," the latex has turned the proper light brown-grey color and about 67 percent of the moisture has been boiled off. Then two men will pour the gum on large previously soaped burlap bags. The gum is so sticky that the men constantly soap their hands while handling it. A wooden wedge is used to scrape out bits of latex left in the pot; dirt and wood scraps are removed by hand. After being left to cool a bit, the chicle is put into soaped wooden molds, kneaded into what looks like a loaf of crude brown bread, and the initials of the chiclero, his employer and, now, FYDEP are stamped on both ends of the loaf with a "devil's key," a wedge-shaped tool made of soft wood. (FYDEP, *Empresa Nacional de Fomento y Desarrollo Económico del Petén*, National Enterprise for Economic Development of Petén, a government agency, took direct control of the chicle industry in 1962, buying chicle from jobbers and acting as the sole agent of sale of chicle to foreign firms.) When the loaves (*marquetas*) cool, they are stored on wet, soapy pole platforms until the time when the employer's muleteers or (since about 1975) pickup truck drivers arrive to take them from camp to a central warehouse. By government regulation, a *marqueta* should be 25 cm by 15 cm and weigh 20 pounds (most weigh between 18 to 23 pounds). The foreman weighs each *marqueta* in camp in full view of the tappers and gives each man a written receipt for each of his loaves. The men are paid according to the weight and moisture content of their chicle.

If a man feels he has not collected enough chicle, he may add other resins to his chicle. However, the practice is not so general as implied by some observers: "Chicleros are fond of slipping earth or stones into the blocks before they solidify since they are paid by weight" (Thompson 1963:153).[12] First, the blocks go through a laboratory or quality control check at the warehouse, and a tapper is not paid for any portion of chicle removed from his blocks owing to impurities. Second, foremen get a small bonus for quality chicle, and although they are usually supportive rather than directive leaders, they do discourage the practice of diluting the chicle. Finally, the cooking is perforce a public affair, and a man who habitually dumps other resins into his chicle will suffer a loss of reputation. Of course, some chicleros do occasionally mix resins, fail to remove wood particles from the latex, and so on, but "to exceed the limits," as chicleros say, "*no vale la pena*" (is not worth the effort). As in many piece goods industries, workers and foremen exercise their own quality control checks for obvious economic reasons. They are paid for what they produce, and nothing else.

The chiclero's equipment is usually supplied by his employer (called the *contratista*—contractor, jobber—or *patrón*). Nevertheless, some men prefer to outfit themselves and to work without benefit of a contractor. In 1974–1975, a man could outfit himself for about Q85 to Q100 (Table 4:1) if he was willing to work without a mule. During 1974–1975, the daily wage rate in Petén was Q1.50 to Q3.00, and closer to Q3.00 if an employer did not provide a worker with meals. Thus, over several months and surely in a year or so, a man who had no unanticipated large expenses could save enough money to work as an independent chiclero. Some of the chiclero's tools are homemade; most of the gear, save for the spurs and cooking pots, are also used for other purposes; none, except spurs and pots, go beyond normal expenses incurred by working men in Petén. Of course, a jobber works on a much larger scale than an independent tapper; for example, in 1960 a jobber who owned twenty mules (worth Q150 each) and employed fifty chicleros had to invest some Q4,000 simply to initiate tapping operations. Few Peteneros would have had Q4,000 on hand in 1960, or would even today. The important point is that almost everyone has always had relatively direct access to the means of production in *la chiclería*.

Before discussing other aspects of this economy, we should consider some of the hardships faced by tappers. Most of the time, a chiclero works alone. Given tapping technology and the dispersed distribution of chicle trees, his work cannot be directly supervised. The work itself is physically exhausting and dangerous. A chiclero may get lost in the woods, fall from

Table 4:1 Chiclero's Equipment, 1974–1975

Equipment	Unit cost	Total cost	Period of use
Machetes	Q 5.50	Q 11.00	Two or more years
Iron files	2.50	7.50	Several years
Rope	2.40	2.40	About two years
Axe	7.00	7.00	Several years
Spurs	4.50	4.50	Several years
Boots & laces	9.00	9.00	One year
Small canvas bags	1.00	4.00[a]	One year
Large canvas bags	2.00	6.00[a]	One–two years
Burlap bags	1.00	10.00[a]	Two years
Molds	Homemade	—	Several years
Devil's key	Homemade	—	Several years
Wooden paddle	Homemade	—	Several years
Chicle cooking pot	19.00	19.00	Two–three years
Brown soap	.10	3.00[a]	—
Scale[b]	Variable	—	Many years
Mule[b]	40–100.00 +	—	—
		Total Q 83.40	

Source: Field Notes. Q = Quetzal (Guatemalan currency, then worth $1 USA). Most chicleros also own a thermos and a mosquito net; a few carry rifles for hunting.

[a]Approximated; need depends on how much chicle a tapper collects.

[b]Scale and mule are optional. A chiclero who purchased both would have raised his investment from about Q83.00 to about Q125–183.00.

a tree, or be bitten by a snake. There are health hazards: overexposure to rain, bad drinking water, organisms that produce fevers, dysentery, parasites, and so on. Of these diseases, the best known is "chiclero's ulcer," a cutaneous leishmaniasis caused by a parasitic fly that lays its eggs, usually, in the nose and ears, leading to erosion of the cartilage. If caught in time, the ulcer can be cured with antimony preparations. (Many older chicleros sport partly "chewed away" noses or ears with some pride.) However, medical aid is always far away. Gone from home for months on end, having contact with the outside world only when muleteers or truck drivers enter camp to pick up chicle and deliver supplies, chicleros worry about their families, hope their patron is paying them the *mensualidad* (the monthly allowance, an amount agreed upon prior to the season), are anxious to know if children are well and wife and daughters behaving properly. In addition, *contratistas* inflate the price of the food, cigarettes, and medicines they sell to chicleros, who have no other source of supply. To complete the list, there may be machete fights in camp, sometimes over the female cook or over a gambling debt. It must be added that the number and severity of these fights is universally and wildly exaggerated, for reasons to be explained later. Although political changes after 1945 and the use of trucks in *la chiclería* after 1975 have improved things for chicleros, the following statement by an older informant captures the problems the men still face.

> I quit working in chicle because it is dirty work, dangerous and hard. It is sacrilegious [a reference to a belief that because the latex is the "blood" of the tree, and because chicleros may kill the tree, their work is sinful as are their wages]. There are many dangers, like the rattlesnakes, and limbs fall from the trees when one is high up, and one must dodge them. A snake forty inches long once darted out of the trunk of a tree, at the bottom, and bit me on the left hand. There are sandflies, mosquitoes, and the damage the cooking of the gum does to the eyes. The cooking takes three hours, and then one works long hours . . . up at 3:00 A.M. and eats and leaves camp by 5:00 A.M. and is back by 5:00 P.M. One goes four or five kilometers in search of good trees, for the trees are scattered about, not in a group. It is all ugly. On Sunday, one does not rest and devote the time to God, but to washing clothes, bathing, and chopping wood for the week. The chicle is cooked on Sunday too. The milpero does not work as hard, from 6:00 A.M. until noon, and then he eats and then he goes back and works until 5:00 P.M. and he can rest on Sunday. It is easier. And chicleros do not have milpas. They must pay what they earn for food and other things. It is useless. The chiclero must pay Q15 to Q18 a month [in the 1970s] for his food, and Q4 to the cook if she cooks for him. The milpa is better, slower, and one does not have to pay for food (Field Notes 1974).[13]

Other older chicleros sum up their experience more aphoristically, for instance, "I worked eighteen years in chicle and came out with nothing but a pair of pants" [and debts to the patron].

Yet in describing their trials, chicleros almost always strike an equivocal note. One such expression of this is the common observation of chicleros that the coffee that warms them in the morning after a cold, damp night in the forest is welcome, but always has a "bitter taste." And, midst the hardships, they enjoy the camaraderie of the camps and take pride in the mastery of forest lore and athletic skills. Most of all, they tap trees because it has the potential to pay them more than other forms of labor.

The history (briefly), ecology, and method of tapping chicle trees, and something of the chiclero's perspective has been described. Now, before discussing how the production of chicle and chiclero labor was organized, the overwhelming importance of this enterprise for the economy and society of Petén in the first three quarters of the twentieth century will be taken up by reviewing statistical data.

Global Statistics on Chicle

There are many problems with aggregated statistical data on Guatemala, and those concerning chicle are no exception.[14] Aside from discrepancies among sources, the Guatemalan government kept few if any records on chicle production prior to the late 1920s. Until about 1930, much of the chicle produced in Petén was smuggled out through Mexico or Belize to Canada and then reexported to the United States. As Grieb (1979:151) says,

> It was simply impossible to police the vast frontier, and despite considerable efforts to do so by the military, small groups of men and pack mules could easly lose themselves in the jungle and slip across the border. Guatemalans were infuriated at the export of chicle from British Honduras, since they assumed that most if not all of this total represented the fruits of smuggling.

To cope with this situation, Ubico substituted exploitation right fees for export taxes and tried, with some success in the case of the chicle, to seal the borders of Petén. In any case, from the late 1920s and especially after 1930, there are relatively reliable and accurate statistics on the extractive economy of Petén.

Between the 1890s and the 1920s the production of chicle increased steadily and rapidly. Problems of resource depletion, that arose, as noted above, by the 1920s, may have led to some decrease in production. The worldwide depression of the 1930s caused a further and much sharper reduction, and production did not pick up until 1936 (Tables 4:2 and 4:3). For reasons discussed previously, production peaked during 1940–1948. Although it decreased after 1948, relatively good levels, with some fluctuations, were maintained until 1979, and for most of the time production never went below 12,000–13,000 quintals per year. Mexican production shows the same pattern, for example, exports decreased from a high of 83,600 quintals in 1945 to to 14,000 quintals in 1974–1975 (Konrad 1981). But by 1979–1980, Petén production decreased to the 1930s depression levels, although Peteneros had been expressing anxiety about the "fall" (*caida*) of chicle several years earlier. During most of the 1980s production

Table 4:2 Petén Chicle Production (quintals, 1,000s), 1919–1985

Year	Amount	Year	Amount	Year	Amount
1919	.10	1944/45	42.00	1965/66	22.24
1920	.08	1945/46	39.00	1966/67	18.08
1927/28	13.90	1946/47	38.00	1967/68	21.45
1928/29	10.02	1947/48	36.96	1968/69	16.94
1929/30	18.35	1948/49	27.00	1969/70	18.07
1930/31	11.99	1949/50	16.00	1970/71	16.61
1931/32	6.41	1950/51	26.80	1971/72	13.36
1932/33	3.44	1951/52	25.00	1972/73	20.00
1933/34	4.14	1953/54	7.80	1973/74	12.65
1934/35	5.28	1954/55	24.00	1974/75	11.38
1935/36	5.93	1955/56	15.50	1975/76	8.64
1936/37	12.92	1956/57	17.00	1976/77	13.57
1937/38	13.73	1957/58	26.80	1977/78	13.11
1938/39	23.27	1958/59	23.20	1978/79	15.62
1939/40	15.05	1959/60	13.62	1979/80	8.35[a]
1940/41	28.31	1960/61	25.24	1980/81	5.48
1941/42	36.77	1961/62	19.55	1981/82	7.50
1942/43	32.89	1962/63	13.68	1982/83	7.50
1943/44	34.00	1963/64	13.01	1984/85	7.42[b]

Sources: Banco de Guatemala 1981a; FYDEP (*Memorias Anuales* and internal memoranda) 1978–1984; Grieb 1979:151; Hoar 1924; Holdridge et al. 1950:4; *Petén Itzá* No. 12, 1971; Pinelo 1937.

Note: Until 1927, production data were scant and quite unreliable. Between 1952–1954, politics interfered with production; reports for 1964–1965 (but cf. Banco de Guatemala 1981a) and 1983–1984 are not clear, hence the figures are estimates. Where possible, figures refer to 1st class chicle. In 1979–1980, FYDEP sold no more than 2,571 quintals, placing the rest in its warehouses. In 1981, FYDEP tried to limit production to 7,300 quintals. By 1985, FYDEP, facing ever growing difficulties selling chicle, had to warehouse 7,000 quintals. There were extended, futile negotiations with Bumbase of Italy (FYDEP rejected an offer of stylish Italian patent leather shoes in exchange for chicle); eventually Mutsui bought some 3,000 quintals.

[a]Production may have been 4,719 quintals; the figure used above may include some chicle collected in previous seasons.

[b]In 1985, FYDEP apparently sold 2,718 quintals, keeping the rest (some 5,000 quintals) in warehouses. In 1986 or 1987, FYDEP sold Mitsui 4,700 quintals, collected during 1984–1985. Recently, a friend wrote to say that 8,000 quintals were collected during the 1988–1989 tapping season.

fluctuated between 3,000 to 7,500 quintals per year (cf. Heinzman and Reining 1988:51). In 1985 FYDEP, short of funds, believed that the sale price for chicle, Q213 per quintal of first-class chicle, could not be lowered,

Table 4:3 Value (quetzales, 1,000s) of Petén Chicle Exports, 1930–1987

Year	Quetzales	Year	Quetzales	Year	Quetzales
1930	105.9	1952	1,710.0	1969	1,747.6
1931	85.4	1953	130.0	1970	1,557.6
1937	306.4	1954	80.0	1971	758.1
1938	510.0	1955	1,357.0	1972	2,052.5
1939	936.0	1956	1,022.0	1973	1,860.8
1940	641.0	1957	888.0	1974	1,636.4
1941	1,226.0	1958	907.0	1975	795.2
1942	1,426.0	1959	2,700.0	1976	2,877.7
1943	1,326.0	1960	2,795.0	1977	4,913.5
1944	1,610.0	1961	2,210.0	1978	4,539.6[a]
1945	2,741.2	1962	551.0	1979	2,075.0
1946	2,956.0	1963	1,115.0	1980–81	1,618.5
1947	3,969.0	1964	1,647.0	1981–82	1,407.5
1948	2,741.0	1965	1,333.0	1982–83	1,407.5
1949	1,844.0	1966	352.0	1987	1,001.1[b]
1950	1,306.0	1967	1,951.0		
1951	2,038.0	1968	413.8		

Sources: Banco de Guatemala 1981a (for 1939–1980); FYDEP 1979; Guinea 1970; Holdridge et al. 1950:4; Pinelo 1937; United Nations 1953–1960. My data differ somewhat (but not by much) from the Bank's, for whenever possible I use values for first class chicle (chiquibul is of limited value).

[a]The reported figure for 1978 (or possibly 1977) may be exaggerated.

[b]This refers to the export value of first class chicle collected during 1984–1985 but not sold until 1987.

yet it was nearly impossible to find buyers at this price.[15] Sales were so low that FYDEP owed Q400,000 to contractors, who consequently could not pay their chicleros. FYDEP's annual budget has never exceeded Q10 million, and was about Q3 million in 1984, hence the Q400,000 was a significant debt. Mitsui eventually purchased enough chicle to cover the debt. In the late 1980s some Peteneros felt the industry might be revived, because in 1987 Mitsui expressed an interest in purchasing about 2,000 quintals of chicle per year and in 1989 Petén produced and exported about 10,000 quintals, nevertheless everything indicates that *la chiclería* will never again dominate the economy of Petén.

From 1932 to 1962, Petén must have exported over Q20 million worth of chicle. Between 1962 and 1987, Petén exported at least Q36 million worth,

Table 4:4 Value of Chicle Exports Relative to Total Guatemalan Exports, 1929–1972.

Year	Percent	Year	Percent
1929	1.3	1957	1.0
1938	3.5	1958	0.9
1942	5.8	1959	2.0 (1.5)
1945	8.5	1960	1.9 (1.7)
1946	8.0	1961	2.3 (2.1)
1947	7.6	1962	0.6 (0.5)
1948	5.5	1963	1.0 (0.7)
1949	3.5	1964	1.5 (0.7)
1950	1.9	1965	0.8
1951	2.7	1966	0.2 (0.1)
1952	2.0	1967	1.0
1953	—	1969	0.9
1954	0.5	1970	0.9
1955	1.4	1971	0.9
1956	0.9	1972	1.9

Sources: Aybar de Soto 1978:318–19; Bulmer-Thomas 1987:834 (who cites a figure of .01 for 1913); *Europa Yearbook* 1959, 1963, 1965, 1972; Fletcher et al. 1970:48; Pan American Union 1948:100; author's calculations based on FYDEP and Bank of Guatemala data (for 1969–1972). Where there is a significant discrepancy among sources, the alternative figure is given in parentheses.

and some FYDEP officials would cite a figure closer to Q44 million. From 1962 on, the rough average is Q1.8 million per year. These are not large sums, but until about 1970 Petén had little else of comparable export value, and for a time the percentage value of chicle exports relative to total Guatemalan exports was rather impressive. In the 1920s chicle was the nation's third most important export (Grieb 1979:64); in 1945 chicle contributed 8.5 percent to the total; between 1953 and 1972, the annual contribution to the total varied from 2.3 to 0.9 percent (Table 4:4). By the 1980s the value had decreased to 0.1 percent and will probably go lower in the future. Of greater importance is that, at times, anywhere from 29 to 50 percent of the economically active population of Petén has been directly involved with *la chiclería*.

For several reasons, estimates of the chicle labor force have often been on the low side. At least since the 1930s labor contractors were supposed

Table 4:5 Estimated Number of Chicle Contractors, 1920–1985

Year	Number of contractors[a]
1920	50
1944	35
1952	60
1974	92
1985	26

Sources: Department Archives, Flores; FYDEP archives; Field Notes.

[a]For several reasons it it difficult to be precise about the number of contractors, e.g., the fuzzy line between contractors and subcontractors, that loggers and others may operate as unlicensed contractors, etc. What may be said is that there were more contractors prior to about 1920 than afterwards. Around 1920, when Chicle Development and Wrigley placed their own personnel directly in Petén, the number of contractors seems to have decreased and stabilized. Chicle Development apparently worked with 15–20 and Wrigley with about 26 jobbers. In 1944, there were at least 32–35 jobbers, but afterwards their numbers increased. By 1952, there were about 60, if not more. In 1974, FYDEP granted contracts to 92 jobbers, 74 of whom collected first class chicle. With the slump of the late 1970s, the number of contractors declined. In 1980, Itzalandia had about 20 members, and in 1985 there were some 26 chicle concessions in the department, i.e., at least 26 contractors. Fluctuations in the number of contratistas reflect market demands for chicle and political conditions in Guatemala.

to pay a fee to the government for each of their foreign chicleros. Some jobbers failed to do so, and this lowered official chiclero censuses. Nor have independent and part-time chicleros always been included in official counts. At other times officials have overestimated the number of chicleros, sometimes to drum up Guatemalan congressional support for the chicle industry.[16] (There also are problems in counting contractors; see Table 4:5.)[17] But the figures even in the cautious approach taken below underscore the importance of the extractive economy to the people of Petén for some 75 to 85 years.

During 1945–1953 the Arévalo and Arbenz regimes made it possible for some Peteneros to improve their economic position by becoming chicle jobbers. For example, from 1920 to 1945 in the pueblo of San Andrés there were two jobbers, an uncle and nephew team. There were five jobbers in town in 1952, and a fluctuating number, seven to ten, by the 1970s. Although after 1945 la chiclería began a secular decline, political reforms did allow some men to improve their economic status.

Relative to the population of Petén, the number of Peteneros working as chicleros has been extraordinary. In the 1920s, in one of two large concessions, as many as 1,000 full-time chicleros were in the field for up to nine months at a stretch, plus an additional 300–400 people working as cooks, muleteers, and so forth (Schufeldt 1950:228). Some Peteneros say that at this time the total number of people involved in chicle may have been as many as 4,000 or 5,000. In 1944, 2,048 men signed contracts with jobbers (at least 70 ran away from their patrons). In 1945, 3,129 men signed contracts to collect chicle; this figure does not include those who worked without a contract. Men working without a formal contract are usually Peteneros who collect relatively small amounts of chicle. In the 1960s there were roughly 2,500 or more chicleros in Petén, of whom 1,000 to 1,500 were resident in the department, representing 17 to 26 percent of the total number of Petén households. From 1970 on, FYDEP has estimated that in any given year there were 1,350 to 2,000 chicleros in Petén. Even in 1985, there could not have been fewer than 900 active chicleros in the department. Konrad (1981) estimates that the ratio of chicleros to support and administrative staff is 5 to 1. Thus, to take the 1960s as an example, when Petén had a population of about 26,000 people, the 2,500 chicleros would have been supported and managed by another 500 people. Almost all staff personnel are residents of Petén. Thus, even if no more than 1,000 Peteneros collected chicle, there would have been some 1,500 Peteneros directly involved in *la chiclería*. Since each of these people usually represents one household (with an average of about 5 to 6 persons per household), anywhere from 29 to 35 percent of the Petén population was directly dependent on *la chiclería* for income (and this excludes merchants indirectly dependent on chiclero customers and chicleros who come to Petén only for the collecting season). The same point may be made by looking at particular communities. For example, in 1960, 39.3 percent of the men in the *pueblo* of San José collected chicle (Reina 1967). In 1961, 38.1 percent of households in the *pueblo* of San Andrés were dependent on chicle for all or part of their income. Although I cannot speak as precisely of San Benito and La Libertad, chicle contractors believe the percentages would have been higher in both towns. Thus, at a conservative estimate, for the first half of the twentieth century, probably 50 percent and more of Peteneros were directly dependent on *la chiclería*. By the 1960s (and here, too, the estimate is conservative) 29 to 35 percent were; by about 1978 (after the demographic explosion of the early 1970s) probably about 7.0 percent were. By 1984 the figure was probably closer to about 5.0 percent. The decline in the percentage of the chicle labor force compared to total Petén population has

Table 4:6 Distribution of Income from Chicle, 1980

Distribution	First class chicle		Second class chicle	
	Percent	Amount	Percent	Amount
Chiclero[a]	43.00	Q91.59	43.00	Q58.91
Contractor[b]	26.00	55.38	26.00	35.62
Air flight	5.16	10.99	10.00	13.70[c]
Land transport	1.17	2.49	–	–
Municipality	5.00	10.65	5.00	6.85
Social Security	1.00	2.13	1.00	1.37
FYDEP	18.67	39.77	15.00	20.55
Total	100.00	Q213.00	100.00	Q137.00

Source: FYDEP. The Bank of Guatemala (1981a) reports a slightly different distribution.
In 1979 or 1980, municipalities began to receive Q6.39 for each quintal of chicle extracted from their jurisdictions, and Q4.16 was distributed to municipalities lacking chicle.
In the 1880s, foreign importers paid about $7.00/quintal of Petén chicle; by 1900, $50.00. Thereafter, the price rose gradually, from Q67 in the 1950s to Q125 in the late 1970s. Around 1980, the price was Q213 (for 1st class chicle). Prices for 2nd class chicle rise with those for 1st class chicle. Suchilma (chicleros' union) receives 1.1 percent of the distribution from FYDEP's share.
[a]Around 1910, chicleros earned ten gold pieces (worth $50)/week (Narciso 1913:317). Between 1910 and 1920, they earned $90–100/quintal of first class chicle. From the 1930s or 1940s until 1973, they usually received Q25–30/quintal (now being paid in quetzales, not pesos). Between 1973 and 1980, they received Q35–45.
[b]Until 1980, contractors received Q20–25 for first class chicle; in 1980 this climbed to Q55.38 for chicle deposited in FYDEP warehouses. In 1973, FYDEP's share was Q18.50.
[c]I am not sure about the exact breakdown of transportation costs but the total for second class chicle is as given above.

been rapid and precipitous, but this is as closely related to demographic trends in Petén as to an absolute decline in the number of chicleros.[18]

Until about 1970 township *cajas* also depended heavily on chicle income. Until 1951 a *muncipio* received Q0.25 for each quintal of chicle removed from its territory. Some Peteneros say that the tax went to Q0.50 in the 1940s, but local archival records offer little support for the claim. In 1951 the tax was raised to Q2.00 per quintal, and the first payments were made in 1953. In 1979 or 1980 the tax went to Q6.39, another Q4.26 per quintal being shared by municipalities lacking chicle (Table 4:6). These funds were very important for the municipalities. Several former treasurers from central Petén *municipios* say that such a large proportion of local government income came from chicle that collection of other taxes tended to be neglected. For example, in 1940 San Andrés had a total income of Q1,767 of which Q871 (49.3 percent) was derived from the chicle tax. Of course this could vary from year to year; for instance, in 1944 San Andrés's total income was Q3,845 of which 74.9 percent was derived from the chicle tax; in 1945 the total income was Q1,134 of which 21.4 percent came from the tax. In 1960 total income was Q13,854, 73.7 percent coming from chicle taxes. In the 1960s roughly 74 to 85 percent of township income came from this source (true also for several other townships rich in chicle trees). By 1985 San Andrés's income, having risen rapidly during the late 1970s and 1980s as did that of other Petén townships, was Q114,562. The portion derived from the chicle tax had declined to 12.0 percent. For many years, Flores, San Andrés, La Libertad, Melchor de Mencos, San José, and Santa Ana, usually in this order, were the main beneficiaries of township tax on chicle extraction.

FYDEP, too, received benefits from taxes on chicle. Until 1977 about 10 to 12 percent of its annual budget came from chicle. Before that year, FYDEP's budget was usually about Q3 million per year, of which Q1.75 million came from the state, and Q1.25 million from its own "private" funds, generated by FYDEP itself through fees, sales of chicle, lumber, and so on. Between 1978 and 1985 FYDEP's budget usually fluctuated between Q3 and Q8 million, to which chicle contributed a high of about 7.3 percent to a low of 1.9 to 3.0 percent toward the end of the period. (Political and economic problems led to a decrease in FYDEP's 1985 budget.)

The record is clear. For most of this century, the economic well-being of most Peteneros and of their communities was based largely on a single activity—the production of chicle for overseas export. Some individuals and some towns (for most of the township income is spent on the *pueblo*) gained more than others, but *la chiclería* affected everyone in Petén. The record also shows that *la chiclería* began a serious decline, the so-called *caída*, beginning about 1976. During the 1970s-1980s a more diversified economy developed in Petén; nevertheless a good many Peteneros were negatively affected by the *caída*. How they were and are organized to produce chicle is described next.

Organization of Production and Labor in *La Chiclería*

In the abstract, the organization of production in *la chiclería* is straight-forward. A certain corporation or individual entrepreneur extends credit to a *contratista* (jobber) who obligates himself to recruit a labor force and to sell the creditor a stipulated minimum amount of chicle. The jobber uses the credit and his own capital to equip labor. The jobber extends credit, in the form of an *enganche* (cash advance), to workers; he agrees to provide their families a *mensualidad* (monthly allowance) and to supply the workers with food, medicine, cigarettes, and so forth during the tapping season. Chicleros sign a contract with the jobber to produce a stipulated minimum of chicle. At the end of the season, the jobber deducts the *enganche*, *mensualidad*, and cost of supplies from the chicleros' total earnings. Government licenses chicle operations, collects fees and taxes from entrepreneurs and jobbers, and decides how to distribute these monies among its several constituent elements—township, department, and central state. The chicle is shipped overseas to locations where chewing gum is manufactured and the finished product is marketed. In practice, the organization of production has been and is a good deal more complicated.

Credit Sources and Arrangements
To begin with, sources of credit changed over the decades. From 1895 to about 1915, Belizean merchants extended credit to and urged their lumber and *hule* jobbers and/or fellow merchants, as well as others in Petén, to collect chicle. Prominent among the Belizeans were Cayo merchants of Lebanese extraction. Mexicans who held logging concessions in northern and western Petén also got involved in chicle tree tapping. Both Belizeans and Mexicans sold the product to United States purchasing agents. In the early years of *oro blanco* (white gold), as chicle was then called, a good many Peteneros worked as jobbers. But the more important ones were Floreños, because they had the closest trade connections with Belizeans. They also held important government posts which brought them into close contact with Mexican loggers as well as Belize merchants.[19]

By the early 1920s, agents of companies in the United States obtained control of the two largest chicle concessions in Petén. American Chicle had a concession in northwestern Petén; Wrigley in northeastern Petén. American Chicle usually shipped its chicle by river to Tenosique, Mexico, and Wrigley shipped by mule to Belize. From the 1920s to 1949, the United States companies operated directly in Petén, extending credit to jobbers. Peteneros unanimously assert that the North Americans brought order into what had been a loosely organized, sometimes violent enterprise. They reduced the number of jobbers, improved terms for them, reliably paid their own workers and jobbers, and provided some medical aid to chicleros. In the early 1920s the national government also began to take more interest in *oro blanco*. In 1922 the state, reacting to reports from the governor of Petén, mandated a chicle extraction fee of $50 ("*oro americano*") to be paid to Rentas in Flores. Somewhat later, the state also established a tax of Qo.25 per quintal to be paid townships for chicle extracted from within their jurisdictions.[20]

In the first twenty-five to thirty years of *la chiclería*, many Peteneros earned previously unimaginable incomes and profits, but some also have bitter memories of this period. Townships as such, as well as individuals, suffered.

> The most bitter and sad experience which the municipality of San José could have suffered occurred during the accursed administration of ex-president of the Republic, José María Orellana . . . 1922–1926, who, abusing his power [and] without obtaining the authorization of the honorable National Assembly . . . gave in monopolistic form the chicle concession to . . . F.M. I_____ and F. J. A_____, who (then) sold the chicle concession to Mr. Percey Wellows Shufledt [sic.] for the derisive sum of five American dollars gold per quintal of chicle that he might export, [but] omitting fiscal and municipal taxes . . . as a consequence . . . the municipalities of this district found themselves on the edge of ruin; the municipality of San José, with the help of its residents, had to plant communal milpas each year so that it could partly support itself [and] not one municipality could carry out a single project; . . . this district was completely forsaken and exploited, the holders of the concession benefitting themselves . . . and the inhabitants of the district suffering (Cahuiche 1964; don Carlos Cahuiche was municipal secretary of San José for many years).

The municipalities of Petén were hardly prosperous prior to *la chiclería*, they did not uniformly and inevitably benefit from it, and as don Carlos reported, were sometimes hurt from the new economy.

To return to the question of credit, after the 1944 Revolution, in 1949, the government made a new agency, INFOP (National Institute for the Promotion of Production), the sole intermediary between chicle producers and foreign purchasers. From 1952 to 1970 the Bank of Guatemala extended credit to jobbers through INFOP, which purchased the chicle and sold it to overseas firms. (This, among other things, led the companies to withdraw their personnel from Petén.) Unlike the past when jobbers had to contract for 1,000–1,500 quintals, now they could make contracts with INFOP for as little as 50 quintals. INFOP set easy credit terms and broadened access to jobbing, so that by 1960 there were more than one hundred *contratistas* in Petén. It is commonly charged that INFOP used political

criteria in distributing credit, that INFOP employees and borrowers sometimes simply defrauded the agency, that it was not efficient in distributing
funds and gave little thought to development problems, not only in Petén
but throughout the country (Silvert 1954:24). There is a perception in
Petén that INFOP's weaknesses led to a reduction in foreign demand for
chicle, although this is at most but part of the story (see above).

By 1959 INFOP's role in chicle production was ended, and a consortium
of jobbers (*Consorcio de Empresarios de Chicle de Petén*) more or less took its
place until 1969.[21] In 1962 FYDEP was given control of the industry. From
1971 to 1980, FYDEP used its own funds, and then in 1980 used credits from
government banks to extend credit to contractors. (In late 1987 President
Cerezo, who took office in 1986, disbanded FYDEP, but as of this writing
the task has not been completed; it is not yet clear which if any state agency
will be given responsibility for *la chiclería*.) FYDEP extends credit to
jobbers (the important ones being members of Itzalandia, the new name
for the Consortium), regulates working conditions in chicle, subsidizes the
chicleros' union, Suchilma(*Sindicato de Chicleros y Madereros del Petén*), sets
production levels, and since 1971 has been the exclusive agent for sale of
chicle (in fact, this role was assumed prior to 1971). Around 1985, FYDEP
seems to have given Itzalandia a global production figure, which Itzalandia
then divided up among its approximately twenty member jobbers. FYDEP
also may have allowed Suchilma to collect chicle through subcontractors.
Following is a description of chicle up to 1985, when I last collected data
directly in the field. Thus, Figure 4:1 is a schematic presentation of the
modern organization of the extractive economy in Petén up to about 1985.

To obtain credit and a contract from FYDEP, a jobber must have
fulfilled all previous contracts with the agency. A newcomer can get a
contract and credit to begin operations on the recommendation of two
established jobbers, or, lacking sponsors, can take out a contract without
being given a credit line. Credit takes the form of a cash advance on the
amount of chicle to be produced; for example, in the 1960s FYDEP advanced jobbers Q15 per quintal of chicle anticipated. If a jobber fails to
make good on this year's contract, his next one will be for a reduced
amount of chicle. If he fails once or twice again, he may be refused subsequent contracts. If the failure is linked to fraud, he is subject to prose-
cution. For many years the paperwork in *la chiclería* was done in Guatemala
City, something jobbers, particularly the less well-capitalized, found onerous. Some *contratistas* allege that political influence, personal relations, and

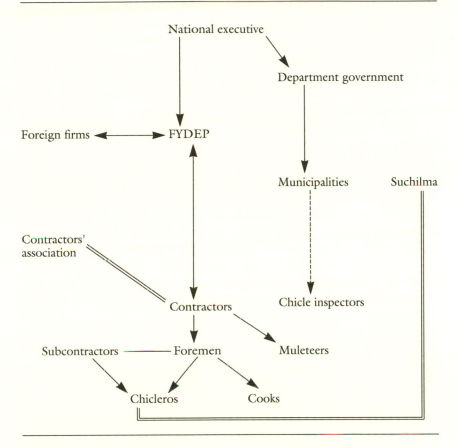

Figure 4:1. Structure of *la chiclería* in Petén. *Source*: Field Notes 1960, 1974–1975. *Key*: Double lines = membership. *Note*: Although municipalities have employed their own inspectors now and then, they have not done so consistently, hence the dotted line.

bribery as much as, if not more, than a record of productive efficiency gain one access to FYDEP contracts and credit. They also claim this was far less likely the case when North Americans operated directly in Petén.

Contractors can also obtain credit or start-up capital from banks and wealthy friends. The friends are usually Flores merchants with whom the borrower has had prior dealings, commonly as a chicle subcontractor, foreman, or muleteer. Interest on loans can be as low as 5 percent, depending on the personal relations between lender and borrower. Although there is talk of 25, 50, and even 100 percent interest rates, in fact a merchant willing in the first place to extend credit to a jobber usually has more to gain by setting a reasonable, "friendly" interest rate that will predispose the jobber to do business with him. In *la chiclería*, friendship and business are two sides of the same coin.

In summary, jobbers have had several changing sources of credit and start-up capital: local and Belize merchants, foreign companies, state agencies. Over time, the role of the state has grown increasingly important. INFOP's liberal or lax credit program both broadened access to contracting, and, in a sense, returned things to what they were prior to the 1920s. *Cuello* (slang for "influence") and social ties have been important for getting credit from state agencies, just as they were important in the early 1900s with merchants in Belize and Flores, and between Mexican loggers and local government officials. Then as now, this situation gave the elite a head start in *la chiclería*. Nevertheless, all jobbers must sooner or later produce chicle. Consequently capable lower-sector men, prior to 1920 and even more so after 1949, have been upwardly mobile, and some members of the elite have lost fortunes.

To produce chicle, a *contratista* normally has to effectively recruit, organize, and manage a labor force. The following quotation from a well-known contractor summarizes some problems faced by jobbers:

> The contractor has to buy equipment and also to have mules and a foreman. He has to buy machetes, ropes, account books, spurs, storage places, paddles [to stir chicle in cooking pots], and cooling troughs. I have forty chicleros in the woods of San Andrés and thirty more men in San José, at Uaxactun. FYDEP gives the contractor an advance. It gives me Q15 for each quintal I have on the contract. I have a contract for 500 quintals. There are many taxes . . . [see Table 4:6] but my profit varies from Q8 to 15 [per quintal] . . . I have to pay dues to my own organization [Consortium, now Itzalandia]. The initiation fee is Q25, and then Q1 for each quintal. This group, a consortium, arranges work and other things, and it has lawyers who work with FYDEP, well, against FYDEP . . . One can get a FYDEP contract on the basis of recommendations from two contractors, or one can start on one's own, but without any money in advance [from FYDEP]. This is the way my brothers and I did it [on their own, but with a loan from a Flores merchant for whom they had worked as foremen and subcontractors; the merchant, in turn, often obtained loans from a wealthy uncle in Guatemala City] . . . If I cannot fulfill my contract, FYDEP gives less next season [that is, decreases the amount of chicle the jobber will be authorized to collect]

... FYDEP will agree to a sale [of one jobber's chicle] to another contractor if one needs cash to buy food for his chicleros ... If a contractor needs cash immediately, he can get it from the merchants in Flores, at 5 percent interest. Before 1944 one had to have a very good recommendation from a *grande* [big shot]) who was well-known in Guatemala City (Field Notes 1975).

He then went on to say that there is a good deal of "deception" in the chicle business, and so one must do whatever is necessary to "defend oneself." For example, a jobber, to please Floreños to whom he is indebted, may claim that chicle collected in San Andrés or San José was collected in Flores, thereby assuring the township of Flores of added unearned tax income. He added that FYDEP owed jobbers money, and that

FYDEP says this money was used to pay for roads, to finance small contractors, and so on, but this is just another way of saying the money was stolen. FYDEP breaks the small contractor because it does not pay him on time, and so small contractors have to borrow money from the rich in Flores ... and so they lose their profit when they are finally paid for their chicle. Sometimes a contractor needs cash. Don C. in Flores pays contractors Q40 per quintal of chicle, but C. pays all the taxes, so the contractor gets Q5 profit [per quintal, after paying the chicleros, interest on the loan, and so on] ... With both INFOP and FYDEP, bribes can help one get a contract, and I know this for certain. In order to get the liquidation papers [at the end of the season] in Guatemala City, one must put some money between the papers one gives the clerk. I received my papers on the same day I went to Guatemala [City], while others there had been waiting eight days. The difference between Guatemala and Petén is that in Petén one gives the money in the other's house, not in a public office (Field Notes 1975).

Labor Recruitment

A *contratista* with equipment, credit advance, and a contract must also put together a labor force. Because of the relatively high labor turnover in *la chiclería*, he has to rebuild his work crews each year. There are three major ways he may do this, and some jobbers use all three at the same time.

First, a jobber can send an agent outside Petén to contact labor recruiters, most commonly in Alta Verapaz or Baja Verapaz. Sometimes the recruiter becomes the crew's chicle camp foreman. Whether he does or not, he is socially responsible for the conduct of the men. The jobber and his agent have little if any personal contact with the crew, although they may have personal ties with the recruiter. This method of labor recruitment has an advantage in that work crews usually come from the same community and ethnic group, factors which, many jobbers believe, make for peaceful chicle camps and tractable chicleros. Moreover, rarely will any of these workers expect the jobber to assist him in any way once the collecting season is over. The disadvantage, aside from transportation costs, is that the jobber knows little about the men or whether they will perform as skillfully as he would wish.

Second, the jobber may decide to work partly or entirely through subcontractors, some of whom may be his foremen—the line between foremen and subcontractors often being thin. (Subcontractors usually live in and manage camps, as foremen do.) The jobber may also work with independent chicleros who organize their sons and other kinsmen to collect chicle. If the jobber gives this sort of independent operator an *enganche* or line of credit, the operator becomes a de facto subjobber. Sometimes a jobber who has a contract with FYDEP and his own crew will also be a subcontractor for another jobber, and the same can be true of his own subcontractors. Thus, arrangements can be complicated, and chicle prices among participants can vary by as much as 33 percent. But the arrangements normally have some common features. They rest on verbal pledges rather than written contracts, in part because they may involve regulatory infractions. The bond between jobber and subcontractor is a personal one. The parties involved trust each other if for no other reason than that verbal pledges are difficult to enforce in court. The advantages of this form of recruitment for jobbers is that they are relieved of labor and operations management. A disadvantage, aside from possible legal problems, is that they must finance the subcontractor, normally to the amount of Q500 to 1,000 or more, before seeing any chicle. The jobber, usually wealthier and more powerful than the subjobber, behaves as if they were nearly equals and old friends, and in fact they may be kinsmen, ritual kinsmen, or friends. Or the relationship may resemble that of patron and client, but roles may also be reversed from one year to the next. Even more important, the tenure normally associated with patronage is often absent. In some cases, the amity and patronage are real and lasting, but in many others they, like other relationships in the chicle business, prove quite fragile.[22]

Third, jobbers may personally recruit foremen and chicleros. Most native Petén chicleros are hired this way, and many jobbers believe that the personal approach increases the chances for a successful operation. Recruitment begins around May or June, lasts several weeks, and involves a number of discussions between patron and worker, after which a formal standardized contract is signed. Irrespective of when they are signed or for what time period, most contracts are dated 1 June to 1 January. They usually call for the chiclero to collect from 5 to 10 quintals of chicle. For some years now, the chiclero's wages have been set by FYDEP (Table 4:6), but *enganches* and *mensualidades* are subject to negotiation.

Several factors condition this third method of recruiting labor. First, contractors and chicleros mutually select each other. The system is not seigneurial; there are many jobbers and subcontractors seeking reliable, able chicleros. Jobbers, including those otherwise united by ties of kinship, friendship, and neighborhood, compete ruthlessly with each other for good chicleros, although the anger this generates seems not to outlast the chicle season (Reina 1965). The rivalry gives the better chicleros an opportunity to chose among patrons.

Second, there is a pervasive belief in Petén that *la chiclería* is a game of *engaño* (cunning and deception), in which everyone—in what can become a chain of self-fulfilling prophecies—is on guard against being duped and may decide to cozen others before he can be deceived. Contractors have been known to short-weight chicle, overcharge chicleros for supplies, falsify receipts, fail to remit *mensualidades* on time, hold chicleros in debt peonage (in the past), and so on. Chicleros have been known to accept an *enganche* from one man and then collect chicle for another (given court costs and, since 1945, the elimination of debt peonage in Petén, jobbers tend to write off these loses without going to law), sell or destroy a contractor's equipment and then disappear into the forest, and so on. For example, in 1949 a jobber, unable to hire enough native Petén chicleros because of his shabby treatment of them during the Ubico period, had to recruit several Mexicans not personally known to him. The Mexicans took the *enganches*, collected about ninety quintals of chicle, sold them to a rival of the jobber, and then left for Mexico with the jobber's equipment. That year the jobber lost a little over Q2,000, no small sum in the context of the regional economy in 1949. Over the years other jobbers are said to have lost much larger sums.[23]

Third, recruitment generates tensions (not all of which are unpleasant) for several reasons: the rivalry and fear of deception mentioned above, the inherent uncertainty of the business (fluctuating market demands for chicle, untoward weather conditions that reduce production, and so on), anticipated hardships in the forest, the social diversity of labor crews (to be discussed below), and high hopes. Despite evidence and cautionary tales to the contrary, tappers and jobbers do have high hopes, intensifying over the days of recruitment, that this time they will realize great rewards. For younger men, this may be the first time they will be away from home and parents for an extended period. They can look forward to working with "strangers," and, before setting off to the chicle camps, they have pocket money from *enganches* with which to drink with veteran chicleros or perhaps to visit prostitutes. Recruitment brings together, particularly in Flores, San Benito, and several other central *pueblos*, men from all over Petén, Guatemala, and Central America: men of different religious, cultural, linguistic, and ethnic backgrounds, some said to be criminals evading the law—"strangers and thieves," as Peteneros say. A week or two before the chicleros leave for the forest, they are expected to go on great binges. The sprees, regarded as an inherent, almost mandatory, part of the recruitment process, add to the excitement.

Thus, if a personal approach to labor recruitment increases a jobber's chances of hiring good, trustworthy chicleros, it is also burdened with many tensions. What makes the selection of personnel so important is that, as described previously, the technology and ecology of *la chiclería* prohibit close supervision of labor. Once in the forest, the chicleros are on their own and work with very little managerial oversight. To make right choices, people must know a good deal about each other as individuals. It was noted in Chapter 2 that Peteneros commonly ascribe personality traits to one another on the basis of community membership, ethnicity, and family background, but in *la chiclería* one must judge the *individual* merits and demerits of others, and in specific relationship to oneself. Recruitment cuts across all social groupings and categories otherwise important. It involves a sharp swing away from social interaction based on ascription, to interaction based on achieved reputation and performance.

The process is not an easy one. A chiclero's or jobber's reputation, that is, past behavior, is a useful but not a sure guide to how he will act in the present. That a chiclero was loyal to a given patron last year does not necessarily mean he will be loyal this year to the same or another patron. A chiclero who believes he was badly treated by his jobber in the previous season may mask his resentment, accept an *enganche*, and then hire on with another jobber. Of course a chiclero who consistently acts badly or lacks tapping skills will eventually find himself without any source of employment, but in the meantime no one can be absolutely sure about him. Achieved reputations must constantly be validated.

Precisely because the *contratista* cannot supervise his workers and often fears they may deceive him, he tries to gain their loyalty, not only by fair treatment, but also by personalizing his relationships with them. Despite the often considerable social and economic distance ordinarily separating them, jobbers may treat some of their chicleros as if they were social equals, friends for whom they are concerned over and above business. Other chicleros may be treated as subordinates, the traditional clients of traditional patrons. In either case, a jobber will warmly encourage his men to buy supplies and alchohol on credit at his store. Reciprocally, chicleros treat their employers with respectful, but not servile, familiarity. Thus, although contractors and chicleros select each other in terms of impersonal performance criteria, the relationship between them is also a personal one.

As implied above, the relationship between a contractor and a chiclero is not always that of patron to client. Although some maintain this sort of tie, most do not. Commonly neither party assumes any special responsibility for the other once the chicle collecting season is over. Labor turnover in *la chiclería* is high, and most chicleros have worked for several jobbers. Konrad (1981) notes that in Yucatán, men with ten or more years of experience as chicleros usually have worked for as many as six jobbers. The high turnover is partly related to rivalry among contractors for chicleros, but also to fluctuations in market demands for chicle, political problems in getting contracts, and so on, which cause a jobber to reduce or change the composition of his labor force from year to year. It is important to note that until recently only rarely would a jobber have been able to offer off-season employment to many of his chicleros, although he might give the best of them small loans or political support to induce the man to continue working for him. Until the 1970s, once the tapping season was over chicleros from Petén returned to their milpas, and jobbers had little need for their labor. As one chiclero put it, "There is no special relation between the contractor and the chiclero in the dry season because the patron is often without money. At times, FYDEP does not pay on time or at all, and so the patron is short of money. He may have to sell to other contractors to get money." Perhaps because jobber-chiclero relations are personalized, Peteneros tend to discuss the absence of patronage and the high turnover of personnel in *la chiclería* in moral terms. Important as moral considerations may be, labor turnover and limited patronage are or were the result of economic conditions in *la chiclería* and in Petén generally. The regional economy and the structure of the chicle enterprise weakened the material ground for sustained patron-client relations.

The relationship between a chiclero and his *patrón* is, then, ambivalent and ambiguous. A contractor who personally recruits chicleros increases his chances of having a successful season. A chiclero who works for a contractor he knows well lowers his risk of being deceived. Hence, mutual selection in recruitment is based on and carried out with displays of friendship and patronage. Each party uses both particularistic and performance norms ("traditional" and "modern" standards, if one prefers) to evaluate the other. The personalization of the relationship is supposed to build trust, and contractors and chicleros usually do deal fairly with each other. Yet mutual suspicion is never far from the surface, often leading to anticipatory deceptions which confirm the necessity for their use, and making the role of patron difficult to sustain. Ambivalence in the relationship was demonstrated during the 1930s and 1940s, when contractors sometimes held their ritual kinsmen, neighbors, and even relatives in debt peonage, coercing them to remain in the forest. People who normally were most trusted became in *la chiclería* those who were most feared.[24] This does not mean that mistreatment and bad faith occurred all the time between all parties. Were this true, the business would not have endured as long as it did. Rather, these things happened often enough to maintain disquietude about relationships in *la chiclería*.

A Case Study of Diverse Relations

A single example drawn from the town of San Martín (pseudonym) illustrates the complexity of relationships in the chicle economy.[25] About 35 percent of adult males in San Martín regularly collect chicle. In 1963, of 290 adult males, 23 were part-time (average age, 39.9 years) and 65 were full-time chicleros (average age, 29.7 years). For the sake of brevity, discussion is limited to the 65 full-time chicleros, 2 jobbers, and 1 subcontractor from San Martín.

Of the 65 full-time chicleros, 46 were Catholic, 13 Protestant, and 6 unaffiliated; 46 were born in San Martín (32 Indians and 14 Ladinos); and of the other 19 men, 2 were born in Petén, 6 in Alta Verapaz, 6 in other Guatemalan departments, 2 in Belize, and 3 in Mexico. Eight of the men were independent chicleros; the others signed contracts for either 5 or 10 quintals of chicle. The 65 full-time chicleros, including the 8 independents, worked for 11 contractors, 4 of whom were from San Martín, 4 from Flores, 1 from Dolores, 1 from San Benito, and 1 from Belize but resident in Carmelita, San Andrés. Thirty-three of the 65 men worked for two San Martineros, don Fulano and Julano.

Don Fulano formally hired 24 chicleros born (17) or now resident (7) in San Martín, and also regularly bought chicle from 4 of the independents. Of the 17 chicleros born in San Martín, several were his *compadres*, and 3 had been his debt peons in the 1940s. Of the other 7, 3 were Cobaneros who had worked for don Fulano since they were teenagers, and 2 were Peteneros who had lived in San Martín for several years. The remaining 2 men, from Guatemala City, were said to be highly skilled "rascals"; in fact, they took don Fulano's *enganche* and sold their chicle to a Flores merchant, don Megano, a *compadre* of don Fulano. One of the rascals gave his reason for doing so as "Don Fulano did not attend me properly." Don Fulano divided the 24 men into two camp groups, one of them composed exclusively of men born in San Martín. Don Fulano's head muleteer, an Honduran, usually resided in San Martín.

Julano, much younger than don Fulano, was much admired by the chicleros, and some of the best tappers in Petén worked for him. He himself had been a skilled chiclero, was liked by the chicleros because he dealt fairly with them and "visited them in the forest," and provided work and small loans to his better, more loyal chicleros during the off-season. Because of his reputation and his regular camp visits he, unlike don Fulano, almost never suffered losses of equipment or *enganches*. In 1963 Julano had a contract with FYDEP and a deal with don Megano, the Flores merchant mentioned above. A politically well connected kinsman of Megano living in Guatemala City used to secure large FYDEP contracts for 500 quintals of chicle, and Megano oversaw the business. Don Megano worked exclusively through subcontractors, one of whom was Julano. The subcontractors purchased their equipment and supplies from don Megano, who claimed that as much of his profit came from these sales as from the margin on the chicle.

During the early 1960s Julano regularly worked with some 40 chicleros. Nine of his chicleros were from San Martín, including 2 younger brothers (another kinsman was his head muleteer). It is interesting that several of these men were Ladinos who, despite the deference they showed Julano (of Indian descent), had never asked him to become a *compadre*. Another of Julano's chicleros was an extraordinarily productive tapper who was quite unreliable. Julano felt he would work out: "If he cheats me, now no one will hire him. He must be honest (*formal*) now. He also knows that if he is not, I am going to get even (*componerlo*)." Another of Julano's chicleros, from Santa Clara, a neighboring township, used to tease that Julano obtained chicle from Santa Clara but claimed it was from San Martín, that is, "cheated" the man's community. "But," the chiclero said, "he is more honest than other contractors, so I have been his chiclero for a long time." Julano, who never denied the charge, usually responded with some sort of counterjibe. Another of Julano's regular chicleros was an excellent hunter; the camps in which he stayed rarely lacked meat. Julano admired the man's forest skills but, despite their long-standing relationship, held and masked a grudge against him because some eighteen months earlier he had had a fist fight (ostensibly about religious differences) with Julano's brother. After 1963 the man went to work for another contractor.

Julano also worked with a San Martinero subcontractor, usually advancing him Q500 at the beginning of the tapping season to collect 50 quintals of chicle.[26] The 50 quintals would be turned over to don Megano. Julano's subcontractor worked with two of his sons, a *compadre*, and, in 1963, a newcomer to San Martín. A third son decided not to work with his father in 1963, but rather to sign a contract with a jobber, "to be more on [his] own."

As remarked, in addition to Julano, don Megano had a second subcontractor in San Martín, Paco, who collected 200 quintals of chicle for him. Paco began as a chiclero, became a subcontractor and eventually a contractor, although some say his chicle business was a cover for archeological relic smuggling. Throughout rural Mexico and Central America, those who become successful are said to owe their fortune to finding buried treasure, to deals with the devil or with goblins, or to some sort of illegal activity. These explanations, of course, lack verity, but at the same time Paco was uncommonly knowledgeable about ancient Mayan ruins. Paco, like Julano, has been upwardly mobile; in addition to becoming relatively affluent, both men have served as *alcalde* of San Martín, but Julano has a better reputation. The difference is that Paco charged his chicleros more for supplies than Julano and in other ways cut corners. Reciprocally, he had more labor management problems than Julano, enough so that he eventually quit contracting altogether. Afterward, in the 1970s, Paco became a trucker, large-scale commercial farmer, and political middleman, but, in part because of endless problems with labor, he has been unable to match Julano's economic success. Nevertheless, for Paco, as for Julano, *la chiclería* provided the means to upward mobility.

Several conclusions may be drawn from the preceding discussion. First, the structure of the chicle economy is complex, and marked by an uneasy mix of personal social relationships and those that are impersonal and strictly economic. Second, a significant proportion of a jobber's profit comes from the sale of supplies to labor, a point that will be taken up later. Third, chicleros have not simply been a servile labor force. As they say, "We, too, have our defenses." Particularly after 1945, when the number of contractors and subcontractors relative to the number of workers increased, along with contractor rivalry, chicleros were in a better position to choose their patrons. Moreover, for technoenvironmental reasons, management has always found on-site supervision of labor difficult in *la chiclería*; if pressed too hard, chicleros could always flee into the deep forest. Nevertheless, contractors not only have usually had the advantage over chicleros but, except for a brief period between 1945 and 1954, the state has supported contractors over chicleros, an issue discussed more fully below. Among this advantaged group, Flores merchant-contractors have had the greatest access to credit and the best political connections to the state.

Chicle Camps and Chicleros' Wages

Before going into more specific detail about labor control, several aspects of camp life and chicleros' wages will be discussed.

As previously remarked, the recruitment process ends with great binges, after which the chicleros depart for the forest camps. Between 1931 and 1975, most flew from Santa Elena to bush airports, little more than cleared strips in the woods, and then usually walked to camps located at least several hours away from even the smallest hamlet.[27] (Since the late 1970s, an increasing number of chicleros have been trucked to or near their camps.) From this point on until the end of the season, the muleteers and truckers who bring supplies and mail to the camps and take out the chicle are the main and sometimes the sole contact between the chicleros and the outside world. Even today, despite the use of trucks and a shorter season, some chicleros are effectively isolated from other people for several months at a stretch.

Modern camps range in size from six to twenty-five chicleros, but most consist of about ten to twenty men and, normally, a foreman and a cook. The cook often has a toddler with her. Some camps consist exclusively of men from the same community and ethnic group (a situation contractors prefer, in the belief that homogeneity reduces the possibility of conflicts among the men) while others are remarkably heterogenous. For example, in 1975, of the seven men in a small camp, one, related to one of Petén's best known families, was a well-educated raconteur who narrated to his camp

Table 4:7 Chiclero Census from Northwest Petén, 1974

Number = 135

Age: Mean 34 years   Median 33 years   Range 15–64 years

Percent married: 39.1

Religion:	Catholic	90 (66.7)
	Protestant	21 (15.6)
	None	15 (11.1)
	Not determined	9 (6.7)

Ethnicity:	Ladino	89 (65.9)
	Indian	41 (30.4)
	Black	2 (1.5)
	Not determined	3 (2.2)

Origin:	Petén	56 (41.5)
	Alta Verapaz	9 (6.7)
	Baja Verapaz	40 (29.6)
	Other Guatemalan departments	13 (9.6)
	Foreign countries	14 (10.4)
	Not determined	3 (2.2)

Number of men sharing a *champa* (lean-to):   Mean = 2   Range = 1–4

Source: Field Notes 1974–1975. Percentages in parentheses; errors due to rounding to nearest tenth.

The table is not representative of the entire chiclero population, primarily because it includes 40 Ladinos from from Baja Verapaz. The chicleros were divided into six chicle camps. There was a female cook in all but one camp. In four camps, the cooks had 1–2 children with them. Konrad (1981) reports that most Yucatecan chicleros are between 21–40 years old, 72 percent are married and have about 10 years of experience in *la chiclería*.

mates abridged versions of novels such as *A Tale of Two Cities* and *The Count of Monte Cristo*; two were Mexicans illegally in Guatemala; a fourth was a seasonal worker of middle class Guatemala City background; and the other three were Peteneros (one of whom was bilingual in Spanish and Kekchí) from *campesino* families from two Petén townships. Most camps fall between these extremes, but consist of men who differ in religion, ethnicity, place of origin (Table 4:7), and experience. Although novice chicleros respect and seek advice from experienced "veterans," as they call them, veterans do not give orders to novices and do not offer them much help unless asked. Despite differences in experience (roughly correlated with age), the men treat each other as peers. However heterogeneous the composition, the point is that during the tapping season a chiclero's reference group, the one with which he identifies and in terms of which he evaluates himself, is a camp unit made up of equals. Chicleros like to say, "We are brothers here" (the men never use any other term of kinship to describe camps).

Aside from common occupation, shared poverty, and isolation, several other factors probably quicken the sense of equality among tappers. Chicle tree tapping is a hand technology attended by uncertain outcomes, most chicleros own a machete (the chief tool of the trade), camp life involves intense face-to-face contact, and worker supervision is perforce limited. Applebaum (1981:135) points out that these circumstances tend to promote independence, self-esteem (if not pride), and equality among workers, such as those in the construction industry. At the same time there is a good deal of quiet rivalry among the men to see who can collect the most chicle, and the most productive chicleros are almost invariably those who say the least about differences in ability.

Internally, a camp is divided into a series of two-to-three man units (*compañeros* or buddies), a foreman, and a cook. Occasionly as many as ten men share a *champa*, an unwalled lean-to with thatch roof, sometimes sardonically dubbed "the hotel of the four winds." There are some chicleros who prefer to live and work alone, but more typically a *champa* houses two or three men. These buddies go off together in search of chicle trees, look out for each other's safety, eat together, share confidences, and so forth. When there are ten men sharing a *champa*, they too tend to break down into two- or three-person units. In the off-season the buddies may or may not reside near and maintain close relations with each other.

Quite commonly, there are kinsmen (and ritual kinsmen) in a camp— brothers, cousins, fathers, and sons—who may or may not share a *champa*. Several sons or nephews of the camp foreman or subcontractor may also be present, but the foreman treats them as he does any other chiclero. To judge from social interaction in the camps, it is almost as if ties of kinship were suspended during the tapping season. Nevertheless, when a senior kinsman is the foreman, his presence may encourage his junior relatives to be on their best behavior.

The foreman (*capataz*) is the first among equals and usually several years

Figure 4:2. Descending a chicle tree.

Figure 4:3. Preparing chicle in front of a *champa*.

older than most of the others in camp. In addition to payment for the chicle he collects, he receives Q1 for each quintal of chicle the other men collect. His major responsibilities are to locate good tapping areas, to decide when to relocate the camp, to maintain internal order in camp, to keep written accounts of each man's production and purchases from the contractor, and to set a work pace. "Most of all," an older chiclero says, "he is also a chiclero." Contractors seek foremen who have both superior technical skills and the respect of others. Today as in the past, contractors hire foremen on the basis of proven performance. Considerations of ethnicity, religion, community, and so on, important during the off-season, are now irrelevant or decidedly secondary.

Successful foremen, normally quiet men, are supportive rather than directive leaders and rarely issue orders. In this they resemble nineteenth-century North American cowboy foremen. "You were supposed to know your business, so the wise foreman never gave orders or made them explicit although indirect suggestions might be made" (Weston 1985:61). As one informant put it:

> The *capataz* is a chiclero, and he must be a good one so that the others [chicleros] will be good too. I have three foremen. The chiclero can ask to work with this or that foreman, and the patron says all right, but if too many want to work with one man, I tell them the camp is full . . . Too many men in one camp will ruin the work there [deplete the trees too quickly], and they accept this . . . Say the men are behind in their work,then you [foreman] . . . say, "Look boys, I want you to help me. I am a chiclero too, and I want three *marquetas* each chiclero in so many days" . . . Then they use their strength, and they are thanked, for example, give all of them cigarettes, and it is a big thing in the forest . . . When one of them says to me, no, because the trees are such and such, I climb up at once [and] afterwards they are ashamed (Field Notes 1975).

In a large, productive, well-run camp, there may be a second man who is quicker than the *capataz* to criticize men who are not using their strength or not behaving properly. The second man, who may be called the *consejero* (adviser), is more intimate with the *capataz* than others, and this is probably why he can get away with carping at the men. His role is not formally recognized, and some chicleros and most contractors would deny it exists, but experienced foremen point out that they, too, need someone to talk things over with (hence, *consejero*) and someone who does what they prefer not to do — speak plainly to malefactors. Chicleros usually esteem foremen, and while they tolerate *consejeros*, they are also irked by them.

It does not detract from the skills of the foremen to remark that the nature of the work practically determines their style. Ecological and technical conditions prevent close supervision of the chicleros. Tree tapping is a solitary activity, and the labor force is dispersed during the work day. Moreover, a disgruntled chiclero can easily leave one camp and attach himself to another or even work by himself (although, as will be seen, the Ubico government took steps to prevent this). Thus, a foreman is almost obliged to be a supportive leader. Even with tyros, successful foremen do not issue orders but rather make suggestions in a soft, often circumspect manner. The foreman comes first, but he really is first among equals.

Because tree tapping is stressful, chicleros turn to the cook as well as to their buddies for consolation. Among nonchicleros, as well as among some chicleros, cooks have a bad reputation. It is often said that they [chicleros] sometimes fight over the cook who is almost always a single woman and a whore. It is rare when the cook does not sleep with the men for money. The men sometimes fight over her because two of them may want to sleep with her at the same time. Generally the fighting is in the form of satire and insults, but a bad fight with machetes is rare. Chicleros are like *compañeros* and brothers and get along well with each other in the forest (Field Notes 1978).

Interestingly enough, the jobber cited here does not allow "loose" women, much less known prostitutes, in his camps, but cultural definitions of gender make it nearly inevitable that a woman, especially if divorced or single, working away from home in an otherwise all-male group will be morally suspect. Chicleros do snub each other and quarrel because of the cook, but more often than not they are competing for her nutrient attention rather than her sexual favors. More chicleros want to talk with her about the day's events, have her add some extra sugar to their coffee, whisper to her of some hurt, and so on, than want to couple with her, and it is this that puts the cook in a position to stir up or to pacify tensions in camp. In any event, in camp the men treat the cook with courtesy and respect.[28]

Endless talk about violence in the chicle camps is even more exaggerated than gossip about cooks. During the first two decades of this century there was some violence connected with chicle collecting, but later tales of such conflict outran its incidence. Today, when a situation becomes very tense, the parties involved are much more likely to avoid each other than to fight. A case in point occurred during 1975 when Mexican and Petén chicleros sharing a camp were upset about the paucity of good trees to tap near their camp. For some reason the cook began to serve larger portions of food to the Mexicans than to the Peteneros, but little was said about this until a quarrel over a card game became the occasion to vent anger over who got how much food. Some men began to avoid each other, and others traded joking insults. Then one afternoon several of the younger men seemed prepared to fight each other, and the foreman had great difficulty in calming them. The next day, without saying anything to the foreman, the Mexicans left and set up a new camp several kilometers away, but the cook remained with the Peteneros. Since apparently there were too many chicleros (thirty-seven) in the original camp relative to the number of chicle trees in the area, the move would have been sensible even had there been no trouble, but everyone defined the situation in terms of the cook's excessive attention to a few of the Mexicans and to Mexican hotheadedness (according to the Peteneros), or to the way Peteneros quietly harbor grievances (according to the Mexicans). In another instance, a cook who had been living with one man took up with his best friend in camp without ceasing to flirt with her original friend. Everyone expected all sorts of trouble, but in the end the men simply changed *champa* mates.

Camps are moved about every six to eight weeks because productive trees in the vicinity are played out. At this point, the composition of a crew may change. Some men may decide to join another crew or to work under another foreman, others may feel they cannot collect much more chicle and are better off returning home to attend their milpas, and so on. Although a plurality of camps largely maintain their composition throughout the season, relocation does give the men socially acceptable occasions to withdraw from unpleasant situations, which also reduces the chances for overt conflict. The men may also become fretful and irritable when there are too few good chicle trees near the camp. This may generate quarrels, which can provide the men with an excuse to split up. That is, social situations can provide rationalizations and occasions for doing what in any case is ecologically/economically prudent.

This is not to deny that there are quarrels in camp. As a chiclero explains:

> There are always little arguments, about *egoismo* [selfishness] because some men get out more chicle than others. But it is not grave, just bad feelings. There are very few ways to enjoy yourself there [in the woods] as the men work long hours and hard. At times they play cards at night for money or cigarettes . . . but not fighting over this with machetes (Field Notes 1975).

Certain things easily attributed to human action, such as a spilled or vanished bag of chicle or a missing article of personal property, are more usually blamed on goblins (*duendes*) than on camp mates. The evidence from direct observation, interviews with chicleros, and court records indicates that despite (or because of) the pressures under which chicleros live and the heterogeneity of camp crews, physical aggression is nowhere nearly as common as the talk about it. Contrary to the evidence, chicleros as well as nonchicleros promote the belief that the chicle fields are places of great violence. The reason for their maintaining this story will be discussed later.

Chicleros are far more concerned with how much money they make than with stereotypes about camp life. In comparison with other rural workers, chicleros have been and are relatively well paid (how much money they keep is another matter), particularly in view of their age and marital status.

Table 4:8 Chicleros and Milperos: San Andrés, Petén, 1975

		Chicleros		Milperos	
Number		53		158	
Age: Mean years		26.4		38.9	
Percent married		47.2		63.3	
Religion:	Catholic	41	(77.4)	124	(78.5)
	Protestant	8	(15.1)	25	(15.8)
	None	3	(5.7)	6	(3.8)
	Not determined	1	(1.9)	3	(1.9)
Descent:	Ladino	15	(28.3)	35	(22.2)
	Maya	36	(67.9)	113	(71.5)
	Mixed	2	(3.9)	10	(6.3)

Source: Field Notes 1974–1975. Percentages in parentheses; errors due to rounding to nearest tenth.

The table compares (i) men who usually worked full-time as chicleros and made no milpa in 1974–1975 with (ii) men who usually worked full-time as milperos and collected no chicle in 1974–1975. The year 1975 was chosen to facilitate comparison with Table 4:7, but data for 1960 show similar results, e.g., mean age of tappers in 1960 was 29.7 years. The sample is representative of religious and ethnic divisions in the town. In 1975, of 15 men involved in other aspects of *la chiclería* (9 jobbers, 1 subjobber, 1 foreman, 1 warehouseman, and 3 muleteers) mean age was 44.3 years; 86.7 percent were married; 73.3 percent were Catholic, 26.7 percent Protestant; 40 percent Ladino, 60 percent Maya. There is a statistically significant difference between chicleros and milperos with respect to marital status ($X^2 = 4.27$).

Insofar as one may judge from San Andrés, and the evidence from San Andrés seems typical enough, the major sociological difference between chicleros and milperos is that the former tend to be younger and less often married than the latter (Table 4:8). In the first quarter of the century, when labor was scarce in Petén, chicleros were "the best-paid laborers of the Republic. They receive[d] $10 gold for each quintal . . . from $25 to $30 United States gold per month" (Hoar 1924:6). In 1904, Maler (1908a:8) noted that woodcutters, chicleros, and *huleros* "receive high wages, free board and . . . many hundred pesos in advance." Their income made them open-handed, hence the saying: *"El chiclero no pide vuelto"* (Chicleros do not ask for change). Forty years later, Whetten (1961:147) reported about the same thing, saying that the high wages were "partly in compensation for . . . long periods of absence . . . from their families, and for the risks from exposure to tropical disease." At that time, chicleros earned about

Q250 (by collecting ten quintals of chicle) in five to six months, and Guatemalan farm workers made Q160 to Q270 per year (Adams 1970:388–90). Chicleros also earned more than Petén milperos (Schwartz 1968:83–86). In the early 1980s, they made between Q500 and Q1,000 per season, or about Q2.50 to Q5.00 per day (see Table 4:6), a wage that compared favorably with Petén farm wages (about Q2.00 per day) and certainly with south coast farm wages (about Q1.04 to Q1.50 per day). (Between 1980 and 1981, the government raised the minimum rural wage to Q3.20 per day, but few employers complied.) Chicleros have not been grandly rewarded, but on average they have earned more than most workers in Petén and the rest of the country.[29]

Since the early 1960s, chicleros have also been able to devote the off-season to the collection of other forest products, shate and pimienta. In 1978, for example, a man who collected shate from February to June (although it may be collected year round), pimienta from July to August and chicle from September to January could earn Q2,736. If he had a wife and two to four children, his annual expenses would come to about Q2,016, and he could net as much as Q720 that year. Most forest collectors did not realize this much for any of several reasons, such as serious illness in the family, unpaid travel time seeking patrons, or drought, but they earned more than milperos.

To optimize income, a forest collector (chiclero, shatero, or pimentero) had to be especially careful about his expenses during the time he spent in the forest. The major outlay was for food, Q22.84 per month, in 1978. (See Table 4:9; the figures are typical of the diet and food costs in chicle camps.) Provided a chiclero cooked and did laundry for himself, did not use tobacco, and did not buy medicine, he spent about Q137.04 during the tapping season and also had about Q90 in *mensualidades* deducted from his wages. Since clothing, medical, and other costs for self and family during the season could easily amount to Q250, only a very frugal and healthy chiclero would have netted Q500; on average Q250 to Q300 is more realistic. Even so, chicleros earned more than milperos because they had another half year to devote to some other income-producing activity. If a chiclero's father or son at home made a milpa for the family, the advantage over the full-time milpero was that much greater. Although an extended dry period and inflated prices for maize could reduce a chiclero's advantage, the conclusion reached here is the same as Konrad's (1981) in his comparison of chicleros with other workers in Yucatán. (Interestingly,

Table 4:9 Monthly Diet and Food Costs for Chicleros, 1978

Food item	Amount		Cost in quetzales
Maize	50 pounds		4.00
Beans	8 pounds		3.20
Sugar	8 pounds		1.44
Lard	8 pounds		5.60
Wheat flour	8 pounds		2.40
Salt	2 pounds		.20
Coffee	1 bottle		4.00
Dry milk	4 cans		6.00
		Total	Q 22.84

Source: Field Notes 1978, including receipts provided by a contractor who regularly works with about 80 chicleros. Following the custom in Petén, pounds are used above.

nineteenth century North American cowboys, who resembled chicleros in some ways, also earned more than farmers.)[30]

Konrad also found that the children of chicleros are better educated than their peers. This is not the case in Petén, but, as mentioned, chicleros have been prominent among upwardly mobile *poblanos* (townsmen outside of Flores), especially since 1945. While some milperos who have never been chicleros have obtained enough formal education to secure, for example, a government post, the more common pattern has been that of chicleros who become foremen, subcontractors, or muleteers, and finally merchant-contractors. They then try to educate their children for careers as bureaucrats, teachers, or professionals. This also often means that the children will eventually move to Flores or Guatemala City.

However, neither the degree nor the frequency of upward mobility must be overstated. *Poblanos* who have improved their economic status through *la chiclería* are not so wealthy as their counterparts from old (Flores) elite families who have succeeded in the chicle economy. (Some old families have also lost fortunes in the business, but their social connections and education usually give them, more than others, opportunities to rise again.) Men who migrated to Petén in the early 1900s and became wealthy in *la chiclería* have usually married into the old elite families, which almost never happens in the instance of upwardly mobile *poblanos*.

Of course, relatively few chicleros were upwardly mobile, and although on average they earned more than milperos, most were not dramatically better-off, and some ended their careers in *la chiclería* "with nothing but a pair of pants." This raises the question of noneconomic motives for tapping chicle trees. Since it has been fully explored elsewhere (Schwartz 1974), a summary statement may suffice here.

No doubt the main motive for tapping chicle trees was (and is) economic, which includes the paucity, until recently, of viable alternatives to farm work. For teen-age Peteneros, however, *la chiclería* also was a passage to adulthood. The recruitment process, as described above, offered adolescent males an exciting opportunity to learn about forest lore and the wider world, to earn some money they could spend as they pleased on sprees and on women, and to free themselves of parental supervision. Now they could be independent workers, associating with all sorts of men who treated them as grown-up equals. Life in the chicle camps had (and has) many liminal dimensions, which sharply constrasted with life at home. The following are but two examples of the contrast. Tapping trees is profane, but making a milpa is, if not quite sacred, then at least morally safe. Peteneros use the idiom of "brotherhood," of equals, to describe their relationships with co-workers in the camps, which are associated with deep forests. But they speak of fathers and sons, of hierarchy, to describe co-workers in the milpa, which is associated with the community. The liquidation process involves a period of reincorporation back into the household, the milpa, and the community, but now as one who has "suffered" in isolated forest camps. For girls, the much celebrated fifteenth birthday publicly marks the transition into young womanhood, but for boys there is no corresponding ritual, except insofar as *la chiclería* can (or could) be secondarily adapted for that purpose, and some Peteneros are explicit in stating that *la chiclería* makes men of boys. In a society where fathers are conventionally defined as "strong and hard," and in fact are often absent from home, and where mothers are defined as "sacred and soft," and in fact constantly keep little boys as well as little girls at their side, perhaps there is a need for some institutionalized mechanism to help boys become men. This is not to argue that needs automatically give rise to institutions that satisfy them, certainly not in the short run, but rather to say that chicleros from Petén incidentally, but perhaps not accidentally, have used and still use what is primarily an economic activity for ritual purposes.

Returning to economic considerations, it should be noted that although the chicleros' employers made money from selling chicle, another important source of their income was the sale of overpriced supplies to their workers. In the past,

> the 'chiclero' had to buy his necessities . . . from the chicle contractor, for there were, of course, no shops in the forest, and the nearest village might have been anything from four to six days' journey . . . The very high prices he paid were partly due to the expense of transporting food to outlying camps, often through great stretches of swamp in which the mules sank sometimes to their knees, partly to the greed of the contractor (Thompson 1963:159).

Even today, a contractor says,

> Much of the profit from chicle, my profit, comes from selling things to the chicleros in the woods. Medicines. The most profitable thing to sell them is penicillin. I get a lot of profit from that (Field Notes 1978).

As nearly as I can judge from observation, from the account books of two contractors, and from conversations with many other contractors, foremen, and chicleros, an impressive 10 percent or more of a contractor's profit in the chicle business can come from sale of maize to his chicleros. In 1978, 55 percent of one contractor's profit came from sales of food and other items to his chicleros. Of course there are times when a contractor can sell his maize and other goods for better prices in a town than in a chicle camp. In this sense the opportunity cost (a benefit given up to obtain a competing benefit) of sales, especially of maize, to chicleros may be unreasonably high, but on average and over time the merchandising end of the business is as important as the contracting end.[31] The contractor cited above, speaking of the "fall of chicle" sums up a good deal by saying,

> I have chicleros [varying from 75 to 100 men in the 1970s–1980s], men who collect shate and pimienta for me, but I have them collecting chicle mainly to keep them working when they are not collecting shate or pimienta. *Pues*, look at the receipts. See, I make more profits from selling the chicleros penicillin, supplies, and cigarettes than I do from chicle. Chicle is nothing now, a problem with FYDEP. They [FYDEP] keep trying to screw us [contractors], so we cannot pay the men. Shate and pimienta are a good business, but not chicle. Just to give the men some work. [Do all of your shateros also collect chicle?] No, not all of them. Some of them work at the [speaker's] farm [and cattle ranch], and the rest *chicleando* [collecting chicle]. Better call them [the chicleros] "shateros" now (Field notes 1985).

Contractors have expropriated the surplus from labor, not only in terms of wages paid relative to the value of the product (and before 1945 by debt peonage), but also by provisioning what amounts to a captive market.

Wages, while hardly munificent, have been comparatively high, but so was the cost of what chicleros perforce purchased from wage payers. In the chicle economy, control of the exchange system was (and is) at least as important as control over the means of production.

Labor-Management Relations

In *la chiclería*, as in any profit-making business, there is a need for a steady supply of labor, from which a surplus is expropriated (Weinstein 1983:29). Despite several changes in labor recruitment and control, discussed below, it is worth repeating that these took place under conditions that did not permit close supervision of labor, did not narrowly restrict access to the means of production, and were not amenable to the introduction of labor-saving devices.

In the first two or three decades of the twentieth century, the heyday of chicle, labor was scarce in Petén because of the isolation and the small population. The situation was aggravated by disease, persistence of oner-ous *téquios* and taxes, political unrest, and resultant emigration. As discussed at length elsewhere (Schwartz 1971), Indians suffered dispropor-tionately from these hardships, and proportionally more Indians than La-dinos fled to British Honduras, although many emigrants returned periodically to Petén to work as chicleros.

If labor was scarce in Petén, so were wage labor opportunities. Milperos engaged in subsistence or simple commodity production had few other ways than tree tapping to earn cash. To attract labor, agents of North American chewing gum companies and *contratistas* offered enticing *enga-nches* and relatively high wages, one consequence of which was to with-draw labor from woodcutting and sugarcane production. Chicle also withdrew labor from agriculture and thus helped to create staple grain shortages. For this reason the authorities ordered that milpas be made, but compliance was not complete.[32] Chicleros had to purchase, commonly from their jobbers, maize and beans at inflated prices. They also purchased luxury goods, in part because they were novelties and in part because there was not much else to buy or in which to invest. In underpopulated Petén, land had little value, there was limited commerce and no industry. The purchases may have strengthened the bonds between contractors and chi-cleros, although not enough to overcome their inherent fragility.

Until the late 1920s violence was supposedly common in the chicle business, and no one was able or perhaps willing to control the situation.

Companies and contractors may have fostered some violence and theft by their willingness to purchase chicle from anyone without inquiring about who originally collected it. Chicleros, too, caused trouble. They "violate[d their] contracts," and this lead to "bloody conflicts between the managers and their men" (Maler 1908a:8). Older Peteneros say that contractors hired gunmen to murder chicleros in their debt, that bandits stole chicle from the camps, and that Beliceños, Mexicans, and Peteneros fought for control of productive areas. In 1916 some fifty Mexican chicleros (or revolutionaries) seized mules and chicle in Plancha de Piedra in eastern Petén to protest injustices in *la chiclería*. Two of the invaders were killed in a battle with Guatemalan troops. In another incident, Guatemalan troops searching for rebels accidently killed a member of an archeological party.[33] The movements of Mexican government and revolutionary forces along the border with northern Petén added to the fear aroused by such events. Moreover, there were said to be among the chicleros many "criminals and drifters from all over the world . . . violent hard-drinking types" (Hendrickson 1976:60), men who did not "reckon an occasional murder as any crime; it [was] just a proof of manhood" (Cordan 1963:115). (Yet, in Quintana Roo, the chicle business actually seems to have helped decrease hostilities between rebel Maya and Mexican forces.)[34] Foreign observers, along with many Peteneros, deplored the violence, the impact of chicle on milpa production and—most of all—what they considered the dissolute ways of the chicleros.[35]

Here something should be said about the image of chicleros as "good-for-nothings" (Morley's view, Brunhouse says)—dissolute, luxury-loving, unreliable, dangerous good-for-nothings (see the authors cited above and in note 35). Most older and many younger Peteneros say the same things about chicleros that foreign writers have said, and chicleros do not exactly reject the image. Yet, insofar as I know, none of the scholars and travelers cited here seems to have noticed that the "good-for-nothing" chicleros, who supposedly *refused* to work during the off-season, could hardly have found any steady work to do until recently. By the time the chicle tapping season was over (February or March, until about 1960), milpas were already cleared, and milperos had to allow the plots to dry during April and then fire them in late April or early May, depending on the weather. Chicleros who made milpas had (and still have) to spend a lot of time inspecting the plots, watching weather signs, and so on, forms of labor which may not appear as such to some observers but which are important tasks. In May they had to look for contractors, and by June they were off to the distant forests. Moreover, if chicleros used to spend large sums on luxury goods, they had until recently very little else in which to invest. More important, the expenditures helped create a network of reciprocity, which was one of the few prudent investment possibilities available in Petén. True, chicleros did and still do go on grand sprees immediately prior to leaving for their forest camps and immediately upon returning from them, but many of them also save a fair portion of their earnings. Some chicleros were and are improvident, but the same thing may be said of some milperos, some merchants and, one may imagine, some of the observers who criticized the chicleros. One need not minimize the gala aspect of the sprees to note that they also were and are ways to build a useful sense of camaraderie among the chicleros. The sprees also are, in part, ritualized ways to mark the transition from farming to tree tapping, from work-related social bonds based on ascription to those based on performance, from simple commodity production to wage labor, and so on (Schwartz 1974). Similarly, purchasing luxury goods or liquor from a merchant who often turned out to be the buyer's actual or potential chicle contractor could be one way to strengthen an otherwise fragile bond between chiclero and contractor. The improvident ways of the chicleros had an instrumental as well as a consummatory side to them. But more than anything else, that so many Peteneros and others used hyperbole to describe chicleros said something about labor-management relations in the business. The image of chicleros as improvident and violent—out of control—not only rationalized the way in which merchant-contractors overcharged and sometimes cheated chicleros but also reminded the former that there were limits to how far the latter could be pushed. The implication that chicleros were out of control may also have reflected the inability of management to closely supervise labor, that is, they were literally outside normal controls. Stereotypes about chicleros resemble those about old-time North American cowboys, probably because of several similarities in working conditions and labor-management relations (see Weston 1985).

As for violence, there is reason to believe that the reports, insofar as they relate to the chicle business, are exaggerated. Official records do not reflect the degree of violence to be expected in view of the stories about it. To illustrate, between 1893 and 1925, during what is supposed to have been the most violent period in *la chiclería*, there was an average of about one violent death or homicide every two years (aside from deaths caused by military

Table 4:10 Death by Violence, San Andrés Township, Petén, 1893–1925

| Age of deceased | Cause of death | | | Military encounter[a] |
	Firearms	Machete	Other	
21–30	5	1	2	—
31–40	2	1	2	—
41–50	1	—	—	—
51 and over	—	—	—	—
Unknown	1	—	—	21

Source: Archivo Municipal, Civil Registry, San Andrés. All but one of the deceased were male.

[a]These deaths occurred at the same time (1916), in encounters between government forces and insurgents.

action) in the township of San Andrés, a major chicle producing area covering 8,874 square kilometers, about 25 percent of Petén (Table 4:10). Even if all these deaths occurred among chicleros, the rate would be roughly 0.5 homicides per 1,000 to 1,500 chicleros per collecting season. The figure does not seem excessive, particularly in view of the isolation and limited law enforcement in the area for most of this period, and the age of the chicleros. Of course there probably were some unrecorded homicides. For example, there are creditable accounts of how in 1943 one Mexican chiclero murdered another over a gambling debt near a *caserío* some 36 kilometers northwest of the *pueblo* of San Andrés. Either because the local authorities had little interest in the event (the Mexicans were not legally in Petén) or because, as people who lived in the *caserío* say, the Mexicans were "*desconocidos y mal elementos*" (unknown or without personal ties to anyone in the *caserío*, and delinquent), the killing went without official notice. It is likely that such omissions occurred during 1893–1925. But even if the homicide rate derived from local archives is discounted, neither do available genealogies support claims of great violence. Older Peteneros from whom genealogies were obtained clearly recall which of their primary kinsmen emigrated, died of a disease or in an accident, and so forth, and there often are corroborative documents in local town hall archives. Questioning a person about his or her genealogy often triggers recollections of many details not immediately connected with kinship. The person may recall, for instance, a year in which the milpas did not produce, the time when a foreign archeologist recruited local labor, or the occasion when a brother's or neighbor's grand spree created a public scandal. Surely, if a kinsman had been murdered in the chicle fields, this too would be recalled, but the genealogies reflect far less chicle-related violence than do more generalized stories. For instance, in extensive genealogies of four San Andrés families (which included many chicleros) covering the years 1860 to 1960 and 196 marriages, among the many incidents of conflict, including those with the authorities, only one probable murder and one attempted murder (unconnected with chicle) were recalled. Most Peteneros and a majority of foreign visitors know of killings, but more often than not they heard of them from someone else who had heard from still another person, in a long chain rarely ending in an eye-witness account (unlike the killing in the *caserío* noted above). Of course, there was political unrest in and near the department, and in a small population even a single murder is frightening. However, the mixture of a few facts and many rumors about violence could have encouraged chicleros to remain close and submit to the discipline of camp life rather than wander off on their own. To the extent that supervision of chicleros was and is inherently limited, that little prevented a man from selling his product to a wide range of buyers, and that labor was scarce, the threat of violence, made real by its occasional occurrence, served the interests of managers.

As mentioned previously, chicleros do not dispute the image of themselves as prone to violence, although they phrase it in terms of "knowing how to defend" themselves. Just as the image of wild, dangerous chicleros served and still serves the interests of managers, it also served the interests of the tappers in that it cautioned that chicleros may not be endlessly "abused"—defrauded, deceived, and mistreated—without risk of retaliation. Nevertheless, management had greater power than labor. Realistic and exaggerated fear of violence cut two ways: it helped management control labor; it also warned management that there were limits to the abuses labor would accept. When Ubico took control of the government (1931–1944), he made several important changes in the chicle business. Faced with the (temporary) collapse of the coffee and banana market during the Great Depression, he took a keen interest in state revenues, including those derived from chicle production. His actions led to the export of chicle through Puerto Barrios, Guatemala, and to a reduction in the number of contractors. Ubico also tried to close the borders between Petén and British Honduras to redirect Petén trade away from Belize and toward southern Guatemala.[36] These and other actions ultimately favored Flores merchants, many of whom were, of course, chicle jobbers. As there was no all-weather road linking southern Guatemala and Petén (and would not be until 1970), in 1933 Ubico inaugurated airplane service between Santa Elena, Flores, and Puerto Barrios. Rustic airstrips were also built to serve chicle warehouse centers, at Carmelita, Paso Caballos, Uaxactún, Dos Lagunas, and elsewhere. This made it easier for contractors to hire large numbers of "Cobaneros" (Kekchí Indians from Alta Verapaz), and, along with the Depression, apparently eased the problem of labor scarcity in *la chiclería*.[37]

Ubico, as is well known, increased the centralization of government and assumed personal command of it. In 1936 he replaced popularly elected mayors with *intendentes*, who were to be appointed by the national executive upon recommendation of departmental governors. As a rule, intendents were not native to the township in which they served. Municipal secretaries who might also be merchants and/or chicle contractors often controlled and commonly had great influence with the intendents. In Petén, and presumably elsewhere, intendents were usually closely allied with or subordinate to local elites.

Intendents and governors helped contractors to control the chicle labor force in several ways. As chicle production recovered, the men had to sign contracts to collect at least twenty quintals. Until a chiclero fulfilled his quota or until the season was over, he could not leave the forest camp without written permission from the *capataz*. If he did do so, the local authorities forced him to return, and the police or the governor might administer a beating to hasten his trip. Some men were taken to the public square in Flores, beaten on the buttocks with a stick, jailed, and then returned to the forest. Others were beaten in the governor's office. The following is a typical report of those days:

> In the time of Ubico . . . one had to fulfill his contract before coming down from the woods, and one could not leave until then, except for illness or something like that. But younger brothers took care of the [milpa] harvest. One had to have the permission of the foreman, a pass for fifteen days or a month. If the soldiers or someone saw you walking around in the *pueblo* during the chicle season and knew you were a chiclero, they would tell the authorities, and then the authorities would ask you why you were in the town and you had to show them the pass. There is no permission [needed] to come down now. Now, it is not demanded, and if they did demand it, the chicleros would run away to some

other place [as some did during Ubico's time] . . . there is less discipline now. Luis Camal [once] came down . . . without permission. When he got here, he went to see his wife who was ill in the house. He saw her and was walking in the streets when the patrol saw him. The soldiers [militia] asked him what he was doing here . . . He did not have a pass, and they hit him in the head with the end of a rifle and took him to the intendent. The intendent scolded him [*le regañó*; in Petén this is very serious; men say, "Do not scold me (*no me regañe*), I have but one father"] and told him to go back to [don Fulano's] camp. The intendents almost worked for don Fulano [a township secretary, who, with his nephew, employed almost all the chicleros from the *pueblo* under discussion between the late 1920s and 1945]. They [don Fulano and his nephew] never paid correctly. They would sell something on credit and then charge three times the correct amount in the books. Some [Indians] could not read too well anyhow. If they decided to go to the Judge of First Instance, don Fulano and don Julano [the nephew] paid bribes. They had stores and chicleros and all the accounts were with them [held by them], but mostly those of the illiterates. The Ladinos . . . could read and write . . . Things were better with Ubico, more orderly (Field notes 1960).

(The "accounts" were the receipts a tapper received at the end of the season for his chicle and supplies purchased in camp, and paper chits (redeemable at local stores and saloons), which, at least in some *pueblos*, contractors gave chicleros in lieu of cash. The merchants were cronies of the contractors.) Although there seems to have been some limit to the brutality (for example in 1939, Ubico removed General Federico Ponce Vaides from the governorship of Petén for excessive cruelty), it is easy enough to understand why many Peteneros refer to this period as "the time of the sticks" (*de los palos*). Certainly the authorities were often heavy-handed before Ubico came to power, but his appointees were rigorous about labor control.

Many chicleros were, besides, held in debt peonage. In 1934 debt peonage laws were officially abrogated (and replaced by equally onerous vagrancy laws), but it was early 1945 before debt bondage ended in Petén (where the vagrancy laws had less affect than elsewhere in Guatemala). At the conclusion of the tapping season, companies, government agencies, contractors, and chicleros did and still do "liquidate" their mutual accounts. Prior to 1945 the receipts for *enganches*, chicle, *mensualidades*, and supplies were held by the contractor. Aside from charging inflated prices for supplies, some contractors falsified receipts and, as one of them explained, "fooled the men on the weights, because illiterates were deceived when *arrobas* were made into kilograms." They also encouraged indebtedness by lending chicleros money to go on binges during "liquidation." Consequently, a chiclero might end the season in debt to his patron. He then was forced to work off the debt at the contractor's milpa or sugarcane field at wages set by the contractor, and to continue collecting chicle for him. When necessary, a contractor called upon the authorities to coerce the chiclero to honor his debts. Although contractors sometimes overextended themselves in lending to chicleros to secure an adequate labor force, and although they sometimes suffered financial losses when chicleros fled to British Honduras, Mexico, or the deep forest to avoid paying their debts, they nevertheless had the better of the situation. The following statement of one worker is almost a refrain among older chicleros and their children:

> In the time of Ubico, there were no such receipts [as are now given to chicleros], not for the chicle nor the food. The chicle was not weighed in camp, but in Santa Elena, in the warehouse of Wrigley (where one could be short-weighted). My father told me one time he had to work to pay a debt, for six years. His patron was don Julano. He came out [at the end of his career as a chiclero] with two pairs of shoes, two shirts, and two pairs of pants. He could not get his liquidation papers, but the gringos did not mix in this. They just paid the contractors, and even gave them big advances if their mules died or they needed money. In those days, contractors got the money for the humidity [content of chicle]. Now, when the chicle is weighed in Santa Elena, the chiclero gets the [bonus] for the humidity . . . [Today] there cannot be arguments over the amount of chicle, as the chiclero sees and signs a receipt at weighing time [and] when a chiclero takes an advance and does not work, it is too hard to take him to court. It costs him [the contractor] too much, but no one hires him if he does this too much (Field notes 1974).

This, too, is reminiscent of the late-nineteenth-century cattle industry in the United States. Managers defrauded prodigal cowboys, and after many years on the trail, cowboys wound up with nothing more than "high-heeled shoes, the striped pants and about $4.80 worth of other clothes" (Weston 1985:37).[38]

As indicated above, most of the men—and they were always men—held in debt peonage were illiterate, which meant that they were more usually Indians than Ladinos. Quite often, debtors were the ritual kinsmen—godchildren or *compadres*—of the lender, and there is no more doubt that some debtors found a measure of security in the bond than there is that some merchant-contractors felt a moral obligation to extend material and political favors to their worker-*compadre*-customers. But the majority of debtors have bitter memories about those days. After 1945 many of them opposed their former patrons in politics and preferred not to work for them, although they still deferred to them in face-to-face encounters. In the early 1940s at least forty chicleros had debts with the two contractors in one *pueblo*, about 16 to 25 percent of their labor force. Of course debt peonage existed in Petén prior to 1931–1944, but it appears to have been more extensive and onerous during these years than earlier. Violence, whatever there was of it in the early years of *la chiclería*, was replaced by more systematic state repression under Ubico.

By 1943–1944 Ubico's personal dictatorship had become less effective, and many of his one-time allies withdrew active support from his regime. This permitted university students and the small middle class in the national capital, along with others, to topple Ubico. The events following the 1944–1945 Revolution had several important consequences for the chicle economy, several of which were discussed previously in dealing with the statistics of chicle production and the organization of chiclero labor.

Freely elected reform governments, led by Presidents Juan José Arévalo (1945–1950) and Jacobo Arbenz (1951–1954), tried to increase lower sector power through open competitive elections, mass organizations of peasants and industrial workers, and judicial and agrarian reform. Arbenz also hoped to give the republic more alternatives in the international arena. In reaction, upper sectors of the society became better organized than before. The Arbenz regime, by concentrating on land reform (which brought it into conflict with the United Fruit Company) and by pursuing closer relations with Eastern European communist nations, challenged Guatemala's traditional oligarchy and the government of the United States. In 1954 a CIA financed counterrevolution initiated a long period of military dominance over Guatemala.

Post-1954 regimes have promoted upper-sector economic interests, including the export of cotton from the early 1960s on and the export of beef from the early 1970s on, and controlled them through regulatory agencies. The elite in commercial agriculture, industry, and finance, powerful though they are, have increasingly relied on government and the military to secure their position. The nation has become increasingly dominated, not so much by an oligopoly as by an increasingly professional military demanding larger shares of the national patrimony. The democratically elected government of President Cerezo (1986–) lacks the capacity to limit military power, although under Cerezo the military have not invariably sided with the economic elite.

As discussed more fully in Chapter 6, from 1954 to the late 1970s, with some fluctuations, the real wealth of Guatemala grew but the central government, the military, and the upper sectors absorbed a disproportionate amount of the economic growth. Lower sectors became increasingly impoverished, despite some gains in the early 1960s, subsequently lost in the 1970s. Military governments and socioeconomic elites have not always had the economic capacity and almost never the political will to respond favorably to the demands of the urban and rural masses. The state and private paramilitary groups have responded with force and terror to popular attempts to articulate demands and to organize for action. The result has been a polarized society and endemic revolutionary and counterrevolutionary violence.[39]

Arbenz's land reforms, important as they were elsewhere in Guatemala, had no effect on underpopulated Petén. There, until the 1970s, there was no pressure on the land, and few highlanders rich or poor had any interest in the distant northern lowlands.[40] For example, between 1945 and 1954, there were 1,497 local agrarian committees set up in Guatemala, but not a single one in Petén. More important was that the 1945 Revolution improved things for chicleros by ending debt peonage and the flagrant use of physical coercion against tappers, by increasing the number of contractors, by enhancing worker access to law, and by permitting workers to organize unions. Additionally, especially between 1945 and 1954, contractors often had less influence with elected mayors than they had had with appointed *intendentes*.[41] At the same time, however, the declining market for chicle weakened chiclero bargaining power.

In 1947–1948 labor organizers from Guatemala City came to Petén to work with local politicians to organize Suchilma, the chicleros and woodcutters' union. Suchilma partisans assert that between 1948 and 1954 the union forced jobbers to honor *mensualidad* agreements, improved medical assistance programs for chicleros, and obtained higher wages for them. In this, Suchilma officials were aided by their connections with regional police officials, Guatemalan labor federations, and important politicians in Guatemala City. Contrarily, Suchilma detractors say that union activity decreased demands for chicle, which eventually lowered wages (this is in part a reference to union dues deducted from wages), that Suchilma cheated jobbers, that its officials were high-handed with mayors, and that union officials (who were not chicleros) were corrupt.[42] Both arguments contain some truth, and chicleros have had mixed feelings about Suchilma. They did and do speak more unambiguously of their "brotherhood" and of their shared interests, as opposed to those of the contractors. Yet, despite what might be called class consciousness, chicleros have not acted in unison, and most of them have not actively supported Suchilma. Several factors weaken chiclero solidarity and union strength.

First, the technoenvironmental conditions that limit managerial supervision of chicleros also make it difficult for Suchilma effectively to communicate with and coordinate the actions of its members during the tapping season. After liquidation, the labor force disperses, and the workers are separated by region, community, and occupation, although most are milperos. Thus, chiclero contact with and support of the union is discontinuous. Second, personalized relations among contractors, subcontractors, foremen, chicleros under contract, and independent tappers inhibit cohesiveness of the labor force. Recall that some chicle camps consist of foremen (or subcontractors) and some of their kinsmen, *compadres*, and friends. If the foreman is antiunion, the men in the camp, facing not just their *capataz* but also their kinsman or friend, ordinarily will not express strong support for Suchilma, although they may do so under other circumstances (a similar situation occurred among cowboys; Weston 1985:26–28). Third, chicleros, subcontractors, and small-scale jobbers are not always sharply differentiated from one another in wealth or social position. Over relatively short periods of time a man may shift from one of these roles to the other. Labor and management are partly interchangeable, and this too dilutes worker solidarity. Fourth, after 1954 some contractors were quick to threaten retaliation against outspoken union backers. The tactic was especially effective with chicleros who had stable patron-client relations with contractors. Also, from 1954 to 1986 the central government was opposed, sometimes violently, to aggressive union activity. Shortly after Castillo Armas came to power in 1954, counterrevolutionary forces killed hundreds of grassroots union, peasant, and reform party leaders. Although this onslaught did not occur in Petén, union leaders and their local political party allies were threatened by the police and the military. That, along with news of what was happening elsewhere in Guatemala, was enough to dampen enthusiasm for the union. Finally, in recent years Suchilma has been partly subsidized by FYDEP so, even aside from the antiunion stance of the government, Suchilma has not been free to press hard for worker interests. Post-1954 military governments have been primarily responsible for weakening unions in Guatemala, and, in the specific case of Suchilma, even prior to 1954 the technoenvironmental and organizational particularities of the chicle industry made unionization problematic. In short, the largest and really the only mass organization in Petén until about 1987 has never been strongly unified or highly effective.[43]

Although patron-client ties helped to fragment chiclero and union solidarity, it bears repeating that in *la chiclería* patronage has been a fragile institution. The primary reason for this was that until about the middle 1960s, when the economy of Petén began to grow rapidly, most contractors, dependent on credit and having to cope with fluctuating international market demands for chicle, did not have enough surplus capital to offer chicleros material support during the off-season or during a downturn in the market. Nor did any of them operate large-scale enterprises, such as commercial plantations, that could absorb labor during the off-season. Before 1945 jobber-merchants, who often also held government posts or had relatives in government, were about the only people in Petén who could play the role of patron. After 1945, however, many small-scale operators entirely without capital reserves got into the business (a situation reminiscent of the first few years of chicle exploitation) and were even less able than pre-1945 contractors to act as reliable patrons. Nor has the role of patron always been rewarding. Even before 1945, to hold a client in debt peonage encumbered resources and put them at risk—some debtors did abscond. Of course, contractors gained more than chicleros from debt peonage, but not without risks and costs. Simultaneously, clientage which involved indebtedness increased the client's vulnerability to *engaños* and coercion. What Weinstein (1983:182) says about the Brazilian rubber economy applies equally well to the chicle economy—that personalized relations (reinforced by *compadrazgo*), paternalism, and physical abuse are not mutually exclusive. Chicleros point up the weakness of patron-client relations by asserting that if a patron-contractor defaults in any of his obligations to his client-workers, the latter may and should renounce their correlative responsibilities. Since contractors almost always default (by charging inflated prices for food, if nothing else), client loyalty is labile. As chicleros say, "If the contractor *no nos atiende* [will not take care of us], we will not take care of him." They add that "In the past [pre-1945] the contractors used to cheat the chicleros, but now, the chicleros cheat the contractors. *La chiclería* is tough and messy. Everybody screws everybody." Rivalry among jobbers for labor also has enfeebled patron-client bonds. Forman and Riegelhaupt (1979:390) refer to relationships of this sort as patron-clientism rather than patron-dependency. After about the middle 1960s, socioeconomic changes in Petén made patron-dependency more attractive for some people, but the depth of the change should not be exaggerated. The regional economy, particularly during the decades when chicle collecting was the major source of wage labor in Petén, did not provide a stable ground for durable patron-client relationships.

There were, however, a few stable patron-client relationships in Petén. A handful of weathy merchant-jobbers and some chicleros, typically Petén residents who sold their surplus grain to the merchants, did maintain such ties. Many Kekchí Indians in San Luis also had patron-dependent relations with a Ladino family there, apparently for two major reasons. First, there was only one affluent resident merchant in the *pueblo*.[44] Second, because of their location, San Luiseños had less access to important Flores merchant-contractors and fewer economic opportunities than most Peteneros. More commonly, Petén chicleros and milperos tried, as they still do, to have reasonably good relations with all affluent merchant-contractors, rather than to become dependent on any one of them. Peteneros are deferent with upper-sector people, but they are not servile peons loyal to particular protective benefactors. Rather than regard the old saw, "I am a chiclero, I do not have to work for anyone," as an expression of the lower-class "vices" of a "ramshackle" lot, as might Maler (1908b:74) and Halle (1941:28), cited at the head of this chapter, it is more accurate to consider it as a reflection of a relative absence of patron-dependence and the presence of a certain autonomy among chicleros. This may be part of the reason Peteneros insist, "There is more democracy here than in the rest of Guatemala."

Concluding Discussion

The collection of chicle for overseas export dominated the economy of Petén for some eighty years, roughly from the 1890s to about 1970. The chicle economy replicated many aspects of nineteenth-century logging and *hule* operations, but on a much larger scale. Although never as important as coffee, banana, (and later) sugar, cotton, and beef production in the rest of Guatemala, for four generations chicle collecting was the major source of wage labor in Petén and an important source of income for Petén townships and even, for a few years, for FYDEP. Practically everyone in the region was affected by the extractive (or enclave) economy.[45] Chicle is still produced in Petén, but now its relative and absolute contribution to the regional economy is much reduced.

Perhaps a decline was inevitable. Peteneros have never had any control over the market for chicle or over the use of alternate resins and synthetics in chewing gum manufacture. But even if the depressed market for chicle had not led to the *caida* of the 1970s, resource depletion probably would have posed problems for the industry. Despite government regulations about tapping and despite concessions granted foreign firms, chicle has been in effect a common property resource, and its exploitation has been nearly unlimited. Certainly by the 1960s the resource was in some danger of depletion, although decreasing demand for it has permitted regeneration of first class chicle trees. One way or another, the industry could not have endlessly maintained early levels of production.

Although an instance of foreign capitalist penetration of a remote, economically marginal region (Konrad 1981), the chicle industry did retain certain precapitalist features, notably debt peonage (until 1945), relative absence of managerial control over primary production, and relatively unrestricted access to the tools of production. The two latter features were related to local ecological conditions. Because chicle trees are scattered in the forest and cannot be cultivated on plantations, labor had to be spatially dispersed and could not be closely supervised. In addition, there was no way to introduce modern cost-cutting, labor-saving machinery into the technology of primary production. These were also characteristics of the Brazilian rubber economy (Weinstein 1983:269). There, too, ecological circumstances directly affected the organization of labor and production and the appropriation of what labor produced. Brazilian rubber traders had even less sway over the productive system than did Petén chicle contractors. Instead, rubber traders dominated labor and appropriated its surplus through "exchange systems" which they did control (Weinstein 1983:29). Something generally similar, though not identical in all details, occurred in Petén.

In both economies, contractors controlled labor in part by exercising control over trade and access to credit. Most contractors, including all the more important ones, were also merchants. Prior to the 1930s, North American company managers, too, were traders, moving chicle from northwestern Petén to Tenosique railheads and returning with trade goods. The jobbers who gave tappers pay advances were the same merchants who sold them goods for cash or credit. Merchant-contractors extracted surplus value from their workers by overcharging them for supplies during the tapping season, as well as during the recruitment and liquidation periods. Merchant-contractors also extended credit to certain chicleros during the off-season. Although a chiclero could shift allegiance from one contractor to another, he could not afford to alienate all contractors, not only because they were the major employers of wage labor in Petén, but also because they were the major traders in the region. This position, more than ownership of the tools of production and control over work processes, gave merchant-contractors some control over labor, and at the same time enabled them to extract surplus value from it.

That merchant-contractors were the patrons of customer-workers did not make them reliable patrons. Foreign companies and, later, government agencies extended credit to labor contractors who competed among themselves for labor. Contractors gave credit and *enganches* to subcontractors, independent chicleros, and chicleros under contract. Credit branched outward and downward, along lines of personalized relationships, which were also used to recruit labor. Decisions about renewing credit and contracts, however, were finally based on more impersonal standards of performance. Because of market fluctuations beyond local control, relationships with merchant-contractors were not secure safeguards against economic distress. Yet, perhaps because there was a personalized aspect to *la chiclería*, chicleros and contractors tended (and still tend) to talk about their relations in moral, rather than in strictly economic, terms. Thus, deception was (and is) said to rupture bonds between jobbers and chicleros—a moral breach terminated an economic relationship—but impersonal overseas economic forces made it impossible to honor faithfully the moral obligations of the relationship. Although it would distort things to discount the way in which Peteneros speak of their experiences, it would be equally misleading to overlook the economic ground of those experiences. In any event, the vicissitudes of overseas markets qualified labor-management relations and labor control in *la chiclería*.

The state, of course, helped contractors to control labor. The government seems to have been most coercive during Ubico's reign. Patronage could buffer political distress, but at the same time the chiclero-client of a contractor-patron was exposed to government "abuse" (the word used in Petén) precisely because of that relationship. After 1954 the state further helped contractors by weakening the union movement. Off and on, local officials also served contractors and foreign firms by less than rigorous collection of fees and taxes. INFOP and FYDEP introduced various changes, increased government regulation of the chicle industry, and led contractors to form a fairly cohesive organization of their own. Neither agency, however, improved labor's position in any basic way. (INFOP might have, but the 1954 counterrevolution truncated that possibility.)

Management's inability to supervise directly the productive process in chicle and to monopolize the tools of production did not give labor the upper hand. For want of alternatives, Peteneros and others had to accept the risks and stresses of chicle work, and until the late 1920s wages were high. Even after airplane service increased the supply of labor, wages were still fairly good compared with other available opportunities. But labor was too fragmented to confront management in a unified way. There were several reasons for this: the seasonal nature of the work; the spatial dispersion of labor during the tapping season; loyalty (on the part of some chicleros) to patrons, subcontractors, and foremen, and some circulation of personnel through these ranks; the individualizing nature of tapping technology; and a political climate usually distinctly hostile to unions. In other words, although tappers constituted a social class in their shared relationship to a form of production, several mutually reinforcing factors inhibited organized class action. Lack of labor unity was one reason individual chicleros could not forego good relations with all jobbers, although patron-dependency was not common in the chicle economy. At the same time, conditions that limited managerial control over work processes gave chicleros some space within which to negotiate the terms of their relationships with management. What Weinstein (1983:31) says of rubber tappers applies equally well to chicleros: "And despite accounts . . . that depict [them] . . . as a dehumanized and defenseless mass, the structure of the rubber trade suggests that the tappers exerted pressure, often successfully, to limit their exploitation and maintain some shred of autonomy." "Shred" is the right word, for while chicleros did have some autonomy, in general foreign firms and contractors supported by government almost always had the stronger hand.

For ecological reasons, the chicle production, despite its scale, did not lead to technological innovations or new socioeconomic relationships (although it did affect ethnic ones) in Petén. In general, it reinforced customary patterns of exchange, all of which was also true in the Brazilian rubber trade (Weinstein 1983:9–15). Yet *oro blanco*, now apparently permanently reduced in importance, did have an enormous impact on Petén.[46]

At the beginning of this chapter I noted that although the chicle economy generated few economic linkages (see next chapter), it did affect many aspects of society and culture in the region. The changes and continuities effected are discussed next.

Chapter Five

The Impact of *Oro Blanco*

"Past and present, sharply separated by the chapter structure, are fused in motifs and unstressed parallels" (DeMott commenting on *World's End* 1987).

"My father says that Indian and Ladino no longer matter, but I do not know. Maybe it is there, hidden" (twenty-five-year-old Petén office worker, Field Notes 1985).

"Good-for-nothing chicleros . . . setting a bad example for the conscientious native farmer" (summary of Morley's views; Brunhouse 1971:149).

Introduction

The exploitation of a new resource, chicle, gave Peteneros a new way to make a living, increased the flow of money in Petén, created partly open opportunities for socioeconomic mobility, and broadened contacts with the wider world. *La chiclería* reduced the salience of ethnicity and, for part of the year, of community. At at the same time, it reinforced the preexisting stratification and exchange systems without generating new opportunities for investment. Peteneros say that *oro blanco*, chicle, transformed Petén, and there can be no doubt that it did qualify a certain range of socioeconomic relations and the ideas Peteneros had about those relations. But there were also profound parallels with the past.

Production, Consumption, and Fiscal Linkages

The immediate impact of *la chiclería* was certainly dramatic. As Peteneros rushed to collect chicle, farm labor became scarce, the price for maize rose rapidly, sugarcane production declined, and the consumption of luxury goods increased. There were political and, many Peteneros felt, undesirable moral consequences.[1] However, the concern here is with more prosaic long-term economic and social effects of *oro blanco*. Hirschman's (1958) concept of "linkages," interdependencies among economic activities, and Partridge's (1979) extension of the idea into the social field provide ways to discuss these matters.

In a region such as Petén where the output of the major economic activity is destined for immediate export and does not require major purchases from other sectors, the chances are slim that the activity will induce new domestic investments, although it may generate tax revenues for local government. This sort of region, sometimes called an "export enclave," has "great trouble in breaking out of the enclave situation" and of developing its economy (Hirschman 1958:109–12). The impact of chicle production on regional development was, as Hirschman anticipated, limited.

Production Linkages

These "occur when the inputs necessary to produce a commodity or the capacity to utilize outputs is inadequate or nonexistent" (Partridge 1979:491). There are forward and backward linkages. A forward linkage (sale to other economic sectors) is created when the output of a given economic activity is used for some other new activity, when the the production of, say, cement leads to "the establishment of a cement block industry" (Hirschman 1958:102). A "backward linkage" (purchase from other sectors) is created when one activity leads to "derived demand" for some other activity, for example, when the cement factory calls forth the production of special packing bags for the cement. Linkages may occur inside or outside a region. (In what follows, the emphasis is on inside linkages.) Thus, if *la chiclería* had led to local production of machetes, this would have been an inside backward linkage; if the production took place elsewhere, it would have been an outside backward linkage. Backward linkages are almost always more important for economic development than forward linkages (Hirschman 1958).

New economic activities can also bring about external diseconomies — harm to existing forms of production. The introduction of new products or new technologies may have negative effects on old "industrial or handicraft establishments" by reducing investment in them (Hirschman 1958:72). Chicle production had this sort of negative impact on sugarcane production; however, government regulations also contributed to the situation.

It is nearly self-evident that chicle production could not have led to significant forward linkages within Petén. Chicle was exclusively destined for overseas export. The capital goods needed for processing could not be assembled in Petén, the materials from various regions of the world required for the manufacture of chewing gum could not be easily transported there, and markets for the product were distant from the region, all of which made it utterly impractical for foreign owned companies to do anything more than import chicle from Petén and adjacent areas. Peteneros did invest in mules for chicle transport, but this was not new—mules had always been used to transport goods. The major linkage impacts of airplane service, initiated in the 1930s, were felt outside the region. The airplanes, of course, were produced outside the region; in addition most airplane maintenance and repair was carried out in Guatemala City, not Petén. (After 1975, with the decline of chicle production and the increased use of trucks, most of the rustic airports in Petén which served no purpose outside of the chicle industry were abandoned.) The use of trucks that now bring supplies to and remove chicle from forest camps was primarily a response to recent increased agricultural production and expanded commerce in Petén rather than to *la chiclería*.[2]

More important for purposes of development, *la chiclería* did not induce significant backward linkages. First, as explained in the previous chapter, methods of production were not amenable to technological improvement. Second, insofar as the activity increased demand for machetes, metal spurs, and other manufactured goods, the impact was felt outside Petén. For example, most of the machetes used in the region were and are produced by the Collins Company of Connecticut. Until very recently Petén's internal market was not large enough to justify local manufacture of such tools, even if the capital and skill needed to make them had been present. The major backward productive linkage induced by chicle collecting was the handicraft manufacture of special ankle-high leather "chiclero's boots." This cottage industry, based on nineteenth-century shoemaking traditions, was owned by the lineal descendants of colonial middle sector families in Flores. There seem to have been six or seven establishments which at their height may have had as many as thirty to forty workers, a respectable number given Petén's small pre-1960s population, but not truly significant.

Beyond increasing investments in chicle collecting or in prechicle commercial operations, there was little in which Peteneros with capital could have invested. This had nothing to do with tradition, for Peteneros were and are practical about economic matters. Rather, because the internal market was small and road access to external markets inadequate, Peteneros had no incentive or opportunity to invest in such things as large-scale agricultural or cattle production. Affluent Peteneros invested in expanded chicle collecting, retail stores, saloons, and inns—most of them located in Flores and San Benito—catering to chicleros, houses in Petén and occasionally in Guatemala City, and the education of their children. Education often proved the most profitable investment. Many of the Peteneros who earned professional degrees took up residence in the national capital, and their relatives in Petén benefited from contacts thereby established in Guatemala City. Affluent kinsmen in the city could extend financial credit and act as political intermediaries for those who remained at home. But additional stores and houses and the exodus of the educated were not productive linkages. Instead, they intensified older patterns of behavior.

Fiscal Linkages

These refer to revenues for government generated by a new productive activity. Two points to consider are whether government sends the revenues outside the local region or allows them to remain within the region, and the uses to which it puts the revenues.

Until the 1960s, the central government did not use its share of chicle revenues to subsidize any productive activity in Petén. The reasons for this lack of investment were that government was more concerned with agroexport crops such as coffee and bananas produced far from Petén, that the state was often short of funds, and that despite the useful connections some individual Peteneros had in Guatemala City, the region was an underpopulated backwater. Peteneros as a group did not have sufficient political or economic power to influence national investment policies.[3] Even for Ubico, for all his interest in chicle revenue, Petén was not nearly so important as the agroexport regions of the country.

As described previously, local government units in Petén did receive a small share of revenues from the chicle economy. This income was important for several townships, but until 1953 it was rarely sufficient for investment purposes. Even after 1953, conditions that constrained individual investment also limited local government investment.[4] Mayors and councils, guided by municipal secretaries, usually spent township revenues in and for their respective central *pueblos*, much to the displeasure of *aldeanos*. (Their wish for improved access to revenue is a major reason that *aldeas* strive for *pueblo* status.) Those municipal corporations receiving chicle income (not all of them did) used their fiscal resources to improve the capital stock of the *pueblo*: town halls, local school buildings,[5] and churches; to build public salons; to purchase dynamos for electricity; to acquire office equipment for the town hall; and/or to cobble streets. Mayors usually hired fellow townsmen to work on public projects, and for many men this was a relatively important supplementary source of cash income. Because chicle revenues were so limited, however, none of the *pueblos* was able to finance public works projects year in and year out or to invest in self-sustaining productive activities.

Townships sometimes quarreled over chicle revenues, particularly before 1953 when tax payments were very low. Neighboring townships accused one another of smuggling chicle across their respective borders to defraud the other of tax income on the product. So long as Flores (or a major concession holder) was not involved, government tended to be impartial in dealing with these disputes, but when a municipality quarreled with Flores, government usually sided with Flores. Thus, in the early 1960s, using the argument that San José lacked the population to need and the ability to manage all of its patrimony, Flores was able to gain from the central government part of what had been San José territory, including areas rich in chicle and the potential for tourism. Just as contractors could usually count on the state in dealing with chicleros, so Flores could count on it in dealing with the *pueblos*.

From the middle 1960s on, FYDEP invested in building an infrastructure for economic development. FYDEP "urbanized" settlements by building schools, health stations, electric plants, and potable water facilities. More important for economic growth, FYDEP constructed roads and bridges within Petén, and in 1970 the agency completed an "all-weather" hard dirt road linking Flores to southern Guatemala. But most of the funds for building roads and social overhead projects were derived from sources having nothing to do with chicle. Over the years, very little of the revenue from chicle was used to invest in productive activities. Fiscal linkages were as limited as production linkages.

Consumption Linkages

These "are generated through demands for imported goods in the host community that, in turn, stimulate producers inside or outside the community to begin supplying the new demands" (Partridge 1979:492). In the first two decades of the twentieth century, the chicle economy certainly generated demands for luxury goods. Chicleros were famous, or notorious, for squandering their wages on such things as silk shirts, fine cigars lit with ten-dollar bills, and expensive cognacs. Several people even purchased automobiles, although road conditions at the time were such that they could not have had much use of them.[6] Such prodigality by itself suggests that there was little in Petén in which to invest. In any case, consumer demands for luxuries rose and fell with booms and busts in *la chiclería*, but they were not as extravagant after the depression of the 1930s as they had been in the early years of *oro blanco*. The critical factor is that consumer demands for luxury items were met by producers outside the region.

Even more telling is that increased demands for manufactured goods for everyday use, such as kitchen utensils, clothing, and metal tools, also were satisfied by importation. Traders, especially those who already had well-established contacts in Belize and Tenosique, benefited from the increase in consumer demand. In fact, the more important traders also became chicle contractors. Growth in trade was great enough to lead a small number of Mexican and British Honduran merchants to take up permanent residence in Petén. Although they grew wealthier, traders and merchants did not invest in the production of goods. The extractive economy increased the volume of trade, but not of production, in Petén.

Social Structural Linkages

The picture may be rounded out by looking at structural linkages which involves considerations of not only what was done with resources, but also who did it. As Partridge puts it:

> When an activity makes new resources available to some segment of the local population which did not have access to them before or more properly when existing resources are now made available to them, and they invest them, this is a structural change (1979:494.)

In this context, it is useful to recall that ever since the Spanish conquest of Petén, access to economic resources (whether eighteenth-century cattle ranches or twentieth-century chicle contracts) and access to political power have tended to be reciprocally related. The acquisition of wealth has as often depended on political power as the other way around.

In late nineteenth-century Petén, members of the upper social class, or social sector, were engaged primarily in commerce and trade. They also owned cattle ranches and sugarcane fields, but apparently very few were logging contractors. Those in the upper sector also occupied most of the major bureaucratic and military positions in the department. Most of them were Floreños, descended from eighteenth-century Creole or Spanish settlers in Petén. They were not wealthy as compared to their counterparts in the Guatemalan highlands, and in this restricted sense, when wealthy Floreños today say their forefathers were "poor " they are correct.

The small middle sector consisted of artisans, lower level bureaucrats, small store owners, and muleteers. The line between the upper and the middle sector was not always clear, for many of the latter had consanguineal and affinal connections with the former. Middle sector people could claim descent from eighteenth-century Creole, Spanish, or Ladino settlers. Although residence in Flores carried more prestige, most lived in the *pueblos*.

The vast majority of the lower sector, or class, were primarily subsistence farmers, some of whom also cultivated sugarcane. In central Petén, they could find part-time work as field hands or cowboys for those of the upper and middle sectors. In the southeast and along the far western rivers, they cut logs for Mexican and British Honduran businessmen. Taxes and corvée fell most heavily on the lower sector, particularly the Indians. Lower sector people, usually Ladinos, who had kinship ties to the middle and even to the upper sector found the connections of limited instrumental value. Although there were ethnic intermarriages, ethnic homogamy was the general rule as much within the lower sector as within other sectors. Ethnicity played a clear-cut role in ritual kin choices—Indians asked Ladinos to sponsor their children at baptismal and marriage ceremonies, not the other way around. Although there were some lower sector people in Flores most of them, of course, lived in *pueblos* and villages.

In ethnically mixed *pueblos*, middle sector Ladinos controlled the town hall and the militia and owned the larger stores. The homogeneous Indian communities of San José and San Luis are qualified exceptions to the rule, because Ladinos rarely lived there. Nonetheless, at least by the late nineteenth century, most of the teachers and secretaries posted to San José were Ladinos from San Andrés, San Joseños often did their militia duty under officers from San Andrés, and they shopped in the larger stores in San Andrés and Flores. Ladinos appear not to have played an active role in the everyday life of San Luis until around the 1930s.

There were and still are various personalized, typically dyadic, ties that cut across social sector, communal, and ethnic divisions. Based on kinship, *compadrazgo*, residential propinquity, privileged friendships, and patronage, these relationships sometimes softened the harsher side of socioeconomic and political inequality, but as might be expected, older people in the lower sector do not recall these personalized bonds being as protective of their interests as do people in the upper sectors.

Sometimes a new economic activity gives a social sector access to resources previously unavailable to it, thereby changing its relations with other sectors. In the Brazilian rubber economy, men of "humble origin," as well as the elite, small traders and lower level bureaucrats, were found among the "first owners and traders," with all this implies for their mutual relations (Weinstein 1983:45–46). In Petén this also was the case, at least initially, as all sorts of people became *hule* and then chicle contractors, but those of "humble origin" could not sustain the role. As described above, the early contractors depended on credit from Belizean merchants, and this gave a head start to upper sector Petén merchants who already had trade relations with the Belizeans. Moreover, because chicle smuggling during the first three decades of the century required the authorities to look the other way, their upper sector merchant-contractor relatives had an additional edge. Prior commercial contacts and political influence enabled the upper sector to benefit disproportionately from the new activity. In the 1920s, when the number of contractors was reduced, people in advantaged positions—rather than those of lower sector origin—continued to work as jobbers for the North American companies. In this manner, the new economy largely reinforced the preexisting social structure.

Yet the chicle industry did make provision for some upward mobility. In 1949 lower sector Peteneros were given more enduring access to chicle contracts, but significant though this was in some ways, its impact was limited. For instance, the change increased the economic status of only a few people—the percent of jobbers went from about 1.3 to about 2.2 to 3.7 percent of the heads of household in Petén. Further, as the number of contractors grew, chicle production declined and the new jobbers were given slices of a smaller pie. By this time many of the older contractors had expanded their commercial operations enough that they retained their economic superiority over all but a handful of new contractors. *La chiclería* also created opportunities for more people of middle and even lower sector origin to enter the field of commerce, although they did not operate on the scale of the elite. Not all the merchants were successful, nor were all better off than the majority—chicleros and milperos. Considered as a social category, however, they lived at higher levels than that majority.[7] *Oro blanco*, then, improved the fortunes of some people, but, more important, it widened the socioeconomic gap between the top and the lower social sectors. After 1900 the rich were richer than before, and the social composition of this sector remained largely unchanged.[8]

This raises the question of whether the poor were better or worse off because of *la chiclería*. Although reliable statistical data are scant, informant accounts and local archives suggest that the majority of Peteneros did not live at significantly higher levels after the advent of *la chiclería*, but it must be granted that informant statements may also reflect some increase in standards of living made possible by chicle income. Yet town archives indicate that until 1953, except in Flores, the provision of public services for education, health, and sanitation were very little if at all improved. For example, towns that had second-grade schools around 1900 had third-grade schools in 1960, and health posts were not built in the *pueblos* until the 1970s. The luxury goods imported into Petén during the early decades of *la chiclería* did not improve levels of living. The majority saw few if any changes in diet, housing, and material possessions, although homemade Yucatecan-style "Indian" dress gave way to imported clothing—not necessarily an improvement. There was an increase in the variety and supply of consumer goods, and chicleros did earn relatively decent wages (although uncertain because of fluctuating demands for chicle). Yet because they were a captive market for jobbers and because chicle collecting reduced crop production (by withdrawing labor from farming) and raised food prices, they had to pay inflated prices for staples and other commodities. The very efforts of the government and the chicle companies to increase maize production attest to the impact chicle had on crop production. In short, because of unfavorable terms of trade most chicleros and milperos were unable to accumulate savings, and although it is not certain that their material situation was worsened by the chicle industry, neither is there any indication it was improved.

Because *la chiclería* widened the economic gap between the lower and the upper social sectors, it may have made the rub of inequality harsher. *La chiclería* increased trade in Petén, but the lack of backward linkages meant, by and large, that those already in commerce added to their stock, sold more, and intensified preexisting exchange relations with others. Labor, however, coping with higher prices and uncertain wages tied to varying demands for a single commodity, could not consistently purchase whatever new goods came to be defined as necessities. Life also may have become

Table 5:1 Social Sectors, Petén, 1900–1962

	Address			
	A	B	C	D
Upper sector				
Merchant-contractor elite	x	x	y	o
Upper-level bureaucrats and politicians	o	x	o	o
Professionals	o	x	y	o
Middle sector				
Larger farmers and ranchers	o	x	y	o
Store owners and small contractors	o	x	x	o
Chicle support staff	y	x	y	y
Subcontractors, foremen, and muleteers	y	y	x	o
Lesser bureaucrats and politicians	o	x	x	o
Artisans	o	x	y	o
Lower sector				
Native Petén chicleros	o	y	x	y
Native Petén milperos	o	y	x	x
Seasonal workers (chicleros) from outside Petén	x	o	o	o

Source: Field Notes; documents cited in chapter. Key: A = outside Petén; B = Flores; C = towns; D = villages. x = most common address; y = second most common; o = least common. (As indicated, two addresses may be equally common, e.g., early in the 1900s, the address of roughly as many big contractors was outside Petén as in Flores.)

Note: During this period, there were few large farms or ranches in Petén. Educators are included with bureaucrats. There were several big contractors in Carmelita but most were in Flores (and British Honduras and Mexico earlier in the century).

more precarious. Peteneros were dependent on an economy subject to the control of foreign markets and, with the use of synthetics in chewing gum manufacture, to modern technology. In this sense, they were at greater economic risk after 1900 than before.[9]

Before discussing the impact of the chicle economy on ethnic relations, community, and ideation, we should note that much of what has been said above of social sectors could have been discussed in terms of ethnicity and community. Briefly, most of the big merchants and jobbers were (and are) from Flores. In the *pueblos*, until 1949, Ladinos—rarely operating on the scale of the Floreños—rather than Indians became contractors. A dispro-portionate number of Ladino townsmen also were in commerce. In gen-

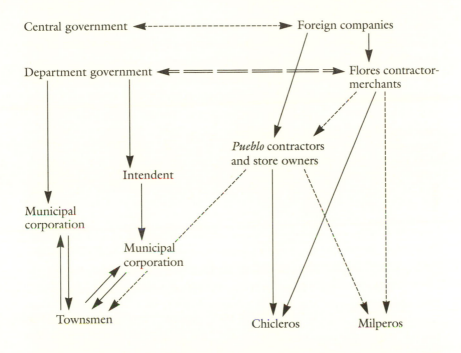

Figure 5:1. Structure of political-economic relations, Petén, 1900–1962. *Key*: Single unbroken line = formal authority and/or contractual relation; double broken line = close, informal relation; single broken line = variable relation, usually informal. Arrowhead indicates subordination; double arrowhead indicates roughly equal power. *Note*: The absence of *aldeas* is intentional, to emphasize that few were large and many were impermanent. The larger ones were usually chicle collecting centers, e.g., Carmelita. The modern intendent system was ended by 1944–1945.

eral, for there were exceptions, Ladinos gained more from the chicle industry than Indians. Because Flores, San Andrés, La Libertad, and San José (until it lost land to Flores) had the richest, largest chicle fields, their capital towns grew wealthier than the others in Petén. Most important, the extractive economy strengthened the position of Flores as the leading settlement in Petén. Thus old correlations between ethnicity, community, and social sector were reinforced.

If *la chiclería* did not transform the social structure of Petén, it did make its society more complicated. Table 5:1 depicts changes, and Figure 5:1 sketches the structure of political-economic relations in Petén between 1900 and 1962, years when chicle collecting dominated the regional economy. The major point made by the table and the figure is that the changes were additive, not fundamental, although *oro blanco* did qualify certain relationships in Petén and the ideas Peteneros had about them. As shall be seen, there is no contradiction in saying that *la chiclería* affected some social relations without changing the basic structure of the society in which this happened.

Ethnicity, Acculturation, and Community

Social Synonyms

The impact of the chicle industry on social relations, specifically ethnic and communal, must be understood in light of the correlations, previously described in several places, between ethnicity, community, and social sector. In Petén, each major settlement has had, and for many Peteneros still has, a distinctive ethnic and social sector signature. Peteneros talk as if and, presumably, think that if they know a person's natal community, they also know his or her ethnic and social identity, and vice versa.[10] Exceptions are acknowledged, but they are treated as just that—irregularities in what is and should be the rule.

The importance of this traditional way of thinking lies in the fact that although Peteneros may appear to have accepted changes in ethnic or other relations, they still make the same (social) distinctions they did in the past. Thus, they say that "now, Indian, Ladino does not matter. We are all the same." But matters are not quite this simple. For example, in 1960 a father might have advised his son not to marry a certain woman because she was a Ladina (or Indian), and in 1985 the father might have told a second son not to marry the woman's sister because her family originally came from the southern half of San Andrés (a synonym for Ladino) or from San José (synonym for Indian). What seems to have changed is the propriety or prudence of openly discussing ethnicity, and although this is significant, it does not prevent people from making the same old distinctions, using an alternative vocabulary. One might argue that ethnicity was less important in 1985 than in 1960, that the example used here is an instance of "culture lag," and that it takes time for ideas about society to catch up with social reality. But the system of social synonyms also makes it possible for Peteneros to assimilate ostensible changes into their traditional ideology.

Peteneros believe that ethnicity, community membership, and social-sector placement all influence social character, and they interact accordingly with one another. Ethnicity is most clearly an ascribed status, but Peteneros also ascribe characterological traits to an individual based on his or her natal community and original social sector (Reina 1965). Although an individual can change his social sector, ethnic identity (usually on the part of an Indian who moves away from his hometown and adopts Ladino behavioral patterns), and community membership, and thereby affect the expectations others have of him, Peteneros nevertheless assume that much of his original social character will endure and affect his behavior. They believe that social personality is largely assigned at birth by the accidents of ethnicity, community, and social sector.[11]

Some ascribed traits are dichotomized. Thus Indians are assumed to be steadfast friends and Ladinos capricious. Other traits are placed on a sliding scale. For example, Peteneros assume that Floreños are "naturally" more urbane than townsfolk who are in turn more urbane than villagers (*aldeanos*), and that within any given settlements Ladinos are more urbane than Indians.

As might be expected, additional factors also affect social action. Proper, albeit "facultative" rather than "firm," relationships (Pitt-Rivers 1954:106) based on kinship, ritual kinship, residential propinquity, and privileged friendship influence interaction, as do smart transactions based on political and economic necessity. These factors and those mentioned above— ethnicity, community, social sector—mutually qualify each other. In any case, the question here is how *la chiclería* affected, insofar as it did, the latter features of the sociocultural landscape.

Acculturation, Assimilation, and Chicle
For the sake of clarity, cultural assimilation (acculturation) will be defined as volitional or forced acceptance of new cultural patterns, and social assimilation will be defined as social participation without regard to sectarian standards, particularly ethnicity. (For a more extended treatment of the distinction, see Schwartz 1971.) Although the issue is complex, one useful indication of assimilation is that people of diverse ethnic identities or background are distributed on occupational, political, and prestige

hierarchies in proportion to their numbers in the total population.[12] By this standard, the Indians of Petén are more acculturated to Ladino culture than they are assimilated in the regional society. For example, although there are affluent Indians and poor Ladinos in Petén, on average Ladinos are economically better off than Indians.

After independence from Spain in 1821, successive Guatemalan governments made efforts to integrate the Indians into the national society, without granting them access to political, economic, or social power. With the expansion of commercial export-oriented agriculture the efforts were intensified, and after 1871 Liberal governments converted communally owned Indian lands to private property (which was then acquired by Ladinos) and forced increasing numbers of Indians to enter labor markets on unfavorable terms. However, "the Liberal Reforms did not register in a uniform way across the country" (Lovell 1988:104). Government officials in Petén discriminated against the Indians, but with less harshness than elsewhere in Guatemala. Indeed, Ladinos sometimes complained that officials in Flores took the side of Indians rather than their side (see Chapter 3).

By 1890, for reasons that are not entirely clear, regional authorities decided to accelerate the pace of acculturation, although the policy was not consistently enforced. For example, in the 1890s governors ordered Indians to adopt Ladino dress, but as late as the 1920s Indians in San José and the northern half of San Andrés were still wearing so-called Indian garb—white knee britches, white short-sleeved collarless shirts, *kaites* (square-toed sandals) for men, and *huipiles* for women. Of greater importance, in the early 1930s governors forbade the use of Maya in public and in school, an order most strictly enforced in central Petén. However, socioeconomic conditions seem to have brought about greater acculturation than government regulations.

The chicle economy contributed to the process in at least two ways. First, for six months of the year Petén Indians and Ladinos lived in the forest with men from highland Guatemala, Belize, Tabasco, Yucatán, and several Central American nations. In general, the chicleros established norms closer to Hispano-American than to Indian traditions. For example, the lingua franca among chicleros was and is Spanish, mixed with some Belizean English phrases. During the tapping season, Peteneros learned about national and even international cultural standards, and the Indians had little opportunity to practice their own customs. Second, labor-management relations in the chicle industry were and still are based on a mix of particularistic and performance norms having little to do with ethnicity. Even contractors who actively discriminated against Indians during the off-season sought out capable Indian chicleros, muleteers, and foremen during the tapping season. Moreover, to advance in *la chiclería*, to become a foreman or subcontractor, an Indian had to acquire what Peteneros define as Ladino traits: literacy, fluency in Spanish, assertiveness, and the ability to "fight with the law, not with fists." At the same time, it is important to recall that during the off season the men returned home, where they could pursue an Indian life-style.

By the 1940s Petén had become one of the more ladinoized departments in Guatemala, although some Indians continued to use Petén Maya and Kekchí at home and to practice some customs Peteneros identify as "Indian."[13] More to the point, until 1944 (as described previously) no matter how acculturated, Indians suffered more social and political disabilities than Ladinos, as in connection with unpaid mail carrier service and corveé. Moreover, chicle contractors and their allies in government benefited from almost any division among workers, including those based on ethnic as well as communal, regional, or national differences. Contractors who ignored ethnicity in the recruitment process also at times invoked it to foment divisiveness among chicleros. Nevertheless, after 1944–1945, overt ethnic discrimination abated not only because of the way management recruited chicleros, but also because popularly elected mayors and political leaders sought support across ethnic lines, and because Suchilma ideology rejected sectarianism among workers. Compared with the trends in other parts of Guatemala, especially the central and western highlands, ethnicity became or appeared to become relatively unimportant in Petén. Contemporary Peteneros reject institutionalized ethnic discrimination, even though ethnicity does continue to affect, often in covert and inconsistent ways, their social relations.

Of course, the absence of formal ethnic discrimination does not necessarily preclude the presence of prejudicial ethnic stereotypes in Petén or anywhere else. The stereotypes common in the region are similar to those used elsewhere in Guatemala.[14] Traits said to distinguish Indian and Ladino, however, are as often phrased in terms of continua as of dichotomies, depending on social context, as in the instance of a Ladino merchant from Santa Ana who says that Indian women chop firewood, but Ladino women never do, and then jokes, "But when we go to Flores, we are all Indians [in the view of Floreños]." More commonly ethnic differences are discussed as if they were contrastive, as in the following several examples: Peteneros say that Indians have "stronger blood" than Ladinos, hence Indians prefer manual labor, and Ladinos office work. Ladinos "are better with words; their heads do not get heated with law." Indians and Ladinos assert that "in the old days, the Indians were not prepared (literate) like the Ladinos . . . the Indians did not believe in education. They said it was not useful. The Ladinos were better pens." Ladinos may add that even today "Indians do not like to learn; they prefer to stay at the milpa." Indians, unlike Ladinos, prefer the tranquility of the forest to the turbulence of the town; Indians "feel" the obligations of ritual kinship and friendship more deeply than Ladinos; and so on. As is often the case, the stereotypes have positive as well as derogatory aspects, as when people say that Indians are "more sincere" than Ladinos, but also more "backward" (*atrasado*), that Ladinos are more "selfish," but also more modern. There are Peteneros who insist the stereotypes are no longer valid: "The Indians are changing" (that is, becoming more like Ladinos); "Now we [or they, depending on the ethnic identity of the speaker] have good pens too."

Yet, there is a sense in which the stereotypes do reflect reality, as, for example, when Indian children are said to be quieter than Ladino young-sters. As a rule, children who live at the milpa, whether Indian or Ladino, are in fact shyer in public than those who remain in town, and a dispro-portionate number of Indian families live at their milpas. There is, then, a weak correlation between quiet behavior and ethnicity, which an observer regards as an artifact of economic position rather than innate character, but which Peteneros see the other way around. The same may be said of the presumed Indian preference for the *monte* and their imputed intimacy with nature. Ladinos who live at the milpas are as close to "nature" as Indians (and Indian office workers are as urbane as their Ladino co-workers) but a greater proportion of Petén Indians than Ladinos reside at milpas. But none of this makes an Indian a Ladino, or a Ladino an Indian. In Petén, ethnic identity is based on ancestry and family background, not life-style or degree of acculturation, except for those who change their community membership and identify themselves as Ladinos in the new place. A woman of Indian descent put it thus: "Everyone here is Ladino, but some are Ladino Ladino and others are Mayan Ladino."

What complicates all this is that the stereotypes about Indians and Ladinos are also used to describe, respectively, milperos and *oficinistas* (office workers, and more generally those who do not work with their hands). For example, both Indians and milperos are *"humilde"* (meek in a negative sense or modest in a good sense, and in either case also implying poor) and parochial. Whether someone uses *humilde* to refer to both poor Indian and Ladino milperos or, particularly when *humilde* is used pejoratively, as a code word only for Indians, depends on the speaker's identity and that of his or her audience. Instances of this sort may suggest that because there are few if any cultural differences between native Petén Indians and Ladinos, ethnic categories are losing much of their former significance, but Peteneros still occasionally use ethnic stereotypes to explain, rationalize, and guide their own behavior and to know what to expect of others.

The situations in which ethnicity may be used as a criterion for choosing a course of action vary from spouse selection to political faction formation. As for marriage, there are Ladinos who favor "the machete in its own case." Indians do not explicitly mention ethnicity in this context, but those who advise their children not to marry "those who used to be abusive " in fact are speaking of Ladinos. The elite rarely raise the issue, because neither they nor anyone else seem to think that marriage between them and people of lesser status is likely, an artifact of which is that the elite and Indians do not marry. Ethnic homogamy promotes and reciprocially is promoted by ethnically homogeneous neighborhoods, privileged friendships, and loosely organized recreational groupings.[15]

There is a strong connection between ethnicity and choice of godparent for a child's baptism. Peteneros almost invariably ask those who are wealthier and more powerful than they to serve as baptismal sponsors, but even so poor Ladinos seek affluent Ladinos rather than equally affluent Indian *compadres*. Indians, on the other hand, look for Indian, Ladino, and Creole *compadres*. Ethnicity can also play a role in civic and church politics. Faction leaders recruit supporters on diverse bases, including ethnicity. Thus, a Ladino faction leader may tell another Ladino that because Fulano is an Indian, hence a "poor pen," he would not make a good mayor or deacon, and an Indian leader may remind his Indian followers that the "haughty" (euphemism for Ladino) who "abused" Indians in the past should not now win their vote. For some leaders these are deeply felt matters, and others confide that they are merely tactics for "those who take such things into account." In any case, although the issue is usually discussed in private, latent ethnic tensions do occasionally become explosively overt. In a recent instance, a large group of San Martineros (pseudonym), including Ladinos and Indians, forcibly removed their allegedly corrupt mayor and tried to install in office Megano C (of Indian descent). Among the men supporting Megano were members of the Civil Patrol, a group that the military government ordered each community to organize to oppose "subversives." During this period, the military also appointed mayors. Although Peteneros, with the exception of San Luiseños, regard the Civil Patrols as a cross between an "imposition" and a farce, the San Martineros thought that by involving the Patrol in the mayor's removal they could get around the military. But the military did intervene, and during a loud, angry public meeting held in the town square they agreed to remove the old mayor and replace him, not with Megano but with Fulano R , a Ladino and a kinsman of a former chicle contracting family which before 1944 had dominated the town and "abused Indians more than Ladinos." (Ever since the 1920s national and regional authorities have selected Rs to represent the community.) Although Fulano is known to be a decent, honest man, San Martinero Indians were upset about his appointment. At the public meeting, they shouted, "We do not want an R to rule us again. You always impose a white man on us. We want Megano; he is one of us!" This unexpected outburst of ethnic animosity split the anti-Fulano forces and angered the military who, making it clear that there were limits to their patience, installed Fulano. Afterward, recent *sureño* settlers said, "It was all nothing. The Cs and the Rs are the same. They rule this place for themselves and do not care about us." In a way they are correct, for since about 1970 Peteneros have often been more concerned about settler-Petenero divisions than about ethnic differences among themselves. Yet, as the young man who was cited at the beginning of this chapter (and who was shaken by the meeting) wondered, "Maybe it [ethnic prejudice] is there, hidden."

Ethnicity does not play a direct role in economic transactions. It is true that an Indian may explain a (Ladino) merchant's sharp trading in ethnic terms, and the merchant may claim that Indians make "foolish" purchases. But for all their talk Indians show no partisan preference for Indian merchants, and Ladino merchants are much more concerned with a customer's economic status than his or her ethnicity. If it suits their purposes, Ladinos will buy and borrow from, sell to, and work for Indians as readily as they will for anyone else, and vice versa. In short, in Petén, except perhaps for choice of baptismal *compadre*, ethnicity tends to be as "facul-

Table 5:2 Socioeconomic Comparisons: Ethnicity and Household

Comparison	Ladino households	Indian households	X^2	p
A Household score				
0–4.0	31 (46.3)	125 (76.2)		
4.5–7.5	24 (35.8)	34 (20.7)		
8.0–11.0	12 (17.9)	5 (3.1)	30.301	<.001
B Cement floor				
Yes	41 (61.2)	67 (40.9)		
No	26 (38.8)	97 (59.1)	7.905	<.01
C Television				
Yes	23 (34.3)	12 (7.3)		
No	44 (65.7)	152 (92.7)	26.996	<.001
D Formal education				
None–3rd grade	32 (47.8)	124 (75.6)		
4th–12th grade	35 (52.2)	40 (24.4)	8.955	<.01
E Primary occupation				
Farming (milpa)	19 (28.4)	100 (67.1)		
Non-farming	48 (71.6)	54 (32.9)	28.913	<.001

Source: Household survey, 1985. *Key*: N = 231. Percents in parentheses.

Note: The contingency coefficient (C) for A = .341. Phi scores for B = .034; C = .342; D = .197; E = .354. Education and occupation are given for head of household. Expert opinion is that one must have at least four years of continuous schooling to retain literacy (Williams 1965), hence the categories used above.

tative" as kinship. However, this hardly means that Indians have attained social, political, or economic parity with Ladinos.

On the regional level, Floreños are overwhelmingly overrepresented among the resident economic elite in Petén. In addition, they very nearly monopolize the top positions in the regional government, civil service, and political parties, and within prestige hierarchies. As a teacher in San Francisco explains, "Prestige is a big word. Truly, to speak correctly, you can use it only in Flores. Here, you should say some people are respected, but no one has prestige." On the local level too, Ladinos are overrepresented and Indians underrepresented within economic, political, and social hierarchies.

The *pueblo* of San Andrés again may serve as an illustration. Precisely because San Andrés has had mayors of Indian descent since 1945, because there are affluent Indians there, because there simply are no overt cultural differences between native San Andrés Indians and Ladinos, and because the public posture is that ethnic distinctions are things of the past, the lack of parity between the two groups is particularly striking. Township secretaries, treasurers, and school directors are almost invariably Ladinos, although San Andreños insist that ethnicity no longer influences appointment to these posts. Despite the numerical superiority of the Indians, between 1945 and 1985 the ratio of Ladino to Indian political party leaders was four to one. Ladinos also are, on average, economically better off than Indians. In 1985, a weighted eleven point "Household Composite" scale based on household construction, service facilities, and material possessions was used to assess household economic level. This measure was used because the household is the relevant unit of production, consumption, and economic decision making in Petén, because the items on the scale reflect differences in wealth in culturally appropriate terms, and because the scale items (for example, floor type) are less subject to respondent distortion than self-reported household income or ownership of productive resources.[16] The households which townspeople consider affluent (and which, in fact, own a very disproportionate share of town productive resources) had Household Scores of 8 and above. Conversely, the "truly poor" had scores of about 4 and below. As Table 5:2 (which deals with native San Andreños) Part A shows, Ladino households were significantly overrepresented among the high scorers, and Indian households among the low ones. San Andreños like other Peteneros set a high priority on cement-floored homes. They also want TVs (available since about 1982), which in 1985 cost Q250 and more. These were expensive items in that average annual household income was about Q1,500. On both counts, Ladinos were significantly better off than Indians (Table 5:2, B and C). There has always been a connection between wealth and education in Petén, and Ladino heads of household have had and continue to have more schooling than Indian heads of household (Table 5:2 D). Peteneros say milperos are less well educated and poorer than others, and with respect to primary occupation, Indians are more apt to be milperos than Ladinos (Table 5:2 E). In short, from any number of angles Ladinos on average enjoy significantly higher political and economic status than Indians. The exceptions are fewer than would be expected, were Indians as assimilated as they are acculturated.

It is easier to point to disparities between Indians and Ladinos than to explain why such inequalities persist, given the apparently attenuated significance of ethnicity, the degree of acculturation, and the absence of discrimination in modern Petén. One might argue that although Indians and Ladinos make milpa, dress, worship, and so on, in the same way, they have different values, hence they make different consumer, educational, and occupational choices. Even were the argument not circular, Indians in San Andrés and, for that matter, in San José and San Luis too, given the means to do so make exactly the same choices Ladinos do. Differences in values, if they are present, do not account for the disparities.

Two other mutually reinforcing processes help to account for persistent inequalities. First, and most obvious, Peteneros of Creole and, to a lesser extent, Ladino descent have enjoyed a historically precipitated edge over Peteneros of Indian descent. The colonial social system, traces of which persisted well into the twentieth century—more often in the form of informal prejudice than formal discrimination—was based on institutionalized ethnic stratification. As a consequence, in postcolonial times non-Indians have had greater access to wealth and power than Indians.

Second, in Petén, as elsewhere, a person's life chances are very much affected by his or her family of orientation. This aspect of ethnic stratification must be seen in the context of Petén's long history of isolation and economic underdevelopment, including a lack of schools. In the absence of well-developed public and parochial schools, training for government employment and commerce (major sources of wealth in Petén) was largely carried out at home. Initially advantaged families could induct their children into useful public and business networks and educate them for success in these fields. Nepotism and education were (and are) two sides of the same coin. The Ortegas (pseudonym), a family of Creole-Ladino descent from central Petén, illustrate a rather common situation. Shortly after the Carrera revolution of 1838, Miguel Ortega, a literate man with affinal kinsmen in Flores, became mayor of San Andrés. One of his sons, Luis, entered the civil service and another became a merchant. The lineal descendants of Luis followed his path. Ever since 1901 they have been teachers and township secretaries, not only in San Andrés but also in San José, San Benito, and San Luis. In 1987 one of them earned a law degree from the University of San Carlos. This sort of intergenerational career continuity is a regular pattern in Petén. To be sure, there have been remarkable Indians who have educated themselves far beyond the norm, but even when they have not had to cope with prejudice and a lack of influential contacts, they have had to compete with equally capable, better-connected non-Indians in a frontier region with limited demand for their talents. Even today, for example, there are not enough positions in the school system for all qualified teachers, a circumstance that favors those with the right family connections or with the wealth to bribe senior officials in the national school administration. Ethnicity, ethnic endogamy, education, inherited wealth, power, and nepotism are all interconnected, and together they perpetuate the inequalities illustrated in Table 5:2.

La chiclería, as should be clear by now, had somewhat contrary effects on the situation. During the chicle collecting season, performance counted more than ethnicity. Although those who were affluent, influential, and literate prior to the introduction of the industry had greater access to chicle contracts than others, some capable Indians also were able to become foremen and, after 1949, contractors. Such Indians became wealthier than most Ladinos even though, overall, non-Indians fared better than Indians in *la chiclería*. In similar contradictory fashion, the extractive economy strengthened preexisting exchange relationships and widened the economic gap between social sectors, with all that implies regarding the perpetuation of ethnic inequalities, while simultaneously fostering cultural homogeneity or acculturation. Even today when there is in Petén a greater demand for educated workers and greater opportunity for economic and sociopolitical mobility than ever, it is still true that differences in educational opportunity and family status enable the children of already educated, affluent families to benefit disproportionately from the changes. Furthermore, the system of social synonyms suggests that at the ideational level, ethnicity will remain at least a latent category in Petén.[17]

Community, Chicle, and Competence

La chiclería also affected community, an important principle of social organization in Petén.

In Petén there are two ways to become a member of a community. One may be born into a community or acquire something like honorary membership through long term residence in and expressed loyalty to it, which can be further reinforced by marriage to a native. But acquired membership is not as secure as membership by birthright, and there are long-term nonnative residents who are never accepted by natives as community members. Nonnative residents express the matter by saying, "Some people always remember that one is not from here" (not born in the community).

As I have said before, a broad range of social relationships is qualified by community membership. Peteneros ascribe to one another a social personality partly derived from community of birth, and they interact on that basis. Traditional political and economic exchanges between settlements appear to be the bases for the stereotypes about character, but Peteneros see it the other way around. The community is also a reference group, a context for self-evaluation (Rubel 1977). For example, men who are most dignified, staid, and courtly in their own community can be frivolous and disruptive in a neighboring settlement. Because community members say, "We are all friends here," and "This place [community] is like a big family," those who misbehave at home are quick to apologize for stepping out of line but resist apologizing when they misbehave elsewhere.

There are, of course, practical as well as moral reasons for identifying with and maintaining a good reputation in one's own community. By custom, members of the community have preferential access to wage labor opportunities on local public works projects, to land controlled by the township, and to the political protection of township officials and local men of influence. The local community, when it is a county capital, also is the one government unit directly responsive to popular will. Further, one's life chances are affected by community, because the state channels public funds and services through this unit. For example, the state provides better schools to some communities than others, and teachers tend to pay more attention to children native to the *pueblo* than to other youngsters, if for no other reason than that their parents have more influence with local authorities than nonnative residents. That townspeople often display greater loyalty to their *pueblo* than villagers to their *aldea* is probably based on the fact that the *pueblo*, rather than the *aldea*, controls income flowing to the *municipio* from the central government.

The virtual absence of voluntary collective organizations in the local communities has no bearing on the importance of community. Household atomism, also a salient feature of Petén social organization, and community are not necessarily mutually exclusive terms. In Petén, the place where one lives, works, plays, and worships, the people with whom one maintains the most important social, economic, and political relations, and the group from which one selects a spouse all tend to coincide, creating a sense of security in that place and a basis for group action. What Munch and Marske (1981:168) say about Tristan de Cunha may be said of Petén: "The individual allegiances of each member of the community are interlinked" and "form a continuous network of individually selected but overlapping and interlocking relationships that in the end covers the entire community." Except that Peteneros do ascribe a collective identity to members of a community and that townships are corporate entities in law, Munch and Marske's additional statement is also applicable to Petén:

> This network is, in fact, what makes this loosely organized aggregate of independent households a *community* in more than an ecological sense, where a person belongs, not by virtue of a collective identity but by virtue of a personal identity expressed and confirmed in those individual allegiances chosen for reinforcement in a pattern of selective reciprocity (Munch and Marske 1981:168).

Paradoxically, recent changes have simultaneously lessened the economic importance and intensifed the psychopolitical significance of community membership. Although Peteneros do not depend on local government for supplementary wage labor opportunities to the extent they did before the late 1970s, the security of being *conocido* (known and familiar in a given place) has been heightened by real and imagined threats from the large number of recent migrants to Petén and, sadly, by the political violence that became widespread in the region beginning around 1982. The community is more than ever a refuge in what has become an unsettled society.

Nonetheless, except for the matter of chicle tax income, the chicle economy has tended to exert a centrifugal force on community ties. Nepotism, influence, and bribery may help a man get a chicle contract, but he will not keep it long if he does not produce chicle, and for this he must hire competent workers, irrespective of their community identity. Hence, within the industry, people relate to each other as individuals rather than as representatives of a particular social category or in terms of ascribed status. They confront one another as economic, not community, actors, and they evaluate individual performance rather than any categorically ascribed personality characteristics.

In other words, contractors and chicleros have a class relationship with one another, although in addition a small minority do have patron-client relationships with one another. Yet despite the fact that economic considerations almost always override personal ones in *la chiclería*, contractors and chicleros talk and occasionally act as if their relations were based on patronage. Insofar as style can shape substance, some contractors and chicleros may be genuinely concerned about each other, but jobbers and tappers are quick to note how often the style is deceptive. To minimize deception, worker and employer may try to personalize their relationship, to act as patron and client, but a contractor will not hire a loyal, servile, but otherwise incompetent tapper, nor will a chiclero work for a decent but otherwise incompetent contractor. In the chicle business, the contract has nothing to do with mutual obligations flowing from community membership or even kinship. A contractor or subcontractor may prefer to hire his relatives or his townsmen, but only if they are also competent chicleros. In his role of chiclero or jobber, each actor builds his own network of instrumental relationships which cuts across, is independent of, and is at times opposed to otherwise important family, ethnic, and community lines.

Chicle collecting also limits the extent to which tappers can make a contribution to the sporadic collective community efforts which do occur in Petén. Chicleros are away from home for months on end and, especially since 1945, work in the chicle fields for varying lengths of time. Thus it is quite difficult to coordinate their joint participation in community activities.

During the tapping season almost everything that defines community is inverted. At home milperos have preferential access to township land by virtue of community membership. In the forest, however, chicleros gain access to trees by their individual efforts and do not have a privileged right to tap trees simply because they are found in their own township. During the season the camp, not the community, is the chiclero's reference group and the physical nexus for his social relationships. Chicleros do not deal with one another in terms of character traits predicated on community membership, but rather as individuals temporarily freed of all ascribed statuses. At home, a man lives among well-known neighbors with whom he usually has settled relations. In contrast, chicle camps are defined as places where people who know little about one another come together, and in fact camps often are diversely composed. At home, a man is normally involved in ascribed hierarchical kinship relationships, as a son or as a father. In camp, his bonds with others tend to be self-chosen and egalitarian. There is also a spiritual dimension to the contrast. Spirit beings associated with settled communities, for example, patron saints, play no role in the camps. Chicleros are more concerned with *duendes* (goblins) which almost never appear in permanent settlements but are encountered in the deep forest, most commonly by chicleros. The chiclero is supposed to be dangerous, prodigal, hard drinking, and locked in struggle with the forest. The milpero at home in the community is peaceful, prudent, sober, and at one with the forest.[18] In fact, they are usually the same person, and it may be that Peteneros dichotomize the roles to clarify and to interpret for themselves their differing experiences in the chicle fields and at home. There are real enough sociological differences and more sharply drawn ideational contrasts between camp and community.

During the tapping season the social reality and ideology of community are muted, but when it is over the routines, relationships, and values of community are reasserted. Both the departure from and the return to the community are marked by grand carousals, in the former case because, the men say, "We will be away for a long time," and in the latter because, "We feel cold, and it takes time to become accustomed to being here [home] again." Although Peteneros drink just as much at other times, chicle sprees are treated as if they were special—rituals of transition rather than ordinary binges. Peteneros ignore any continuities between camp and community. For example, although a camp may include fathers and sons or men from the same community, in camp the men do not interact as kinsmen or fellow townsmen but rather as chicleros. This is part of a more general structural pose in which the organizational principles of the camp and those of the community are discussed as if they were completely contrastive. Because where the camp is, the community cannot not be, and vice versa, they are mutually explicit opposites. By weakening the social bonds and ideational significance of community part of the year, the chicle economy strengthens them the rest of the time, if for no other reason than once the tapping season is over people must resume and reaffirm the roles and relationships appropriate to community.[19]

Class, Ethnicity, and Community

By this time it should be apparent that the social class or social sector system of Petén resembles that found elsewhere in Hispano-American society, although it has some distinctive features.[20] Social class, in the broad rather than the restricted economic sense, is determined by wealth, access to institutional political power, family ancestry, and *educación*, in the double sense of formal schooling and refinement of manner and speech. Differences in social class are manifested in such things as dress on festive occasions, size and location of house, material possessions, elaborateness of sepulchers (those of the Flores elite are palatial enough to bear the names of their architects), and assigned position in religious processions. Social clubs have never had much success or permanence in Petén, but elite

Table 5:3 Social Sectors in Contemporary Petén, 1985

	Address			
	A	B	C	D
Upper sector				
Commercial and contracting elite	y	x	y	o
Large-scale ranchers and farmers	x	y	y	o
High-ranking government bureaucrats	x	x	y	o
Professionals, particularly physicians	y	x	y	o
Middle sector				
Lesser contractors and store owners	o	x	x	o
Medium-sized farmers (some with small herds)	o	y	x	o
Foremen, office workers, salaried and skilled labor	o	x	x	o
Lower level bureaucrats	o	x	x	o
Lower sector				
Wage workers (in construction, saw mills, stores, etc.)	o	y	x	y
Forest collectors (chicleros, shateros, loggers)	x	y	x	y
Native Petén small-scale farmers	o	y	x	y
Recent settler small-scale farmers	o	o	y	x
Landless farm workers and unskilled labor	y	o	x	y

Source: Field Notes. *Key*: A = outside Petén; B = Flores; C = towns; D = villages; x = most common address; y = second most common; o = least common. (As indicated, two addresses may be equally common, e.g., the address of roughly as many important bureaucrats is outside Petén as within it.)

Note: Big farmers may crop 40–50 hectares, medium farmers 6–39 and milperos about 5 or less. Upper and middle sector ranchers typically own at least 225 hectares of pasture (plus farm land), and 160–300 cattle. Peteneros among them are often merchant-contractors.

exclusiveness is apparent in private celebrations, particularly birthday parties, and, since the early 1970s, in several restaurants in central Petén catering to wealthy Peteneros and tourists. Other Peteneros who can afford the prices in the restaurants but who lack prestige say they would feel uneasy dining in places reserved for the "big shots" (*los grandes*).

With these criteria, Peteneros distinguish between (a) *los ricos* (the rich), or *los grandes* or *gente de categoría* (distinguished people); (b) *gente buena*, sometimes also called *gente fina* or *buenas plumas*—respectively, respectable, refined, or literate people, who usually also have *sus centavos*, "their pennies," that is, some money (*los grandes* share the first three traits but are in addition rich and distinguished); and (c) *los humildes*, "humble people," also implying they are poor milperos or forest collectors who, *grandes* and *gente buena* say, speak *pujado* (rustic Spanish). In several *pueblos* members of old Ladino families may distinguish between *gente buena* (themselves) and *gente baja* (Indians), and the Indians may refer to *naturales* (native Petén Indians) and *los egoistas* ("selfish" Ladinos, sometimes meant to imply undeserved pride; in an intercommunity context, the word refers to Flores merchants). As the use of these terms indicates, the lines between the sectors are somewhat blurry. Thus, a family may have upper sector ancestry and refinement, but if it is not affluent it will not be counted among *los grandes*. However, marriage with an upper sector family is possible. At the same time, the lines are stiff enough so that an affluent family of lower sector (and particularly Indian) ancestry would have to be wealthy, well educated, and refined for several generations before marriage with an old middle sector family would be possible, and marriage to someone of *gente de categoría*, though not formally prohibited, would remain decidedly improbable. Upward and downward social mobility occurs in Petén, but not easily. Finally, although wealth and occupation by themselves do not determine social status, there are strong enough connections between them to describe social sectors in economic terms (Reina 1964; Tables 5:1 and 5:3).

There are several distinctive features of the Petén stratification system that merit mention. First, and perhaps most singular, no one, including the elite, denigrates manual labor. This may reflect the fact that until the 1920s no one in Petén was extremely wealthy and everyone at one time or another had to work with his or her hands. Moreover, and perhaps in connection with this, wealth—no matter what its source—commands respect. Sometimes people will say that the respect accorded, for example, an affluent Indian chicle contractor who is not above tapping trees may be feigned, whereas the respect given a teacher of "refined" ancestry who also "has his pennies" is genuine. Outward expressions of deference, however, are the same in both cases. Second, ownership of farm or ranch land is not a prerequisite for high status, although it may have been during the colonial period. By the 1840s, when ranching declined, commerce became more important than land as a source of status and wealth. In the twentieth century, chicle contracting became another nonlanded source of wealth. It is true that most upper sector families have always owned large farms and ranches, but not all of them do. They have usually derived more wealth

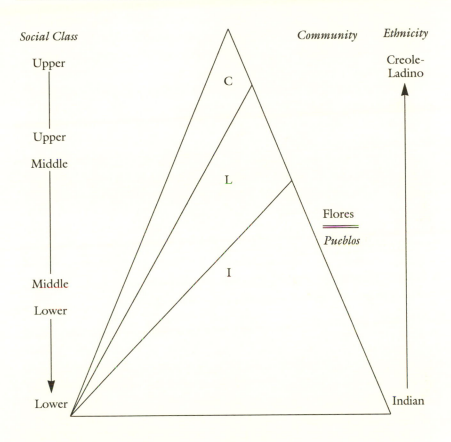

Figure 5:2. Class, community, and ethnicity. *Source*: Field Notes. *Key*: C = Creole descent; L = Ladino descent; I = Indian descent. *Note*: The figure depicts proportional distribution of class, etc., rather than population ratios. The line at the far right, "Ethnicity," refers to acculturation.

from trade, contracting, and politics than from farm production. Furthermore, the sort of rivalry found between merchants and owners of large estates in other parts of Guatemala has not occurred in Petén (although very recent economic developments may lead to a change).

Third, the stratification system has been integrated with ethnicity and

Community   Socioeconomic status

Position: High

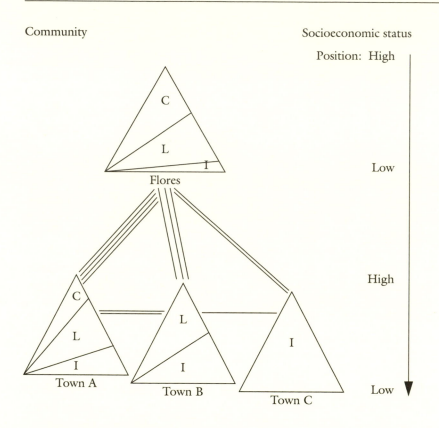

Flores

Low

High

Town A

Town B

Town C

Low

Figure 5:3. Community, ethnicity, and socioeconomic status. *Source*: Field Notes 1960–1985. *Key*: C = Creole descent; L = Ladino descent; I = Indian descent. *Note*: The figure depicts correlations among community, ethnicity, and socioeconomic status. Ethnicity, wealth, political power, level of formal education, and social prestige are congruent with each other. Moreover, townsmen tend to have more political-economic exchanges with Floreños than with people in other towns.

community. Figures 5:2 and 5:3 depict the connections between socioeconomic stratification, ethnicity, and community. As shown in Figure 5:2, which considers the region as a single unit, most of the upper class or upper sector are of Creole or Creole-Ladino descent and from Flores. Although most Ladinos are in the lower sector, a disproportionate number of them compared with Indians are in the middle sector. Rare is the society which bars all social mobility, and Petén is no exception. Thus there are affluent, well-educated, universally respected people of Indian descent in Petén, but the vast majority of Indians are poor farmers, forest collectors, and/or wage workers from the *pueblos* and *aldeas*. Figure 5:3 views the system primarily in terms of settlements as settlements, but also considers the individuals within them. Figure 5:3 shows that towns as such have more ties to Flores than to each other. Put another way, the figure shows that the number of relationships that cut across community lines increases with socioeconomic status of people within the community. For example, taken collectively, wealthy upper class Floreños have more economic and social (particularly ritual kinship) ties with non-Floreños than San Joseños have with non-San Joseños, and so on. The ties between individuals within any given community usually have more strands than those between individuals from different communities, but the upper class in Flores has a more extensive network of ties with non-Floreños than non-Floreños from the towns have with each other, and so on down the scale. Thus there are people of high social class status in town A (for example, La Libertad), but hardly as many as in Flores (and now, Santa Elena). Taken collectively, the upper class in town A have fewer ties with people from other communities than Floreños have, and additionally more of their ties are with Floreños than with people in town B, and so forth. Few of the local elite in town B (for example, Santa Ana) and certainly none of the local elite in C (for example, San José) qualify for membership in the regional level upper sector, hence they have correspondingly fewer cross-community ties. Moreover, the small number of the local elite in the towns who do qualify decreases across settlements as the number of people of Creole and/or Ladino descent in them decreases, for which reason town A is drawn a bit higher than B, and B than C. The figures may also help to show why, as has already been observed, it is difficult to affirm or deny that the significance of ethnicity is declining in Petén. Although there are Peteneros who contend ethnicity no longer matters, they also say that no one in San José is in the upper sector. They argue that contrary to what other Peteneros may say, this has nothing to do with ethnicity, but rather is due to the circumstance that San Joseños are milperos who have not had access to advanced education. Yet no matter what the explanation is, San Joseños remain *humildes*. Similarly,

Figure 5:4. Intercropped (maize, beans, squash, etc.) farm plot.

San Joseños valorize what they call "our customs," now in terms of community tradition and then in terms of ethnicity. But under either banner they continue to maintain a separate identity in Petén. Again, just as there are times when community appears to be increasingly less important in framing interpersonal relations, there are also times when Peteneros explain those relations in terms of stereotypes about social character based on community membership. In Petén there is a good deal of change without loss of continuity.

   Important as the preceding considerations are, they should not obscure the fact that in the last analysis Peteneros are more concerned about the welfare of the household—typically, a conjugal pair and their children—than anything else.[21] A man's first and major obligation is the material support and defense of his household against the outside world, and a woman's is proper internal maintenance of that same unit. Unless other-

Figure 5:5. Intercropping *jícama* (a tuber, *Pachyrrhizus tuberosus*) in a milpa.

wise very clearly demonstrated, Peteneros assume that whatever a person's ethnic, community, or social identity, he or she is fully competent to fulfill the primary responsibility, which—particularly for males—involves the ability to make a living in a variety of ways. As a household's economic status rises, it usually expands and thickens its ties to kinsmen (especially siblings) and others from its own and other communities, but loyalty to one's own household and usually to that of one's parents is categorical. Beyond this all other loyalties are contingent upon circumstances which Peteneros regard as inherently labile and equivocal. That the chicle economy placed a premium on individual effort may have contributed to the salience of the atomistic household, but whatever the reason, it is at the center of the Petenero's concerns.

To speak of events up to about 1970, life in Petén was hard but not miserable. On the one hand, most of the time householders were able to fulfill their major obligations. Certainly the majority were poor (and the

Figure 5:6. Backyard garden and semi-domesticated deer foraging in yard.

Figure 5:7. House, external kitchen, and yard orchard.

small middle sector far from affluent) and had to work ceaselessly to make ends meet, but more often than not they were able to satisfy their basic needs for food, shelter, and clothing. There was no pressure on the land, and a man could make as large a milpa as permitted by his age, health, available household labor, and time devoted to extractive work and, prior to 1945, corvée duties. Most farm households making three to five hectare milpas produced about 150 to 250 quintals of maize for household consumption (at least since the 1940s, average household size has been five to six persons) and for sale—a positive picture compared to the rest of Guatemala. If, for social or political reasons, life in town became too difficult, a household could retreat to the forest. Life there was a solitary one, but as Peteneros say, "The *monte* was tranquil, and there was always a lot to eat." Chicleros had to cope with all sorts of trials, but not being subject to close supervision they found ways to resist excessive abuses. On the other hand, even aside from the necessity for unremitting labor, there were periodic famines and epidemics, medical care was inadequate, particularly for infants and toddlers, and there was political oppression, which if not as harsh as that in southern Guatemala was onerous enough. Perhaps the combination of material and political hardships, along with open access to land and the possibility of flight to the woods, helps account both for the constant concern—really an underlying anxiety—about authority and about producing enough food for the household, and for the equally constant refrains, "The forest will provide for us" and "Petén is democratic, unlike the rest of Guatemala." Peteneros are resigned to hardships, but they are not defeated nor made disconsolate by them. They have a robust appreciation for the small pleasures of everyday life, such as savoring the aroma of freshly cut pimienta, enjoying late afternoon conversations with friends, or watching the progress of the milpa. For all their adversity, one of the most characteristic sounds, at least in central Petén, is that of laughter. The mix may also help explain several other characteristic patterns of belief and behavior.

Kearney says that the Ixtepijians of Oaxaca assume that "the individual is essentially alone in a hostile [natural and social] world in which nothing is secure" (1972:44). In Petén, the assumption rather seems to be that the individual, supported by the household but otherwise alone, must confront an ambivalent world in which nothing is certain. Children can depend on their parents, but beyond this relationships are facultative, not firm, and everything is equivocal. An elderly informant explains that "*el más amigo es el más traidor*" (one's best friend is the most traitorous) — your most intimate friend knows your secrets, the better to betray you. In their poems chicleros define the tapping season as *"sagrada y mala"* (sacred and sacrilegious), a time to make money for the household, but by killing trees. The season is the epoch of *"alegría"* (joy) and of *"peligros funebres"* (gloomy dangers), *"cruel"* (grim, brutal), *"pero él que sufre es él que no muere"* (but he who suffers will not die). After a damp, cold night in a forest camp, they say, "The coffee that warms us (also) tastes bitter." Chicleros are relatively well paid, but the work is physically and morally dangerous. Farmers do not earn as much, but their work is peaceful, safe, and proper. Office work is respected, safe from physical accident, but socially and politically tense and often venal. Even the tranquility of the milpa is equivocal; it is a welcome respite from the social entanglements and morally perilous temptations of life in town, and for the same reasons *triste* (sad, dull). It is prudent to be *conocido* (well known) in a community because people more readily help *conocidos* than strangers, but this also means putting up with the nettlesome scrutiny of neighbors. One should be concerned about the community and be willing to serve on the municipal council, but doing so means compatriots will suspect one of dipping into public funds. (This reflects the circumstance that councilmen are expected to honor the moral norms of the community and the legal rules of the state, which contradict each other, so no matter what they do councilmen violate some standard.)

The same sort of ambivalence marks other socially standardized roles and relationships. For example, Peteneros value both autonomy and competence, yet the realization of one state undermines the realization of the other. A man becomes most independent and most able to live without social embroilments by working at the milpa, but this usually means that to sustain his household he will have to find off-farm work. He must be sufficiently competent to engage in different types of wage labor, at the cost of yielding some of his autonomy to meet the demands of his patron. Since the men usually work alone or with the aid of unmarried sons at their milpas, or alone in the chicle fields, the value placed on independence and competence is consonant with the organization of labor in Petén. But the point is that the values of independence and competence often are inversely related. The Petenero's outlook may reflect historical experience as well as modern circumstances.[22] In the colonial period, precisely because those who lived in settled communities considered the forest dangerous, it could be a sanctuary for those who could not put up with alien rule; likewise, the

Figure 5:8. Flores.

chicle economy had its own ambiguities and uncertainties. Such (equivocal) attitudes and patterns of behavior may be responses to modern macrosocial conditions and historical events, or they may be self-chosen ways of being that are compatible with those circumstances. Precisely how the ideational, including its moral dimension, and the situational interpenetrate, however, goes beyond our immediate concerns.

Concluding Discussion

From the 1890s to about 1970, chicle collecting dominated the economy of Petén, but without stimulating its economic or social development. The basic conditions and socioeconomic patterns laid down in the early eighteenth century persisted, with modifications to be sure, into the mid-to-late 1960s. Until then, the region remained isolated, underpopulated, and economically marginal. Transportation and communication were rudimentary, and Petén was neglected by the state. Society was led by a small group of families who were affluent but not rich, based in Flores and descended from Creole (with Ladino admixtures) soldiers, bureaucrats, ranchers, and merchants who settled in the region between 1700 and 1750. Although notable families, always willing to make marriage alliances with able, ambitious newcomers, might gain or lose status, theirs was largely movement up and down the higher rungs of the social ladder. Their descendants are quick to point out how much Petén "suffered" from the material conditions noted above. Those circumstances, however, prevented the stratification system from becoming as inegalitarian and, after the initial military conquest and consolidation, the political system from being as harsh as elsewhere in Guatemala, small comfort though this may have been to Indians and lower-sector Ladinos. Flores was (and is) the physical, political, economic, and social center of the hinterland, the center of a "multicommunity" system (Reina 1965) incorporating the settlements around the Lake and on the savanna, but increasingly less linked to settlements progressively further from central Petén. The particular economic relationships of each community with Flores apparently generated and sustained durable stereotypes about the social character of its inhabitants. Although the impact of the extractive economy was not all of a piece, it did not substantially change, but more usually reinforced, these patterns and the relationships between social sectors in Petén. Here and there the mold was dented, but its overall shape held.

The traditional upper sector was the major local beneficiary of the chicle business. The enterprise ran on credit, and the upper sector's prechicle commanding position in the regional exchange and political system (this itself a colonial heritage) gave it superior access to private and public lines of credit. For technoenvironmental reasons, management could not rely on ownership of the means of production to control and extract a surplus from labor. Foreign companies (from about 1920 to 1945) and the upper sector, aided by state authorities, dominated and took a profit from labor as much by control of commerce and credit as from surplus value (i.e., commodity price for chicle less wages and costs). What added to the importance of exchange relations was that given the ecology of chicle production, profit could not be increased by technical modernization or by increased labor productivity. In any event, traditional exchange relationships were strengthened, much to the advantage of the upper sector. True, between 1949 and 1954, the state broadened access to credit, but by this time it was too late to narrow the increased socioeconomic gap between social sectors that had been engendered by the chicle industry.

If the chicle economy enriched upper sector merchant-contractors and, particularly after 1949, opened the door a bit to social mobility, it did not lead to economic development in Petén. Most of the wealth from *oro blanco* flowed outside the region to foreign companies that processed and marketed chewing gum. Petén's role was restricted to primary production and export of chicle. Although it may be argued that chicle production as such, for all its booms and busts, represented increased economic output and did increase the volume of trade, the industry did not generate productive or significant fiscal linkages in Petén, and eventually, of course, chicle production itself steeply declined. Moreover, development refers not only to economic growth but also to an improved quality of life for all sectors of a society, as measured by such factors as rising levels of real income, improved nutrition, shelter, medical care, and education.[23] Although *la chiclería* did not erode material conditions of life for the majority, and although chicleros often earned higher wages than other Guatemalan rural workers, their gains were just as often offset by higher prices for maize and imported goods and indebtedness brought about by the industry. In effect, chicle collecting did little to improve living conditions in Petén. Rather, it increased economic disparities between social sectors.

Economic growth brought about by primary production of chicle for export was not accompanied by "structural changes to induce complementary growth or by institutional changes to diffuse gains in real income among all sectors of the population" (Clower, Dalton, Harwitz, and Walters 1966:vi; although they are speaking of Liberia, they might as well have been describing the situation in Petén). While it lasted, chicle production increased total wages in Petén for tappers and increased revenues for government, but the wages did not lead to the creation of local industries to satisfy consumer demands. Instead, chicle production raised imports of consumer goods. Furthermore, since most of the time most of the revenues were spent outside Petén, they could not increase productive capacity in the department.

Nor did the chicle economy lead to another sort of modern development—the emergence of an organized class of workers. Tappers were conscious of their shared position in the productive process and were not a servile labor force, but they were not able to take unified action in opposition to management. Between 1945 and 1954 national regimes supported unionization, but the same organizational and technoenvironmental conditions which made it difficult for management to supervise labor

also hindered labor unity, and efforts to organize chicleros remained unsuccessful. After 1954 union activity became extremely risky. Until the early
1980s the isolation of Petén from the highlands and the spatial dispersion
of the chicleros insulated labor there from the full measure of the state-
sponsored terrorism against unionists so common elsewhere in Guatemala.
The potential for violence, however, along with the isolation, dispersion of
labor, and organization of chiclero-contractor relations, completely debilitated all organized attempts to express the class interests of labor. Short-
term patron-clientism was not only compatible with ecological, technical,
and social conditions in the chicle industry, but also had no safe alternative.

Oro blanco did contribute to the various processes promoting ladinoization in Petén, and during the tapping season ethnicity had little meaning.
But acculturation has not brought about assimilation, in the sense that, on
average, Indians have not achieved socioeconomic parity with non-Indians,
and native Petén Indians still maintain a separate ethnic identity, most
overtly in San José and San Luis, where ethnicity and community corre-
spond to each other. Outside of these two places, ethnic distinctions may
be used or ignored in making a wide range of personal decisions. Yet even
where consideration of ethnicity seems a thing of the past, political tensions may evoke overt expressions of otherwise latent biases. Although
Indians and Ladinos have shared a common position in relation to chicle
production, and although they have farmed, as they still do, in the same
way, many have retained either a hidden or overt sense of ethnic distinctiveness.

La chiclería did not diminish the importance of community as a principle
of social organization. Perhaps as a reflection of the inherent instability of
the industry, Peteneros regarded chicle collecting as parlous and profane.
In self-defensive response, each individual built a personal network, which
during the tapping season cut across and muted ascribed group allegiances,
including communal ones. Salient as these networks were during the tapping season, when it was over community reassumed its organizational
vitality. Of course, the territorial-administrative structure in Guatemala
assures the weight of community. In addition, in a type of schismogenetic
process, community and personal network in *la chiclería* alternately sustained and drained each other. This, too, contributed to the continuing
significance of community.

Yet the case for different types of continuity must not be overstressed.
Clearly, there were many changes in Petén between the early 1700s and late

1960s, including those traceable to the chicle business. The recall of no more than a few instances will make the point. Thus there is a difference between the legalized racism of the colonial period and the overt ethnic discrimination of the post-1821 period, and an even greater difference between the latter and the covert, wavering prejudice of modern times. San Joseños still regard themselves and are still regarded by others as a distinct ethnic group in a separate community. However, San José teenagers no longer speak Maya, are culturally indistinguishable from other youngsters, and go beyond the sixth grade. This subtly shifts the weight of their distinct identity from ethnicity to community, reshuffles their negotiations with non-San Joseños, and broadens their personal options. Again, although Peteneros worked as hard after the abolition of corvée and debt peonage in 1945 as before, the change not only gave them more disposable time, it was also celebrated as the lifting of "impositions." In a typically equivocal appreciation of the change, an informant observed (in 1961) that "In Ubico's time, there was order here. Now the *palos* are gone and there is freedom and disorder. No one has to obey his patron." With the decline in chicle production, even the popular image of the chiclero has changed. In 1960 hicleros were "powerful" men, admired for their sylvan skills and hardiness, men who could not be pushed too far. By the late 1970s they had become merely ordinary workers.[24] If *la chiclería* did not develop Petén, it did give some few chicleros a chance (granted, a slim one) to improve their material condition. Chicleros who were able to purchase radios or extra clothes or to become subcontractors certainly felt better off, even though increased trade and production primarily served upper sector merchant-contractor interests. Similarly, at least a portion of the revenues from chicle, particularly after 1953, provided for some additional public amenities in several towns. Nothing said here is intended to minimize the force of these or other changes not immediately germane to this discussion.[25]

Rather, the point is that however important, the changes did not transform the region. Local government did not get enough of the surplus from chicle collecting to make major investments in the productive infrastructure of the department. Although foreign companies took most of the profit from chicle production, Peteneros—primarily merchant-contractors—did trap some of it. However, they had very limited opportunities for investment, and for technical and ecological reasons they could not improve per capita productivity in *la chiclería* to increase their share of the surplus. They did expand their exchange operations, but this did not generate new productive activities. Only when the era of chicle was ending did FYDEP invest some of the profit from chicle in the regional infrastructure. Even if there should be renewed demands for chicle, post-1970 demographic and other changes in Petén (described in the next chapter) make it quite unlikely that *la chiclería* can ever regain its former preeminence.[26] Generalizations about the eighty-year history of a major economic activity in a vast region must admit of exceptions, as the late investments of FYDEP indicate. Yet, despite the long-term centrality of the chicle business and despite whatever benefits it gave some Peteneros, it did not generate socioeconomic development in Petén and did not end its isolation.

Nor did *oro blanco* seriously affect commutative relations between social class, community, and ethnicity, or household atomism. The industry had little effect on the stratification system other than, partly because of the role of exchange relations in the chicle economy, strengthening the position of the upper sector and of Flores. It also may be noted that in comparison with many other areas of Guatemala, while political and economic conditions in Petén were undeniably hard, they were not viciously harsh. Despite all the shifting complexities of region's history, the basic postconquest sociocultural patterns persisted, and in this sense life in the hinterland was settled. For a variety of reasons, concurrent with the decreased importance of *la chiclería*, Petén was "recolonized" and life there became unsettled.

Chapter Six

Conclusion: Continuity, Change, and a New Turn

"After all, the Peten was then [1895] and is now [1940] a region almost unoccupied, little developed, and of small promise" (Jones 1940:82)

"May your dreams come true" (old curse usually attributed to the Chinese).

Introduction

This chapter carries the narrative into the 1980s. It will not be as detailed as the earlier chapters, because what has happened in Petén since about 1970 is so complex, so many-sided, that a complete account would require a second volume. Instead, the description will outline what has happened lately, in an effort to explain why the old dream of incorporating Petén into the nation has become a nightmare for too many Peteneros and new colonists, why what once was a stable—and in this sense a settled—frontier society most lately has become recolonized and unsettled.

To underscore similarities and differences between selected aspects of life in Petén before about 1970 and after, the first section will recall what has been said so far. Then more recent events will be discussed. As will be seen, the contemporary recolonization of Petén is reminiscent of the late seventeenth-century conquest and early eighteenth-century colonization of the region. True, there are profound, sharp changes taking place in Petén, and some of them are probably irreversible. But in some ways the story nearly comes around to where it began.

Continuity, Change, and "Democracy" in the Lowland Forests

The first major theme of this study has been that for some 250 years, roughly from the 1720s to the 1970s, the sociocultural system of Petén endured with noticeable continuity, not in spite of changes, but to an important degree because of them. The second major theme has been that although Petén inevitably shared much in common with the rest of Guatemala, circumstances also made it distinctive from the rest of the nation. One important difference has been that over time and until very recently sociopolitical conditions for the lower sectors of the population were—if not benign—improving.

Until recently, Peteneros put it another way. Two of the first things they used to tell newcomers are, "The forest is rich and provides for us," and "Petén is more democratic and tranquil than the rest of Guatemala." Only on longer acquaintance did they talk about hardships in the forest, poverty, injustice, and inequality. What follows is a concluding statement about the historical warrant for these maxims.

In 1697 the Spanish conquered the Indians, but not the forests, of Petén. Thereafter, Peteneros entered the forests to make a living and to find a sanctuary from oppression. Unlike too many other rural Guatemalans, poor Peteneros, whether Indian or Ladino, were *not* increasingly alienated from the land, pushed deeper into poverty, subject to ever harsher repression, and finally driven to violent revolution. In general, socioeconomic and political inequalities were not so extreme nor so brutally maintained as in several more populated areas of the country. A colonial castelike system that included forced labor is hardly a happy base from which to begin, but Peteneros did not have to choose between abject submission to the lords of wealth and power, and armed opposition to them. For many Peteneros ethnicity does remain a principle of social organzation, but for the last several generations it has not been a euphemism for stark racism. Most Peteneros are still poor, but few go hungry; most defer to elites, but few are slavish. In turn, there is no way to mistake the wealth, power, and prestige of the regional elite, but they are not openly "contemptuous" (Manz's word) of the poor or of Indians, as they are elsewhere in the republic (Manz 1988:141). Peteneros want more than this, but given the national economy and structure of power, they have not been served a Barmecide feast. Their maxims about the forests and about democracy make sense.

To recognize the continuities in postconquest Petén is most emphatically not to minimize the discontinuities. The social history of Petén has been no more orderly or immutable than that of any other place. Since 1697 there have been many changes, including, of course, traumatic military conquest in the late seventeenth to early eighteenth century; formation of a new polity, economy, and society in the early colonial period; an important shift of trade and contact away from Spanish-speaking Campeche and toward English-speaking British Honduras after the 1830s and 1840s; large-scale capitalist penetration (*la chiclería*) in the late nineteenth century; revolution in 1944, counterrevolution in 1954, disorderly colonization since 1970, and civil war in the 1980s. Yet, except possibly for post-1970 events, these and other changes reinforced major sociocultural patterns initially laid down in the first two or three decades of the eighteenth century. The process was not smooth or free of exceptions, but there were strong continuing central tendencies. From the early eighteenth to the last third of the twentieth century, there was relatively little change in the socioeconomic composition of and the relationships between Petén's various social sectors, ethnic groups, and communities. The unequal distribution of wealth, power, and prestige within and across settlements was stable. Social groups occupied relatively unchanging, status-congruent positions within economic, political, and prestige hierarchies.

In some places there is a master "mode of social categorization"—caste or community or class—that "overrides all other social categories and operates as *the* basic source of systematic human distinctions" (Gilmore 1976:99). This was not (and is not) the case in Petén, except perhaps in colonial times when ethnicity may have overridden all other social categories. But thereafter social sector (or class), community, ethnicity, and, for some Peteneros, patron-client ties cutting across categories became roughly equally important principles of social organization. For example, although no longer decisive in all contexts, ethnicity is still critical in some, such as spouse selection, and to say that context determines when it is primary is simply another way of noting that no single principle is *the* basis for systematic social distinctions.

That community, class, and ethnicity are, or were until recently, equally important and commutative appears to be causally related to material circumstances. If we refer back to but one example, we recall that even if relations in *la chiclería* could be described solely in terms of social class— and they cannot be—Peteneros were not only (chicle) wage workers, but of necessity also independent peasant farmers. In some contexts, community was at least as important as class and more important than ethnicity for one's economic welfare. Until very recently everyone had access to land, but farm location was determined primarily by community, and to whom one sold surplus crops was in part structured by community as well as by class and personalized relations (Reina 1964:275). Moreover, access to wage labor opportunities on public works projects was based on community membership. Thus, to an extent, income differences, particularly in the lower sectors, were affected by location of community and by community membership. As a result, for most of the twentieth century and perhaps even earlier, householders in, for example, San Andrés were on average better off than those in Dolores or San Francisco. In short, to rank one principle of social organization over another, although appealing, would be an oversimplification and distortion.

From colonial to modern times, the regional elite lacked incentives and opportunities to exercise unlimited dominion over land and labor. By the time the colony was established, *encomiendas* were no longer granted, and the major productive activity in the colony—livestock raising—was not successful and did not absorb labor. Then and later, undeveloped infrastructure, sparse population, and probably soil conditions prevented development of large commercial plantations. In sharp contrast to those in the rest of the nation, Creoles and Ladinos in Petén had no need or motive to deprive Indians of access to land. Even when chicle was the mainstay of the economy, the elite could not completely control labor, partly for technoenvironmental reasons and partly because they had to compete for workers. From the early 1700s on, the dominant social sector turned to commerce for want of alternatives, having more to gain from that than from direct control of land and labor. Even in colonial times and more so later, milperos had to supplement farm income with off-farm wage labor to purchase the minimal necessities of life such as salt, metal tools, and cloth, all of which were imported. The more affluent merchants, and at times government too, controlled this trade. Within the constraints imposed by exporters and government, the merchants also set the terms of trade and thus helped determine the need for supplemental wage labor in Petén. In addition, particularly after 1821, they provided milperos with the largest number of off-farm wage labor opportunities. In this sense, upper sector control of trade and commerce was a nonviolent substitute for more directly coercive methods of labor control. Major economic changes, such as the secular decline of livestock trade after the 1830s and the introduction of *la chiclería* in the 1890s, increased the importance of commerce for the elite. In a long history of sluggish economic development, they relied less on control of productive resources than on preeminence in the exchange system.

Lack of economic development was also consequential for status continuity. Those in the lower and middle sectors had no significant opportunities for economic mobility, with all that means for perpetuating the status quo. Few entrepreneurs had reason to invest in or to migrate — except as refugees — to Petén; the regional upper sector faced no rivals from that quarter. The upper sector also worked at protecting its position, through marriage alliances with the few successful immigrants who came to Petén and through pursuit of multiple careers in commerce, in the professions, and in government. The upper sector also practiced nepotism to gain access to these careers and to credit, whether it was rationalized in terms of family ancestry, social class, ethnicity, or ubiety. After 1945 popular mayoralty elections and broader access to chicle contracts led to some changes in several *pueblos* (but not in Flores). However, the reforms were not permanent nor deep enough to have a major impact on the composition of the social sectors or their historically precipitated enduring relationships.

Economics, broadly, influenced the particularities of ethnic relations in Petén. Most noticeable in view of what happened elsewhere in Guatemala, the lot of Indians in Petén improved over time. As mentioned, the reasons for this include the absence of interethnic competition for land and the absence of a need for an army of dependent laborers, the opposites of which have been disastrous for Indians elsewhere (Lovell 1988; Swetnam 1989). After 1821 government extracted unpaid labor service from poor Ladino *vecinos* as well as Indians — a warped advance in ethnic relations. More positively, postcolonial elites perforce made little if any distinction between Indians and non-Indians in ranching, logging, *hule*, and chicle operations, and able Indians could and did become foremen in all these enterprises. In contrast, post-1870s capitalist development in highland Guatemala worsened conditions for Indians (Carmack 1983:222–25, 242–43). After 1945 political reforms gave exceptionally able Indians in Petén access to chicle contracts and to political power in several towns. In addition, a long history of competition for customers among upper-sector merchants lessened overt ethnic discrimination. Merchants were unable to treat their customers, Indian or otherwise, too roughly, if for no other reason than that customers could take their trade elsewhere.

At this point, let me repeat that despite such improvements things were not easy for Indians. Colonial society was based on ethnic stratification, and after 1821 Indians continued to suffer disproportionately from political and economic injustice. Although Ladinos complained that Creole authorities used the law to favor Indians over them, in general Ladinos fared better than Indians, who had reason to fear and resent non-Indians. Yet, largely for economic reasons, ethnic discrimination and prejudice gradually lessened.

In general, since the end of the colonial period, upper-sector treatment of lower sectors (including Indians) while not benevolent was usually relatively temperate. Even affluent merchants, operating in a limited-growth market, were not usually high-handed or abusive with customers. In this situation, relations between customers and merchants paralleled those between forest workers and contractors. In both cases the lower sectors had some (limited) opportunity to negotiate the terms of their relations with superordinates. In neither instance was the upper sector able to rely simply on client-dependency or coercion to retain customers and workers, although they did use these methods. By the 1870s and until 1944, in most of Guatemala seasonal labor for commercial plantations "was recruited by a variety of coercive techniques," including (after 1936) "restrictive vagrancy" laws (Swetnam 1989:2), but there were no plantations in Petén and vagrancy laws were not as uniformly and rigorously enforced there as elsewhere in Guatemala. Postcolonial relations between lower sector customers and workers and upper sector merchants and employers more commonly were optional and personal. The personal aspect was fragile because the same economic conditions that tempered relations between social sectors also "forced" merchants "to exploit coldly" their "narrow possibilities" and to curtail their willingness to assume the burdens of patronage. Merchants and customers, employers and workers agreed that it was "every man for himself" (Reina 1964:275). Patron-client and personal economic ties across (and within) social categories were limited in range and duration.

From about the 1720s—that is, after the traumatic conquest of Tayasal and brutal consolidation of military gains—to about 1980, levels of violence were in Petén relatively moderate—if that may be said about such events—compared with the conditions in the highlands. Of course, a relatively peaceful situation may mean that rulers have effectively suppressed all overt dissent and have thoroughly cowed the ruled. Perhaps this was roughly the case in colonial Petén and for a long time afterward, although the nervous reaction of the authorities to any sign of what they perceived as rebellion suggests that they did not feel themselves securely in control of those they ruled. In addition, until the late 1970s, there was not much to fight about. Ethnic groups, towns, and/or social sectors had no need to fight each other over land. After the 1890s, struggles over chicle concessions and taxes could not be settled by violence but rather by legal and political action in Flores and Guatemala City. To be sure, contractors deceived chicleros and governors treated them harshly. A public beating of a chiclero by a governor must have had a widespread minatory effect, but the mode of chicle production and the violent reputation of chicleros did limit the use of coercion. Equally important, after 1821 and possibly before then, the Flores upper sector normally had no incentive to control affairs within the *pueblos*. Other Peteneros complain that "selfish big shots" in Flores have never cared about their welfare, yet as a result of neglect people were (until the 1980s) increasingly free to arrange their own local affairs.

Any attempt to describe the social history of postconquest Petén must take note of contrarieties. If the forests were sheltering, they could also be unforgiving. The social environment, too, had and has a hard side. Peteneros had their share of forced labor, economic abuse, poverty, authoritarian rule, social inequality, racism, and violence. Yet, they also experienced gradual, though never steadily progressive, release from labor extractions and institutionalized ethnic discrimination. They had access to land; especially after 1821, the ruling group had to be relatively moderate in dealing with the ruled; and violence was not endemic. Seen in the context of Guatemalan national history, these are not inconsiderable circumstances.

In the midst of other changes, some benign and others harmful, there were deep continuities. Aside from household atomism, the most notable ones concern social structure and (lack of) economic development. The composition of social sectors, ethnic groups, and communities, and their mutual relations endured for over 250 years. There has been a stable integrated multicommunity system, with Flores at its hub. The preeminence of Flores, initially based on military conquest, subsequently derived from the wealth, political power, and social prestige of its residents. Peteneros observe the contrariness and also the permanence (as they thought) of the forests; they celebrate ambivalence and impermanence in social relations as well as the durability of what observers call the social system. The way of being in Petén was organized around stable, familiar—at times hard, at times "democratic"—certainties. For nearly three centuries, postconquest Petén was an almost unoccupied frontier and a settled society. Peteneros dreamed of a time when their isolation would end, their economic opportunities expand, and their level of living improve. As the dream approaches fulfillment, their society is becoming unsettled and their lives are imperiled.

Colonization of Petén—The Second Conquest

To appreciate what has happened in Petén since the 1970s, the national context must be discussed. In some places it will be necessary to skip ahead of the story.

National Context

During the 1960s and the early 1970s, the Guatemalan economy grew and developed rapidly. Although urban-based industry expanded, growth was led by increased production of beef and of agricultural commodities, particularly cotton, for export. (Coffee, however, remained the single most important export crop.)[1] This growth increased the size of the commercial and financial middle class and of organized urban labor, but the benefits accrued primarily and disproportionately to the traditional landed elite, upper class urban bankers, industrialists, traders, professionals, and a growing number of multinational corporations with interests in Guatemala (and eventually to high ranking military officers). Expansion and, to a lesser degree, modernization of plantations and ranches were accompanied by the displacement of smallholders. Land, already quite unevenly distributed, was further concentrated in the hands of the elite, and the position of smallholders grew worse. For example, between 1964 and 1979 the proportion of farms less than 0.7 hectares (too small to support a farm family) increased from 20 percent to 41.1 percent of all farms in the country, and the average size of these units decreased from .38 to .24 hectares. During the same period, the number of landless rural households increased from 278,985 to 414,999 (Early 1982:68–69). As population grew, at about 3.2 percent per year, smallholders were forced to subdivide their small plots among family members, to migrate to Guatemala City and other cities, or to seek land in the north. A combination of factors, including high rates of demographic growth, limited urban-industrial employment, and growth-induced inflation, increasingly worsened conditions for the dispossessed in the countryside and redundant labor in the cities. The economic status of the poor deteriorated absolutely as well as relatively. By the late 1970s, they were truly desperate.[2]

In 1973 the international oil crisis slowed Guatemala's economic expansion. Following a brief recovery, the economy turned down for several reasons, including the collapse of the Central American Common Market, a devastating earthquake (1976), a second oil crisis (1978), continuing inflation, and falling prices (beginning about 1975) for export commodities, particularly coffee and cotton. In 1979–1980, there was an upturn, followed by an economic crisis which continues into the present. From 1978 to 1982, the economy was further distorted by extraordinary corruption in the government, civil war, and, by 1982, unofficial currency devaluation. All this led several multinational corporations to withdraw from Guatemala and local capitalists to send their liquid assets abroad. The state was faced with a huge foreign debt, a recession, reduced revenues for social welfare, growing rural and urban unemployment, and insurrection.

From 1954 to about 1978, elite groups and the state answered lower and middle class demands for economic and political reform with repression. The lower sectors, often aided by priests, tried to form grassroots, class-based organizations to articulate their demands, but the dominant groups were completely unwilling to yield any power, thus pushing increasing numbers of the poor to the political left. Brief reference to Izabál and Zacapa (where the majority of the population is Ladino) in the 1960s illustrates what was happening. In 1961, the United States government, partly in connection with the Alliance for Progress, raised Guatemalan beef export quotas to the United States, and this stimulated large cattle growers to expand down the Motagua River Valley into Izabal and Zacapa. In the process, many Ladino smallholders lost their land, and some of them turned to a guerrilla group, consisting of perhaps 500 men. As the insurgents stepped up their activities, the military, apparently backed by U.S. special forces, responded with fury. Although no one knows the exact figure, it is estimated as many as 8,000 to 16,000 people may have been killed (Williams 1986). It mattered little whether they did or did not sympathize with the guerrillas. The point of this action was to completely cow the population and still all opposition to the prevailing distribution of wealth and power (Williams 1986). Thus, in the late 1960s, the military and right-wing paramilitary groups attacked not only insurgents in places like Zacapa and Izabal, but also middle class reformers, moderate politicians, unionists, and rural grassroots organization leaders. The 1974–1978 regime was somewhat more moderate than the regimes that preceded and followed it, but the degree of moderation should not be exaggerated, as the infamous incident in Panzós (1978) shows. Government troops and armed landowners there killed as many as 100 Kekchí Indians demonstrating over land rights. Word of the massacre spread rapidly, and all sorts of people—middle class, clergy, urban poor, Indians, and others—were genuinely shocked. Many were politicized as never before. This, along with similar events and general conditions in the country, led increasing numbers of Indians to support insurgent forces (with information, food, and so on) or to join them. Thus, by the late 1970s it was an increasingly polarized polity and society that had to cope with a deepening economic crisis. In 1982 a worldwide recession that threatened elite economic interests aggravated an already explosive situation.

> Triggered by natural disasters and world-system shocks outside the control of anyone, conflicts between the two great camps intensified. At precisely the time when elites were most threatened by the loss of lands to the banks in the city, the peasants were moving onto lands in the countryside. At a time when profits were being squeezed by exploding prices of oil, fertilizer, pesticide, and credit, the labor force was demanding higher wages (Williams 1986:165).

More than a decade earlier, the guerrillas had decided that swift, dramatic strikes by small armed groups, designed to galvanize the countryside to join the revolution, had not and would not work in Guatemala. Rejecting this so-called *foco* theory, they planned instead for a lengthy struggle. During its first stage they would keep a low profile, organize popular bases of support throughout the countryside, and work to overcome racial, ethnic, and regional divisions, which had debilitated previous insurgency movements. Thus, by the late 1970s and early 1980s, the guerrilla forces had established a wide base of support among rural Ladinos and Indians. They built, for the first time in the twentieth century, alliances between ethnic groups, and soon thereafter controlled large portions of the western and northwestern highlands of Guatemala where Indians were the majority. From 1978 to 1985 the state waged a brutal, indiscriminate war against the popular classes. For a time it seemed a "crime" to be young, to be poor, and to be an Indian (Black, Jamail, and Stoltz 1984). The state was particularly anxious to prevent Indians from building up their local economies and withdrawing from seasonal employment on plantations (Lovell 1988:106). In early 1980, the sugarcane cutters and cotton pickers strike, followed by a coffee pickers strike later in the same year, caused the regime to raise minimum wages for rural workers from Q1.12 to Q3.20 per day. No one incident triggered the war, but the strikes in particular made normally sane, though hardly liberal, socioeconomic elites and members of the middle class willing to put up with the worst sort of excesses by the state and military. The Indians took the brunt of the war; tens of thousands were killed and perhaps up to one million Indians were displaced. By 1985 the guerrillas had lost the latest battle in an apparently endless war.

The military then permitted free elections, hoping this would lead foreign lenders, repelled by gross human rights violations and military mismanagement of the economy, to renew aid to the country. With the elections, they also in effect shifted responsibility for multiple and seemingly intractable problems to the civilian regime of President Cerezo, a Christian Democrat, who took office in 1986. Of course Cerezo's problems had deep historical and structural roots, including what some scholars term "dependent capitalist development." He also faced a long list of immediate problems: shortages of foreign exchange capital; a huge public debt; seesawing prices for coffee, which remains the critical export crop; inflation that ran as high as 35 percent (in 1987) and affected the price of food staples; high unemployment rates, officially admitted to be 16 percent, with underemployment at 46 percent (again in 1987); demonstrations by unions and popular organizations; campaigns of disinformation from the left and the right; and the reemergence of deadly, clandestine right-wing paramilitary groups. In 1986 the gross domestic product showed negative growth, and in mid-1988 Cerezo officially devalued the currency (Q2.27 = $1 U.S.), which was then about Q2.80 to the dollar on the parallel market. He was also able to make some tax reforms, because the military supported the move, against the wishes of the upper classes. The military still hold supreme power in the society. For ideological and economic reasons connected with Guatemala's dependent capitalist development, the military and various powerful elites continue to reject genuine reforms, including those needed to address the most immediately pressing problems—the role of Indians in the national society and the extremely unequal land distribution.

In brief compass, then, this is the larger environment within which the colonization of Petén has occurred. Around 1960 Guatemala, like several other Latin American nations, began to settle and develop its tropical lowlands, including Petén, in part to ease the problems described above, including, as mentioned, growing land scarcity in the highlands. Land reform was out of the question, but lowlands settlement was not. The state was also responding to the economic ambitions of the military who had limited access to land in the highlands (because it was already held by traditional elites) and to growing international capitalist interest in lowland oil, minerals, and forest resources. By opening the lowlands to settlement the state hoped to increase production of food staples, to exploit raw materials, and to ease political tensions. Toward these ends, in 1958 the state gave FYDEP extensive and in practice exclusive authority over Petén, leading FYDEP's critics to dub it "a state within a state." In view of the national context, the chance to achieve equitable and sensible colonization seemed and turned out to be slim.

Years later, in October 1987, President Cerezo, responding to charges that FYDEP was corrupt, that it had created large estates in Petén, and that it was inefficient, more or less fulfilled his campaign pledge to disband FYDEP. Influential Peteneros who had once found fault with FYDEP now rose to its defense; nevertheless a "Committee of Liquidation" was established to reallocate FYDEP's various functions to appropriate ministries of the central government. For example, in 1987 FYDEP's road building equipment and its responsibilities for road maintenance were turned over to the Department of Roads within the Ministry of Communications, Transportation, and Public Works. In early 1988, FYDEP's main installations, located in Santa Elena, were apparently turned over to the adjacent Henry Danilo Military Base. Despite these and other actions, the liquidation committee found it could not complete its work within the time initially set for dissolution of FYDEP. Thus the tenure of the committee and its authority over several matters, including that related to land distribution, were extended to April 1990, when the "liquidation" of FYDEP was finally achieved. Whatever the future may be, for over a generation FYDEP was the most important unit of government in Petén.

FYDEP: Responsibilities and Activities

When it was organized, FYDEP was charged with responsibility (1) to build an infrastructure to foment agricultural, industrial, and touristic development in Petén; (2) to administer and to exploit Petén's resources, except oil, for domestic and overseas markets; (3) to sponsor colonization and to provide landless peasants with land and thereby increase production of food staples; (4) to settle farmers along the Usumacinta River in an effort both to bar a proposed Mexican hydroelectric project from flooding Guatemalan soil and to prevent Mexican colonists from encroaching on Guatemalan land; and (5) to promote medium-scale capitalized cattle ranching in south-central and central Petén. The area north of parallel 17°10' (roughly 33 percent of Petén), several small forest reserves in the south, a thin strip of land running along Petén's southern border, a military zone in the southwest, and a number of archaeological parks—a total of roughly about 1,517,023 hectares—were exempted from colonization. The northern reserve was set aside for "controlled" logging and collection of forest products such as chicle, allspice, and shate palms for domestic and foreign markets.

The state did not invest heavily in frontier development. For example, from 1974 to 1986 FYDEP's annual budget varied from about Q3 to Q10 million, the central government usually contributing from 26 to 53 percent per year to the budget. The rest was generated by FYDEP's "private" activities, such as commercial logging, land sales, fees and taxes derived from sale of chicle, taxes on forest products such as shate, and various licenses. At least from the 1970s on, income from logging was usually the single most important source of revenue for FYDEP, although in some years sale of land was. Since the early 1970s, logging has accounted for no less than 16 percent, and sometimes as much as 54 percent, of its annual budget. Since about half of FYDEP's revenues were usually spent on wages and administration, in any given year it could dedicate no more than 50 percent of its total income for development purposes.

Foreign technical experts, for example, those from from FAO (Food and Agriculture Organization of the United Nations) advised FYDEP that Petén's fragile forests and many of its thin tropical soils were better adapted to controlled logging, exploitation of nontimber forest products, and cattle ranching, than to farming. They concluded that about 48.1 percent (17,951.5 square km) of Petén should be restricted to forest exploitation, 32.8 percent (12,229.5 square km) should or could be devoted to ranching, 17.6 percent (6,568.0 square km) devoted to mixed ranching and farming, and 1.4 percent (536.0 square km) used for "urbanization" (FAO/FYDEP 1970; Latinoconsult 1974; figures given for Petén's area range from 35,854 to 37,285 square km, the smaller figure commonly used in land tenure documents and the larger one most commonly found in global planning documents). FYDEP estimated that the average six-person farm family needed about twenty-one hectares to maintain itself, hence it felt that Petén could not support many people. In the 1960s FYDEP officials argued that because so little of Petén was "suitable" for agriculture and because colonization and demographic growth must be well planned and gradual, the population should not grow beyond 50,000 in the near future. Only after many decades of development might the department be able to assimilate 150,000 people (Casasola 1968:56–61). They also argued that Petén needed ranchers, "well-prepared" farmers who would know how to protect the forests, and so on, rather than Indians, such as the Kekchí, many of whom were then moving from Alta Verapaz into San Luis. The argument also implied that the native Petén swidden agricultural system was not conducive to sound management of the forests or, in general, to sound development.

FYDEP began to exercise the full range of its authority in about 1962–1964. Since then, it has engaged in a wide range of infrastructural activites, building by itself, or in conjunction with other governmental entities, hospitals and health stations, tourist facilities, potable water systems, schools, sports facilities, municipal salons, markets, and roads. Although the amount varied from year to year, most of the time FYDEP invested about 20 to 42 percent of the 50 percent of the budget available for development (see above) in road and bridge construction and maintenance. For example, in 1978–1980 FYDEP invested Q3,161,218 in infrastructural and urbanization projects; about 60 percent of this was for road repair and new road construction. Depending on terrain, drainage, and so forth, from 1974 to 1984 the cost for constructing a washboard dirt road in Petén varied from Q715 per km on flat land to Q7,143 on rough upland terrain, averaging a cost of about Q3,000 to 4,000 per km. Costs to maintain roads and improve trails varied from Q29 to Q2,500 per km per year, averaging Q390 per km in 1974–1978, and Q1,845 per km for roads and Q594 per km for trails in 1984. The costs were so high relative to FYDEP's income that it could barely construct more than 60 to 320 km of road per year. Thus, between 1972 and 1975, FYDEP built about 90 km per year, and in 1984, 128 km. At the same time, FYDEP and the central government, with international donor aid, did invest Q22 million in an international airport in Santa Elena, just opposite Flores, and a paved road from the airport to the famous archaeological site of Tikal. The airport and road were completed in 1982. The main beneficiaries of the investment were the Flores elite and several wealthy highlanders who own the better hotels and restaurants in Flores, Santa Elena, and Tikal, gas stations, tourist bus facilities, and a tourist airline. This combination of budgetary constraints and investment policies goes a long way in explaining why in 1985 hundreds of some one thousand small rural settlements in Petén lacked feeder roads and were isolated during part of the rainy season. Perhaps FYDEP's most consequential accomplishment was the opening, in April 1970, of an all-weather dirt road linking central Petén to southern Guatemala. In 1970, for the first time in modern history, Petén farmers shipped maize and beans to highland markets. By 1975 Petén led the nation's twenty-two departments

Table 6:1 Place of Origin and of Residence of Heads of Household, Township of San Andrés (Center and Three Villages), 1985

Place of origin	San Andrés #	%	Sacpúy #	%	Chunya #	%	Ixhuacut #	%	Total #	%	Percent excluding Peteneros (N=489)
Central Highlands											
Guatemala	2	.5	5	1.8	1	1.2			8	1.0	1.6
Sacatepequez											
Chimaltenango	6	1.4	1	.4					7	.9	1.4
Midwest Highlands											
Sololá											
Totonicipán											
Central Pacific											
Esquintla	7	1.7	15	5.5	1	1.2	9	20.9	32	3.9	6.5
Suchitepequez	6	1.4	6	2.2	3	3.6	1	2.3	16	1.9	3.3
Retalhuleu			10	3.7	3	3.6			13	1.6	2.7
West Pacific and Highlands											
Quezaltenango							1	2.3	1	.1	.2
San Marcos			1	.4					1	.1	.2
Eastern Highlands											
Jalapa	5	1.2	14	5.2	4	4.8			23	2.8	4.7
Chiquimula	8	1.9	38	14.0	6	7.2	1	2.3	53	6.5	10.8
Eastern Pacific											
Santa Rosa	15	3.5	12	4.4	2	2.4	7	16.3	36	4.4	7.4
Jutiapa	12	2.8	43	15.9	3	3.6	3	7.0	61	7.4	12.5
Northwest											
Huehuetenango	1	.2	2	.7					3	.4	.6
El Quiché	1	.2	1	.4	1	1.2	4	9.3	7	.9	1.4
Northeast											
Baja Verapaz	4	.9	16	5.9	1	1.2	1	2.3	22	2.7	4.5
El Progreso	6	1.4	7	2.6	2	2.4	8	18.6	23	2.8	4.7
Zacapa	19	4.5	21	7.7	4	4.8	3	7.0	47	5.7	9.6
Far Northeast and North											
Izabal	5	1.2	17	6.3	9	10.8	2	4.7	33	4.0	6.7
Alta Verapaz	33	7.8	20	7.4	28	33.7			81	9.9	16.6
El Petén	280	66.0	37	13.7	14	16.9	1	2.3	332	40.4	
Honduras	2	.5	2	.7					4	.5	.8
El Salvador	3	.7	2	.7	1	1.2	2	4.7	8	1.0	1.6
Mexico	2	.5							2	.2	.4
Belize	4	.9							4	.5	.8
Not determined	3	.7	1	.4					4	.5	.8
Total	424	99.9	271	100.0	83	99.8	43	100.0	821	100.1	99.8

Source: Field Notes (census) 1985. Error due to rounding to nearest tenth.

in maize and bean production. In that Petén has become a major supplier of food staples for Guatemala, one FYDEP goal has been realized.

Between 1966 and 1970 FYDEP allocated land to sixteen cooperatives and four villages along the Pasión and Usumacinta rivers. By 1966 FYDEP had began to sell land to individual colonists and Peteneros, but it was not until December 1974 and January 1975 that legal titles were actually distributed to holders.[3] Until 1966–1974, private land ownership in Petén was insignificant. Pre-1944 governments had given titles to fifty-four Petén notables, 90 percent of them from Flores, but they held only 1.5 to 2.0 percent of Petén's land area; the rest was a "national estate." The 1944 revolution and 1954 counterrevolution had no impact on land tenure in the department. Prior to 1966, access to land was based on usufruct and township permission to work the land.

Growth and Development in Petén, 1966–1986
In the 1960s the central government pressured FYDEP to colonize Petén rapidly, in part to ease demands for land in the highlands. Although high-ranking FYDEP officials felt this was unwise for reasons discussed above, they could not resist the pressure from the central government. By 1966, according to internal FYDEP memoranda, the scramble for land had become "anarchic." "Irrational" swidden farmers from the south (*sureños*) were taking possession of the land, and population was growing too fast. In 1972, there was another invasion. Kekchí Indians from Alta Verapaz "invaded" San Luis and Sayaxché, in part because international corporate development of the Northern Transversal, the region immediately to the south of Petén, had increased the value of land there and led to conflicts between powerful national interests and poor farmers, violent social unrest, and the subsequent flight of Kekchí Indians. However, most migrants are Ladinos from the most ladinoized parts of Guatemala. Even in a place like San Andrés, which has not received as many migrants as the southern townships of Petén and which has a relatively large number of Kekchí colonists, most of the newcomers are from the more ladinoized parts of the country (Table 6:1). The township also is typical of the post-1960s settlement process in that native Peteneros are in the majority in the *pueblo* (center) and the newcomers are in the majority in the *aldeas* (Sacpúy, Chunya, and Ixhuacut) and smaller settlements. Moreover, most of the demographic growth here and throughout Petén is due to in-migration from southern Guatemala. Between 1960 and 1986, the population of Petén

grew from about 26,000 to about 300,000 or more people—an increase of over 1,100 percent in twenty-five years!

Economic growth has been equally dramatic. For example, in 1960 there were about 40 commercial establishments in the Flores-Santa Elena-San Benito triangle. In 1985 there were over 900 (Table 6:2), selling everything from modern electrical appliances to pizza.[4] In 1960, there were 2 inns in Flores and Santa Elena; in 1985 there were 14 inns and hotels, including 3 luxury hotels. In 1960 there was no reliable, let alone year-round, overland transportation from Flores to the highlands; in 1985 several passenger buses went to the south *every day*. In 1960 Aviateca, the national airline, usually made 2 roundtrips per week between Guatemala City and the rustic airport in Santa Elena. In 1985 at least 4 airlines were making daily flights between Guatemala City and the new (1982) airport in Santa Elena, which can accommodate most large civilian jet planes. In 1960 muleteers handled cargo hauling in, for example, San Francisco; in the 1980s there were at least 8 long-distance truckers operating out of the *pueblo*. In 1960 Poptún had 1 inn, no market and few stores; in 1985 it had 2 hotels, 5 inns, a modern market, and about 330 commercial establishments. In 1960, 19 (9 percent) of 210 households in the *pueblo* of San Andrés possessed a radio; in 1985, 351 (82.8 percent) of 424 households had a radio and 36 (8.5 percent) a television set. Between 1960 and 1985 the population of the town doubled, from 1,202 to 2,382 people. During the same period municipal income increased nearly ninefold, from Q13,854 in 1960 (of which 82 percent derived from chicle taxes) to Q114,562 (of which 13 percent derived from chicle taxes).

A more systematic although equally abbreviated review indicates the scale of economic growth. In 1959 Petén exported chicle and some lumber, but nothing else of note. As for the agrolivestock sector, in 1974 a government agrarian development bank, BANDESA (*Banco Nacional de Desarrollo Agrícola*), concluded that there was a sufficient number of farmers and ranchers in Petén with documented title to land to warrant opening branch offices there. The first BANDESA branch bank in Petén was opened in Santa Elena in October 1974, followed by a second one in Sayaxché in August 1975 and a third in Poptún in January 1979. By 1985 there was a BANDESA bank in Melchor de Mencos, primarily serving ranchers in eastern Petén, and three small rural offices in San Luis, the *aldea* of El Chal, and the *aldea* of Las Cruces. By 1975 Petén was the leading producer of maize and black beans in the nation. In 1985 Petén produced some 2.4

Table 6:2 Commercial Establishments, Petén 1985

	A			B			C			D			E				F				G				H			Total
	A1	A2	A3	B1	B2	B3	C1	C2	C3	D1	D2	D3	E1	E2	E3	E4	F1	F2	F3	F4	G1	G2	G3	G4	H1	H2	H3	
1. Flores	4	1					3		9	23			2	8	1	1	5	2	5	2	3	1					2	72
St. Elena	5	2	3		1	2	5	12	12	53			4	11	3		5	2	2	5	10				1	1	2	141
2. San Benito	9	3	8	15	28	2	78	33	22	186	28	39	5	45	26	4	5	10	14	36	25	55	12	10	2	11	1	712
3. San Andrés				5			2			39	2	1	2	3	4	1		3	1	2	9	2	1		3			80
Sacpúy										40			(1)	5						2	4	2						53
Carmelita							1			12										2	10							25
4. San José										14				3							3		(1)					21
5. San Fᶜᵒ				8		2	2			31		10		4	1	1				2	3	2	1		1			68
6. St. Ana					1					20		1			1	1					3	1	1					29
7. La Libertad	1			2	2	1	4			20		1		4					1	3	5		4		1			49
Las Cruces				2		1	5	4	4	20		9	1	5				1		1	5		1				1	60
8. Dolores				1			1			22		2	1	3						2	3		1					36
El Chal	1			1			3		1	16		6	(1)	3						3	4					1		40
Mopán									1	15		1	2	1							3							23
Ocote									1	14		3	(1)								1							20
Sabaneta				1			1		2	5		2		1				1		3	2							20
San Juan								1		8		1	(1)	1						1	2			1				16
Colpetén				2					1	6				1						2	1			1				14

Table 6:2 (Continued) Commercial Establishments, Petén 1985

	A			B			C			D			E				F				G				H			Total
	A1	A2	A3	B1	B2	B3	C1	C2	C3	D1	D2	D3	E1	E2	E3	E4	F1	F2	F3	F4	G1	G2	G3	G4	H1	H2	H3	
9. Poptún	2	1	3	19	2	2	26	6	13	115	14	18	3	27	19	2	2	5	3	15	25	5	1	1	1		1	330
10. San Luis	2			6	1		4	6	1	53	5	8	2	6	2		1	1		7	7	1	1	1	1			116
Chacte	1				1	1				12	3	3	2	3							2			1			1	26
Chinchila										18	7	7			4				2	2	3							34
Ixbobo										15	1	1	1		3				3	3	1							24
11. Melchor	3	1	1			1	36	10	6	72	3	7	3	ND			1	2	3	13	15	4			1	2		184
12. Sayaxché	2				ND	1	14		5	13	9	10	2	4			1			14	6			3	1	1		86
Total	23	14	16	59	41	12	186	71	78	842	61	129	38	104	97	10	20	27	29	118	155	73	26	14	10	13	13	2279

Source: Rentas Internas, Flores, Petén; Field Notes 1985.
Key: A1 = Wholesale establishment, A2 = Agro-veterinary supply, A3 = Distributorship (soda, beer, etc.).
B1 = Long distance cargo hauling, B2 = Passenger service, B3 = Gas station.
C1 = General store, C2 = General goods stall, C3 = Specialty store.
D1 = Grocery, D2 = Food stall, D3 = Butcher shop or bakery.
E1 = Pharmacy, E2 = Repair store, E3 = Nixtamal, E4 = Private school.
F1 = Hotel, F2 = Pension, F3 = Restaurant, F4 = Diner.
G1 = Saloon, G2 = Drinking stall, G3 = Cinema, G4 = Brothel.
H1 = Private sawmill, H2 = Factory, H3 = Bank.
ND = Not determined
(For the expanded Key, see note 4, this chapter.)

million quintals of maize, about 8.3 percent of the national total, and it also led the nation in honey production. Since the late 1970s marijuana has become an important though illegal export crop. There are no reliable statistics on cattle production, but between 1957 and 1964 there were said to be 6,000 head in Petén (Latinoconsult 1968). In 1977 FYDEP reported that there were about 21,000, and two years later some officials claimed there were 75,000. By 1980, according to one report, there were 150,000 head of cattle in Petén (Zetina O. 1980:11).

Of extractive industries, logging is the most important. Private companies and FYDEP employ thousands of seasonal loggers as well as about 1,200 sawmill workers, some of them year-round (except between 1983 and 1984 when FYDEP ordered a halt to logging). Some twenty clandestine sawmills in Mexico use Petén wood and employ workers from Petén, Mexico, and Belize. There are also said to be some 5,000 independent small-scale loggers, who combine woodcutting with other income-producing activities. Chicle production has decreased (see Chapter 4), but since 1960 Petén has exported more and more shate and pimienta gorda. In 1960, according to official figures, Petén exported 50 quintals of shate; in 1985, perhaps five to ten thousand seasonal cutters collected 11,284 quintals of shate for export. The actual figure is probably ten times the official one (Heinzman and Reining 1988). Shate processors in San Benito provide factory employment to some 190 women and 10 men. In 1954 Petén exported 45 quintals of pimienta, and in 1985 3,037 quintals. As indicated, actual export figures are much larger than official ones, because producers and exporters grossly underreport the amount of shate and pimienta they collect and sell overseas to avoid paying township and other taxes. In 1960 the export value of nontimber forest products, principally chicle, was worth

Figure 6:1. Thatched roofed and laminated roofed houses.

Figure 6:2. Sawmill, central Petén.

Figure 6:3. Market, Melchor de Mencos.

about Q3.0 million; by 1985–1988 it was worth at least Q16.8 million (R. M. Heinzman and C. Reining, personal communication). In southwest Petén, oil companies employ several hundred men, although their operations are periodically interrupted by guerrillas. Commerce and services also have grown enormously (Table 6:2). Rapid population growth, commercial expansion, and multiplication of military and government installations (primarily in Santa Elena, San Benito, Poptún, Melchor de Mencos, and Sayaxché) have led to a boom, probably temporary, in construction, which FYDEP estimates provides work for about 1,800 people. Tourism grew rapidly from the late 1960s until about 1982, when political unrest nearly eliminated it; it has picked up again since 1986. Until about 1986 government employment was a growth industry, with FYDEP employing 1,565 people in 1976 (reduced to 842 in 1987 when FYDEP was supposed to be, but was not, liquidated), the Institute of Anthropology and History employing 400 to 500 workers at Tikal National Park, and the townships employing about 240 civil servants. The Ministry of Education and other central government agencies with outposts in Petén employ up to 800 or 1,000 more.

Impressive as these figures are, structural change and development have not kept pace with growth. Economic growth has not generated significant internal backward productive linkages. Petén has very few industries that provide stable employment. The sawmills—the major industrial component—finish little of the lumber cut in Petén; there are, however, efforts to remedy this situation. The sawmills depend on resources (mahogany and cedar trees) that need at least fifty to a hundred years to be renewed. So far, reforestation programs are token at best, although the Cerezo government has taken some initial steps to conserve the forests. The other extractive enterprises are constantly threatened by shifts in distant market demands, by synthetic substitutes, by natural depletion, and by competition from other countries (for example, Mexico also produces shate for the North American market). Although the percentage of proletarian wage workers has grown since 1960, most of them employed as farm hands, loggers and forest collectors, the available evidence indicates that most households still remain dependent on milpa for all or part of their income. In 1974 in the town of San Francisco, for example, about 75 percent of the employed adult population were dependent on farming and ranching (Table 6:3). Between 1960 and 1983, in San Andrés as in most of the other *pueblos*, the percentage of households dependent on milpa dropped—primarily because of the increase in the percentage of loggers who did not make milpa (Table 6:4). In 1985, however, when the sawmills

Table 6:3 Primary Occupation of Employed Adult Males and Females, San Francisco, Petén, 1974

	Percentages	
Occupation	Male	Female
Agriculture (milpa) and ranching	73.5	3.6
Unclassified common labor	4.1	—
Artisan	6.4	28.6
Professional and technical	3.6	10.7
Managerial and administrative	1.0	—
Office staff	3.0	1.7
Commerce and sales	2.0	39.3
Other services	4.6	—
Transportation	1.8	—
Total	100.0	100.0

Source: Lic. Ruben Ayala, FYDEP. The table refers to women employed outside the home, not to 100.0 percent of adult women in the town. Lic. Ayala's count refers to adults, not to heads of household.

were closed and most of the loggers had moved away to find work elsewhere, 71.1 percent had to combine farming with another occupation. An even greater percentage of *aldeanos* rely on milpa. In 1985 over 95 percent of male heads of household in two typical rural settler villages farmed or combined farming with some other income producing activity (Table 6:5).

Labor-management relations and working conditions in shate and in log cutting are similar to what they were in *la chiclería*. Increased farming and forest exploitation have increased demand for commercial output, but most of the supply comes from Guatemala City and from overseas, rather than from local craft production. Moreover, even in the major population centers, a large percentage (39.6) of all business establishments are small grocery stores or food stalls (Table 6:2), many of which simply supplement farm or wage labor income. In the 1980s, because the state had so many economic problems, government employment proved quite unreliable. Rapid growth has not led to economic development.

Furthermore, the elite have captured most of the growth. In the 1980s five entrepreneurs from Guatemala City controlled logging concessions in Petén. Land has been increasingly concentrated (see below), and new roads, as observed in the case of the paved road from Santa Elena to Tikal,

Table 6:4 Occupation of Male Head of Household, San Andrés, 1960–1983

Occupation	1960		1983	
	Num.	*Percent*	*Num.*	*Percent*
Dependent on Milpa				
1 Farmer	67	34.5	91	19.7
2 Farmer and farm hand	10	5.2	45	9.7
3 Farmer and non-farm wage laborer	3	1.6	42	9.1
4 Farmer and forest collector	47	24.2	29	6.3
5 Farmer and other	32	16.5	83	17.9
6 Farm hand	4	2.1	—	—
(Sub-total	163	84.1	290	62.7)
Not dependent on Milpa				
7 Non-farm wage laborer	2	1.0	73	15.8
8 Forest collector	13	6.7	27	5.8
9 Other	16	8.2	73	15.8
(Sub-total	31	15.9	173	37.3)
Total	194	100.0	463	100.0

Source: Field notes 1960–1983.

Note: In 1960, almost every category of employment included chicle tappers, foremen or contractors. By 1985, the number of households decreased to about 424 because so many *sureño* loggers relocated when the sawmills closed. In 1983, most non-farm laborers were loggers. In 1960, all collectors were chicleros; by 1983, most were shateros and pimenteros. "Other" includes ranchers, artisans, civil servants, teachers, merchants and transport workers. Employment in every category except that of merchant doubled between the 1960s and 1980s.

often favor elite interests. Commercial ownership also has been highly concentrated. To illustrate, in the 1980s an old elite family from Flores owned a large beer distributorship in San Benito, a large wholesale/retail emporium, a luxury hotel, several smaller businesses and a large cattle ranch. Another old elite family, also from Flores, owned a large retail emporium, four specialized stores, including one in Melchor, four hotels in Flores and San Benito, part of an airline company, two cattle ranches, apiaries, and numerous houses in central Petén and in Guatemala City. In 1974 the family's enterprises grossed about Q180,000; in 1984, more than Q1,000,000. In 1985 one family in Melchor owned 9.6 percent of all commercial establishments, except small groceries, in town. The significance of the family's assets for commercial distribution and off-farm employment in and around Melchor was even more impressive. It owned the

Table 6:5 Occupation of Male Head of Household in Two Petén Villages, 1985

Occupation	Num.	Percent
Dependent on milpa		
1 Farmer	21	30.4
2 Farmer and farm hand	—	—
3 Farmer and non-farm wage laborer	4	5.8
4 Farmer and forest collector	22	31.9
5 Farmer and other	20	29.0
6 Farm hand	—	—
(Sub-total	67	97.1)
Not dependent on milpa		
7 Non-farm wage laborer	1	1.4
8 Forest collector	1	1.4
9 Other	—	—
(Sub-total	2	2.8)
Total	69	99.9

Source: Field Notes 1985. Error due to rounding to nearest tenth.

Note: One village is in the *municipio* of San Andrés, the other in Flores. All the farmers, including those with other occupations (artisan, deputy mayor, grocer, pastor, and small-scale shate contractor) considered farming their primary occupation. Until the saw mills temporarily shut down, about 12 farmers also worked as loggers. The non-farm laborers are loggers; the forest collectors are shateros/pimenteros. Note, too, that in some years the figure for forest collectors (with or without other sources of income) rises to 45.5 percent.

two pharmacies in town, a building materials distributorship, four relatively large *tiendas* (general stores), numerous houses, a sawmill, which until it closed in 1985 was the major source of wage labor in town, a cattle ranch, and several farms. Nearby *aldeas*, as is true of most of Petén's approximately 300 *aldeas*, possess at most a rustic saloon (*cantina*), a small grocery store and, less commonly, a small *tienda*, so most *aldeanos* made their major purchases in Melchor and from the above mentioned family. (Of some 595 *caseríos* in Petén almost none possess any kind of commercial establishment.) The same pattern of concentrated control over distribution and nonmilpa production occurs in almost every other important *pueblo* in Petén, most noticeably in the Flores-Santa Elena-San Benito urban center, San Andrés, La Libertad, Sayaxché, and perhaps Poptún.

Between the 1960s and the 1980s the economy of Petén grew rapidly, but except for the important circumstance that the concentration of wealth and socioeconomic inequality increased sharply, many structural aspects of the economy did not change. However, the process of settlement did initiate several—probably irreversible—changes, which will be discussed after a review of recent winners and losers.

Winners and Losers

In general, metropolitan elites, the military, and local elites have benefited disproportionately from the second conquest of Petén. The old regional merchant-contractor elite was particularly well placed to take advantage of the demographic growth and its implications for commerce. Large-scale logging operators, sawmill owners, and shate contractors (including among them members of the old regional elite) also have benefited from the colonization process.[5] For one thing, it has provided them with a plentiful, relatively cheap supply of labor. For another, even if FYDEP had wished to supervise their activities and collect its fair share of taxes from them, it has not had sufficient financial resources and personnel to do so, in part because (as discussed above) the central government did not invest much in new lands settlement. Thus, FYDEP has had to rely heavily on income derived from its own and private logging operations to finance infrastructural investments. There are charges, widely accepted in Petén and in the Cerezo government, that logging companies have evaded taxes, failed to honor FYDEP regulations (for example, to plant ten trees for every one they fell), bribed officials, and so on, but the same lack of resources that has more or less forced FYDEP to depend so much on income from logging has also made it difficult for it to control the industry, even when some particular *promotor* (head of FYDEP) has wished to do so—and not all *promotores* have. In a sense, those who have scored FYDEP for permitting too much (unregulated) logging and for not building feeder roads to isolated farm settlements have been talking at cross-purposes. Despite limited collection of taxes, and so forth, road building and social overhead investments in Petén have depended in part on logging.

Since the late 1970s, winning and losing for most of the population has been more directly related to land distribution. As noted below, it also has a connection with logging. This is particularly the case for lower sector settlers, the largest number of whom migrated to Petén for the express purpose of acquiring land so that they could devote themselves to farming. Several conclusions about land distribution based on previously published

Table 6:6 Land Tenure, Petén, 1975–1980

Num. of cases	Average holding in hectares	Average cost per hectare	Occupation of holder	Num. resident in Petén
14	600	Q7.20	Unclear	1
68	511	8.50	Professional, merchant, gov't. offical	4
39	506	7.70	Agriculture	1
19	496	8.50	Professional, merchant	19[a]
10	480	7.70	Student	0
15	470	8.70	Military	0
16	390	7.50	Agriculture	16[b]
47	54	9.60	Milpero	47[c]
36	40	—	Milpero	36[d]

Source: Land Registry Bureau, Guatemala City; FYDEP; Field Notes 1974, 1985.

[a] Eleven are Flores merchants; 6 are or were FYDEP officials who have taken up permanent residence in Petén.

[b] All were born in Petén. An agriculturalist operates on a large-scale, in contrast to a milpero.

[c] All are *sureño* settlers.

[d] All but one are *sureños*. They had applied to FYDEP for parcels, but no price had been set at the time of this survey. Settlers tend to have larger holdings than native Peteneros, for whom the average holding (usually held in usufruct) is or was in 1985 closer to 23 hectares.

studies are summarized here. For extended discussions of land tenure and land ownership, see Góngora Zetina (1984) and Schwartz (1987).

First, the affluent have gained more from colonization than the poor. FYDEP has catered to the interests of military officers, members of the middle and upper classes in Guatemala City, affluent Peteneros, and its own officials. In line with expert advice to establish well-capitalized ranches in Petén, and because of political pressure, FYDEP has sold these people relatively large, well-located (for example, with respect to roads, soil quality, and so forth) parcels of land at low cost. Although by regulation one could not buy more than 675 hectares (reduced to 225 hectares in the late 1970s), in practice estates at least three times this size have been built, including those held by absentee owners. For example, in the late 1970s three brothers each bought 500 hectares in southeast Petén, placing the entire 1,500 hectares under the management of one brother while the other two remained in Guatemala City. In another case, apparently unknown to anyone in FYDEP, a lawyer from the highlands acting for several members of her family put together a 2,500–hectare estate in a relatively inaccessible northwestern sector of the department. The purpose of this was avowedly speculative. The lawyer (correctly) believed that FYDEP lacked the personnel and vehicles to monitor her activities. In contrast, poorer colonists, nominal cooperativists, and Petén milperos have acquired small, often isolated 21– to 45–hectare farms, paying more per hectare than the wealthy pay (Table 6:6).

Before turning to the second conclusion, regarding land concentration, some comparisons between ranchers and milperos will illustrate what favoring the interests of the affluent has meant.

As noted above, after the late 1970s FYDEP limited (in theory) sales of land for ranches to 225 hectares, 20 percent of which is supposed to be kept in undisturbed forest. In north-central Petén and probably along the fertile Mopán river valleys, one who properly manages a 225–hectare ranch with improved mixed criollo-Zebu, Brahman and/or Swiss Bronze herds and who sells 80 to 100 steers per year can net as much as Q10,000 to Q25,000 per year. But many ranchers are not this fortunate. For several reasons, including high start-up costs, low stocking rates, lack of year-round surface water (in parts of Petén), fluctuating market demands for beef, and inexperienced or careless management, returns from cattle production can be low or negative. In 1980 a rancher had to invest about Q84,000 (for land, start-up herds, pastures, fences, and so on) to establish a modern 225–hectare ranch, and had to wait nine years before seeing a profit on his investment (Banco de Guatemala 1981b). A rancher who stocked the average 0.5 to 0.6 head per hectare could net Q108 per hectare from cattle (adjusted to 1987 prices). In comparison, a farmer cultivating maize and beans could net Q151 per hectare, without taking into account the value of food equivalents. A shate plantation owner, in theory, could net Q500 per hectare (Heinzman and Reining 1988). For all these reasons, some novice ranchers, unfamiliar with Petén, have lost considerable sums of money, and many more have reduced the scale of their operations. On the surface, ranching does not seem to be so good for ranchers, nor, because it converts forest to pasture, for Petén. This view, however, overlooks several advantages that a clever rancher, knowledgeable about lowland conditions, may exploit, including returns from land rents. For one thing, more experienced ranchers know how to initiate operations for far less than the Banco de Guatemala figure, how to turn a profit within two to three years, rather than nine, and how to stock 2 to 3 head per hectare, rather than 1. For another, there is the matter of scale. A ranch family with 180 hectares in pasture can net close to Q20,000 per year, but a farm family cannot crop more than about 6 hectares. To crop more than this, the farm family has to hire workers, which may drive per hectare returns below that realized by the rancher. As for shate, it is vulnerable to the "notorious volatility of the market" for primary nontimber tropical forest products (Heinzman and Reining 1988:52). In addition, ranchers can sell their timber, and titled land can be used as collateral for low-interest BANDESA loans. Given the rate of inflation in Guatemala in the 1980s, the cost of a loan is relatively low. The loan can then be invested in a profitable nonagrarian enterprise, and if the borrower has sufficient *cuello* (influence), he can delay timely repayment of the loan. Moreover, between the 1970s and the mid-to-late 1980s, land values in Petén rose from less than Q10 to Q27 per hectare to about Q45 or more; and FYDEP regulations notwithstanding people do sell their land. Even a depleted ranch can be sold for a profit, or kept for speculative purposes. Finally, a rancher does not have to deal with a large labor force, as does a large-scale agriculturalist or shate contractor.

In contrast, a milpero who prudently manages a 45–hectare farm and crops 5 to 6 hectares per year may net about Q755 to Q975 per year (in 1985), not including the value of food equivalents, largely from sales of maize and black beans. This will—just barely—sustain the average six person household, but it will not permit the accumulation of capital. A milpero may increase crop yield and farm income by shortening the fallow and by reducing intercropping in favor of maize and beans, but under current tropical Petén milpa regimes, this encourages pest infestation and rapidly depletes soil productivity. The situation is further aggravated by terms of trade for staple crops and consumer goods. Thus the milpero, or an unmarried adult son residing with him, must seek off-farm employment, typically as a seasonal woodcutter, chiclero, pimentero, or shatero. For example, in 1973 Blas and his unmarried seventeen year old son, who usually try to crop about 6 hectares, had a very poor milpa harvest. This left him almost without any cash reserves, so in 1974 Blas decided he and his son should devote most of their labor time to off-farm work. In 1974 they earned Q1,302 collecting shate and Q514 collecting pimienta. The total household expenses for the year were Q1,224, of which Q320 were used to pay a man to help Blas with his milpa. Although Blas and his son worked at the milpa when not collecting forest products, they needed to hire labor because of the time they spent off-farm; in particular, the pimienta collecting season conflicts with peak demands for labor at the milpa (shate may be collected year-round). Because there were no major illnesses in his household, Blas was fortunate enough to net Q592. He says, that because of the price of food staples, if "I had not been able to pay for the milpa, I would have come out with nothing." Although other men have gone further than Blas and have found that by combining shate, chicle, and pimienta collecting and/or logging they can earn enough to forego farming, there is a constant risk that if the price of staple grains rises too high they will face serious economic problems. The most common strategy is to combine milpa with some form of wage labor (Tables 6:3 to 6:5). One result is that the thousands of smallholders who also work as woodcutters perforce oppose attempts to curtail logging, even though many of them fear that deforestation will eventually harm their interests. Another result is that given the large number of men in Petén and elsewhere in the country who must seek off-farm seasonal work, lumbermen, contractors, and other employers are assured an adequate supply of cheap labor, which for political and economic reasons remains unorganized. That labor is in a weak position to negotiate wages is in part a result of the land distribution system.

Second, land for small-scale farming is becoming increasingly scarce. One reason for this is the growing concentration of land in fewer (affluent) hands. Based on a 10 percent sample of landholders in 1980, 50 percent of them held 22 percent of the land, and the other 50 percent held 78 percent. By 1983, based on a 30 percent sample, the first 50 percent now held only 13 percent of the land, and the other 50 percent held 87 percent. More to the point is that 56 percent of the land was held by 5 percent of the owners (Góngora Zetina 1984:125–31). FYDEP officials have criticized Góngora Zetina's results, although they are generally consistent with a smaller, but more detailed, data set collected by other methods (Schwartz 1987). FYDEP notes, for example, that she has mixed pre-FYDEP titles with FYDEP-sold titles, that she has included Kekchí farmers around San Luis who "prefer" smaller than average milpa plots, and so on. Nevertheless, the data indicate a strong trend toward increasing land concentration which, although not as extreme as in the highlands, is reminiscent of conditions there.

There are additional reasons for an increasing scarcity of land for small-

Figure 6:4. House set on cement platform, with exterior kitchen.

holder cultivation: the expansion of ranching, the acquisition of farms by the thousands of landless peasants from southern Guatemala, road construction, urbanization, and political violence which makes it unsafe to farm in certain areas. Uncontrolled commercial logging, tree felling for household fuel use, especially for cooking, and shortening of fallows also decrease the amount of good land available for milpa, but not necessarily for ranching. Scarcity increases the value of farms (and ranches) with good road access. Between 1974 and 1985–1987, the price for 45 hectares went from a low average of about Q432 to about Q2,025. But milperos who sell their land voluntarily or under pressure enter an unreliable labor market. To leave farming makes sense for those who can find relatively secure, well-paying jobs, such as operating heavy machines or certain positions in the civil service, but most cannot do so. Instead, landless peasants who come to Petén to farm their own land often wind up landless wageworkers. In short, land scarcity places at risk those small farmers and colonists who desire to become smallholders.

Third, although the affluent have benefited disproportionately from FYDEP policies and the recent economic growth in Petén, the impact on the lower sectors has not been uniform. Some have fared better than others. Substantial numbers of lower sector native Peteneros, especially those who reside in the *pueblos*, have profited from initial "founder" advantages in gaining access to an expanded white-collar job market, from knowledge of how to exploit forest resources such as shate, and from increased *cabildo* disbursements. Those with superior entrepreneurial skills have gained from expanded regional commerce. Moreover, although FY-DEP's infrastructural investments, such as in roads and communications, primarily benefit those with political infuence and wealth, they have co-incidentally improved the life chances of many *poblanos*, former *poblanos* who have entered the ranks of the middle sector, and smaller numbers of colonists. Other Peteneros are absolutely, as well as relatively, worse off than they were prior to the 1960s or 1970s, and one important reason for this is that they no longer have open access to good farm sites. (Nation-wide economic problems such as currency devaluation and inflation also have hit hardest at the poorest people in the department.) Many Petén milperos were initially reluctant to buy land because they felt it already belonged to them by right of traditional occupancy. They also believed the colonists would not remain in Petén, hence they did not need to buy what was theirs in the first place. Nor was FYDEP eager to sell land to "irra-tional" slash-and-burn cultivators, whether from Petén or elsewhere. In the middle 1980s, no more than 13 to 16 percent of native central Petén milperos had land titles. Now, with 56 percent of nonforest reserve land held by 5 percent of owners, they are encountering difficulties in finding good land to farm. The same range of variation occurs among the colonists, except that a far larger percentage of them bought land. Some *sureños* (and even some Kekchí, who are on average poorer than any other group in Petén) say they are better off here than they were at home. Despite problems of adjustment to Petén, they point out that here, unlike where they came from, at least they have access to land and a chance to produce enough food for the household.

Unfortunately, there are thousands of others for whom migration to the lowlands has been a disaster. The experiences of colonists along the Pasión and Usumacinta rivers in western Petén and, for comparison, in an *aldea*, Cascajal (pseudonym), in the east illustrate what has happened to many other settlers throughout Petén.

As mentioned earlier, between 1967 and 1970 sixteen nominal cooper-atives and four villages were allocated land along the western rivers. Be-cause they were settled there to prevent Mexican encroachments on Guatemalan soil, the colonists were hastily organized, given no training in collective work (each farmer usually works his land alone), and provided with few infrastructural facilites. Moreover, with some truly heroic ex-ceptions, extension, medical, and other government personnel have been loathe to reside in the impoverished, isolated riverine settlements. Perhaps the greatest hardship was a lack of feeder roads which forced (and still forces) many settlers to rely on riverboat middlemen to buy and sell goods and produce at unfavorable terms of trade. In 1975, when maize sold at Q7 to Q10 per quintal in Sayaxché, middlemen bought it from riverine settlers at Q3 to Q4, less than the price of a work shirt. In 1981 BANDESA calculated that in the rural areas outside the town of Sayaxché, the cost of producing 50 quintals of maize per hectare was Q309, but riverine farmers could not sell their maize for more than Q6 per quintal and often had to settle for Q4 per quintal. (In 1985 riverine farmers were still selling maize for Q6 to middlemen, who then resold it for Q15 to Q20.) Thus, farmers had net losses of Q9 per hectare or more. Two things offset this dismal picture: BANDESA set the opportunity cost of a day's labor at Q3, but farmers relied on household labor with lower opportunity costs, and they also sold other crops such as black beans and rice to middlemen. Nevertheless, many—perhaps most—riverine farmers were as poor in 1981 as they had been in 1972, when most of them lived below the poverty line established by the government (Carranza F. 1973). Moreover, even if a settler who cropped 5 hectares had an excellent harvest and managed to net as much as Q319 (a figure based on optimistic assumptions) for his surplus maize, and perhaps twice that for his beans, he would have been hardpressed. Given the terms of trade, he would have been unable to put aside anything to improve his material condition, pay FYDEP for land surveys, cope with a medical crisis, and so on. By 1972 —*before* the civil war of about 1978 to 1985—physical hardships, rumors that the central government might build a hydroelectric facility in the area, flooding 12,000 square kilometers and wiping out years of pioneer sacrifice, and political unrest drove about 26 percent of the original co-op membership to abandon their homesteads. Some lands cleared and then abandoned by cooperativists and other pioneers have been occupied by wealthy farmers and ranchers. Because of unfavorable conditions the settlers have, in effect, underwritten oil and lumber company workers in Sayaxché with cheap grains and have subsidized affluent ranchers by clearing forest for them.

Because Cascajal is adjacent to a major road, farmers there have had a solid advantage over the cooperativists, but this has also drawn many settlers to the village. Around 1966 they began to arrive in Cascajal, the site of an old hamlet that was abandoned in the early twentieth century. The overwhelming majority came from ten different departments in eastern, central, and southern coastal Guatemala, and most were strangers to one another. Some came with moderate resources, and many more were very poor. Several settlers had bad memories of failed land-settlement schemes on the south coast. A substantial minority of them had been members of unions and peasant organizations. By 1980 there were approximately 1,800 people in 300 households, four rival Protestant chapels, a Catholic prayer house, many small stores, and a third-grade school in Cascajal. All but one man was a settler (mean time in Petén was 9.4 years, and in Cascajal 8.8 years), and almost all of the adult males were full-time farmers, cropping on average between 6.7 and 7.0 hectares. By this time many farmers were reducing (but not eliminating) intercropping to grow more maize and beans, because truckers who came to Cascajal from the highlands had next to no interest in other crops. A Cascajal farmer could net about Q52 per hectare of maize and Q250 per hectare of beans, which, while not grand sums, were more than what a farmer on the Río Pasión could earn. Under optimally favorable conditions a farmer who planted his first year plots (most farmers cropped two plots a year) half in maize and half in beans could net Q1,046 and (a la Carranza 1973:83) the equivalent of Q515 in "auto-consumption." Moreover, certain types of beans and other cultigens can be planted in fallow fields. This was enough to live above subsistence and perhaps enough to save some money, although prices for consumer goods such as cloth, tools, and so forth were and are higher in Petén than in the rest of the country. Under the same optimal conditions, a Cascajaleno could practice a 2 to 4 year crop-fallow ratio, which meant he needed, as FYDEP estimated, about 21 hectares to make a living.

But optimal conditions are not normal ones. In Petén second-year plots commonly yield up to 35 percent less maize than first-year plots; second-year plots demand more labor because of weed intrusion, and many fields may have to "rest" 5 to 6 or more years before they can be profitably replanted. After about 10 to 15 years of farming around Cascajal, a substantial number of the farmers found that their soils were not as productive as they had been initially. Moreover, by 1980 some farmers were having serious problems with crop pests. There seemed to be two reasons for this. Cutting back on intercropping optimizes conditions for pest infestation. As temperatures in humid Petén are relatively high throughout the year, the pests are always present, and they can spread more rapidly in a plot lacking a variety of cultigens that would otherwise impede their progress. Furthermore, plots around Cascajal lack wide separation by dense, extensive corridors of mature forest, which can form barriers to the spread of crop

Figure 6:5. Children.

Figure 6:6. Boy's birthday party.

insects (Wiseman 1978:93). Partly for these reasons, most farmers said they needed to control 45 rather than 21 hectares to make a living.

Cascajalenos were using a variety of strategies to cope with their growing farm problems. Some were working off-farm as woodcutters and collectors of nontimber forest products, but most were not, largely because they had little prior experience with these types of work. Some were intercropping more and planting less maize, but because of the market this was decreasing their cash income. Others were intensifying maize and bean production, usually by shortening the fallow, although this placed additional burdens on household labor to combat weeds and degraded the thin tropical soils in the region, increasing the pressure on farmers who chose this option. To maintain long fallows as well as adequate levels of crop production, several better off farmers were increasing the size of their holdings to grow more maize and beans and/or to convert some of their land to pasture for stock raising. Usually they bought land from poorer farmers who came to Cascajal in the late 1970s. But precisely because so much of the land near the road and around Cascajal was already occupied and because land prices were rising, poor latecomers found they either had to move deeper into undisturbed forest areas far from the road (which raised the costs of transporting crops to the roadside and thus reduced their farm income), or take advantage of rising land prices, sell out, move to less densely settled areas to farm, or enter the wage labor market. In addition, several younger men were beginning to grow marijuana. For example, a thirty-four-year-old father of three young children, after three poor maize harvests in a row, decided that he owed it to his children to begin cultivating the crop.

As the farmers in Cascajal and in nearby villages, as well as several large ranchers, spread out, hundreds of square kilometers of forest in the vicinity were cleared. Despite low population density (lower than ten people per square km), by 1980 holdings with good soil and good access to the road were becoming scarce and increasingly concentrated in fewer hands. In Cascajal, this led to land disputes, several of which turned violent. To cite but one case, Fulano, who came to Petén from the south coast of Guatemala in 1975, bought 35 hectares near Cascajal, but because of "politics" (his word) he wanted to sell the land and move to northern Petén. In addition, he discovered that the soil was not as fertile as he had initially thought. He was also having endless problems in getting clear title to the land from FYDEP and was spending too much of his time and money going back and forth to the FYDEP land office in Santa Elena. Megano, a wealthier neighbor who came to Cascajal from eastern Guatemala around 1967, had been a relatively successful farmer before coming to Petén and was able to buy 90 hectares in Cascajal. Megano claimed that a portion of Fulano's land was really his; because of an error in a FYDEP land survey, they had overlapping claims to the disputed land. In late 1979 Fulano offered to sell what he claimed was his land to Megano, but the latter had no intention of buying what he felt was his. Membership in rival Protestant groups added to the tension between them. In early 1980 one of Megano's sons punched Fulano after he and Fulano had traded some insults over their respective pastors. Fulano then told several people he was going to shoot Megano. At this point, a local military commissioner who occasionally worked for Megano and was his coreligionist denounced Fulano to the army, claiming that he was a "communist" and that one of Fulano's adolescent sons was providing the guerrillas with food. Insofar as the youth did boast of all sorts of things, including contacts with guerrillas, there may have been some truth to that charge. By the summer of 1980, an angry, frightened Fulano claimed that "politics" and FYDEP's preference for "the rich" were the causes of his ordeal. To be safe, he was planning to leave Cascajal, even if he could not sell his land. For his part, Megano said that he might have allowed Fulano to crop his (Megano's) land, but because of his own farm problems and because land near the road was so scarce, he had to occupy the site. By 1985 Megano, now a rancher and merchant as well as a farmer, had increased his holding to 175 hectares. Fulano was working in a large *tienda* in San Benito for Q2 a day, barely enough to cover his household's daily food costs. All in all, Fulano has fared as badly as many of the riverine settlers.

By the late 1970s FAR (*Fuerzas Armadas Rebeldes*, Rebel Armed Forces), the guerrilla group that operates in Petén, had become more active. Although FAR does not reveal the identity of its members, it seems to be led by people of urban middle class background. Most ordinary members appear to be recruited from poor, politicized countrymen, including those who have seen their dreams of a new life in Petén ruined. There seem to be few native Peteneros in the group. Having spent years quietly cultivating a network of informants and sympathizers among disillusioned rural colonists, particularly in far western Petén, FAR apparently felt it could strike out more openly in the late 1970s. Along with attacking army and police outposts and oil installations, planting Claymore mines on roads, and destroying between Q0.5 to Q1.0 million worth of FYDEP road-building equipment, FAR kept stressing two things to settlers: that the revolution would give them land and that it was not opposed to religion. FAR won, as indicated above, some adherents among the desperate riverine settlers, whereas others were willing or felt obliged to supply FAR with food and information. FAR, however, almost always paid for the food and never physically abused anyone it defined as a poor peasant. By about 1980, two years later, after the state declared war on the poor in the highlands, the military in Petén responded to FAR and to poor settlers with devastating violence. Hundreds, perhaps thousands, of settlers were killed, and FAR was unable to protect any of them. At first, settlers in the southwestern and far western parts of Petén (in the *municipios* of La Libertad and Sayaxché), and soon afterward in east-central Petén, suffered the heaviest casualties. As a result of death and destitution, several co-ops were completely abandoned, some as late as 1983. Some settlers fled to Mexico, and others joined what became a surplus labor force in central Petén. Between 1982 and 1984 the war in Petén peaked, and in 1985 the military "resettled" some refugees in one or two new riverine sites, and others in a fortified hamlet (a "development pole") farther east, that is, closer to the township capital of La Libertad.

In mid-1983 in Cascajal, a group of better-off farmers reported to the army that some forty of their poorer neighbors were FAR sympathizers. Although some of them may have been, the entire matter was complicated by overlapping-land disputes, intense religious antagonisms, personal disputes that in a heterogenous settlement of strangers such as Cascajal are not easily resolved, and so on. Stories are told that one day "someone," whom no one will identify, warned selected villagers to keep a lamp burning in their windows all night, but not to tell the so-called FAR sympathizers about this. Just before sunrise of the following day, a group of men (again, no one will identify them but several people hint that they were soldiers) entered the village, dragged out men who did not have a lamp burning in the window, gave them a severe beating, and then killed a number of them. Many people fled to the safety of central Petén (Flores-Santa Elena-San Benito). In 1985 Cascajal had half the number of households it had had in 1980, and some landowners had enlarged their holdings. Some gained, some lost. A settler, who has become fearful of working away from home and barely makes a living by backyard gardening and some carpentry, expresses the despair and demoralization of defeated settlers in Cascajal and elsewhere as well as anyone can:

You see, well, the government is like a parent, and when we were disobedient they had to correct us, like a father beats a rebellious child. We were stupid, beasts, so the army had to beat us. Now, well, I just try to find work. I do not know where Rafa [his oldest son] is. The army is not bad, but severe, as they must be with people who behave like drunken animals. Now I know better. I just want to know where Rafa is. [His wife interrupts to say that one beating left her husband with "nerves," and that is why he cannot make a milpa at his farm, located about one kilometer from the village.] (Field notes 1985).

The site he had farmed has been occupied by another, initially somewhat better-off settler who has become a small-scale rancher. The entire process is reminiscent of the war waged against the Indians and their subsequent removal to "reduced" settlements in early eighteenth-century Petén, except that this time the losers cannot flee to unexplored forest sanctuaries.

In 1980 it seemed as if the military were clearing regions where oil had been or seemed likely to be discovered. But the war between FAR and the army soon spread throughout Petén. For a combination of reasons, the army struck hardest, as previously mentioned, at villages in western, southwestern, and east-central Petén. Several Peteneros have suggested that in addition to combating FAR, the army wished to depopulate certain specific areas so that privileged elements could expand their holdings, or for some other similar reason, but the matter is far from clear. Of course, in certain instances, the violence, by intention or not, did benefit better-off land owners, but in other instances it prompted their peers to depart Petén. What is clearer is that a predominant majority of these villages were and are, except in parts of San Luis, populated by post-1966 settlers, so in attacking these villages the army was also necessarily attacking settlers more often than native Peteneros. FAR's strategy has been to build bases of popular support in rural areas among poor farmers who suffer most from inegalitarian land distribution, lack of adequate infrastructural facilities, and so on. During the period under discussion, there were few and often no soldiers posted to the villages. Army commanders may have thought it unwise to spread their forces too thin; in addition there is some evidence to suggest that they doubted the capacity and/or the willingness of small units stuck in villages distant from large military bases to engage with FAR. Thus FAR could more or less safely enter the villages in force to collect supplies and to hold "educational" meetings with the local population. If the occasion arose, they also could eliminate whatever small government force might be there, deepening the reluctance of soldiers to be stranded in such places. While FAR sometimes assailed military com-

missioners (ex-soldiers and reservists responsive to the army) and suspected anti-FAR informants, and more often forced villagers to attend the
meetings, they did not injure "poor, innocent" *campesinos*. In general, the
latter were not frightened of FAR. However, they did not necessarily have
faith in FAR's "talks" about land for the poor and respect for religion, or
FAR's queries about how wealthier people in the vicinity treated the poor,
from which some villagers inferred that FAR might settle accounts with
unjust patrons, merchants, and so on. Although many settlers had no
sympathy with FAR, a certain number of others, including those who had
been unable to obtain title to land, could not lift themselves out of the
poverty that drove them to Petén, or had been politicized before moving
north, provided FAR with information or food, or at least gave it a
hearing. Even more responsive were some settlers who had been involved
with insurgents before coming to Petén, and (at least in Cascajal) some
idealistic youngsters who believed that FAR would eventually and somehow ease the poverty and oppression suffered by their families and friends.
Regardless of the response, however, the army struck at any village that
FAR visited, as the air force was still doing at least as late as 1985 or 1986.
The mere presence of FAR placed a village at risk.

Reactions to army attacks—to property destruction, indiscriminate beat-
ings, and death—varied. Although I am not able to quantify the reactions
or to speak of more than several villages, certain observations are possible.
Some villagers welcomed the army, for ideological reasons and/or for more
material ones (as was in part the case in Cascajal, if indeed it was the army
that attacked the village). A greater number wanted nothing more to do
with FAR, because the army demonstrated that the guerrillas could not
protect villagers. Others, as already remarked, fled to larger, safer towns or
departed Petén. Above all else, villagers were terrorized. Yet, it must be
noted that the attacks also gained vengeful recruits for the insurgent forces.
By its actions the army stilled, at least temporarily, the voiced demands of
the poor, and also kept alive what it wished to eliminate.

The army did not attack the towns (the municipal capitals) of Petén,
where the majority of the residents are native Peteneros. Here, too, there
were several factors at work. There are large military bases near the major
towns—Flores and the Lake-side *pueblos*, Melchor de Mencos, Poptún, and
Sayaxché. These bases, with the exception of Sayaxché, which is near very
dense forest cover, limit FAR incursions and, correspondingly, army re-
prisals. Moreover, most native Peteneros display no more sympathy for

FAR (perhaps because they have no tradition of violent land conflicts) than they do for civil patrols mandated by the state (an exception is the San Luiseños, who seem to take patrol duty more seriously than other Peteneros). Besides, as the result of the recent economic growth, a visible minority of native Peteneros have prospered. For economic reasons, as well as for personal safety, they tended and still tend to want peace at almost any price. Men who before the 1960s scratched out a living by making milpa and collecting chicle, in the 1970s and 1980s could earn higher incomes in other ways. For example, a householder who used to be a milpero now might be working full-time as a mason, while one of his unmarried adult sons is a truck driver and a daughter is a clerk in a government or private office. Men who were small-scale chicle subcontractors are middle sector agriculturalists, merchants, or shate contractors. Many gave up farming (Table 6:4), and it is for this reason that settler farmers in small villages rather than people in towns such as San Andrés now constitute the "maize basket" of central Petén. The new petit bourgeoisie (like the traditional elite), whose views influence less prosperous kinsmen, clients, and fellow community members, wanted (and want) to keep their new-found but not yet completely secure prosperity and to educate their children for professions. They tended to oppose any group threatening to destablize the orderly pursuit of wealth. Furthermore, examples of what was happening in settler villages, deaths of native Peteneros caught outside the relative safety of the larger towns, the menacing disorderly behavior of off-duty soldiers, rapid population growth, which by itself can strain the fabric of society, combined to frighten them and other Peteneros, stilling any inclination they may have had to express sympathy with insurgents. In short, the army had little reason to mount organized assaults on the *pueblos*. By the end of 1984, having cowed FAR sympathizers and many others besides, the army had, for the moment, the upper hand. But as of this writing, FAR's reduced forces do continue to operate in Petén.

By 1985 many native Peteneros and new settlers believed that FAR had been weakened by the army and perhaps too by in-fighting among its own units. However, whatever the future of FAR, it is probable that it or some other guerrilla group will remain active in Petén, as guerrillas will throughout the country, because the deep, historical conditions that brought them into being in the first place and that subsequently have provided grounds for their actions have yet to change in any significant way.

Figure 6:7. Settler's kitchen, Cascajal.

The least favored, poorest settlers have suffered most from the process of colonization and from the civil war. As in the case of the riverine cooperativists, their situation was both a brutal continuation and a result of pre-1980 events. It is important to note that even before the civil war began, colonization processes worked to their disadvantage. Later, in the war, many lost their lives. By 1985, as shown by an examination of the records of a religious group in central Petén that aided some of the victims of the war, there were over 2,000 orphans in southwestern and southcentral Petén alone. Some caution is needed to interpret the numbers, because the church considered as orphans fatherless, but not necessarily motherless, children, siblings were not clearly distinguished from nonsiblings, and in some instances the father appears to have abandoned his family rather than to have died. Nevertheless, the records and interviews at the church indicated that almost all of the children lost their fathers as a direct or indirect result of the civil war, and that most of the households in which they lived were either extremely poor or completely destitute. According to a church worker, the predominant majority of the children came from settler families which, precisely because they were settlers, had few if any kinsmen to whom they could turn for help. In the midst of so much social and political unrest it was not possible to be precise, but it appeared that perhaps as many as 500 or more households suffered the loss of an adult male. By inference, there must be at least several hundred more orphans in the rest of the department. Other families lost their land and fled Petén or moved to the major towns of the region where, as has been mentioned, they have entered a cheap labor market, to the profit of middle and upper class ranchers, merchants, and entrepreneurs. Even if this development did not by itself trigger a growth in unemployment, by the early 1980s it certainly aggravated the situation in the more urbanized areas of Petén. Although far fewer native Petén milperos have been killed, those among them who failed to purchase land must now cope with land scarcity, unreliable wage labor markets, and increasing socioeconomic differentiation. As remarked, a number of lower sector and larger numbers of middle and upper sector *sureños* and Peteneros have benefited materially from economic growth and relatively cheap land sales, and indeed from the civil war, but now they must live with heightened fear. Another consequence—for some the purpose—of the hideous violence has been to make the *status quo ante bellum* and worse seem tolerable, thus stilling overt dissent and undermining even mild reform efforts. In this milieu, personal conflicts peripheral to the basic causes of political instability, such as family feuds carried over from the eastern highlands of Guatemala to Petén, or what once would have been squabbles between native Petén store owners, have been pulled into the main arena and dealt with violently. Violence connected with unprecedented levels of common crime, increasing cultivation of marijuana, land disputes, and private feuds has become enmeshed with everything that provoked the civil war. It is as if having been defeated by the state, the society has turned against itself. A densely reticulated social and economic situation has become overlaid by apparently endless civil-political violence.

Even as violence and colonization have become twisted around each other, there also has been economic growth and development in the region. Although relatively few of the people who live in the riverine cooperatives, hamlets, and smaller *aldeas* have benefited from the economic changes, for *pueblo* residents (the majority of whom are native Peteneros in most *pueblos*) there have been certain gains. There now are increased educational opportunities, up to and including college education, with all this implies for upward mobility; increased access to health care and potable water; growing numbers of households with cement floors, which seem to improve the health of infants; electrification, which if not always reliable is present; and expanded markets for farm and nontimber forest products. There is a more diverse (though not reliable) job opportunity structure, and there is a wider range of consumer goods from which to choose. Although Peteneros still feel that the central government neglects them, for example, that it has failed to invest in road construction, which they consider essential for further development, the changes mentioned above have been rapid and have deeply impressed them. Yet they need to be assessed alongside at least one other aspect of the situation.

In the 1760s an unskilled manual laborer in Petén earned about two reales per day and a skilled (Indian) artisan earned about three reales per day. Although the price for a quintal of maize varied, as it still does, by season and by location, it appears that on average an unskilled laborer had to work 2.0 to 4.0 days and an artisan 1.0 to 2.0 days to buy a quintal of maize (see Chapter 2). Two hundred years later, around 1985, an unskilled laborer rarely earned more than Q3.00 to Q3.50 per day, when wage work could be found; a skilled sawmill machine operator could earn about Q17.30 per day. In central Petén maize cost on average about Q10 to Q12 per quintal, and in some other parts of the department the cost was higher. Thus, an unskilled laborer had to work 3.0 to 4.0 days and one of the most highly paid types of skilled worker 0.6 to 0.7 days to buy a quintal of maize. To be sure, these calculations are rough, and many townspeople have been decreasing their reliance on maize because there now are permanent markets in which to buy other foodstuffs such as rice, potatoes, packaged broths, and so on. Nevertheless, maize remains the staple item of the diet. Thus, in historical perspective, in an elementary sense the most highly paid workers have realized some gains from the most recent, post-1960s, economic changes and developments in Petén, but ordinary people have not. Moreover, the economic gap between skilled and unskilled labor appears to have grown wider. If the economic status of people living in the cooperatives, hamlets, and most of the *aldeas* were considered, it would be difficult to speak of "development" in any sense. Of course, the lack of economic progress cannot compare with the added misery caused by civil war, but it nonetheless colors the lives of Peteneros.

Ecological Consequences

Deforestation is yet another result of colonization, and ultimately of the inequities, injustice, and repression that led to the "anarchic" settlement of Petén. Between 1962 and 1975, about 12 to 20 percent of Petén's forests were felled; by 1985, 38 percent of the department was deforested (also see Saa Vidal 1979); and in that year severe erosion was apparent in parts of southeast Petén (also see Góngora Zetina 1984:48). In 1985 deforestation in Petén was not as extreme as in other parts of Guatemala, but everything indicated that the situation would worsen. One important fact was and is that despite regulations to the contrary, there are extensive milpas in the "protected" northern forest reserve, for example, around Paso Caballos, Carmelita, and old Chuntuquí. In 1989, a mere five years after my latest field data for this study were collected, there were reports that 60 percent of Petén had been degraded (*Prensa Libre* 13 May 1989:8). This figure still needs to be verified, but it is clear that the pace of deforestation has been rapid.

Native Petén milperos and chicleros say that removal of forest cover has led to increasingly lengthy dry seasons over the past fifteen years. As reported in Chapter 1, recent studies of rainfall patterns in Brazilian rain forests lend support to what Peteneros say. In Amazonia, the forests themselves generate a good deal of the rain that falls on them. When extensive areas are cleared of trees and replaced by grasses, the amount of moisture available for evaporation and transpiration is decreased; there is less water vapour in the atmosphere and a significant reduction in the amount, but apparently not the intensity, of precipitation; hence unprotected thin top-soils are washed away (Salati 1985:45–46). The grasses and the cattle ranging on the land tend to compact the soils, overexposing them to the sun, reducing soil permeability, and increasing water run-off (Salati 1985). In combination, all these circumstances can sharply deplete soil nutrients, scarce to begin with in regions like Petén. Although certain pasture grasses used in Petén, such as those introduced from Africa (for example, *Cynodon plectostachyus*), are drought resistant, it is not clear whether they are capable of sustained growth. If they are not, ranchers will have to clear virgin forest, decrease herd size, or force small farmers off the land. In addition, because some poor settlers from the highlands need quick returns from farming, or because they have not yet learned how to adapt to the low-lands, or because they are under great economic pressure to maximize production of basic grains, they do not, or cannot afford to, intercrop properly and maintain proper crop to fallow ratios. Failure to follow both of these practices leads to pest infestation and reduced soil fertility. As Wiseman (1978:76) observes, if the fallow is too short, "heavy rains unre-

stricted by [forest] canopy or leaf litter, carry [organics and minerals] away
. . ." decreasing soil fertility. Weeding, which loosens the soil, accelerates
the process. Moreover, without protective tree cover, the rains can drive
nutrients too deep into the soil for crop roots to reach them. An additional
unfortunate circumstance is that many of the more fertile soils in Petén are
on well-drained slopes which, when cleared of trees, are susceptible to
erosion (Sanders 1977). As the soils are progressively exhausted, the carrying capacity of the region will be significantly reduced. Soil regeneration
depends on reforestation, and the forests are being degraded at a rapid rate.

At least several experienced Petén farmers believe that deforestation is an
exponential process. They say that if a cleared plot of about 5 hectares is
cropped two years in a row and then fallowed for four to seven years, there
will be sufficient forest regrowth for many additional, satisfactory 2:4 to 7
year crop to fallow cycles. But if several hundred adjoining hectares are
cleared of primary or secondary forest and cropped for two years, the land
may have to rest fifty or more years before it is sufficiently reforested for
cropping purposes. They have also observed that the trees on the edges of
such areas are gradually reduced, so that once deforestation crosses some
as yet unknown critical threshold, it may become self-perpetuating. They
add that the land may even become a grassy plain suitable for pasture or
for the cultivation of fruit trees, but not for milpa. One implication of their
comments is that FYDEP's regulation that a landowner maintain 20 percent of his parcel in forest may be futile. For example, in an extensively
deforested area, keeping 60 hectares of a 300–hectare ranch in forest may
not be enough to assure long-term conservation of the woody patch. If the
farmers are correct, then the growing number of *contiguous* farms in southern (and in some parts of northern) Petén, covering hundreds and hundreds of hectares of land, will lead to an ecological disaster. It is not
altogether clear why the process is exponential. One contributing factor
may be that certain seed-carrying birds and bats, and perhaps other animals, are so highly adapted to specific trees that they will not cross extensive areas lacking those trees (some birds will not even fly over wide
roads), thereby limiting forest recovery. But, because of the environmental
diversity in Petén (see Chapter 1), a word of caution is needed. For example, in southern and southwestern Petén, where deforestation is extensive, there are many milpas that have been cropped and fallowed in a 1 to
2:3 to 5 year cycle for twenty years (as of 1985) and have fairly consistently

produced 23 to 40 quintals of shelled maize per hectare the first year of cultivation and 12 to 30 quintals the second year. The higher average, 40 quintals per hectare, is a relatively high production figure for rain-fed tropical swidden cultivation. Thus more time is needed to assess accurately the impact of current land clearing and farming practices on the environment. However, if current practices do exhaust soil resources in the near future, time for assessment will have to yield to relief efforts.

Since the late 1960s and early 1970s there has been a tremendous increase not only in swidden cultivation and ranching, but also in (uncontrolled) logging in Petén. In 1970 there were four logging concessions, in northwestern, eastern, and southeastern Petén. By 1987 there were seven in the southeast and in the "protected" northeast. The number of authorized sawmills has varied over the years, from seven to eleven, including three or four owned and operated by FYDEP, not to mention the twenty or so clandestine mills. Just how many trees have been felled in recent years is uncertain. Between 1979 and 1987 FYDEP reported that loggers felled 103,544 mahogany, cedar, and other trees, about 60 percent of which appear to have been sent overseas. Some Peteneros suggest higher numbers. For example, in one year one logging company alone is said to have felled and trucked out 3,600 to 5,400 cedar and mahogany trees, and it is not known how many trunks may have been left to rot because heavy rains made it impossible to haul them. Furthermore, many noncommercially valuable trees are felled to cut down a single valuable one. To assure that a big mahogany tree will fall freely, loggers may have to cut up to 12 to 17 adjacent trees. Because across Petén the average number of mahogany trees is less than 2.5 per hectare (although there are up to 12 per hectare in parts of the northwest; Lamb 1966:52), loggers have to open many logging trails and roads, cutting down a large number of trees in the process. Adding to the ecological damage are the logging roads that enable farmers, some of whom also work for lumber companies, to move deeper into the woods where they will clear even more of the forest. In Petén, there is a kind of negative symbiosis between loggers and colonists.

Another little studied source of deforestation is the use of hardwoods for domestic fuel. Although a growing number of households in Flores and Santa Elena use propane gas and kerosene for cooking, elsewhere in Petén over 95 percent of households instead depend exclusively on hardwoods. Wiseman (1978:81–82) estimates that,

In an equilibrium model, three hectares of sustained-yield land could supply the energy requirements of each person. If an expansionist model were used, in which regeneration is not assumed, 0.6 hectare could support a person's fuel requirements [or 3.6 hectares for a six person household].

Wiseman notes that his calculations are crude, but the point is that without taking anything else into account, the dramatic population growth of recent years by itself exerts severe pressure on the forests.

Given current cropping, ranching, and logging practices, there may not be enough land left to support many more people than already live in Petén. Some reformers and radicals have suggested that FYDEP should have distributed land evenly (see Manger-Cats 1971; also see writers cited in Schwartz 1987), but such a policy might have been as ecologically unwise as it was politically impossible. In 1962 FYDEP had some 34,344 *caballerías* (1,545,480 hectares) to sell. Since, under current milpa regimes, a farmer needed about 21 hectares and, despite what FYDEP says, more usually needed 45 to make ends meet, even had all the land been evenly distributed, Petén could not have supported many more than 300,000 people directly on the land. Furthermore, the scale of deforestation implied by these figures would have raised the problems of resource depletion noted above, and that would not have served the interests of smallholders. In any event, land was not evenly distributed, some lands in southwestern Petén were occupied by the military, and land consolidation is increasing. As land becomes scarce, milperos may—some already do—shorten the fallow, thus depleting soil productivity. This can force them to sell or relinquish their land to ranchers and largeholders, move deeper into the forests, and repeat the cycle. The process is complicated by the extensive logging, expanded ranching, dependence on hardwoods for domestic use, and civil war.

The grossly unequal distribution of land south of Petén also affects Petén. In addition to the situation described earlier in this chapter, in Guatemala about 2 percent of the farms control 72 percent of all agricultural land, and 1 percent of the holdings account for 34 percent of the cropped land (Manz 1988:51). To make matters worse, "access to arable land per capita declined from 1.71 hectares in 1950 to .79 hectares in 1980" (Manz ibid.). As long as the distribution of land in general remains so skewed, land-hungry countrymen will continue to migrate to Petén. All this has led informed Peteneros to fear that in the next twenty to thirty years the forests may disappear, with disastrous ecological and social consequences.

There still may be ways to turn the situation around. There is widespread agreement in Petén, in Guatemala, and in international donor agencies that the remaining forests of the northern lowlands must be preserved. To cite but three examples: In 1989 the central government, with the approval of most Peteneros, prevented a US oil company from drilling an exploratory oil well in the El Seibal archeological park in southwest Petén, to safeguard ancient Maya structures there. Recently the Cerezo government also has recreated protected forest zones in Petén, primarily north of latitude 17°10′. CECON (*Centro de Estudios Conservacionistas*, Center for Conservation Studies, National University of San Carlos) has been entrusted to study and manage at least 3,000 square kilometers of forest, and in general to provide technical advice to CONAP (*Concejo de Areas Protegidas*, National Council of Protected Areas). CONAP is a member of the *Comisión Nacional de Medio Ambiente*, National Commission for the Environment, whose head is appointed by the national executive. How these entities will prevent settlers from making milpas in the protected zones and how well-funded any of them will be is still not completely clear. Finally, West Germany has conditioned its promise to finance construction of an asphalted road between Petén and southern Guatemala on the impact of road construction on the ecology and on protection of forests and archeological sites.

Of course more can be done. Among other things that might help are the development of sustainable small rural industries to lessen dependence on farming, some form of land reform, the revival of several ancient Maya agrotechnologies, careful regulation of logging, and cultivation of non-traditional products that place relatively little pressure on the land.[6] Improved agroforestry, including balanced combinations of milpa and cultivation or collection of nontimber forest products on smallholder farms (Heinzman and Reining 1988), too, could help. For example, preliminary studies indicate that under proper management, cultivation of shate is compatible "with maintaining the integrity of the larger ecosystem" (Heinzman and Reining 1988:6). In that the net present value of land under shate cultivation is greater than that of land used for milpa, extractive economies also might improve smallholder living standards (Heinzman and Reining 1988:64). Add in other nontimber forest products, for example, chicle and allspice, and the argument for such economies becomes stronger. Moreover, Peteneros are familiar with many tree crops, root crops, and medicinal plants that could be cultivated or extracted on a commercial scale. Unfortunately, the most profitable nontraditional crop is marijuana. In contrast, "continued expansion of *milpa* may be both economically inefficient and ecologically nonsustainable" (Heinzman and Reining 1988:6).

There also may be ways to intensify agricultural production without necessarily depleting soil resources. The ancient Maya intensified production by complementing swidden cultivation with a "complex and diverse range of agrotechnologies," including raised fields, terraces, irrigation systems, and kitchen gardens. They also may have developed intercropping systems that help sustain soil fertility and lengthen field productivity (Santley, Killion and Lycett 1986:128–31) and relied more heavily on root crops and orchards than modern populations do. Although it is less certain that they used fertilizers, there are modern Petenero farmers who experiment, for example, with bat guano to cultivate papaya trees, apparently with some success. In addition, alley-cropping and hedgerows on hill slopes might limit erosion.

Of course, ancient Maya society in Petén eventually collapsed because of complex interactions between several factors, including agricultural intensification, increased monocropping, demographic instability, limited access to external sources of energy, and disruption of interregional trade (Santley et al. 1986). The point here, however, is that it may be possible to learn from the ancient Maya, without endangering the resource base in Petén.

Unfortunately, it is always difficult to implement apparently sound development policies. The Mexican government designed plans (similar to Guatemala's for Petén) to protect the Lacandón rain forests of Chiapas—the region immediately to the west of Petén—which have not yet been successfully implemented (Ross 1988). Moreover, the Guatemalan government may permit logging companies to ship logs out of Petén instead of processing them there. (As it is, relatively few logs are processed in Petén.) Influential Peteneros claim this will have a negative impact on local employment. In the meantime there are thousands of poor people who depend on logging for part or all of their income, and they will have to accept work on whatever terms the logging companies offer them. The government saved El Seibal, but at El Naranjo, La Libertad, Basic Resources International Ltd. wants to build a small refinery in another protected area (Biotopo Laguna del Tigro-Río Escondido), over the objections of CECON and many Peteneros, including members of the upper class (*Central American Reports* 1989). Although Peteneros agree there is a need for a refinery, they are upset about where Basic Resources wants to build it. Many if not all of the suggestions made previously about improved farming and extractive technologies are designed to protect the ecology and to help the poor. Those who make these suggestions assume that producers would have secure land titles. Without this stipulation who would invest labor in, for example, hedgerow construction? Smallholders also need access to feeder roads, cheap and reliable transportation, extension services, secure markets, and, of course, better terms of trade. But even with access to roads, markets, and so on, extractive economies are almost always unstable, and their products may be displaced by synthetics. In addition, buyers usually have multiple sources of supply, which increases the vulnerability of producers. For example, between 1979 and 1987, as Guatemala's share of the US shate market declined from 37 to 17 percent, Mexico's share went from 63 to 83 percent, because of cost differences (Heinzman and Reining 1988:44). There are ways to improve Guatemala's share of the market, but given the booms and busts in extractive economies, most householders will not risk relying on them to the exclusion of swidden, not because they have some special love of farming, but rather because their first goal is to ensure themselves a reliable source of food.

The difficulties of effecting recommendations about shate, nontraditional crops, better agrotechnologies, and so forth are not simply lack of secure markets, not the risk-aversive strategies of the poor (for they do experiment on a small scale with crops), not the failure of people in Petén to recognize current threats to the environment (for they do), not that all development strategies have advantages and disadvantages. Rather, the fundamental obstacle lies in the fact that those who gain disproportionately from the colonization process will, of course, not voluntarily give up privileges and practices that drive them, as well as the poor, to remove the forests. Effecting change will be stalled so long as profit from forest degradation remains possible, and this in turn is related to the national political economy. Ultimately, the problems of the losers in frontier settlements, and possibly those of the winners, are tied to the problems facing the entire nation. They require solutions not only at the regional but also at the national and international level. Gloomy predictions alone are not useful as they can foster passivity. However, even the brief review of the national context presented at the beginning of this section and immediately above indicates the tremendous scale and complexity of the challenge. If it is not met, the second conquest of Petén may be even more devastating than the first.

Concluding Discussion

I have argued that the sociocultural system of postconquest Petén has been conditioned largely by ecological, geographic, and economic circumstances beyond the control of the Peteneros. Yet not everything can be explained this way. As Bullitt says in a different context, no single analysis can account for the "multifariousness . . . the perpetually shifting facts of experience" (1966:144).[7] Nothing illustrates this better than the Peteneros' attachment to community which, though based in part on material considerations, is also invested with meanings that exceed those considerations. Peteneros, like everyone else, are the subjects as well as the objects of history, but just when they are one or the other is far from immediately obvious.

There once were parts of Guatemala where local people could live with a measure of freedom from political repression, without "being despoiled of their land," and with some control over their own lives. For Indians, this usually occurred where they greatly outnumbered non-Indians and where there were no large plantations of any sort, as in Chichicastenango (Bunzel 1952:12). For somewhat different reasons, postconquest Peteneros, too, saw some gradual improvement in the sociopolitical, if not the economic, conditions of their lives.

After the military conquest, a diverse group of people living in this isolated, tropical hinterland went about the business of creating a way of life for themselves under new conditions. The new native Peteneros had to cope with natural and social hardships, including those of ethnic and class inequality and injustice. However, the political economy of the region (including the absence of large commercial plantations and related neglect by the state) within the intimacy of a small society gradually tempered relations between rulers and ruled. Peteneros constructed a new stable society, marked by the continuity of social status and commutative relationships between ethnicity, community, and social class. Although there was a harsh side to this society, there was also a degree of security in its stability and sense of permanence.

The late nineteenth-century intrusion of foreign capital affected many aspects of the society, but it did not develop the region. Perhaps for that reason *la chiclería* did not change preexisting social and economic relationships, although it did qualify them. The industry increased the wealth and power of the traditional elite, reinforced preexisting exchange relations, mitigated ethnic injustice part of the time, and, without weakening attachments to it, had contrary effects on community. Supported by the regional government, management dealt harshly with labor. But the chicleros were hardly defenseless. In the vast forests of Petén, the technology and ecology of chicle production largely determined the organization of labor in the industry, which in turn gave the chicleros some opportunity to defend themselves against management. Moreover, the chicleros from Petén could always fall back on the land. They had open access to that basic resource. The region remained undeveloped and basic sociocultural patterns endured. Petén still seemed to be "of small promise" (Jones 1940:82), and Peteneros—the poor majority and the affluent few—dreamed of an end to their isolation.

The dream has become reality. Petén has been colonized, the economy has grown, and the region is increasingly integrated with the rest of the nation. As a result, Peteneros of all classes have more material possessions than they ever did. In the late eighteenth century, a man had to work about two to four days to earn enough to buy a quintal of maize, and in the late twentieth century he has to work three to four days to do so. Today, there are more goods to buy and to sell, more ways to earn a living and, as Peteneros say, more things to see and do. However, the price of progress has been high. The elite are amassing more and more land and wealth and becoming further removed from the lower sectors. Along with greater class conflict, there are heightened tensions between the regional elite and metropolitan logging and petroleum interests. Growing numbers of Peteneros and colonists are threatened by lack of access to land. For some, new wage labor opportunities more than offset the loss, but most must still combine small-scale farming with insecure seasonal employment in highly vulnerable extractive industries. Worse, thousands of displaced colonizing smallholders have been forced to enter a growing, unorganized rural proletariat which provides cheap labor for the extractive industries.[8] Demographic and economic growth have not led to structural development. Some colonists have tried to resist, and the state has responded with ruthless violence on a scale not seen in Petén since the late seventeenth-century conquest.

The second conquest of Petén resembles the first, but this time things may not settle down. If, as is possible, several changes prove irrevocable, they will generate endemic instability. The changes include the mutually reinforcing relationships between deforestation and resource depletion, increasingly unequal land ownership, expansion of ranching, which does not create employment, growing socioeconomic inequality, and deepening poverty among the lower sectors. By 1980, before the civil war forced thousands of smallholders off the land, these factors led to unprecedented levels of unemployment in Petén. As the working class grows in size and as people of diverse origin learn to live together in the same community, ethnicity appears to become less important and social class membership more important, with fewer ameliorating personal ties cutting across class divisions.[9]

Furthermore, if conditions worsen, social unrest and investment in military-police repression will feed on each other. Except for the receding role of ethnicity, the outcome of colonization may be that the social, economic, and political structures of the Guatemalan highlands will be irreversibly replicated in the lowlands of Petén.

Petén is no longer an isolated hinterland. The frontier has been settled, and the society has become unsettled. After the seventeenth-century conquest, the new Peteneros gradually moderated their relationships with one another and rejected extremism, perhaps as much by an act of will as by the force of circumstance. Now, as they cope with a second conquest, Peteneros argue that there is still time to save the forests. There also may be time to rebuild a more humane, stable way of life in the lowlands. The hope is that the loss of the past for a grim present does not need to spell the loss of a chance for a better future.

Appendix: Status Continuity in Petén, Eighteenth to Twentieth Centuries

Status by Century

18th, vecinos A	19th–early 20th, notables B	20th, professional C	20th, upper class D
1 —	A+	—	—
2 B	B	B	—
3 C	—	C	C
4 D	D	D	D
5 E*	—	—	—
6 F	F	—	—
7 —	G+	G	—
8 H*	—	H	H
9 —	—	—	I?+
10 J	J	J	J
11 K	—	K	K
12 —	—	?	L
13 —	—	M	—
14 —	N+	—	—
15 O	—	—	—
16 P	—	—	P!
17 —	Q+	—	—
18 —	—	R	—
19 S	S	S	—
20 T	T	T	T?
21 U*	—	—	U
22 V	V	V	V
23 W*	W	W	W
24 X	X	X	X
25 Y?*	—	Y	Y
26 Z	—	—	—
27 —	—	AA	—
28 —	—	BB+	B

Status by Century *(Continued)*

18th, *vecinos* A	*19th–early 20th,* *notables* B	*20th,* *professional* C	*20th,* *upper class* D
29 CC?	CC	CC	—
30 —	DD	—	—
31 —	—	EE*	EE
32 —	—	FF	—
33 GG	GG	GG	—
34 HH?	HH	HH	—
35 II?	II	II	—
36 JJ	JJ?	JJ	JJ

Sources: AGCA documents cited in text, such as *Ramo Criminal* 1822–1899; *Rentas Internas*, etc.; also see references to authors, such as Boix-Torres 1936; Narciso 1913; Pendergast 1967; Soza 1970, etc.; Field Notes (including genealogies, family traditions, and notes abstracted from certain church records; *Revista Petén Itzá* 1937–1986, and several other annuals (published by the *municipios* of San Benito, Poptún and Melchor de Mencos). For further description of sources, see below.

Key: * = The colonial family was of "humble," possibly Ladino and/or Pardo origin.

+ = The founding ancestor was not a member of a Petén colonial family and was not born in Petén.

! = It is not completely clear if the modern family has any genealogical connection with the colonial family.

Note: After considerable thought, I decided to use symbols rather than actual surnames.

What the table does not show is that most of the families are related by ties of affinity and consanguinity, and most of them also reside in the same community or nearby, that is, Flores, and some in Santa Elena or, less commonly, San Benito. Affluent, highly educated Peteneros who reside in Guatemala City not listed here.

Column A lists some, but by no means all, relatively important colonial families, e.g., those who served as chief administrators of San Felipe, were army officers, and so on. Also listed are families who seem not to have held such high positions. Most of these families were of Creole origin. Of special value here were AGCA sources, church records, Soza 1970, and family traditions.

Column B lists names based on cross-tabulations with AGCA documents and Soza (1970:171, 229–334). At least two–thirds of the people Soza lists were born in Flores. Like all of us, Soza had his predilections and prejudices, and he does omit several relatively important people born in and residing in other *pueblos*, but most Peteneros would agree with him, and the documents usually support him. The documents and Soza refer to people born between 1801–1925.

Column C (derived from Soza 1970:334 and my own field work) refers to professionals born after 1925 and active in the 1950s and 1960s. Some would want to add other names, but after about 1965, the number of professionals has grown so long that it is not possible to list all of them.

Column D is based on data collected for the period 1960–1985. To be a candidate for Column D an individual (representing himself or his immediate family) had to appear on two of the following lists. (a) *Economic*: The individual owned a large business employing at least several (and some had many more than several) workers who were not kinfolk, and the economic importance of the business had to be confirmed by examining *Rentas Internas* archives. (b) *Political-bureaucratic*: The individual held or had held important elective (congressman, mayor), and/or non-elective political or bureaucratic posts (e.g., governor, chief educational administrator, FY-DEP executive, high ranking military officer, etc.), and/or the presidency of an important regional organization (e.g., cooperative, ranchers' association, apiarists' association, and/or chicle contractors' consortium, etc.). (c) *Sociocultural*: The individual was named at least once in some important department-wide "cultural" activity (e.g., editorship of *Petén Itzá*, winner of an essay contest, etc.). This procedure yielded a list of 56 individuals grouped into 18 (often interrelated) families. Most of them appear repeatedly on all three lists. It is important to note that the procedure also *failed* for one reason or another to include several wealthy, influential Peteneros, e.g., in La Libertad. It also omits wealthy newcomers to Petén who may have little need for or interest in regional socio-cultural activities or departmental bureaucratic positions, e.g., a banker who is an absentee landowner, at least one member of a famous family from Guatemala City who owns a great deal of property in Petén, high ranking military officers with land in Petén, etc. Families listed in Column D that are not of colonial origin are related by marriage to Peténeros of colonial origin, and Flores is almost always their address. It should be added that there are relatively wealthy and politically influential individuals and families in *pueblos* outside the urban triangle of Flores-Santa Elena-San Benito who are not included in Column D because they never appear on the sociocultural list and very infrequently or never on the political-bureaucratic list. Perhaps to be expected but still of interest is that they rarely have kinship ties to the families listed in Column D.

There are, as also might be expected, lower as well as upper sector members of most of the families listed in Column D, although in some instances the genealogical connection is unrecognized or minimized by the people involved, especially by those more fortunately placed.

Notes

1. Comments in the text do not imply that because Peteneros can enjoy the environment, they also must value living "in harmony with nature." In 1975, the Kluckhohn-Strodtbeck (1961) "Values Orientation Schedule" was administered to 78 adult native Peteneros and 13 migrant Kekchí Indians in a central Petén town. The sample included 24 Petén Ladino, 26 Petén Indian, and 10 Kekchí males; and 8 Petén Ladino, 20 Petén Indian, and 3 Kekchí females. No dimension of the schedule distinguished ethnic groups from each other, however, with respect to the "Man-Nature Orientation" (mastery over, in harmony with, or subjugation to nature) the Petén Indian group did choose "subjugation" to a nearly significant degree, and open-ended interviews suggest that they tended to feel more subject to nature than others but did not necessarily value this state (Schwartz and Eckhardt 1979).

1. For additional details, see Bricker 1981; Harris and Sartor 1984; Hellmuth 1977; Jones 1982; Nations and Nigh 1980.

Western and most of northwestern Petén remained beyond the reach and really the concern of colonial and national regimes until the 1830s, and even then these zones were not brought under (relatively weak) government control until the late 19th century. Today, although insurgent forces operate in all parts of the department, the western forests immediately adjacent to the Pasión and Usumacinta Rivers are particular guerrilla strongholds. Both areas were very sparsely populated until the late 1960s. The nineteenth- and twentieth-century Lacandón speak a language mutually intelligible with Yucatec and Itzá Maya (Harris and Sartor 1984:32). As they did in colonial times, Peteneros refer to these Indians as "Lacandones" or "Caribes." Peaceful relations with the Lacandones in Petén were firmly established between the 1830s-1840s, and the last Lacandón resident in Petén died around 1960. Other Lacandón, of course, continue to live in Chiapas, Mexico.

2. Indians identified as Cehach were settled in San Andrés and in San José as late as the mid-nineteenth century.

3. All of this may have been complicated by Kekchí reluctance to aid the Spanish in the subjugation of the Manché. The Kekchí had first-hand experience of Spanish brutality and also wished to protect their own cacao and achiote trade routes, hence the reluctance (Wilk 1981:30, 48–50).

4. In the sixteenth and seventeenth centuries, the Kekchí were occupying Manché Chol lands in the Río Dulce region. It is possible that Cahabón and Lanquin Kekchí also occupied whatever Manché areas spilled over into Petén, but

hardly in sufficient numbers to reestablish the pre-conquest demographic status of southeastern Petén. There are Mopán today in Belize, and a small number of Mopán still live as a minority among the modern Kekchí of San Luis, Petén.

5. Tipú has recently been identified as Negroman, Belize (Graham, Jones, and Kautz 1985). The Tipuans submitted to the Spanish between 1695–1707, helped in the conquest of the Itzá and then, in 1707, were removed to the shores of Lake Petén Itzá (Graham et al. 1985:207–10). The Muzul, residing near and perhaps some of them in Tipú, also seem to have been removed to the Lake shores and elsewhere in Petén at this time, and certainly other Muzul were rounded up later, for example, in 1754–1756, and resettled in and around Santa Ana, San Luis and (a few) San Andrés. The Muzul may have been a component of the *"indios del monte"* (wild Indians) referred to in eighteenth-century documents, until 1756 that is (Comparato 1983:210; Jones 1983:81; Mazzarelli 1976a:168–70).

6. The British or perhaps more properly the English had penetrated the coast of Belize perhaps as early as 1638, and by 1677 this area was an important haven for pirates and an important source of logwood. Not only did the English despoil Spanish ports in Belize and Campeche, for example, in 1659 and in 1678, but their capture of Roatan Island increased their control over much of the coastal Caribbean area (Comparato 1983:125; Mazzarelli 1976a:153–54; Woodward 1985:52, 288). The English and the Spanish struggled with each other for control over Belize in the seventeenth, eighteenth, and nineteenth centuries, and in a very real sense the struggle, now between Belize and Guatemala, still goes on.

7. European introduced diseases include smallpox, influenza, various dysenteries, and malaria. Peteneros still suffer from what was introduced so long ago. "The whole department of the Petén is a notorious hotbed for malaria" (Thompson 1970:58), and 94 percent of the mid-twentieth-century population had intestinal parasites, which rendered them more vulnerable to malaria than would otherwise be the case (Thompson 1966:25). Hookworm, malaria, intestinal parasites, amoebic dysentery, and TBC are still—in the 1980s—very widespread among the population.

8. An earlier fort, at Poptún, was abandoned on the orders of the President of Guatemala, who had little if any interest in the conquest of Petén (Comparato 1983:21, 233–37). From 1700 on, Remedios (renamed Flores in 1831) continued to be the main center of Spanish population and the main military stronghold in Petén.

9. The population of Belize was 2,656 in 1790; it did not reach 25,000 until 1861, and did not exceed 120,000 by 1970 (Bolland 1977:3). In 1733, the Spanish drove the English from Belize, but they soon returned. In 1754, the Spanish once more tried to oust them; the invasion failed, but as a result of the attempt, the English constructed a fort at Belize to prevent further attacks (Comparato 1983:393; Woodward 1985:66). The borders between Guatemala and Belize were regularized in 1783 and again in 1860, but Guatemala has never given up its claim to the country. Rumors about violence between the two countries are as common today as they were in the past. With reference to the 1710 rumors, see Valdavida; for 1765, see AGI Guatemala 859.

10. Compare, for example, AGI Guatemala 859, 1765; AGCA A1 Leg. 5919, Exp.

51134 ("El Comandante del Petén, don Jose de Gálvez, informa que el precio de un novilla en la jurisdicción de su mando, tan solo alcanza a 22 reales, debido a la falta de caminos para conducir el ganado a otras zonas," 1795); AGCA A1.22.33 Leg. 15510, Exp. 2160 ("El Vicario del Petén, Pbro. Domingo Fajardo solicita providencias para construcción de un camino que una al Petén con Verapaz," 1812); González 1867; Soza 1957; *Prensa Libre* interview with Governor Castellanos Góngora 23 February, 31 May, 8 and 19 June, 1986. Petén's economic problems have consistently been attributed to a lack of good roads (what Comandante Gálvez said in 1795 sounds very much like what Governor Castellanos had to say in 1986. Soza, speaking of this "distant, isolated and abandoned department," adds that "It is said that previous governments never preoccupied themselves with" road construction in Petén (1957:294). Travelers and government personnel on official inspections were forever noting that Petén was "almost uninhabited" (Berendt 1868:420), so "abandoned to its own resources for 150 years" (González 1867:76) that "nothing at all was known about the distant region of Petén" in the 1870s (Boddam-Wetham 1877:212), and in the mid-19th century the people of Flores lived "in profound ignorance of all that takes place in the world outside" (Morelet 1877:212). In 1940 as in 1883, Petén was "almost unoccupied, little developed and of small interest" (Jones 1940:81–82), and until the late 1960s, few Guatemalans wished to settle there. "Of outsiders [*foraneos*], that is to say people born outside El Petén who resided here [there were] only the governor [*jefe político*], the judge of the first instance, and now and then a physician, other public offices being in the charge of Peteneros, because no one from elsewhere dared to penetrate a place so distant and unknown . . ." (Soza 1970:288).

11. Valdavida (1975), relying primarily on colonial church records, lists the *northern* settlements between San Andrés and San Felipe (the first Mexican settlement across the modern border). The Valdavida map refers to 1720 (see also the maps in Morelet 1871 and Scholes and Roys 1968). The Rivas document — dated 1724 — discovered by Dr. L. Feldman (Francisco Rivas, "Razón del Presidio de Petén," Royal Library, Copenhagen) supports Valdavida, except that Rivas says Chivalche rather than San Felipe was the first town in Campeche. The settlements listed immediately below persisted — with some variations—throughout the colonial period (AGI 859 Guatemala, 1765; Fajardo 1812 above, note 10) and into the nineteenth century (Berendt 1868:424; González 1867; Valenzuela 1879). After the 1840s, the northern route, as noted, declined in importance. Continued political turbulence in the north helped keep population low along the northern portion of the *camino real*. In 1924 or 1926, political troubles in Yucatán spilled over into Guatemala, and the last families living in Chuntuquí—who still spoke Maya—left for San Andrés. Until 1882, when it was ceded to Mexico, a triangular piece of Petén jutted north by northwest into southern Campeche; it seems never to have been under effective control of any Petén government. Following the Valdavida map, the settlements (those marked with an asterisk said to possess a church) were: San Andrés*, San Miguel*, Santa Rita*, San Martín*, Sahich (?), Chuntuquí, Batcab, and San Felipe*.

For 1720, Valdavida (1975) lists the following settlements, other than Remedios, along the southern branch of the *camino real*: Santa Rita*, Santo Toribio*,

Dolores*, Poptún, San Luis*, Chimay, Tzunkal, Santa Isabel and from the last named on to Cahabón, Alta Verapaz. (Rivas [1724] says it took 14 days to travel from Santa Isabel, the last settlement in Petén, to Cahabón; Royal Library, Copenhagen.)

Fisher (1974:79–80) says that the Cobán-Cahabón-Bolonco-Tuila-San Luis route was replaced by the Cobán-Chisec-Chinajá-Flores route; the latter may have become the main Cobán-Flores route as early as 1826 and as it certainly was by the 1850s. The national government had great problems keeping open the Chinajá-Flores route, and off and on it became seriously deteriorated (Boddam-Whethem 1877:240; González 1867:86–88; *Petén Itzá* 1938; Soza 1957:315).

12. The western routes, from Flores to the Pasión-Usumacinta region, took 6–12 days to traverse. The routes grew important with logging, apparently in the 1860s. This also led to an increase in population, but the entire west and northwest was underpopulated until recently. Flores and La Libertad in particular benefitted from logging (Maudslay and Maudslay 1899:230; Mejía 1904; Morelet 1871:190; Valenzuela 1879). After the chicle companies built rough—to put it mildly—airstrips in places such as Paso Caballos (Paso Petén), Carmelita, Uaxactún, Dos Lagunas, and so on, in the 1930s, these northern and northwestern footpaths declined in importance.

The eastern route from Flores to Belize passed through Macanché, Yaxhá, modern Melchor de Mencos (formerly Fallabón and Plancha de Piedra) in Petén, and Benque Viejo, Cayo, and so on in Belize, on to the port of Belize. In the 19th century, the trip from Flores to Belize apparently took some six days, with post-stations found every 16–24 kilometers along the route (Berendt 1868:423–24). Although not the easiest passage (as Caddy noted in 1840 [Pendergast 1967:160]; also see González 1867:86–88), Peteneros traded moccasins, hides, and cattle for cloth and luxury items from Belize from at least the 1840s and 1850s on. In the late nineteenth century, the chicle industry greatly enhanced the importance of this route, and in the 1930s Ubico's attempts to seal the Petén:Belize borders were only partially successful. From at least the 1880s until the 1960s, coming from Cayo one reached the small and often deserted village of Remate, at the western end of the Lake; then one took a canoe rather than following the footpath around the Lake to reach Flores.

In the nineteenth century, the side trails from Dolores to Belize, a three day trek, seem to have been more traveled than the Cahabón-Belize trail (González 1867:77–78; Valenzuela 1879).

13. Between 1821 and 1845, the southern branch of the *camino real* deteriorated and in 1847–1848 was "utterly unavailable for commerce" (Morelet 1871:227). Political turbulence in Guatemala and increasing use of the port in Izabal apparently contributed to this situation (Griffith 1965:11). Colonial and post-colonial documents constantly refer to the need to maintain this difficult passage (e.g., AGI Guatemala 859, 1765; AGCA Geográfico: Hemeroteca D for the years 1831, 1848, and on; also see Berendt 1868; Morelet 1871:278–86; Soza 1957:315). In 1879, Valenzuela, who seems to have been a plain, practical man not easily made physically uncomfortable, felt the road was in fair condition, but others obviously did not share his

view. As late as 1961 the land trip from Flores to Guatemala was interesting if not easy. One took a canoe from Flores to the mainland, then, the rains permitting, a jitney bus across the savanna (the road never seemed to be in the same exact place twice in a row, but the land is flat enough so that the driver, who fortunately had lost his right rather than his left arm so that he could steer while his daughter worked the gears on his right side, always found some way to cross the area) to Machaquilá. There, if the river was too high, passengers used a rope bridge to transfer to another bus going to the ferry crossing at the Río Dulce. (Sometime the jitney went no further than Poptún, and the trip to San Luis was made by horse or military jeep.) From the Río Dulce the bus went to Morales, and from there by bus or railroad to Guatemala City. With luck, the trip from Flores to the City took 2 to 3 days.

From the early eighteenth century onward, paths linking Flores-La Libertad-Santa Ana were well-traveled, and late observers (e.g., Mejía 1904:29) claimed they were the best roads in Petén. Flores and San Andrés (and San José) were linked by canoe, and even in 1985 passengers preferred the motorized canoes to the land route.

There are now roads linking Flores and Sayaxché, Flores-La Libertad-Naranjo (in the far west; from Naranjo one crosses into Mexico), San Andrés-Carmelita, and so on. The major road from Flores to the southeast passes over the old *camino real*. Old place names which fell into disuse in the early to mid-nineteenth century are reappearing on the maps of Petén.

14. Clerical and secular authorities mutually accused each other of abusing their respective authority and power. For example, see AGCA A2.2 Leg. 37, Exp. 751 et seq. (*Autos criminales . . .*, 1708); AGCA A 1.23 (from the Crown to "Mi Gobernador . . . y presidente de mi Audiencia Real," ordering the authorities to cease forcing and conning Indians from their assigned locales, 1716); AGCA A1.21.7 Leg. 185, Exp. 3788 ("Don Juan Jose Hurtado de Mendoza, alcalde y castellano de El Petén, rinde informe sobre el estado del Petén Itzá," 1725); Comparato's (1983:393) description of how in 1754 Mencos' soldiers on their retreat from Belize treated Indians; AGCA A1.12 Leg. 5466, Exp. 46932 (Josef Ubano Mendoza, "Misión Itzá . . . ," 1812); AGCA A1.17.1 Leg. 188, Exp. 3843 ("El Vicario del Petén, Pbro. Domingo Fajardo rinde informes sobre el estado economico y religioso de los Pueblos del Petén," 1819). The most brutal period of colonial rule seems to have been the earliest (1700–1708). The tenure of Gov. Coronel Juan Antonio Ruiz y Bustamante (1708–1718) was apparently a good deal more humane in relation to the Christianized Indians (Comparato 1983:320, 385; Hellmuth 1977; Soza 1970; Valdavida 1975). But the Indians were a conquered people ruled by foreign clergy and military, and all through the colonial period at least some of the Indians were disposed toward flight and resistance (see especially AGI Guatemala 859, 1765 and AGCA A1.15 Leg. 5465, Exp. 46917 ("Rama sala de crimen," 1803).

15. AGCA A1.21.7 Leg. 185, Exp. 3788 (Gov. Hurtado "Informa a vuestra Señoría . . . ," 1725); AGCA A1.6 Leg. 3799.5 (Gov. Francisco Joseph García de Monzaval, "Autos hechos en virtud de su Magestad . . . ," 1754); AGCA A1.6 Leg. 3799.15

(Gov. Manuel de Amate, "Informe . . . ," 1757); AGCA A3.1 Leg. 11, Exp. 207 ("El castellano de la forteleza . . . ," 1783); AGI Guatemala 859, 1765; Valdavida 1975; census 1778; *Comisión de Limites* 1929.

16. See AGCA A3.2 Leg. 11, Exp. 207, 1783 cited above. The *Comisión de Limites* (1929) maps do not show any settlements in the far west until about the 1890s (see Bianconi map of 1891 and Sapper map of 1894). Bianconi's map shows a settlement just about where modern Sayaxché is located. Most of these settlements sprang up in the 1860s, in connection with logging activities.

17. On the *situado*, see Soza 1970:281–82, 592–94; Wortman 1982:141. Soza says that *situado* payments did not end until 1874, when they were replaced by taxes on lumber and rubber extracted from Petén. See Farriss (1984:359) on the *cajas*. Ursúa did not want tribute imposed on the Indians of Petén; see also AGCA A3.1 ("Tributos: Recaudación," 1795). Comparato (1983) mentions labor scarcity in post-conquest Petén; see also documents in AGCA, Vicars Fajardo (1812) and Mendoza (1812), and Gov. Hurtado (1725), cited above. See also AGCA A1.11.24 Leg. 3793, Exp. 185, 1743; Leg. 5919, Exp. 51130, 1778 respectively ("Construcciónes Templos"); A3.1 Leg. 590, 1794. It should be noted that the clergy used to ask the secular authorities to prevent non-Indian settlers from using Indian workers so that they, the clergy, could have them nearby to more readily convert them, but failed to mention the labor they, the clergy, extracted from the Indians.

18. For this paragraph I have relied heavily on AGI Guatemala 859, 1765 mentioned above; aside from the financial accounts of the crown estates, the 1765 document seems to be the longest report on colonial Petén. Information on the estates comes from numerous documents—AGCA A1, A1.21.7, A3.3 et seq. and B5.7,"Cuentos de los productos de la hacienda de San Felipe," "Inventarios de la hacienda de San Felipe," "Gastos de la hacienda de San Felipe," and "Minutas de la hacienda de San Felipe." AGCA documents on San Felipe are listed further on. Names of soldiers and other non-Indians in colonial Petén are taken from a wide range of AGCA documents: San Felipe accounts; census data; AGCA Appellidos drawers; requests for *bayucos* (military salaries), requests for tavern licenses, and so on in AGCA *Ayuntamientos del Petén* for 1706–1817.

19. See Commandant Amate, AGCA A1.6, Leg. 3799.15, 1757; Caddy 1839 (Pendergast 1967:102); Soza 1970:229–324; interviews with people in Flores.

20. There are references to the "*parroquias del norte*" in the Flores archives at least until 1754, but "their" priest or priests resided most of the time in San Andrés, e.g., AGCA A1.12.11 Leg. 186, Exp. 3803 ("Casique Ylario Zib, Alcalde ユ Chí y Regidor Thom° Pott, Representación del°s Casique y Just. del Pueblo de Concepción del Petén," 1763) and Valdavida 1975. For other AGCA documents on the church in Petén: see A3.3 Leg. 29, Exp. 569, 1732 and Leg. 33, Exp. 677, 1732; A3.1 Leg. 1285, Exp. 15480, 1771; A3.1 Leg. 11, Exp. 207, 1783; A1.21.7 Leg. 2159, Exp. 15480, 1785; A3.3 Leg. 36, Exp. 731, 1787; A1.21.7 Leg. 2159, Exp. 15489, 1795; A1 Leg. 5919, Exp. 51134, 1795; A3.1 Leg. 978, Exp. 18039, 1795; A1.21.7 Leg. 2158, Exp. 15492, 1797; A1.6 Leg. 2158, Exp. 15492, 1797; A1 Leg. 5919, Exp. 51191 and 51197, 1813; A3.3 Leg. 43, Exp. 867, 1818; A1.44 Leg. 2160, Exp. 15528, 1821; and B5.7 Leg. 67, Exp. 1827, 1882.

21. AGCA A1.23 Leg. 10080, Exp. 1525, 1714, from crown officials to the Guate-

malan Royal Audience. The shortage meant that any given parish, except for Remedios, might be without its priest for longer or shorter periods, for example, San Andrés had no resident priest in 1768–1778 and again in 1810–1818.

22. See Vicars Fajardo AGCA A1.22.33, Leg. 15510, Exp. 2160, 1812 and Urbana Mendoza AGCA A1.12, Leg. 5466, Exp. 46932, 1812 cited above, and Vicar don Pedro Ponce de León, AGCA A3.1 Leg. 590, Exp. 11700 ("Al proximo real tribunal audiencia . . . ," 1795); de León laments that the *vecinos* could raise no more than 122 pesos for church repairs. From 1743 on, many of the ornaments in the *capilla real* (main church, in Remedios) needed to be replaced and/or mended, but as in the case of the garrison, supplies and funds were slow to reach Petén and, in the view of civil and regligious authorities there, never in sufficient quantity. In 1806, the community of *pueblo* San José had 66 head of cattle, selling several to subvent religious ceremonies. Valdavida (1975) discusses church ranches.

23. See AGI Guatemala 859, 1765; and documents in AGCA, Comandante Hurtado 1725; Vicar Mendoza 1812; and Casique Zib 1763, all cited above; Valdavida 1975. See also MacLeod 1985:490 and AGCA Tributos:Recaudación, A3.1 Leg. 1316, Exp. 22296 ("La Contaduría Mayor de Cuentas es de parecer que se den instrucciones al Comandante del Petén y a los curas reductores para que traten de imponer algún tributos a los indios a favor del rey, eso si sin amenazas ni opreciones, para evitar que los indios se fugen a las montañas," 1795).

24. See various eighteenth-and nineteenth-century "Cuentos" and "Gastos" for San Felipe. See also documents in AGCA, Vicars de León (1795), Fajardo (1812) cited above, and Valdavida (1975). Farriss (1984:414) notes that "Although no longer technically missions, the parishes in Peten in the early nineteenth century were still partially supported from the royal exchequer." She also notes that in 1776 the Yucatán Bishop's share of tithes was 4,351 pesos, a tremendous amount by Petén standards. The Petén parish priests' salaries rose to 360 pesos per year in 1782. Patch (1985:28) gives "some indication . . . of prices and purchasing power" in eighteenth-century Yucatán which "were considered standard throughout the century, although short-term fluctuations occur." Maize cost 2 reales/*carga*; cotton 6.25–10 reales/25 pounds; sugar 0.5 reales/pound; cow or bull 5 pesos (rising to 6–7 pesos in the early nineteenth century; Farriss op. cit.); and mules 15–18 pesos. Patch (op. cit.) says that a *carga* was a "local unit of measurement approximately equivalent to the *fanega* widely in use elsewhere, i.e., 1.5 bushels." In the USA today a bushel of shelled corn with 15% moisture content weighs about 56 pounds (25.2 kilograms), but in colonial central Mexico the *fanega* seems to have been closer to 176 rather than 84 pounds (Gibson 1964:600). In colonial Petén, *fanega* and *carga* seem to have been used interchangeably, and a *carga* apparently weighed between 80 and 100 pounds (the *carga* was half that in the highlands). Although prices for maize and livestock were roughly the same in colonial Petén and Yucatán, prices tended to be somewhat higher in Yucatán, the difference probably owing to Petén's greater remoteness.

25. Colonial census data and ethnic labels used in them must be treated with caution (Wortman 1982:288). In the counts, "Indians . . . became ladinos. And ladinos were frequently confused with mestizos in documents. Mestizos, on the

other hand, were sometimes included in Spanish documents. It is clear that no estimate is possible for the caste population of the colony" (Wortman 1982:290). Indians who entered the ranks of the mestizos or Pardos did not pay tribute, although they were otherwise part of the "unskilled labor force" in Yucatán (Farriss 1984:114). Ethnic and cultural boundaries were "nebulous," and despite a rigid caste system, in many ways mestizos, Pardos and Maya were "indistinct" (Farriss 1983:17–18).

26. A very good description of the food supply situation in colonial Petén is found in AGI Guatemala 859, 1765; see Reina 1967 for a discussion of frequent reports of maize shortages in post-conquest Petén.

27. In addition to documents cited above and Valdavida (1975), there are several series of documents on the royal ranches. After 1775, the documentary record becomes relatively complete, perhaps because of the complaint, e.g., in 1771, AGCA 3.1 Leg. 1285, Exp. 22109 ("Los officiales de la Real Contaduría, informan acerca de que solamente existen en su oficina cuatro documentos relativos a la propiedad que tiene el Rey sobre la Hacienda de San Felipe, en la jurisdicción del Petén"). The AGCA documents, listed below, concern various aspects of San Felipe, and some report on communal ranches:

A3.3	Leg. 29,	Exp. 569	1732	A1.21.7	Leg. 2158,	Exp. 15492	1797
A3.3	Leg. 33,	Exp. 677	1732	A1.6	Leg. 2159,	Exp. 15492	1797
A3.1	Leg. 1285,	Exp. 22109	1771	A1	Leg. 5919,	Exp. 51192	1813
A3.1	Leg. 11,	Exp. 207	1783	A1	Leg. 5919,	Exp. 51197	1813
A1.21.7	Leg. 2159,	Exp. 15480	1785	A3.3	Leg. 43,	Exp. 867	1818
A3.3	Leg. 36,	Exp. 731	1787	A1.44	Leg. 2168,	Exp. 15528	1821
A1.21.7	Leg. 2159,	Exp. 15489	1795	B5.7	Leg. 67,	Exp. 1827	1827
A1	Leg. 5919,	Exp. 51134	1795	A1.44	Leg. 2160,	Exp. 15528	1808
A3.1	Leg. 978,	Exp. 18039	1795	(which gives herd size for 1797–1806).			

In general, the reports say more about cattle than horses and mules, although Petén's hard-hooved horses and mules were highly esteemed in Yucatán and highland Guatemala. From at least 1765 on (see AGI Guatemala 859), officials and vicars suggested and recommended that the crown estates be sold because they were not profitable, were difficult to operate, and so on. Even so, in 1795 Commandant Gálvez said that the major source of garrison and community income is ranching. If true, the communities "de yndios" must have been quite poor, for example, Gálvez reports their "goods" as follows: San Andrés—151 cattle, 25 horses/mules; San José—50 cattle, no horses/mules; Santo Toribio—40 cattle, 18 horses/mules; Dolores—150 cattle, 15 horses/mules; San Luis—80 cattle, 10 horses/mules. The total is 471 head of cattle and 68 horses and/or mules. Of significance is that Gálvez noted that these "pueblos" have no other common or community goods.

28. Although Bourbon administrators, especially after the 1770s, seem to have maintained better records and apparently to have been more scrupulous than Hapsburg administrators, who were more lax and more willing to live with local autonomy or decentralized government (Farriss 1984:358–61), in Petén there may have been corruption in the sale of horses and mules. Although the documents on

cattle sales are clear and straightforward, those for horses and mules are not (references in preceding note).

29. With reference to exaggerated claims about the numbers of unpacified Indians in colonial Petén, see Bricker 1981; Feldman 1982:225; Hellmuth 1977; Valdavida 1975; Comparato 1983:263, 398.

30. See Rivas 1724 ("Razon del Presidio del Petén"); Valdavida 1975. Means (1917) dates the Torres-Landa map to 1750, but Villacorta (1942:399) to 1740, and Reina (1966) to 1735. The map shows some 18 communities (but not Poptún), the crown estates and ranches in the vicinity of La Libertad (then Sacluk) and San Francisco (then Chachaclun, sometimes spelled Chachalum).

31. In 1975 workers erecting a water tank in San Andrés uncovered what appeared to be a Post-Classic Maya structure. The site, near the top of a slope, contained post-classic figurines and stamp rollers or seals. After some discussion, the workmen decided not to inform the authorities about their find, in part because they did not wish officials to take the seals and figurines from them but primarily because they thought the authorities might delay completion of the water tank and thus inconvenience them significantly. The site was filled with concrete and a concrete water tank erected over it. For the possibility that San Andrés may be the site of a Cobox village, also see Stone 1932.

32. AGCA A1.24 Leg. 10244, Exp. 1580 ("San Andres de lla Nueva Provinicia del Itza. 15 de Mayo 1713. RP Titulo de Gobernador del San Andres, a favor del casique don Bernardo Chatha, quien habia cooperado en la reduccion de los indios llamados Quexaches," 1713). Later, other Chatás were named as Governors of San Andrés, for example, in 1795. In 1960, the oldest (in his 70s) member of a Cohouj family correctly claimed that his ancestors had been "caciques in this place," but that "those who thought they were lords of the earth [Ladinos]" and had "good pens" came to dominate the Indians of San Andrés.

33. Soza (1970:468) says that among the earliest settlers of new San Andrés were people named Acosta, Aldana, Cano, Manzanero, Muñoz, Puga, and Vanegas. The Aldanas most probably were Creoles; others may have been. The Canos and Pugas may have come to San Andrés later in the eighteenth century than Soza would have it; in any case, some modern Canos and Pugas claim Creole descent from "blue-eyed" (*ojos sarcos*) Campechanos, and blond hair and hazel eyes are relatively common in intermarried Cano and Puga families. I am fairly sure that Soza errs in placing the Muñoz family among the early eighteenth-century settlers of the *pueblo*. The surname, as far as I know, never appears there in the eighteenth- or nineteenth-century archives, and the modern Muñozes came to the town from a northern Petén village in the early 20th century, as the result of border disturbances connected with the Mexican Revolution; some members of the Muñoz family subsequently moved to San José. The oldest man in San Andrés in 1960, ninety-six-year-old don Leandro Cano, who could trace his genealogy back to about 1815, told me that in his youth all the people of San Andrés spoke (Yucatec?) Maya, but "we, the Ladinos, also spoke Spanish. Not the Indians here; they spoke Maya, just that. Maybe some of them knew some Spanish, but they spoke Maya. Well (*pues*) we all did, but we spoke Spanish too."

34. Although the ethnic composition of San Andrés may have been more complex than that of other major Petén settlements, almost all of them show a similar mixing of peoples; see the 1778 census. San José may be an old pre-conquest village of the Tut family, refounded by the Spanish. Reina (1962:27) says that many of its inhabitants are "probably descendants of the early Itzá," but the early post-conquest villagers were joined by Cehach and Muzul Indians (Thompson 1977 [about the Tut family]; Valdavida 1975; García 1754 in AGCA). The tradition in Petén is that Santa Ana was settled with Muzul Indians, but there may have been Mopanes among them. Dolores, perhaps the site of an aboriginal village refounded by the Spanish, contained Mopánes and Yucatecans. Apparently, some Muzules also were placed there. Santo Toribio contained indigenous Petén Indians, Muzules from Belize and Yucatecan Ladinos. As noted, early in the colonial period, the families of the Spanish and possibly Ladino managers of the crown estates also may have resided in Santo Toribio. (Santo Toribio became a village subordinate to Dolores in 1929.) San Luis was most likely a pre-conquest settlement. The Mopán Indians there were joined by Muzules, perhaps some Manché-Choles, and Kekchí early in the colonial period (Valdavida 1975). La Libertad, in the vicinity of the earliest private estates in Petén (Comparato 1983:303), has a complex ethnic history. Apparently Yucatecan mestizos worked on these ranches as early as 1728, as did Petén Indians. Then, around 1795, wealthy Yucatecans expanded livestock operations there, bringing with them Indians from Yucatán. Thus, the first post-conquest settlers were Mopánes, soon joined by Muzules and Yucatecan mestizos, and thereafter reinforced by other Yucatecans. During the Caste Wars (beginning 1847), more Yucatecans came to La Libertad, although not all of them stayed, and in the 1840s several Englishmen from Belize resided in or near La Libertad. In 1880 the Yucatecans—perhaps to acclaim their status in what was then called Sacluk and Guadalupe Sacluk—renamed the *pueblo* La Libertad. The community had a common pasture of some 271 *caballerías*, at least until 1902 (Martínez Uck 1971; see also Comparato 1983:210; Mazzarelli 1976a:153–63; Ramírez 1980; Thompson 1977:5–25; Valdavida 1975). San Francisco has a somewhat similar settlement history. Sayaxché, a village subordinate to La Libertad until 1929, well may have been founded around 1860 by Kekchís, "Lacandones" and Belizean blacks, although I cannot find it on any map until the 1890s (see Sapper map of 1894 in *Comisión de Limites* 1929). Poptún must have been populated with a mixed group of Mopán, Muzul and other Indians. Melchor de Mencos became important in connection with the chicle industry and reflected the ethnic diversity of that activity. Finally, as discussed below, San Benito was founded as a settlement for Belizean blacks.

35. See in AGCA Mendoza, Fajardo, and Real Sala de Crimen cited previously. Interestingly, Fajardo also accused the commandant of failure to stimulate trade in portable commodities (cacao, achiote, vanilla and tobacco), some of which figured prominently in pre-1697 Tipú-Tayasal trade.

36. Gov. Amate, cited above, AGCA A1.6 Leg. 3799, Exp. 15, 1757, and Commandant Gálvez, AGCA A1.21.75 Leg. 5466, Exp. 46935 ("Relativo al Oficio de V. C. de 3 de Octub.e Ult.º Sob.e Ayuntamt.to . . . ," 1813).

37. Mazzarelli (1976a:171) suggests that some Petén Indians who took to the

woods may have joined others who raided loggers in Belize as late as 1788 and 1800. As for the so-called Lacandón in western Petén, formal peace treaties were concluded between them and Petén government officials only in 1837–1846, as noted above (Soza 1970:236).

38. Colonial documents refer to the black fugitives as "Mulatos" and "Negroes," thus distinguishing them from Pardos. Their presence in Petén during the colonial period is noted in AGI Guatemala 251, 1727 and AGI Guatemala 589, 1765; see in addition to other documents noted below, the following: AGCA A3.1 Leg.11, Exp. 207, 1783; A1.56 Leg. 12, Exp. 209, 1789; A1.56 Leg. 17, Exp. 818–2356, 1795; A1.56 Leg. 3809, Exp. 186, 1800; and B10.2 Leg. 158, Exp. 3312, apparently from 1825.

Most of the "Negroes" entered Petén from southwestern Belize, sometimes with arms. In absolute terms there numbers were not great, e.g., San Benito had a population of 233 people in 1845, about 200 in 1879, and 300 in 1904 (Petén census 1845; Valenzuela 1879; Mejía 1904), but given Petén's small population they were a significant minority. Some blacks also lived in a small hamlet or ranch called "Cimarrón" (in American Spanish the word means "wild, slave or fugitive") close to San Benito. Cacique Chatá's petition is in AGCA A1.1 Leg. 217, Exp. 5110 ("Comun del Peten sobre que no se repartan Yndios para las lavores Mulatos, que estos vivan fuera de la Reducción; que sé reparen los edificios Publicos; y otros particulares," 1795). Attached to this document are others (AGCA A1.56 Leg. 186, Exp. 3809, 1795–1800) dealing with various considerations that went into deciding to settle the blacks in San Benito.

39. With reference to the practice of selling blacks back to Belizeans, see AGCA A1.56 Leg. 8 and 201 ("El Senado Federal . . . contra el Comandante del Petén Luis Vera por haber entregado a ciertos esclavos . . . ," 1778); and for 1818 see A1.56 Leg. 818, Exp. 2358; for 1825 see B10.8 Leg. 3483, Exp. 79641 and Leg. 158, Exp. 3312. Some 32 armed blacks tried to reach what became San Benito as early as 1795 (AGCA A1.56 Leg. 1256, Exp. 17818). On blacks who came to Petén in 1813 and 1825, see Bolland 1977:78. At least some of the notables involved in selling blacks back to the English were bureaucrats and members of the leading commercial and merchant families in Remedios.

40. González (1867) and Valenzuela (1879) report that the blacks in San Benito held apart from others, and also that people from Remedios rarely went to San Benito, despite its proximity to Remedios, except on official business.

41. Most of the data for this section are from central Petén, especially San Andrés. With respect to ethnic intermarriage and endogamy, for the early and middle eighteenth century, I must rely primarily on family oral traditions. For the late eighteenth and early nineteenth centuries, I have drawn on AGCA documents, including an 1845 census (the first detailed household-by-household survey I have found for Petén, recording age, given name, and surnames for all members of each household), and civil registries in Archivo Municipal, San Andrés. These documents plus interviews with elderly Peteneros ranging in age from 68 to 96 years (in 1960) permit the reconstruction of genealogies reaching back to the late eighteenth century. Complete genealogies were collected from three large families of Ladino and/or Creole descent and three large families of Indian descent whose members

reside in San Andrés, San José, and Flores. The Hispanic tradition of using double patronyms is useful for tracing genealogies and ethnic intermarriages. For example, AGCA A1.20 Leg. 1507, Exp. 9983, 1817 records that Juan Baldizón, the son of Leonardo Baldizón who was born in Panamá and María Díaz a Petenera, married María del Carmen Pinelo; thus Juan's full surname is Baldizón Díaz, and his children would be Baldizón Pinelos. To take another example, Juana Aldana—born 1780 and 65 in 1845—was the widow of a Chatá, hence her children were Chatá Aldana. The 1845 census (*padrón*) records that Juan Aldana, 63, was married to Guadalupe Toraya, 51 (born in 1782 and 1794, respectively), hence their children are Aldana Torayas. Some care must be taken in identifying ethnicity, e.g., Juan Paredes (pseudonym), born in 1786, was wed to Juaquina Ytzá, born in 1791, but this is not a case of ethnic heterogamy for Paredes was an Indian surname. By cross-checking marriage records with the 1845 census and with ninety-six-year-old don Leandro Cano, mentioned above, it became clear that his grandfather's brother was one León Cano, born 1811. Don Leandro remembered León and said that León told him that his (León's) father came to San Andrés from Mexico, which, if correct, would seem to conflict with Soza's comment (1970:468). Don Leandro is probably correct—his memory for kinsmen he knew in his youth was quite sharp and consistent with documentary evidence (his memory for more recent events was not so clear). In the event, this pushes matters back to the late eighteenth and early nineteenth centuries, but hardly clarifies everything. For example, Guillermo Quixchán was born in the *pueblo* of San Andrés in 1830 (Civil Registry in San Andrés). Don Leandro and an eighty-year-old Quixchán disagreed about the origin of Guillermo's paternal grandfather. Don Leandro was sure the grandfather was born in San Andrés in the 1780s, but the elderly Quixchán was equally sure he was born in Campeche. In short, I am able to trace some families back to the 1780s, but beyond that things become blurry. It should be added that the names of bureaucrats, crown ranch managers, and soldiers given in this section were obtained, as noted elsewhere, from AGCA "Ayuntamientos del Petén" for 1709–1838, supplemented by other documents listing officials, for example, AGCA A 1.4–7 Leg. 2160, Exp. 2160, 1806; "Pago de sueldos en las reducciónes del Petén"—A1.12.11 Leg. 333 and 334, 1696; A2.1 Leg. 303, 1707; A1.22.33 Leg. 2160, 1709; A1.12.6 Leg. 4060 [104], 1805; and A3.1 Leg. 1285, Exp. 22109, 1771. AGCA A1.44 Leg. 2160, Exp. 15527, 1821 ("Padrón de . . . 1821") which in fact does not contain a census but does list crown bureaucrats and crown managers. Now and then, a license or permit also proved useful, e.g., A1.2.15 Leg. 5917, Exp. 51042, a "Licencia otorgado a Antonio Baldizón para que abra una taberna," 1772.

42. As noted in various documents cited above, clergy and at times commandants expressed great concern about excessive use of alcohol by the Indians, although they could not (or would not because of *vecino* economic interests?) curtail the habit. To give another instance, in 1813, Comandante Gálvez (AGCA A1.21.75 Leg. 5466, Exp. 46935) notes that Petén had few men capable of discharging high office, and adds that "rare are the *naturales* (Indians) . . . who are not given to great

drunken excess." Incidentally, he—or his scribe, Lucas Pinelo—adds that Indian village authorites communicate with Remedios through translators, i.e., the Indians do not command Spanish.

CHAPTER THREE

1. Gálvez offered each perspective foreign settler one *caballería* (45 hectares) of land, the same amount modern smallholder colonists in Petén say they need to make ends meet.

2. Gálvez also relied on a head tax. Indians paid 2 pesos/year. Non-Indians were taxed according to their occupation, as follows (from Wortman 1982:225):

Servant . . . . .0 pesos, 4 reales	Artisan. . . . . .6 pesos, 0 reales
Farmer. . . . . .0 pesos, 4 reales	Shopkeeper . . . . .1 peso, 4 reales
Small proprietor . . . . .1 peso, 0 reales	Spirit seller . . . . .5 pesos, 0 reales
Medium proprietor . . . . . .5 pesos, 0 reales	Innkeeper . . . . .6 pesos, 0 reales
Large proprietor . . . . . . .20 pesos, 0 reales	Merchant . . . . .20 pesos, 0 reales
Cattle purveyor . . . . . . .2–7 pesos, 4 reales	

3. In 1934, the Ubico government formally ended debt peonage, perhaps because the combination of the depression of 1929 to the late 1930s (which caused a decline in coffee production) and demographic growth led to reduced need for forced labor. Besides, the government instituted "a vagrancy law that achieved the same end" (Weeks 1986:38). The vagrancy law required that those not engaged in a trade or profession or not cultivating a certain minimum of land were to find wage labor 100–150 days of the year. "In practice, the law was applied only to the indigenous population" (Weeks op. cit.). Vagrancy laws were abolished in 1945; since then Guatemalan landowners have used other, often equally coercive, methods to control labor.

4. As mentioned in Chapter 1, in the nineteenth century there were two main trails north to Mexico from Flores the old *camino real*, over which traffic diminished after the 1840s, and a route from Flores to Tenosique (for the 1890s, see Maler 1908a and 1908b). The Flores-Tenosique trail went south from Flores to Sacluk (La Libertad), then west from Sacluk to the Pasión and Usumacinta Rivers, and then it turned north to reach Tenosique in Tabasco, Mexico. There also was a trail running almost directly east from Flores to British Honduras, and two southern routes. The first southern passage went from Flores to San Luis and then to Cahabón, Alta Verapaz and from there to Cobán. For many years the easiest passages were those going north from Flores to Mexico (Morelet 1871:168–72). Soza (1970:287) says that from the mid-nineteenth century on the Flores-Chinajá route was the most important of all trails in Petén, and this was certainly true with reference to official communication and mail between Guatemala City and Flores, but even this trail deteriorated off and on throughout the nineteenth century (Boddam-Whethem 1877; Soza 1970:229–334). The southeast route, from Flores to San Luis to Cahabón, part of the old *camino real*, apparently lost some importance, and in the 1840s Morelet found it useless for commerce (1871:227), but it continued

to be used all through the nineteenth century (González 1867; Valenzuela 1879). Certainly by the mid-nineteenth century, the Flores-British Honduras (Belize) route was important, even if the trail was not very good. *La chiclería* made it the most important trade route in Petén between the 1890s and the 1930s. In the 1930s Ubico tried, with some success, to redirect Petén's trade away from Belize toward Guatemala, via a Flores-San Luis-Izabal passage and by Flores-Guatemala City airplane traffic.

5. See Karnes 1961:5; King 1974:285; and Table 1:1 above. Although one may doubt the complete accuracy of these data, and although there were uncounted people in Petén, for example, Lacandón Indians in the far west and Maya in the northeast, they do confirm that Peten's frontier status remained unchanged in the nineteenth century.

6. In 1825, *diputados* (roughly equivalent to territorial or provincial congressmen) from Guatemala and elsewhere in Central America were sent to the Federal Congress. Petén (which in 1825 was made a "district" formally subordinate to Alta Verapaz) was apparently represented by the Verapaz *diputado* (Thompson 1829:509–10). Even before it was elevated to the level of a department, Petén sent its own congressional representative to the 1848 Constituent Assembly of Guatemala (Estrada Monroy 1977:107).

7. Between 1826 and 1844 the chief executive officer of Petén was called *jefe político*, from 1845 to 1871 *corregidor*, from 1872 to 1943 *jefe político*, and from 1944 to the present, *gobernador*. Since all had about the same duties, authority, and power (until about 1958–1959), it is convenient to use the same word ("governor") for all of them.

8. Sources for Table 3:3 include AGCA censuses; González 1867; Mejía 1904; Reina 1966; Soza 1970; Valdavida 1975; Valenzuela 1879. In addition to these sources, *cabildo* archives in the *pueblos* and court records from 1822–1899 (see below), censuses and *padrónes* (a census was a simple population count; a *padrón* counted people by household, giving age, occupation, church post and political office for each member of the household) taken in Petén in 1845, 1848, 1856 and 1863 are invaluable for working out the number and sociology of the *pueblos* in the 19th century. Also useful are AGCA A1.4–7 Leg. 2160, Exp. 15506 ("Cuenta de lo invertido en la vacunación de las habitantes de los pueblos del Petén," 1806), and AGCA "Visitas Judiciales" (e.g., "Libro de actas de la visitas de esta Ciudad [Flores] y pueblos del Distrito del Petén practicados por el Jues del 1ª Ynstancia en el año de 1862"). At this time, 1862–1864, the *Corregidor Comandante*, José Eduvigis Vidaurre, also doubled as the Judge of the First Instance for Petén.

In the 1740s-1750s, there were some 10 other settlements, most of them located around Lake Petén Itzá and the *camino real*, and also the crown ranches (San Felipe). What became San Francisco and La Libertad may have been ranches in the very early 1700s, and by the 1740s they appear as *estancias*. Poptún, too, was a ranch site in the eighteenth century, but it may have become one after the other two were established. From the early nineteenth century on, the route northwest, from San Antonio (in San Andrés) to Dzilbalchen (in Yucatán, about 90 kilometers southeast of Campeche), seems to have been sparsely populated (AGI Mexico 2692, 1806).

The 1845 census (see Table 3:9) omits Concepción and probably several other small settlements adjacent to the *camino real*, north of San Andrés. In 1867, González listed most of the settlements given for 1879, plus 10 small ranching settlements, including Xex, Juntecholol, Machaquilá, and Poptún. González remarks that San José and Santo Toribio are "unimportant" towns. Valenzuela (1879), who traveled more widely in Petén than almost any other official, mentions some 13 settlements on the Flores-Yucatán route, including San Antonio, Thubucil, Nojbecan, Concepción, Santa Clara, Santa Cruz, and Yacché (there was also a Yacché in eastern Petén). There does not seem to have been much trade between these places and Flores although, Valenzuela notes, the people north of San Andrés would have welcomed more contact with Flores. He also notes that the authorities in Flores are unnecessarily fearful of visiting these settlements; despite their reputation the people were pacific. I suspect reduced trade and fearfulness were related in chicken-egg fashion.

Mejía (1904) notes that at this time Flores had 6 *aldeas* and 2 *caseríos*. San Benito had 1 *aldea*, Cimarrón, probably modern San Antonio, but not to be confused with the San Antonio north of San Andrés. San Andrés had 2 *aldeas* and 4 *caseríos*, most of them strung along the old *camino real*, north of the town; San José had 2 *caseríos*; Santa Ana had an *aldea*, the old Juntecholol; La Libertad had an *aldea* and some 19 *caseríos*, which seem to have been *monterías* (usually impermanent logging sites). One of these *monterías* can be identified with Sayaxché, and others—after interrupted occupancy—have become *aldeas* and/or riverine cooperatives, for example, San Juan Acul and La Union. Santo Toribio had an *aldea*. Santa Barbara, today known as Machaquilá, was then a (short-lived) county capital, and Mejía says Poptún was an *aldea* within its jurisdiction; Santa Barbara also had a *caserío*.

Today Santo Toribio and San Juan de Dios are *aldeas*. By 1805, San Benito seems not to have been an *aldea* of Flores, but later on reverted to that status, until 1873. Fallabón and Plancha de Piedra, on the border with Belize, grew together and became Melchor de Mencos, which until 1962 was a Flores *aldea*. In August 1985, the (military) government granted Santa Elena, on the mainland just opposite Flores and adjacent to San Benito, *municipio* status, perhaps because the military were annoyed with Flores's refusal to maintain a civil patrol unit, but this was also related to tensions between Flores and Santa Elena, which in part seem to reflect social class (elites versus the middle and working classes) antagonisms rather than a split within the upper class. In 1986, the national executive rescinded the order and the national judiciary refused to hear legal appeals from Santa Elena, to the fury of many people there.

9. During Valenzuela's visit, *Rentas* did collect $4000–5000 in taxes, but he was sure it should have collected much more. By 1872 officials were making attempts to collect taxes on felled trees, and—like crown officers before them—they were concerned about illegal cutting by British Hondurans, e.g., see AGCA Legajo 15834, Exp. 121 B ("Sobre la reclamación del valor de la madera cortada fraudulamente en el Distrito de Petén por vecinos de Belice," 1846). In 1876, the tax was $1 (one peso) per ton of lumber. Valenzuela (1879) reported that managers of the logging operations ridiculed those sent to measure the wood, cut more trees than

allowed by their licenses, mismarked trees to confuse inspectors, falsified records, and, if pressed too hard to pay the tax, threatened to abandon Petén. Given the profits *caoba* brought to the Mexican lumber companies, Valenzuela considered these to be empty threats. He felt they would have continued to operate even if taxes were raised, as he recommended they be. Valenzuela based his comments on first-hand inspection of 10 logging camps strung along "ten leguas" of the Rio Lacantún. Valenzuela also hinted at official corruption — $3,000 in *caoba* taxes were collected in 1878, and $8,000 should have been. He felt that if in addition to full collection of *caoba* duties officials collected all they should have from the Belize-Petén trade, *Rentas* could easily bring in $16,000 per annum, roughly 4 times what it was amassing. His report could have been written in 1985.

In reading the above, it is useful to note that during the colonial period and for some time afterwards, Guatemalans used coins from various countries. In 1851, the U.S.A. dollar was made legal tender, and in 1925 the quetzal took the place of the peso. Until recently, the quetzal was equal to the U.S.A. dollar (J. Sexton, personal communication).

10. For this paragraph see Archivos Municipales de San Andrés 1864, "Libro de Cargos y Data . . . de la sala Municipal," Flores, for various years; and Secretary Morales' letter from Santa Ana to the Governor, 10–29–1864. Also see *Petén Itzá* 1940:54–55; Reina 1967; Valenzuela 1879; AGCA, Vidaurre 1862, cited above in Note 8.

11. Jones (1977:57) says that Peteneros could sell crops to non-farmers along the Belize River, work as carriers and do some *caoba* cutting. Another reason some Peteneros left home and headed for the Belize River in the 1830s was a rumor, connected with Gálvez' colonization scheme, that the English were going to be thrown out of British Honduras (Griffith 1965:123). This was a "pull," but the "push" came from the government at home (e.g., see Soza 1957:27).

As for epidemics, the following apparently incomplete list indicates how often they hit Petén: smallpox (*viruela*) in 1810, 1862, 1890, 1909, 1918; whooping cough in 1847 and perhaps in 1882 (*tos ferina* was reported to be widespread); cholera morbus in 1851, 1868 (with *grippe*), 1939; malaria in 1898. Compounding medical problems were food shortages and crop failures, for example, in 1848 around Dolores (Morelet 1871:266), in the 1860s, 1882, 1895, 1901, 1909 (when locusts became a massive problem as they did in 1924), and so on. For epidemics and crop failures after the colonial period see Berendt 1868; Jones 1977:55; Morelet 1871:266; *Petén Itzá* 1939:49; Reina 1967:15–16; Vidaurre 1862 above.

On Mopán flight to southern British Honduras, see Comparato 1983:345; Howard 1977:15; Thompson 1930:38; and Wilk 1981:57–58. By the 1860s, after centuries of moving north, the Kekchí were numerous between San Luis and Poptún (González 1867), that is, there were surely many Kekchí in San Luis in the 1880s, but there is no record that they joined the 1883 Mopán exodus. I wonder if what appears to be the 1880s numerical superiority of Kekchí over Mopán contributed to Mopán unhappiness.

12. AGCA Leg. 1–19, *Organismo Judicial, Ramo Criminal, el Petén, Juzgado de Primer Instancia*, hereinafter referred to as *Ramo Criminal* 1822–1899.

13. AGCA B9.1 Leg. 153, Exp. 3260 ("23 de noviembre de 1838 El Jefe Político de Verapaz, informe al gobierno que durante la noche de 11 de octubre, el jefe político del Petén Jose Baldizon y Manual Ozaeta se pronunciaron a favor de la faccion de Rafael Carrera," 1838); Caddy in Pendergast 1967:90–95, 159; Guzmán 1984.

14. AGCA Gobernación, Legajo 28637, 1873, deals at length with the Matus sedition case; see also *Petén Itzá* 1938.

15. *Huites* may derive from the verb *huir* (to flee, to avoid), that is, Indians or others who took flight and evaded subjugation. *Huites* might also be an alternative to *Guites*, also used in Petén, for example, in reference to mulatto raiders from British Honduras who threatened people in southeastern Petén in the eighteenth and nineteenth centuries (Valdavida 1976). Or *guite* may derive from *guitón* (tramp). I have heard the word *huits* used to describe a rascal who was never sober away from a chicle camp and who would fight with other men who called him "Indian," "*huits*," and some other choice words. Also see AGCA Leg. 18557, Exp. 1410 ("Corregidor de Peten a Ministro Gobernación sobre la reclamazión que hizo con respeto a crimen cometido por los barbaras de Yucatan en San Andres," 1852).

16. See also Bolland 1977; Clegern 1962; Comparato 1983:315; Maler 1908; Mazzarelli 1976a and 1976b; and particularly Jones 1973.

Refugees from the War of the Castes arrived in relatively large numbers, but many of them appear not to have remained in Petén (see AGCA B Leg. 28577, Exp. 057 Folio 1, "El Corregidor del Depto. de El Petén, Señor José E. Divides (sic.) Vidaurre, informa al Ministro de Gobernación que al pueblo de Dolores han llegado a avencindarse individuos procedentes de Yucatán y que próximamente llegaría 80–más . . . ," 1859). In the censuses, the Yucatecans were often counted apart from Peteneros. Although their presence frightened the authorities (e.g., in AGCA B Leg. 28584, Exp. 093, 1861, where the Corregidor Vidaurre informs the central government that the "barbarian Indians" from Yucatán threaten to invade the "pueblos de Concepcion, San Antonio y Dolores"), the refugees committed few crimes and shed little blood.

17. For Ladino and/or Creole-led attempts at rebellion see AGCA *Ramo Criminal*, Leg. 1, 1861; Leg. 2, 1868; Leg.1, 1873. For what follows, also see Jones 1940:77–81; Soza 1957:292–95.

Although one may not read the present back into the past, either time can provide cautionary tales for the other, and experience dictates that rumors of invasion and war in Petén be regarded judiciously. In 1960 there were reports in Guatemala City that 500 armed British Hondurans were entering Petén; the "army" turned out to be some 19 Beliceños, most of them teenagers, led by an elderly "mulatto" with an even older shotgun—the sole weapon the "army" possessed. The group illegally crossed the border to seek work as chicleros, and were captured and returned to British Honduras. In the 1970s there were rumors in Petén that combined Guatemalan and Israeli forces were poised to invade British Honduras, there to do battle with an army of British and black Beliceño troops. Older Peteneros were genuinely upset by the "coming war to return Belize to Guatemala," but younger men seemed positively happy about the prospect. They were just as happy a few weeks later when the excitement fizzled out.

18. Compare AGI Guatemala 859, 1765 with Reina 1967.

19. Cowgill (1962) and Reina (1967) report lower average yields, but they may have omitted *mulco* (unstorable or blighted maize which is shelled immediately upon being reaped, and then consumed by people and/or fed to animals). Of course, it may be that between the time they did their fieldwork—in the late 1950s and early 1960s—and the time I collected maize production data—in the 1970s and 1980s—changing market demands led farmers to increase production, but I believe the first reason is more likely. Unless Petén milperos are specifically and explicitly asked about *mulco*, they tend not to mention it when asked about *maize* (which is not blighted and can be stored) yields. Another way to discuss *mulco* is to ask about or to weigh a *saco* (a small sack into which *mulco* is placed during the harvest) as distinct from a *costal* (a larger, coarser sack into which maize is placed). The point is that *mulco* can come close to 10–30 percent of the total corn harvest (Schwartz 1985).

20. For example, Caddy in Pendergast 1967:76–78; Morelet 1871; also see Soza 1970:281. In the 1870s it apparently cost a Ladino soldier in the central highlands about 3 reales/day or $136/year to feed and clothe himself (Boddam-Whethem 1877:81–82). That is not too much more than what, 100 years earlier, it took (1–2 reales/day) to sustain a soldier in the Remedios *presidio*. In 1830, a "servant" in Guatemala City needed about 1.25 reales/day to feed himself (Parker 1970:248). By these standards, the milperos were certainly quite poor.

21. Morelet (1871:168, 224–25) complained that in 1847 mules were very difficult to obtain in Flores (but not in Tenosique, Tabasco) and that beef was costly. Yet, Caddy (in Pendergast 1967) says that in 1840 it was relatively cheap. This, too, suggests some decline in ranching after the 1840s.

22. Reina (1967, 1968) attributes the absence of *cofradías* in modern Petén to the time-consuming problems of swidden cultivation, and—because farming does not produce a surplus beyond what is needed for household consumption (and sometimes not even enough for that)—the need to supplement farming with wage labor. Off-farm wage labor takes men away from the community. These two conditions—limited grain production and wage labor—prevent Peteneros from giving time to coordinated group activities such as *cofradías* (and show how modern conditions may illuminate the past). True, outside of San Luis, there are no *cofradías* in modern Petén, but there were *cofradías* there in the colonial period and well into the nineteenth century, for example, in Flores at least until 1876. Over the course of the nineteenth century they declined and eventually disappeared, except in San Luis. Reina's argument seems not to explain their presence in San Luis. In contrast, I suspect that the general decline in ranching had a negative impact on *cofradías*. In the colonial period and afterwards *cofradías* were sustained by livestock raising; as ranching declined, perhaps so did the economic reason for the existence (and support) of the *cofradías*. For example, in 1862 the *cofradía* in San Juan de Dios owned only 9 head of cattle (AGCA Vidaurre, *Visita*, 1862). The Kekchí in San Luis may have maintained *cofradías* for cultural reasons, but note that in San Luis

cofradías seem to have had little connection with ranching. Because of the problems connected with drawing inferences about the past from the present, it seems best to say that reasons for the disappearance of *cofradías* in most of Petén require more investigation.

23. Maudslay and Maudslay (1899:230) described woodcutters (in 1880–1882, at La Libertad) as a "thriftless folk" who wasted their advance money. This is very much the same way travelers have described chicleros. Also see Berendt 1868:421; Caddy in Pendergast 1967:46–47; Morelet 1871:116–17; Valenzuela 1879.

24. To avoid cluttering Table 3:12, sources and notes under superscripts are placed here. Sources for the table are *padrón* records for 1845–1863; AGCA *Ramo Criminal* Leg. 1–19, 1822–1899; AGCA Geográfico: Hemeroteca D ("Titulo de Ciudad de Flores y de su camino de Cobán a Petén," 1831; "Informes sobre restablecimiento del Presidio en el Petén. Apertura del Camino a Verapaz," 1848); Andrews 1983:96–101 (on salt trade); Berendt 1868; Caddy in Pendergast 1967 (for 1840); González 1867; Maudslay and Maudslay 1899:230 (on western Petén); Maler 1908a:4–28 (on black loggers in Sayaxché in the 1890s; he also mentions "half-breed negroes" at Remate, a village at the eastern end of Lake Petén Itzá); Mejía 1904; Morelet 1871:151–68, 257–73 (for 1847); Pinelo 1941 (on the Lacandón); Soza 1957, 1970; Valenzuela 1879; Wauchope 1965:185 (on trails in western Petén).

[a] Apparently the chief areas for *hule* exploitation were in the municipal jurisdictions of San Andrés, Flores, and La Libertad, this probably related to river transport systems on the Pasión, Usumacinta, and San Pedro rivers as much as anything else. With all respect to Soza, there are documents in local *cabildos* which date *hule* tapping from 1866, rather than 1874.

[b] San Andreños, who preferred military service to other forms of *téquio* (at least the Ladinos did), also served as mail carriers, but the chore usually fell on the Indians; San Joseños were even more commonly made to carry out this most onerous task. A string of small settlements, most of them on or near the old *camino real* north of San Andrés, traded forest products with Peteneros in return for manufactured goods (as did Lacandón Indians in the west with loggers and chicleros until the 1920s-1930s) and probably *aguardiente*. People in these small settlements also supplied food and lodging to merchants and others traveling from Petén to Yucatán. After 1847, some of these places were inhabited by so-called "rebel" and/or "wild" Indians.

[c] In San Francisco, La Libertad, Santa Ana, and Dolores people had (and still have) large complex backyard gardens. The steep, uneven stony slopes of San Andrés and San José limit making such large gardens. Gardens in San Benito are smaller than those in San Francisco, etc., but larger than those in San Andrés and San José. Valenzuela (1879) noted that San Francisco had more farmers than La Libertad; the former also had far fewer cattle, because (Valenzuela says) of the limited and bad water supply there. Nonetheless, he believed that many more cattle than he found could have been stocked. At various times between 1821 and 1944, Peteneros were ordered by the government to plant coffee, cotton, henequen, and tobacco, but for socioeconomic and ecological reasons, these crops were either better tended or more important in San Francisco (in the great savanna) and in

several other communities in the southeastern hills of Petén than elsewhere in the department. Oral history suggests that the poorer the community was, the more likely it was that these crops were important, but the matter is far from clear.

d Yucatecan refugees from the War of the Castes found the area around La Libertad quite congenial. As late as the 1880s, so-called "wealthy" Yucatecos were setting up ranches there. Coffee also may have had temporary importance there.

e Lacandón Indians also were called "Caribs" and "Jicaques." Until the time of chicle tapping, there were few trails in their area, or at least few known to older Peteneros. After the "peace treaty" between the Lacandón and the Flores authorities was concluded in 1837, there was more trade, or more likely more barter, between Lacandón Indians and people from La Libertad and perhaps from Flores, but there was little social intercourse beyond that needed for trading. Capuchin missionaries worked with the Lacandón in Petén between 1837–1882, but the border treaty between Mexico and Guatemala truncated their mission. Pinelo (1941) reported some 3,000 Lacandón in western Petén by the mid-nineteenth century. I believe they may be the "nomads" referred to in some census documents (e.g., in 1879); however, the matter is not completely clear. Mejía (1904) claimed there were but 100 Lacandón left by the turn of the century. In 1960, there was one Lacandón family, residing in San Benito, left in Petén. It is of course possible, indeed probable, that other Lacandón who lived in Mexico continued to pass back and forth across the western Guatemala border with Mexico, without official notice.

f It is possible that Sayaxché was settled by black loggers who came directly from British Honduras, or by black people from San Benito. Near the end of the nineteenth century, there were about 12 households in Sayaxché (Maler 1908a:11).

g From about 1840–1847 on, travelers and government inspectors reported that once prosperous Dolores, like Santo Toribio, had fallen on hard times, but Dolores continued to be parish headquarters for much of southeastern Petén, and by this time San Luis was included in the parish. Poptún was something between an estate and a ranching village for most of the nineteenth century. Shortly after 1847, there were 20 Yucatecan families in Dolores. The largest landowner in the vicinity of Dolores was a Floreño who eventually obtained formal title to his estate from President Estrada Cabrera (1898–1922).

h From the 1840s on, if not before, the Indians of San Luis were visited less and less by officials from Flores. The central *pueblo* was very small, and the majority of the people lived dispersed in rural neighborhoods. They had far closer economic, social, and, of course, cultural ties with Cahabón and Cobán than with Flores or other Petén towns. This in part was because from 1821 to the 1930s the roads from central Petén to San Luis were wretched, particularly from Poptún or the crossing at the Río Machaquilá and on south to San Luis, yet it must be said that the roads from San Luis to Cahabón were worse. Perhaps ecological differences (the area around San Luis is more mountainous than other parts of Petén, somewhat different species of tree are common, etc.) giving rise to a different mix of crops (or different proportions of the same crops) than are commonly found elsewhere in Petén also tended to turn San Luiseños south to Alta Verapaz. In addition, the Kekchí in San Luis had sociocultural ties with Alta Verapaz, not to mention a desire to avoid the non-Indian authorities in Flores. In the nineteenth century, the experiences of Kekchí coming to San Luis from places such as San Pedro Carchá, etc. must have reinforced fear of non-Indian authorities, much as contemporary events still do (see Chapter 6).

25. The usual fine or fee for a year's exemption was $8 (Archivo Municipal, San Andrés 1894).

26. AGCA Geográfico: Hemeroteca D, Leg. 32863 ("Proposicion del Gobernador Indigena del Petén. Venancio Puc. En el que solicita que sus subditos pueden entrar a negocios de comercio. Acuerdo 4 de dic. de 1850").

27. See Bolland (1977:78) for up to 1825; see also Caddy in Pendergast (1967:94–95) for the 1840s, and the Maudslays (1899:231) for the 1890s.

28. See Ramo Criminal, Leg. 1, 1860; Leg. 2, 1863; Leg. 2, 1868; Leg. 3, 1871. I wish to thank Dr. Ruben E. Reina for generously sharing his Ramo Criminal data and his insights into these documents with me. He and I are planning a monograph based on these documents, in which we will examine the culture of nineteenth century Petén, with special emphasis on Peteneros' philosophic conceptions of (male and female) "human nature," community, and so on.

29. Court cases such as Ramo Criminal, Leg. 2, 1863, make it clear that Indians understood Ladinos would forbid their children marrying Indians. Table 3:14 provides me with an opportunity to correct a previously published count of homogamous unions (Schwartz 1971:298).

30. AGCA Ramo Criminal records, cases of misdemeanors in town court archives, and life history data suggest that men and women were most apt to fight with kinsmen in their own community. Male cousins were most apt to fight when both of them were inebriated. The documents support the suggestion that extended family relationships were not inviolate, but at the same time they also suggest that not only did one's everyday companions tend to be kinsmen but also that one's secondary resources tended to be the same kinsmen, rather than patrons of higher socioeconomic standing.

CHAPTER FOUR

1. Grieb 1979:64; Narciso 1913; Sierra Franco 1940.

2. Revista de San Benito 1975:11–12; Schwartz 1974; Soza 1970:275–76; Stravakis 1979:48. Anti-Cabrera revolutionary forces led by Valdés and Prado Romaña invaded Petén, and were defeated (at Plancha de Piedra, San Juan—near Paso Petén, Chuntuquí, etc.) by government troops led by regular army officers and Floreños. The chicleros were part of the revolutionary forces. After 1920, both Prado Romaña and Valdés served as governor of Petén, but the latter got in trouble with President Orellana for protesting a North American's (Schufeldt) alleged acquisition of land in Petén (see below, notes 20 and 39). Some elderly Peteneros assert that Mexican troops may have been involved in the 1915–1916 invasion, which was in fact supported by Carranza of Mexico.

3. As noted previously, it is not possible to be accurate about how many people lived in and left Petén at this time. For one thing, Holmul group Maya, Yucatecan refugees, Mexicans in logging camps on the Pasión and Usumacinta rivers, and

unidentified "nomads" (Lacandón Indians?) were not regularly counted. For another, primary sources are not in complete agreement. Even as late as 1940 population figures for Petén varied from 10,566 to 11,475. After 1950, disagreements among sources declined appreciably, although problems emerge as census data are aggregated upward from township to department to central government. But *all* sources do agree that between about 1880–1918, the population of Petén declined (see sources cited in Table 1:1, Narciso 1913:320; Soza 1957:27). Soza argued that the post-1920s increase in population was a direct consequence of the initiation of regular airplane service to Petén. Correct or not, it is true that the airplane service was an artifact of *la chiclería*.

4. Banco de Guatemala 1981a; Hendrickson 1976:191–95; Hoar 1924. Although the exact composition of modern chewing gum is a closely guarded secret, 60 percent of the product is sugar, 20 percent synthetic plus natural gum bases, 19 percent corn syrup, and 1 percent flavoring. The favored synthetic in the 1970s was and presumably still is styrene butadiene (Hendrickson 1976:195; cf. Banco de Guatemala 1981a).

5. Hendrickson 1976:67–76, 107.

6. For these figures, see Hendrickson 1976; Hoar 1924; Konrad 1981. The most important manufacturers of chewing gum were and still are Wrigley Import, American Chicle (a corporation formed in 1899 when several companies including Adams' merged) and Beechnut. Chicle Development Co., as well known in Petén as Wrigley, became a joint subsidiary of Beechnut and American Chicle. In 1962, American Chicle merged with Warner-Lambert Pharaceutical, and Beechnut became part of the Squibb Company. By 1969, the companies using chicle resins— albeit not in amounts used before 1945—included Herman Weber & Co., W. Wrigley Jr. Co., Wrigley Import Co., American Chicle (all USA firms) and Mitsui and Co.; after 1976, the latter became the most important importer of Petén chicle. Other countries importing chicle from Petén are Belize, Canada, Virgin Islands and the U.K. (Banco de Guatemala 1981a:14).

7. Chicle is called *tuna* in Nicaragua and *níspero* in Panamá and parts of Mexico. The tree is called the sapodilla, naseberry, and/or dilly in the USA. Konrad (1981) suggests the word "chicle" may derive from the Nahuatl *tzictli* (glossed as chewable substances of plant or animal sources) rather than the Maya *sicte* (white resin of zapote fruit). *Tzictli* was chewed in pre-Columbian times, and—because chicle is "inflammable and produces an odor between that of copal and rubber"—Blom "surmised that the Maya could have used chicle for incense" (Brunhouse 1976:192). In the nineteenth century, Peteneros used raw chicle to slake their thirst and to fashion little figurines for children's Christmas gifts (Soza 1957:88).

8. Thus, the richest areas for chicle are in the townships of La Libertad, San Andrés, San José, Flores, and Melchor de Mencos. Chiquibul is found in Santa Ana, Dolores, Poptún, and San Luis, as well as in the departments of Izabal and Alta Verapaz. Unlike chicle trees which can be profitably tapped only during the rainy season, chiquibul can be tapped almost year round, however, it is not first class chicle and for some years now has not contributed much to total chicle production.

9. The maximum concentration is or was 100 trees/hectare (Holdridge, Lamb,

and Mason 1950:47). Also see Lamb 1966; Góngora Zetina 1984:29; Hoar 1924 (for the 13.6–15.9 kilo latex yield/tree figure). Figures for contemporary latex yields are based on interviews with chicleros and observation, but also see Hendrickson 1976:58–65. Some chicleros say that ideally a tapped tree should be allowed to "rest" for as long as 15 years.

10. Hendrickson (1976) uses the 15 percent depletion rate; also see Holdridge et al. 1950; Karling 1934:171–72; Lundell 1937 op. cit. Chicleros are aware of the "death" rate of chicle trees and its negative impact on long-term production, but they also are concerned about current income. They know that the current income they receive from a given quantity of latex may be worth less in the future because of inflation. In a sense, the chiclero's willingness to "kill" trees today depends on what he thinks the price of chicle and the discount rate of money will be in the future. Thus, from the point of view of the individual chiclero, killing the trees is not necessarily an (economically) irrational act.

11. This chiclero insists that "A tree can be reused once in four or five years" (cf. Karling 1934).

12. Chicleros also are said to mix inferior resins with chicle (and to cover themselves from head to foot when they add *chechen* resins). Some claim that these practices helped reduce USA demand for Petén chicle (Banco de Guatemala 1981a), but it seems clear that the use of synthetics played the greater role in decreasing demand. Blaming chicleros for decreased demand sounds like a rationalization.

13. Older chicleros in particular believe it morally risky to tap chicle trees, for one may drain their "blood" and thus risk killing them.

14. See, for example, Fletcher, Graber, Merrill, and Thorbecke 1970 on farm production data; Karnes 1961 on demography; and McIntosh 1980 on land tenure. Problems stem from lack of funding and personnel, use of different data categories for same or different time periods, political interference, and so on.

15. To round out Table 4:6, between 1910 and 1920, one quintal (100 pounds) of chicle cost $190 (pesos; Soza 1970:89). In 1967, a quintal of first class chicle cost buyers Q67; in 1973 the price was Q83.50–84; in 1974 it jumped to Q108, and between 1979–1980 rose to Q213. Second class chicle prices rose in tandem with first class chicle, going from from Q70/quintal in 1973 to Q137 in 1979–1980.

16. The chewing gum companies claim they have not retained records on such matters, one major company writing me to say that as for "basic information," we "haven't retained such information about chicle in our files and the people who were really knowledgeable about it have now retired from our company" (letter dated 3 December 1975).

17. Official records concerning the number of contractors are not always clear, in part because of the sometimes fuzzy distinction between contractor and subcontractor. Nevertheless, putting together data from *Memorias Anuales del Departamento de el Petén* (Flores), *Memorias Anuales de Flores*, *Rentas Internas*, FYDEP archives, and records from Itzalandia (an association of contractors) yields a reasonably accurate figure for the number and identity of contractors, and the size of the labor force. The following two examples are typical of what the records show: (a) in 1945, right before Arévalo assumed the presidency of the nation, the Gua-

temalan Ministry of Agriculture granted chicle exploitation licenses to 32 contractors, of whom 23 were Guatemalans and 9 were foreigners; (b) in 1946, the Ministry granted licenses to 45 contractors, of whom 36 were Guatemalans (at least 15 of them from Flores) and 9 foreigners. Of the 45 contractors, 19 sold chicle to Chicle Development, and 26 sold to Wrigley.

18. Data for 1945–1946 are especially well documented and precise, at least for chicleros under contract. Of the 3,129 men who signed contracts, 2,329 (74.4 percent of the total) were Guatemalans; 500 (16.0 percent) were Mexicans; 168 (8.6 percent) were British Hondurans; and the remaining 32 (1.0 percent) were from Honduras (15 men), El Salvador (11), Nicaragua (5), and Jamaica (1). In 1961, there were 516 chicleros working in the township of San Andrés; they accounted for 35–40 percent of chicle production that year, from which it is reasonable to deduce that there were probably at least 1,290–1,474 chicleros in the field (without including the men who collect small amounts of chicle in and around their own milpas), exclusive of support and managerial personnel. In 1961, of 288 resident adult males in the town of San Andrés, the primary source of income for 59 (20.4 percent of the total) was chicle collecting, and another 104 (36.5 percent) collected some chicle. These percentages remained relatively constant until about 1975. By 1985, of some 409 male heads of household, some 29 (7.1 percent of the total) were chicleros, but only 11 of them considered chicle collecting his primary occupation (the others listed shate and pimienta collecting as the primary occupation). Another 10 men (2.4 percent of the total) were involved in chicle (plus shate and pimienta) contracting, but few of them considered chicle jobbing as their major source of income. Thus, until about 1975, more than 50.0 percent of San Andreños were dependent on chicle for all or part of their income. Thereafter, the number declined to 9.5 percent. It should be noted that the percent of men working in chicle is higher in San Benito and La Libertad than in San Andrés. In 1964, when the economically active population in Petén 7 years of age and older was 8,025 (7,421 males and 604 females; Dirección General de Estadístico [*Anuario Estadístico*] 1972), FYDEP estimated that there were 2,500 chicleros (to which must be added another 500–600 people on the support and managerial side) working in Petén.

19. Soza (1970:89) implies that the chicle business in Petén began in 1898, but in July 1890 a man named Pacheco asked the authorities in Flores for permission to extract chicle from San Andrés (R. E. Reina, personal communication), and at a 4 March 1895 council session in San Andrés, the mayor and the council ordered that all those who took chicle from the township had to pay the *cabildo* one real/quintal. Soza is usually accurate, but his oversight in this case is probably related to the fact that during the first two decades of the twentieth century, authorities in Flores—not to mention those in Guatemala City—did not closely regulate chicle collecting. Moreover, in most matters, rules enforced elsewhere in the nation reach Petén late, for example, reales were used in Petén at least until 1910 (Martínez Uck 1971:7). Narciso felt that "To demonstrate the peculiarity of that region [Petén] and its commercial independence [from the rest of Guatemala], it is enough to explain that its monetary system is not the one common . . ." in Guatemala (1913:330); The quetzal was not universally accepted in Petén until the early 1930s.

Mazzarelli (1976a:298–99) reports that Lebanese families in Cayo were *caoba* jobbers who also dominated trade in Cayo. By Guatemalan Congressional Decree 1813 (1936), Arabs among other foreigners were not permitted to open a business in Guatemala, but as late as the 1980s, one of the Lebanese families was still active in Petén logging, usually working through a Guatemalan partner.

20. Some Mexicans, for example, Arthes & Sons, Otero Logging Co., etc. exploited chicle trees under old logging concession rights and, stimulated by market demands for chicle, also obtained new concessions or simply expanded operations into new areas. Federico Arthes, whose concession was in the northwest, worked with Mexican contractors resident in Petén and also with native Petén contractors. Arthes sold his chicle to American Chicle (that is, Chicle Development Co.). Around 1920 P. W. Schufeldt, the friend of Morley, acquired the Arthes concession either in his own name or that of Chicle Development (another man, probably an Englishman from British Honduras, also had a chicle concession in the area, which was cancelled after Arthes concluded the deal with Schufeldt). The other large concession, in the northeast, was that of José Wer which Schufeldt, having left American Chicle, obtained in the 1920s for the benefit of Wrigley. Concessions were granted and renegotiated on a yearly basis. Many older Peteneros recall these events, and for these and related matters also see Anderson 1950:224; Brunhouse 1971:150; *Revista de San Benito* 1975; *Revista Petén Itzá* No. 10, 1971; Schufeldt 1950; Thompson 1963:234–66.

21. In 1980 there also was, at least on paper, a chicleros' co-op (Los Cenotes) headquartered in Dos Lagunas, Petén, claiming 600 members and the ability to produce 5,000 quintals of chicle per year.

22. The following typified contractor-subcontractor arrangements. The speaker, a contractor, noted that it was a "relief" to have subcontractors manage his operations, even though he must finance them. He went on to say that "The subcontractor handles all the work and gets Q45 per quintal [in the 1960s-1970s], and out of this he must pay the chicleros, foremen, mules, and everything, and get the chicle to the warehouse. His profit is about Q5 each quintal, and it was like this in Ubico's time, and later too. There were about 30 contractors, more or less, who worked in [the township of] San Andrés in Ubico's time, and there are about 100 . . . now." The informant said that Floreños in particular work through subcontractors, to whom they advance Q700–1,000 in a lump sum. "Feliciano worked for me [last year]. He did not have a contract, but I gave him Q200, and he agreed to get some men, about six, and to bring in about 20 quintals of chicle, but his real income comes from selling food and other things to the chicleros . . . Alberto [also] works for me, as a foreman, more or less. He gets the chicleros himself and works as a subcontractor. I give him Q500 at the beginning of the season . . . Somebody who just brings in chicle and sells it [to a contractor] does better than the chiclero on contract because he get Q35 a quintal [at the time chicleros were paid Q25–30/quintal]. This is illegal, but it is good for the contractor because he has no responsibilities to this type of chiclero [and saves on transportation costs] . . . My father was a subcontractor for N [of Flores] in Uaxactún. My brother was a subcontractor, too, and his *patrón* helped him get a contract and lent him three mules. He had

another three of his own. His *patrón* was Chencho [of Flores], and my brother had been a foreman for don C [of San Andrés]. Then my brother, when he became a contractor, helped me and F [another brother] get a contract with INFOP, without an *enganche*, for 100 quintals. My father worked the mules, and I, F, and M [yet another brother] got out 118 quintals that season. My brothers and I work together in *la chiclería*, but any other business we do alone. Each by himself" (Field Notes 1975).

23. There are stories dating from the 1920s and 1930s of *contratistas*, including some from Flores, who lost Q56,000 and even Q200,000 in the chicle business. Although the stories are well known and may be accurate, they are difficult to corroborate with documents (receipts, personal account books, etc.). In contrast, the loss of the Q2,000 noted in the text has been documented. The contractor in question did not attribute his loss to his own past conduct but rather to INFOP's failures and the loss of "order" after the overthrow of Ubico.

24. Evidence that contractors held kinsmen, *compadres*, etc. in debt peonage and called on the government to force them to stay in the forest comes from municipal archives in Petén, interviews with older chicleros and contractors (particularly those who worked in central and northwestern Petén), and genealogies. Indeed, the most vivid memories were evoked when genealogies were collected, however, whether debt peonage was as bad in the 1920s as it was later is not entirely clear.

25. Because of the legal implications, the name of the community and the exact year have been altered. The pseudonym (San Martín) should not be confused with the colonial settlement of the same name.

26. There is some variation in how much a subcontractor gets from a contractor—it depends on their relations, the subcontractor's need for income (the greater the need, the harder the bargain the contractor can drive), and transportation costs assumed by each of them. For example, during the 1960s and the early 1970s, don Megano usually gave his subcontractors between Q40–45/quintal of chicle, and Julano paid Q35, the difference largely due to don Megano's proximity to the main FYDEP warehouse, which reduced his transport costs. In either case, the subcontractor would normally realize a net profit of Q5–5.50/quintal of chicle, plus whatever he earned selling supplies to chicleros.

27 No later than the 1940s, chicleros were flown to the bush airports in twin-engined DC3s (C-47s), the "flying boxcars" of World War II. Some of the planes, no longer produced, are still flown in Petén, but not with tourists on them. Replacements are obtained by cannibalizing other planes. Given the condition of the DC3s and of the airports, there have been remarkably few accidents, but a trip from Santa Elena or Cobán to, for example, Carmelita can be unnerving, even though the bush pilots are first-rate and chicleros stoical.

28. As for sex, veteran chicleros claim that after about six weeks in the forest, men about thirty-five years old and older experience a reduction of sexual drive. Studies of relationships among hormones, environmental stress, and behavior are contradictory, but there is some evidence to suggest that environmental stress does lower testosterone levels. In any case, some younger men rather than solicit the cook for sex "make the trip alone," as chicleros say. There are also hints that some chicleros

practice homosexuality in the forest, but the evidence for this is slim, which is not to say that it never occurs.

29. In 1980, BANDESA (Banco Nacional de Desarrollo Agrícola, a government agro-development bank) used Q3 for bank loan accounts in central Petén, but in fact day laborers were more typically paid Q2/day and would accept less if they were provided with 1–2 meals/day and/or assured of work for several months. At the time, Petén municipal corporations paid unskilled labor Q2.50/day for short-term (usually two weeks) employment on public works projects. Sawmills were paying Q2.50–3/day, and special machine operators could earn up to Q8/day. Artisans (masons, master carpenters, etc.) charged Q3/day. It is difficult to calculate annualized daily wages for milperos because of things like fluctuations in crop prices, but they counted on earning Q1.50–3/day in cash plus the value of crops consumed at home. Unskilled oil exploration company labor could earn Q5 and more per day, for the normal 6 day work-week. In 1980, given what a chiclero can or could earn in 5–6 months, they were as always and taking everthing into account comparatively well-paid.

30. Reina says chicleros are not better off economically than milperos, primarily because the yield of resin "depends on adequate rainfall" (1967:14). But milperos are no less dependent on weather conditions. The difference is that in some but not all cases even if the weather is bad, a milpero will reap some maize, but at the same time a chiclero may not obtain enough chicle to pay for his maize (the price of which will rise in a year when the weather is bad), unless he has children who make a milpa. Yet, although Peteneros say the milpa is more dependable than chicle, they also say that chicle "brings in more money," that is, more cash and often a better income than milpa. By saying that chicle is less reliable, Peteneros are referring not only to economics but also to morality—making a milpa is "safer" than tapping trees because there is not the moral risk that attends killing a chicle tree. This aspect of *la chiclería* is discussed at length in Schwartz 1974.

31. As for profit, when FYDEP purchased chicle for Q65/quintal, contractors received Q20–25/quintal, and their net profit varied from Q8–15 (without taking into account depreciation on or loss of equipment or mules). Since most contractors sold 200–500 quintals to FYDEP, they could net between Q1,600–7,000. When the price of chicle went to Q213, the contractor received Q55.38 and could net between Q5,000–12,500. Put another way, 40–45 percent of what FYDEP paid the contractor was net profit, less depreciation costs and losses. In 1978, it took about Q3 to produce and transport to market a quintal of maize (by 1981, BANDESA estimated the cost was Q3.70 in parts of Petén), and since contractors sold maize to chicleros for about Q8, they made a profit of Q5/quintal. If, as was usually the case, a chiclero bought a 5–6 month supply of maize from his contractor, the latter made a profit of Q12.50–15.00 on maize sales to each chiclero. Each chiclero normally collected 5–10 quintals of chicle, thus providing the contractor with between Q40–150 in profit from chicle. That is, maize sales to chicleros could account for 10–37.5 percent of a contractor's profit from the chicle business. But matters do not stop there. Contractors sold chicleros clothing, medicine, etc., at a considerable mark-up. For example, in 1978, a contractor bought work shirts for Q1.50 each,

reselling them to his chicleros for Q4. After deducting transport and storage costs, the contractor cleared at least Q1.50/shirt. (The same thing occurs in shate camps, where the mark-up for food may be 500–1,000 percent; Heinzman and Reining 1988:40). Thus, it is no surprise that the contractor's account book indicated that total sales (food, shoes, clothing, medicine, cigarettes and other incidentals) to his chicleros netted him more (55 percent) than the sale of chicle (45 percent) to FYDEP during the tapping season. To be sure there is no reason to assume that all chicle contractors made (or make) this much from trade with chicleros, but sales to them have always been a significant part of the contractor's business.

As remarked in the text, opportunity costs of sales, especially of maize, to chicleros also must be considered. In 1978, maize rose to Q9/quintal (but was sold to chicleros for Q8), and transporting maize from, for example, central Petén to San Benito is roughly half as expensive as transporting it to chicle camps in, e.g., northwest Petén. Thus, there are times when a contractor might be better off selling maize in San Benito, but as one contractor pointed out, his men must be supplied with food and his mules must go to the camps to bring out the chicle, so they might as well go with victuals for sale. In short, even in a worst case situation (as in 1978), the opportunity cost of selling maize, etc. to chicleros is relatively low.

32. The chicle collecting season originally extended from about June/July to February/March but has since been reduced to 4–6 months. The tapping season has always conflicted with important farm tasks such as *la dobla* (bending maize stalks) carried out in conjunction with the second milpa weeding, harvesting *elotes* (green maize) in August and September, and harvesting and storing mature dry maize from October to December.

Although Maler tended to exaggerate, his observations had some validity: "No one will plant a milpa (and) . . . a general famine occurs nearly every year in Peten, which would otherwise yield an almost over-lavish abundance" (1908b:74). Maler added that for this reason, the authorities compelled people to plant some maize every year. The people also had to do *téquio*, carry mail, serve in the militia, and work on the roads (Narciso 1913:315), all of which further reduced the time available for milpa. Soza (1970:618) says that chicle had a negative impact on sugarcane production and that "the owners of *trapiches* (rustic sugarcane mills) abandoned their farms" to collect chicle. Thompson (1963:155) and Gann (1925:51), speaking of western British Honduras, make similar observations and lament the impact of chicle on the Indians.

Among the consequences of all this, "the price of food soared . . . in former days maize was $1 to $1.50 per cargo; now it is $2 to $4; . . . the price of labour has doubled; now, as a chiclero, if he will condescend to do any work outside the chicle season, he demands at least $1.25" (Gann 1925:52). Chicle had similar affects on maize prices and labor costs in Petén. Even in the 1940s, some people claim, the price of maize in Petén could climb to nearly ten times what it cost in Guatemala City.

To cope, until 1946 the government obliged each chiclero to plant about one hectare of milpa during the tapping season, and contractors were supposed to plant a similar amount of land for each of their foreign workers (Gobernación Petén,

Oficio 54; 24 January 1946), but it was relatively easy (and common) to evade compliance. The chicle companies seem to have had more success than the government: "I told Morley that in my then [1920s] several years of experience in the chicle business, I had supervised the felling and burning of many hundreds—I might say—thousands—of acres of forest lands . . . for the purpose of planting *milpas*" (Schufeldt 1950:225). For example, near Laguna Perdida, western Petén, as many as 350–450 hectares were cleared. American Chicle also cleared many hectares of trees near their Paso Caballos field headquarters, on the San Pedro river in the northwest (the company used the waterway to ship chicle to Tenosique, Mexico and to return with supplies and luxury goods for the chiclero market). Incidentally, Schufeldt's comments suggests another cause in addition to tapping and logging, that is, farming, for the depletion of chicle and other trees near the Río San Pedro, which Lundell (1937:15) noted as early as the 1930s. Companies and contractors also engaged in logging; chicleros who also worked as woodcutters spent most of the year in the forest, and perforce often made milpas there.

It remains to add that despite all the government, companies, and chicleros did, there was, as one informant put it "a sharp division (from the 1920s to 1945) between people who worked in the milpas and those who worked in chicle. One could not do both types of work." And an elderly woman recalls that "When I was a child [in the first decade of the twentieth century] . . . little maize was planted in June, and in March the chicle season was over . . . and the men could not work the milpas under the existing laws, the tyranny. In April and May, they were preparing in order to go [collect chicle], and so many men did not make milpa, and often there was a maize shortage, at least some times" (Field Notes 1961).

In short, relatively high wages, lack of markets (other than chicleros) for farm produce, and perhaps government pressure, led or forced men to relinquish farming for chicle collecting.

33. The invasion of Plancha de Piedra was said to be against the "Guatemalan government for injustices in the chicle business" (Brunhouse 1971:10), but also see note 2, above. Dr. LeFleur, a member of Morley's team, was apparently accidently shot by Guatemalan troops, although the Guatemalans never acknowledged this (Brunhouse ibid.).

The movements of the Mexican troops are reported in *Revista Militar* (Guatemala) 1929. As noted elsewhere, one result of the movements was that around 1924 or 1926 people from Chuntuquí fled to San Andrés. The oldest man of the group says that the Mexican troops often crossed the ill-defined border. Soza (1970:276) says that Ubico tried to seal the Petén-British Honduras border not only for economic reasons but also to curb border violence.

Thompson (1963:154–55) relates the sort of event one hears about violence in the chicle business. He was told about a Mexican contractor who sent two men to retaliate against "some chicleros who had skipped across the frontier and signed up with a Guatemalan contractor after receiving his advance." The contractor's men allegedly killed four chicleros.

34. The rebel Maya of Quintana Roo needed money for arms and ammunition, which they purchased in British Honduras, bringing them into contact with British

Honduran loggers and chicleros. In 1902, the Mexican desire for access to, among other things, chicle led the central government to establish the Federal Territory of Quintana Roo. Shortly afterward, rebels became chicleros, and General May, their leader, became a contractor. In 1915, a government army forced the rebel Maya to leave Santa Cruz (today Felipe Carrillo Puerto) and to accept a peace treaty. The troops then left, and the rebels reasserted control until 1929. After 1929, May devoted himself exclusively to chicle contracting (Konrad 1981). One may argue that, in this case at least, chicle was an alternative to violence rather than a cause of it.

35. Foreign observers—not to mention Peteneros—have always deplored the influence of chicle on local populations, especially Maya Indians who, observers claimed, gave up milpa and community to tap trees. Despite high wages, chicleros were so improvident that they wound up in poverty: "At the start of the rainy season, a 'chiclero' would receive an advance of $100 or $150 . . . but at the end of three or four days it was usually all gone on what passed for wine, women, and song in El Cayo, Benque Viejo . . . The real trouble is that the Maya who goes into chicle is uprooted" (Thompson 1963:154–55). The work paid well and left the men "with half their time available for loafing in the small towns, drinking, love-making, gambling, and fighting [and demanding] imported shoes and stockings," for "Chicleros are extraordinarily improvident, and swayed solely by the whim of the moment" (Gann 1925:52, 82). Even Morley, the famous friend of Peteneros, who relied on chicleros as forest guides, felt they were "good-for-nothing" (according to Brunhouse 1971:149), simply "squandering their advance pay on women and liquor . . . and setting a bad example for the conscientious native farmers." Gann (1925:53) says the contractors too "soon gambled or dissipated away" their money; "in fact, the only beneficiaries . . . are a few large *concessionnaires* and the great companies to whom chicle is consigned in the far-off U.S.A."

36. See Guatemalan Government Decree 1538, 26 June 1934. Ubico's interest in chicle was also based on his belief that its exploitation was less damaging to the ecology than logging and that chicle collecting, unlike logging, did not require road construction (Grieb 1979:50). Ubico could not get the Americans to cease buying contraband chicle from British Honduras, so he opted for "annual fees for exploitation rights in lieu of export taxes hoping that this would salvage some revenue" (Grieb 1979:151). Yet, there is some evidence that these fees were collected before Ubico came to power.

37. Preoccupied with roads, Ubico tried to link Petén with southern Guatemala. The road, opened in 1937 or 1938, went from Guatemala City to Rabinal to Cobán and finally reached Sebol, Alta Verapaz, but it never entered Petén. The entire project came to a halt in 1940 (Grieb 1979:134). Ubico inaugurated airplane service to the department in 1933. In 1926, the first airplane landed in Petén; in 1930, there were several flights from the south to Santa Elena, Flores, however, regular flights did not begin until 1938. From then to the late 1960s (when tourist traffic and Aviateca's acquisition of modern jets increased flights) there were two weekly flights from Guatemala City to/from Flores. Several former labor recruiters say that the real increase in Kekchí chicleros began in 1938, rather than earlier. They also say

that airfreight costs from Petén to Puerto Barrios ultimately increased the cost of chicle for North American companies, but I have been unable to find corroborative documents for the last statement.

38. Perhaps the best sources of information on indebtedness (aside from informant interviews) come from local *cabildo* archives, particularly official correspondence and the *Libros de Actas de Demandas*. In the 1940s, most debts were in the Q20–100 range, equivalent to 30–100 days of labor at what were then prevailing wages (Q1/day) in the *pueblos* of central Petén. Archeologists, too, noted how often and how heavily in debt chicleros were (e.g., Maler, cited above).

39. The literature on Guatemala and Central America has grown tremendously in the past 15 to 20 years, and there are many accounts of the so-called "current crisis" (roughly from 1978 to the present), but for this section, I have relied primarily on Adams 1970; Handy 1984; Sexton 1985; Weeks 1986; and Williams 1986.

40. Arévalo did want to colonize Petén, to which end in 1945 he initiated a colonization project in Poptún and eventually invested a good deal of money in housing there, but the project failed because of the lack of roads to and the isolation of Petén, "scarcity of arable lands, and the disinterest of the second revolutionary government" (Aybar de Soto 1978:129).

Until the late 1960s, there were very few land disputes in Petén. True, there is the well-known Clovisland-Ixcha case, but this involved a few wealthy people and had little meaning for ordinary milperos. In 1912, President Estrada Cabrera gave a member of the Berges family a 29 *caballería* land grant (Clovislandia, located partly in Flores and partly in San José), and in 1916 gave Cor. Julián A. Pinelos 14 *caballerías* (Ixcha, today Santa Elena), located in Flores and San Benito. After Cabrera's regime ended, the government tried to rescind some of the grants, which led to several land sales, some of them fraudulent, and litigation. Most of the litigants, including a North American, were *contratistas*.

Estrada Cabrera and later Ubico made land grants to 54 (Góngora Zetina 1984:86 says 56) Petén notables, most of them descended from early- to mid-eighteenth-century Petén Creole (or Spanish) families from Flores (over 90%). By the 1970s, through inheritance divisions and sales, these lands were owned by some 82 people.

Until the 1970s, most land disputes were not about land per se but about about crop damage by animals, usually cattle. Usually, the owner of the animals would offer some compensation to the complaining milpero, but if this did not resolve the matter, one of the parties simply relocated—land was too ample and too cheap to fight over. For example, between 1930 and 1944, there were no more than two or three "serious," as people say, land squabbles in San Martín (pseudonym):

Lupe, a Maya speaker who migrated to the *pueblo* from the north as a result of 1916 border tensions, made a milpa next to that of don Fulano M's milpa (Fulano was a chicle contractor). Don Fulano's cattle ate Lupe's maize. Unable to settle matters with don Fulano, Lupe went to the intendente who ordered that both men build fences to separate their farms, but the fences proved inadequate, and don Fulano's workers testified that Lupe failed to put up a fence. Lupe now offered to sell his land (legally to sell his crops, hut, etc., since at this time land other than that held as private property by the notables could not be sold) to don Fulano and also asked don Fulano to pay for his damaged crops; don Fulano offered Lupe 60 percent of what the latter asked, and the intendent agreed Fulano's offer was fair. In some heat, Lupe appealed to the Judge of First Instance in Flores, and finally the matter was taken to the Supreme Court! The Supreme Court, upon hearing testimony from an agronomist hired by don Fulano, decided against Lupe, who then appealed directly to President Ubico. Don Fulano asked his cousin, —the township secretary and a man with powerful connections, to speak with Ubico. Ubico ordered Lupe to accept don Fulano's offer. Lupe did so and then moved to San Juan. Lupe's brother then shot don Fulano—a superficial arm wound. The authorities were relatively lenient with the brother.

Don Fulano and his cousin won a second very similar case against another Maya-speaking household. The details are almost identical, except that the case was not appealed to the Supreme Court or to Ubico. The major difference is the don Lito (the head of the defeated household) used to insist (in the 1960s) that both he and Lupe were victims of ethnic discrimination. (Although Lupe agreed, he also felt that the land disputes were an instance of how "rich" people unite to "mistreat *los humildes*.") After 1945, don Lito became a local political faction leader, usually allied with the Cs (see below). Don Lito used to recruit followers in part on the basis of ethnicity, telling people of Indian descent to "remember the abuses our parents suffered" at the hands of "selfish people who thought they owned everything [Ladinos]." In these discussions, he offered as part of his evidence Lupe's and his defeat in the land conflicts with don Fulano, that all formal education was in Spanish (he felt Maya too should be taught), and so on.

In the third "serious" case occurring in 1933, don Fulano M and his uncle had a dispute with a Ladino (or Creole?) family, the Cs. The governor, presumably with Ubico's approval, had sold or granted to the Ms a piece of land that overlapped land the Cs had worked for years. Insults were exchanged and a legal suit initiated which eventually went to the Supreme Court. The Cs say "we lost because we were too poor to pay for a lawyer," but Ubico did urge (not order) the Ms to be considerate with the Cs.

To deal with another town, based on a sample (64 cases) taken from the Archivo Municipal, San Andrés, *Libro de Sentencias Económicas*, land dispute simply was not much of an issue until recently. In the 64 cases, only 2 involved land, and 33 (51.6 percent) concerned brawls (rarely serious), usually between inebriated men. Note, too, that despite inequalities of power, Lupe did get 60 percent of what he felt was due him.

It goes almost without saying that land issues were and are critical in the highlands, where as early as 1950 some 72 percent of farm land was held by about 2 percent of farms; a mere 22 farms held 13 percent of the nation's farm land.

41. The power of local elites and the alliance between contractors and *intendentes* must not be exaggerated—the latter two sometimes fought one another, as in the following instance. For no very clear reason other than that he was drunk, C—the nephew of a contractor— hit an *intendente*, and the Court of First Instance seemed likely to sentence C to a lengthy jail term. Thus, C's mother (J) and uncle (M) gave the judge (M's *compadre*) a Q300 bribe. For some inexplicable reason, the judge

gave M a receipt for the money, and then sentenced C to jail. Now at this time the judge and the governor were at odds, so M gave the receipt to the governor, who then "denounced" the judge. An order came from Guatemala City to arrest the judge, M, and J. C was sent to jail there. M and J went to the national capital, where M tried to get two *compadres*—the governor and a military officer, close to Ubico, to help them, but nothing availed. C's father (L, also a chicle contractor) now went to the capital. According to L, J and M were visiting C in jail where they encountered the judge (now a prisoner) and everybody began to shout at everybody else; in the confusion, the warden jailed everyone present (although the courts had not yet decided if J and M were to be jailed). Eventually L paid fines to secure the release of J and M; about the same time the governor was removed from office for "abuse of power," including illegal detention and beating of chicleros. C was remanded from the capital to the jail in Flores, not the worst outcome under the circumstances. L says the entire incident embarrassed his family, and *los humildes* love to recount the event, which among other things suggests that though affluent chicle contractors had high level contacts they did not always win.

42. Suchilma was one of some 1,420 unions that came into existence between about 1945 and 1951. The counterrevolutionary government of Castillo Armas declared most of them procommunist. For years, members of a San Andrés family held important offices in Suchilma. One was Suchilma treasurer in the early 1950s, and another headed the union in the late 1970s, but—typically enough—neither was a chiclero. Typical of charges and countercharges about union corruption is one connected with the frightening days of the 1954 counterrevolution. In 1954, a Suchilma official fled to Mexico, taking union funds with him. Suchilma supporters claim he was safeguarding the funds (and in fact after delegalizing the unions, Castillo Armas did freeze their funds in government banks), and detractors say he was simply absconding with them (and in fact the funds seem never to have been returned).

43. In 1960, Suchilma officials claimed 2,600 members. In 1974, they claimed 1,800 members, very few of whom paid their dues. At the end of the tapping season, dues are collected by union officials in the presence of FYDEP personnel. Many men would not pay the dues were it not for the presence of the FYDEP men. Even with this inducement, no more than 60 percent and more usually less than 40 percent of the chicleros pay. In the late 1970s, fights among Suchilma officials also weakened the union. But, it must be said that the union did improve conditions and wages for chicle camp cooks.

Comments in the text are not meant to imply that mass organizations cannot succeed in Petén, and, as noted elsewhere, chicleros have tried to organize themselves to secure FYDEP contracts. In June or July 1987, an organization called *Sindicato de Trabajadores Peteneros* (Union of Petén Workers), STP, noting that there was no genuine wage laborers' organization in Petén, tried to form one that would include shateros, carpenters, masons, milperos, plumbers, drivers, electricians, shoemakers, mechanics, and so on. STP also hoped to diversify sources of employment for workers. STP planned to cooperate with the Guatemalan Confederation of Union Unity (CUSG) and at least initially to meet at Suchilma headquarters in San Benito. In view of what has been said about status continuity, it is worth pointing out that most if not all top Suchilma and STP leaders are direct descendants of old colonial Creole and Creole-Ladino families.

44. Of course, patron-dependency may or may not involve affection. There is some inconclusive evidence suggesting that the head of the dominant (Ladino) family in San Luis was murdered by one of his clients.

45. Economists might object to the word "enclave." Over the last twenty years, they have challenged the validity of the "enclave economy" concept. An enclave economy may be defined as a system of production which has few socioeconomic linkages with its host region and which is usually geographically remote from host and foreign centers of industry, trade, and population. Enclave economies do not stimulate local industry, do not process what they produce, and export earnings "suffer from short-term price instability and long-term real price deterioration" (Hojman 1985:29). *La chiclería* fits the definition fairly well, but economists have shifted attention from production to fiscal linkages, have stressed that many "enclaves" are now owned by foreign-host partnerships, and so on, that is, they question whether much is added to analysis by calling an overseas productive system an enclave economy. By whatever name, *la chiclería* did not stimulate local production or fiscal linkages. Processing plants were located outside the host region and owned by foreign concerns, and export earnings were vulnerable to market demands beyond local control. Thus "enclave" does describe the chicle business in Petén.

46. The Bank of Guatemala (1981a) and Suchilma officers would disagree. They say that chewing gum companies want to increase the amount of natural gum bases in their product, thus *la chiclería* can be revived. Perhaps so, but not much chicle was collected during 1985–1987. In July 1987, FYDEP divided Q160,000 among some 19 contractors, and in September 1987 distributed Q186,244 derived from chicle among the 12 Petén *municipios*, but these monies came from sale of chicle collected in the 1984–1985 season. For 1987–1988, FYDEP planned to award contracts for collection of 2,000 quintals of chicle. In 1989, about 10,000 quintals of chicle were collected and sold, but even if *la chiclería* were revived, and that is after all possible, its relative importance for Petén would be less than what it was because since 1965 so many other aspects of the regional economy have grown so much: commerce (related to dramatic population growth), logging, cattle ranching (although the growth here may be limited), honey production, shate and pimienta collection, oil exploration and production, tourism (which was interrupted in early 1980 but was reviving by 1985 and may grow dramatically if the planned Ruta Maya paved road linking Petén with tourist routes in Belize and Mexico is completed), agriculture, and (since the late 1970s) marijuana cultivation.

CHAPTER FIVE

1. In addition to writers cited in Chapter 4, also see Rodríguez 1967; Wauchope 1965; and Wyld Ospina 1956.

2. In 1985 of the twelve gasoline stations in Petén, several were owned by mer-

chants who had previously owned mules used to transport chicle. Most of the stations are in central and eastern Petén.

3. There is general agreement that social overhead capital, especially electrical power and transportation "facilities are essential preconditions for economic development practically everywhere" (Hirshman 1958:84), and it is usually government which makes the necessary investments. But until very recently, the Guatemalan government lacked the resources to build even all-weather dirt roads in Petén (Grieb 1979; McIntosh 1980). Besides, airplanes satisfied the central government's major interest in the region, that is, the export of chicle from Guatemalan ports.

4. During Ubico's reign, municipal corporations lacked bursary autonomy. They had to have the approval of the national executive for even the smallest purchases, such as stamps and stationery. After 1945, they were granted bursary autonomy, subject to the law and to scrutiny by higher authority. During the period from 1960 to the 1980s, the national executive and national-level township associations have given municipal governments increasingly larger amounts of money. In Petén, FYDEP has also shared a portion of its income, primarily from land sales, with municipalities.

5. Until the late 1960s, the *pueblos* (save Flores) had but third grade schools. Educational upgrading almost always begins in Flores. Thus, in 1956, the first public kindergarten in Petén was established there. In 1965, a normal school was opened, with help from FYDEP, in Santa Elena, Flores. In 1971, an extension of Mariano Gálvez University was founded in Santa Elena with 63 students, and in 1987, the University of San Carlos opened an extension division in Petén. A majority of the first 63 students to attend the Mariano Gálvez extension school are descended from colonial Creole and Ladino families. Most of them came from Flores and La Libertad, with some others from San Benito, San Francisco, San Andrés, Poptún, and possibly Santa Ana. None came from Melchor, Sayaxché, San José or San Luis. Department education supervisors are almost always Floreños descended from colonial Creole or Creole-Ladino families. In 1985, in general native Peteneros were much more eagerly taking advantage of new opportunities for formal education (and white collar jobs calling for formal schooling) than *sureños* and Cobaneros. This is in part related to "founder advantages" and to the fact that a higher proportion of the latter two live in villages and hamlets than the former.

6. British and American loggers stationed in Petén also imported luxury goods, for sale not only in Petén (Fisher 1974:81) but also adjacent Chiapas.

In 1926, a chicle contractor purchased the first automobile seen in Petén. By 1941, there were a total of five cars in the department, operating between Flores and La Libertad (Halle 1941:34). In 1960, a bus operated—now and then—between San Benito-San Francisco-Poptún, and there were two gas stations in Petén. Between 1970–1980, dirt roads were built linking all the major settlements in the department, but each year the rains wash out portions of the roads, bringing truck and bus traffic to a halt for several days or more at a stretch.

7. Some families did and still do open a small store to compensate for economic problems in farming, etc., and may be poorer than the majority, but on average,

merchants and store owners were better off than the majority. Because land was nearly a free resource until 1974, household type and household possessions were better (albeit proxy) measures of wealth and level of living than the amount of land cropped. Thus, in 1960, in San Andrés for example, there were 37 houses with a *lámina* (laminated zinc) roof, 17.6 percent of the 210 households in the *pueblo*. The 17 merchants in town owned 12 of these houses. Merchants, chicle jobbers, and subcontractors together owned 25 of them; all the other houses had thatch roofs. Of the 17 merchants, 11 were of Ladino, 5 of Maya, and 1 of Kekchí descent. In 1960, there were 79 adult male Ladinos and 149 adult male Indians in the town, thus the former were overrepresented among the merchants ($X^2 = 6.15$, $p < .05$).

8. As mentioned in several places, when the more successful contractor-merchants are compared with the colonial elite, early twentieth-century notables, 1930s notables, and the contemporary elite, the degree of family status continuity is unmistakable (for specific names see Soza 1970; Narciso 1913; Boix de la Torre 1936). The middle sector has been more labile than either the upper sector or the lower one, but during the last 55 years (1930–1985), with one possible exception, no lower sector individual has become a member of the upper class.

9. Population growth (or that portion due to natural growth), from about 8,000 to 10,000 around 1900 to around 25,000 in 1964, may indicate an improvement in level of living, or increased need for farm labor related to the withdrawal of labor from milpa and its redeployment in chicle. If the latter is the case, although wages were relatively good in *la chiclería*, the work also put labor pressure on households. For example, in May 1925 in the town of San Andrés, 93 men planted a total of 170.3 hectares (range = 0.9–3.5 hectares; mean = 1.8; mode = 1.3), but two men (chicle contractors) accounted for 12.2 percent of the 170.3 hectares. In 1928, 101 men planted 237.4 hectares (not including another 22.0 hectares planted by Chicle Development), and the two contractors accounted for 16.7 hectares, or 6.5 percent of the total. In 1928, the mode for the milpas was 1.4 hectares. Since the 1950s, the mode has never fallen below 2.0 hectares, for the *cosecha* milpa. It appears that the increase is in part related to changes in the chicle business. After 1945, although San Andreños continued to collect chicle, they were freer to come and go from chicle camps, thus they had more time for their milpas. Prior to 1945, they did not have this opportunity and had to turn to "younger brothers" (often literally younger brothers, but by this people also may be referring to members of one's own household in general) to tend the milpa. This may have induced people to have more children. Thus, prior to about 1945, while *oro blanco* increased wages it also reduced cropping, and in this sense demographic growth from 1900 to 1945 may not indicate improvement in level of living.

10. "Peteneros" is a shorthand expression for "a majority of people interviewed and observed in a variety of settings over an extended period of time." It does not mean "everyone and/or all Peteneros all the time." Also note that the system of synonyms is most common in the oldest *pueblos*.

Since the late 1960s, *aldeanos* have identified themselves and been identified by others more in terms of place of origin rather than ethnicity, largely because most *aldeanos* are not native to Petén—most are *sureños* (from southern Guatemala) or

"Cobaneros" (Kekchí from Alta Verapaz). Many people living in *pueblos* regard them as poor rustics, but officials and Floreños qualify this by asserting that *sureños* in general are better and more dedicated farmers than native Petén milperos from the *pueblos*.

11. Family background also influences personality, but this is implied in social sector placement. Education or training at home and in school are said to influence character.

Some older Peteneros, mostly males, believe that a man—but not a woman—can also influence his child's personality by what he deliberately looks at or thinks about at the moment of "conception."

12. A distinction may also be made between assimilation and sociopolitical and economic integration. A group may be integrated into the large society without being acculturated or assimilated, as Gonzalez (1986) points out in her review of Mesoamerican Indian acculturation, assimilation and integration. Similarly, a group may abandon all outward symbols of ethnic identity and be assimilated into the larger society without losing its ethnic identity.

13. Petén was one of the most ladinoized departments in the country, in, for example, the ratio of Ladinos to Indians in the population, the percentage of people who were monolingual in Spanish, and literacy rates (Adams 1957:275–78; Whetten 1961:262–63, 370).

14. For example, the stereotypes recorded by Hawkins (1984) are also used in Petén, where in addition there are stereotypes about blacks (said to be more violent and less moral than Indians and Ladinos) or—alternately—San Beniteños. Older Peteneros still use "San Beniteño" as a euphemism or synonym for "black," although they equation no longer has sociological validity.

15. Ethnic homogamy has several unintended consequences for community social organization. Peteneros have a strong, explicit preference for virilocality, but at least one married son often resides close to the parents (and in theory, the youngest male inherits the paternal home). This results in residential clusters of primary and secondary kinsmen, and even though these clusters are not corporate in any sense, people do tend to find their best friends within the cluster, a neighborhood cluster does tend to be the core of an informal recreational group, and so on. In this way, ethnic homogamy tends to build intra-ethnic unity based on household propinquity, recreational groupings, and networks of friendship.

16. The "Household Composite" index measures investment choices. Scores were based on the following point system:

Item	Score		
Roof type	Lámina = 2.0	Wood = 0.5	Thatch = 0
Floor type	Cement = 2.0	Wood = 0.5	Earth = 0
Water supply	Indoor = 0.5	Public = 0	
Service	Septic tank = 2.0	Latrine = 1.0	Hole = 0
Cooking fuel	Kerosene = 1.0	Wood = 0	
Possessions	Television Yes = 2.0	Sewing machine Yes = 1.0	
	Refrigerator Yes = 1.0	Radio Yes = 0.5	

The index is not perfect, for instance, there is a difference between a small house with a deteriorated cement floor and a large house with a well-maintained one. Nonetheless, there is agreement between informant ranking of households and the ranking which resulted from use of the index. There also is a statistically significant correlation between "Household Score" and self-reported household income for households headed by native San Andreños (N = 231, r = .5057, z = 8.09, p < .05).

Household economic status was also measured by a weighted "Productive Resources" index, constructed as follows:

Item	Score	Item	Score
Hectares cultivated	0.25	Truck/motorized canoe	2.00
Cattle/head	0.50	Large general store	2.00
Pig	0.05	Pharmacy	2.00
Fowl (small flock)	0.05	Saloon/inn	2.00
Worker (adult)	1.00	Small grocery store	1.00
Worker (minor)	0.50	Comedor (eatery)	1.00
		Maize grinding mill	0.05

An attempt was made to calibrate the items, e.g., a steer sells for about 10 times what a pig does. There is a statistically significant relationship between "Productive Resources" scores and self-reported household income (N = 254, r = .3251, z = 5.18, p < .05).

In 1985, there were 255 households in the *pueblo* headed by native San Andreños, but because some piece of information was missing on 24 of them, the N in Table 5:2 and above is 231. The total number of households was 424 (plus another 21 in which the householders, all single men, were so rarely in town that it seemed best to exclude them from the census). Between 1982 and 1985, when three sawmills in the town were temporarily closed, another 54 families, mostly of *sureño* origin, left town. Of the 169 households not headed by native San Andreños, 31 were headed by Kekchí from Alta Verapaz, 106 by *sureños* (most of them from southeastern and Pacific coast Guatemala), and 32 by a diverse group of others—Peteneros from other townships, and people from Mexico, Belize, and El Salvador.

17. Lutes (1987:17), some of whose words are paraphrased at the end of this paragraph, has reported somewhat similar continuities among mestizos and Indians in Sonora, Mexico. In Petén, the continuities also are seen in what may be called honors lists. For example, from 1931 (when the annual departmental fair was officially inaugurated) to 1986, the departmental Queen of the Year has almost without exception been descended from a colonial Petén Spanish, Creole or Ladino family. That wealth as well as beauty determine who will be Queen simply reaffirms the point about status continuity.

18. For an extended discussion of the inversion, see Schwartz 1974.

Scholars and missionaries have often made the same distinction between milperos and chicleros that Peteneros and other Guatemalans make. Some scholars and missionaries also have identified milperos with Maya villagers and chicleros with a semi-nomadic motley of no particular ethnic identity, sometimes overlooking, as I have already said, that the villagers also worked part of the year as chicleros. The inversion may have somehow helped make easier the transition from one role to another.

For graphic negative descriptions of chicleros see *Awake* 1959; Blom and LaFarge 1926–1927:204–05; Brunhouse 1971:149; Gann 1925:32. For more positive images, see González Salas 1984; Shattuck 1933:157.

19. Obviously the community does not vanish into limbo during the tapping season, but personnel and social organization do change. For example, until recently, when during the tapping season as many as 35–50 percent of the adult males in some communities were away for six months, adult women played a more commanding role in everyday life than when the men were at home. I have stressed the impact of chicle on men, but there is no doubt it also affected women and children in this and in other ways.

Some may wish to see the contrast between camp and community as an (attenuated) expression of pre-Columbian native cosmological views about the distinction between the "civilized," safe social world and the wild, dangerous forest one, and so on, but there are reasons to be wary about this view. The camp-community contrast noted here and in Schwartz 1974 is based on what can be observed and connected with experiences occurring in the same time frame, whereas linking the contrast to pre-Columbian systems of thought involves temporal disjunctions and would require considerable exegesis. Besides, contrasts of the camp:community and town:forest sort are common in many places in the world—there is nothing, I suggest, specifically Maya about it, although it is an expression of the specific historical experiences of Peteneros of Maya *and* Ladino, black and Creole descent.

20. See, for example, McVay and Vogt's (1988) description of San Juan Villaseñor, southern Mexico.

21. In 1985, household census data for a municipal center and three *aldeas* (all three mostly composed of post-1965 settlers) showed the following:

Community	Number of households	Percent virilocal
San Andrés	424	72.0
Ixhuacut	43	83.7
Chunya	83	80.0
Sacpúy	269	70.3

These data indicate that new settlers like native Peteneros prefer virilocal households.

22. The great value placed on autonomy (or independence) also may be reactive compensations to overcome dependence on mother, fostered in children. Children are trained to be independent, but they also are expected to be obedient and competent rather than simply independent, and in many ways mothers train children to be dependent on them, including mother-child co-sleeping patterns and affectionate but inconsistent feeding patterns. The social distance between fathers and children and the physical absence of fathers for extended periods also feeds into the process.

23. Econonic growth is defined as a "steady process by which the *productive capacity of the economy* is increased over time" (Todaro 1985:582; stress in the original), and as a process in which levels of real income increase at a rate exceeding population growth. Economic development refers to economic growth plus generation of linkages and structural changes, including increased access to goods and services for all social classes. Many of the causes of economic growth and development, such as increased per capita productivity, technological modernization, stable commodity prices, and growth of internal markets (Clower et al. 1966; Keiser 1975) were not present in Petén during the period under discussion.

24. Peteneros and foreign observers also have had positive (as well as negative) images of chicleros, admiring especially their sylvan skills and hardiness. Only the chicleros, they say, can cope so well with the adversities of the deep forest: isolation, poor diet, hurricanes, insects, poisonous snakes, chiclero's ulcer, accidents, and endless rain. In his famous novel *Guayacán*, Rodríguez Macal praises the chicleros in an ambivalent way, noting their "ambition, fatalistic resignation, . . . will to survive, primitive cruelty and generosity" (1967:6). Petén intellectuals share this qualified admiration of the chiclero who lives in what some call the forest "hell." Most interesting is that with the decline in *oro blanco*, the image of chicleros has changed. The same people who in 1960 spoke of chicleros as "dangerous," "powerful," and so on, in 1985 were more apt to describe them as ordinary laborers who were unable to organize for collective action, and so on. In a sense, chicleros are less "dangerous" now. They are less economically important, at least for the time being, for and in Petén, and the change is reflected in less sharply drawn (negative or positive) images.

25. Among other changes, between 1900 and 1950 in several towns education was upgraded from second to third–sixth grade (chicle revenues helped defray part of the cost for larger school buildings). In the late 1920s, Nazarene missionaries began to work in Petén, and other pentacostal sects arrived in the 1960s. Few of the political reforms of 1945–1953 endured, but the bursary discretion granted *municipios* did. To cite but one more example, after 1945, infant mortality rates decreased, probably because of DDT spraying. After about 1963–1965, deeper changes were brought about by FYDEP, as described in Chapter 6.

26. For example, shortly before this book was turned over to the copy editor, I learned that during 1989–1990 some 10,000 quintals of chicle were collected and sold for more than $2,000,000—this after a yearly average of 3,000–4,000 during the 1980s. Since each chiclero collects between 5–10 quintals per season, this level of renewed demand would provide work for 1,000–2,000 men. Without minimizing the importance of increased demand for the tappers or for the regional economy, even if we assume each tapper represented one household in Petén, only about 2–4 percent of households would be directly affected, which obviously does not compare with the percent affected in earlier eras.

CHAPTER SIX

1. Although the export value of coffee declined between 1960 and 1985, coffee

remained the country's most important export crop and never dipped below 25.0 percent (in 1975) of "total export value" (Wilkie, Lorey, and Ochoa 1988:434).

2. See, for example, Adams 1970; Dixon 1987 (on physical quality of life indices); Sexton 1985; and Williams 1986.

3. Because of the way the original enabling legislation concerning FYDEP sale of land was written, there are some legal ambiguities about land titles, but people do hold title to private parcels and register them as such.

4. The expanded key for Table 6:2 is as follows:

A1 = Large, well-capitalized wholesale and/or retail establishment selling major modern appliances, hardware, construction materials, heavy machinery, etc. Each employs at least several people, none of whom are kin to the owner.

A2 = Agro-veterinary supply and/or service establishment (including an apiary supply and service store) selling hybrid seeds, medicine for livestock, etc., and dispensing advice on farming and livestock care. Usually employs several people, none of whom are kin to the owner. One is a subsidiary of the Bayer company.

A3 = Distributor and/or bottler of soft drinks, beer and liquor, usually employing several people, none of whom are kin to the owner. The largest are in Santa Elena (Flores) and San Benito.

B1 = Long distance cargo and/or log hauling. Hauler is usually an independent *sureño* operator with 1–3 trucks.

B2 = Passenger service. Two Flores-Guatemala City operators and a Sayaxché-Sebol (Alta Verapaz)-Guatemala City operator. Buses also run from Flores to Melchor, Sayaxché, Poptún, and Naranjo (La Libertad). (By 1987, there were five more minibus operators, not included above, going from Flores to Poptún.) The column includes an inter-urban line (operating in the Santa Elena-San Benito area), motorized canoes, and taxis (all the taxis are in the Flores-Santa Elena-San Benito urban triangle). There are also motorized canoes at Sayaxché. Something reminiscent of a 76 Truck Center is located at Sabaneta (Dolores), almost on the old *camino real*. The biggest company is owned by a Petenero from San Andrés.

B3 = Gas station, with or without automotive supplies and/or mechanic. Those with the best stocks and with repair services are in central Petén.

C1 = *Tienda* (general store). A small-scale version of A1, but family-operated, or as a rule with no more than 1–3 employees, unrelated to the owner. *Tiendas* vary in size and composition of stock. Some are in the front room of the owner's residence, and others are not.

C2 = General goods stall. Typically sells clothing. Those in the markets of Santa Elena, San Benito (33 stalls), San Andrés, Melchor, San Luis, and Sayaxché look solid, but those outside the markets look flimsy.

C3 = Specialty store. Typically sells a wide range of goods, but concentrates on one item in particular. The column includes appliance, tire, paint, hardware, furniture, fishing gear, photography supply (often with attached portrait studio), stationery, book, record, party favors, radio, special parts stores, and boutiques. Stalls with a special line of goods are few in number. Most of the fancier stores with luxury items are in the urban triangle (Flores-Santa Elena-San Benito), with Poptún and Melchor distant seconds. In smaller settlements, the stores are usually clothiers.

D1 = *Pulpería* (grocery). As with F1, F3 (below) and C3, the largest are in the urban triangle. As in the case of D2–D4 (below) a grocery is almost always a family operation and usually located in the front room of the owner's house. Quite commonly, a woman runs the grocery, while her husband (if she has one) works in some other line.

D2 = Food stall. Sells locally produced fruits, dairy products, fish, sweets, ice-cream, and also vegetables imported from the highlands.

D3 = Butcher shop, bakery, etc. Included are four fish stores (in Sayaxché) and cheese-butter stores (in San Benito). Bakers often own small trucks, used to hawk wares in town and rural areas.

E1 = Pharmacy. Fully stocked ones are found in *pueblos*, partially stocked ones (in brackets in Table 6:2) in *aldeas*. Pharmacists also dispense medical advice.

E2 = Repair, service, and/or artisan store. A very general category. The store usually sells the item it repairs, but it leans more toward repair and/or service than sales. Included are barbers, beauticians, photographers, rental and sales agents (only in Poptún and Santa Elena), morticians, lawyers, accountants, agronomists, Petén's one stable printing house (in Flores), two radio stations (Flores and Santa Barbara Island, Flores), and so on. There are repair stores for machinery, radios, watches, electrical appliances, and shoes. Artisans include tailors, silversmiths, blacksmiths, and leather workers. Almost all of these establishments are family operations, the one exception being a store in Flores that employs 6–9 young men to repair shoes and make chicleros' and hunters' boots (the business goes back to the nineteenth century).

E3 = Nixtamal (to grind maize, but in Poptún also other grains). Almost always a family operation and located in the front room of the owner's house. The number of mills used to be (and still may be for larger towns) a good proxy for population density, for which reason they are placed in a single column.

E4 = Private school. Teaches modern office skills.

F1 = Hotel (minus those at Tikal). Most of the first-class and all the luxury hotels are in Flores and Santa Elena. With one exception, they are owned by Peteneros, usually from Flores.

F2 = Pension, inn and/or dormitory.

F3 = Restaurant. Most large ones are in Flores and Santa Elena. Usually employs several people, none of whom are related to the owner.

F4 = *Comedor* (eatery) and food stall. *Comedores* and stalls are usually rustic, family operations.

G1 = Saloon. Some are also small distributorships.

G2 = Drinking stall. Usually limited to sale of beer and/or soda.

G3 = Cinema. Includes a San Joseño who owns a projector and shows films in several places but does not own a permanent theatre. Since about 1982, TV and political unrest have negatively affected cinemas. Billiard parlors (male gathering places) are excluded and appear to be disappearing, probably because in the early 1980s it was risky to hang around them in the evening.

G4 = Brothel. Several double as saloons, with or without *comedores*.

H1 = Private sawmill. Between 1970 and 1985, the number varied from 7 to 14.

Because FYDEP prohibited logging in 1983–1984, it was difficult to determine if a mill was temporarily or permanently shut-down. Listed are private mills, which were operating in 1985 or appeared to be gearing up to renew operations. When operating at capacity, the mills employ from fifty to several hundred people. With one or possibly two exceptions, the mills are owned by foreign or metropolitan (Guatemala City) entrepreneurs and companies. The five major logging concessions are also in the hands of metropolitan interests. Omitted are chicle concessions—at least 22 in 1985.

H2 = Factory. The largest, in San Benito, processes shate and has a stable work force of 200. There is a concrete block plant in San Benito. *Rentas* classifies as factories several small shops that make coffins, dairy products, and ice-cream.

H3 = Bank. Location of banks roughly parallels that of major medical and dental clinics, hospitals, and military bases (Santa Elena, Melchor, Poptún, and Sayaxché, but there is a Kabile base at Polvora, between Flores and Melchor.)

ND = Not determined. Stalls in particular are undercounted. Data on stores in villages and hamlets were obtained from *Rentas*, but they are too numerous to list. In 1985, there were about 300 *aldeas* and some 700 or more hamlets and rural neighborhoods in Petén, many of which had 1–2 groceries, perhaps a saloon and—less often—a *tienda*. For example, in San Luis township there were at least 40 small settlements, each of which had 1–4 stores. The distribution of establishments reflects not only the poverty of the small settlements but also settlement hierarchy in Petén: in 1982 there were 24 settlements with a population of 1,000 or more people, about 24 with 500–999 people, and 840 with fewer than 500 people. Private and public commercial and service establishments are concentrated in—by numerical order—(1) the urban triangle of Flores-Santa Elena-San Benito (and within that, in San Benito), (2) Poptún, (3) Melchor, (4) San Luis, (5) Sayaxché, and (6) San Andrés. Actually the concentration is greater than a mere count shows, for instance, 50 percent of the stores in San Andrés are small *pulperías*.

In a more complete survey, Cayo, Belize, which is close to and has commerical connections with Melchor, would be included. Had it been, the Melchor-Cayo zone might have looked more important than that of Poptún.

5. I say "in general," because several medium-scale loggers have failed. In addition, one large foreign-owned sawmill closed down completely during 1983–1984, when FYDEP forbade all logging in Petén.

6. For example, in recent years honey has become an important product (although it is in fact an old, now revived one in Petén). In the 1940s, there were no commercial hives in the department, but by 1985 registered bee-keepers produced 7,849 quintals of honey worth Q300,000, and non-registered bee-keepers may have produced an equal amount. To cite another parallel example, at least one large-holder in southwest Petén is cultivating *hule* on his estate.

7. Nor has the present analysis covered everything, for example, there is a need to know more about exactly when and how colonial settlements became communities in a sociological sense; pre-1820s genealogies for the lower sector; pre-1930s chicle production, and so forth, and much more could have been said about the role of women in the society.

8. Despite Suchilma and the *Frente de Trabajadores de Petén* (which claims to represent some 10,000 Petén laborers), wage workers and smallholders are not effectively organized to protect their interests.

9. Stereotypes based on place of origin are beginning to replace ethnic ones, perhaps to express competition between newcomers and old-timers for scarce resources. Like ethnic opposition, tensions between Peteneros and settlers fragment the lower sector, to the benefit of the wealthy, who did not invent the stereotypes but may exploit them. There seems to be a set of free-floating images in Guatemala, which most commonly attach to Indians and Ladinos but which can attach, with appropriate modification, to almost any opposed social pair. Some of what once was said of "wild" Indians and later on of chicleros is now said of settlers, particularly Ladinos from the south coast and eastern highlands—they are violent, dangerous, and (less commonly) rustic. Similarly, what Petén townsmen say of Flores merchant-contractors, *sureños* and Cobaneros now say of Peteneros (including townsmen)—that they are selfish, urbane, and so on. The stereotypes persist, but the social categories to which they refer change, in part because many village settlers have socioeconomic relationships with Petenero townsmen that parallel relationships the latter have had with the Flores upper class.

Glossary

Aldea. Administrative-territorial division of a *municipio*; headed by an "auxiliary mayor" appointed by the mayor of a *municipio*; a rural village.

Cabildo. The building in which the municipal government is housed; roughly equivalent to a town hall.

Caja (*de comunidad*). A strongbox in which community or *municipio* funds were kept in the colonial period; the term is still used in parts of Petén.

Cofradía. Religious confraternity, dedicated to the care of one or more saints, including the patron saint of a community.

Milpa. Clearing for a maize field, which is almost always intercropped with other plants; form of slash-and-burn or swidden cultivation.

Milpero. In Petén, a small-scale farmer.

Pimienta gorda. Allspice (*Pimenta officinalis*) an aromatic spice; it is a New World tree with a slender, smooth, grey trunk. It can reach 30 meters in height.

Real. A silver coin equal to one-eighth of a *peso*.

Shate (*xate*). A *Chamaedorea* palm; tiger fur, used in floral arrangements. Two species are collected in Petén: (1) *C. oblongata*, locally called *jade* (jade, green) or *macho* (bot.) male; strong, and (2) *C. elegans*, locally called *hembra* (bot.) female; delicate.

Téquio. Obligatory service Indians owed to the colonial government; labor tax imposed on a community, which persisted into the Independence period.

Vecino. Non-Indian or citizen in colonial times; resident of a community; neighbor.

Visita. Official tour of inspection and/or inquiry; also a subordinate settlement of a parish.

Bibliography

Abbreviations:

AGCA = Archivo General de Centro América (Guatemala City)
AGI = Archivo General de Indias (Seville)
FYDEP = Empresa Nacional de Fomento y Desarrollo Económico del Petén (Guatemala City and Santa Elena, Flores).

Note: Bibliographic references to collections and individual documents in AGCA, AGI, FYDEP (with two exceptions), *cabildos*, local courts, the governor's office and *Rentas Internas* in Flores, parishes, magazines published in Petén, and *Prensa Libre*, a Guatemalan newspaper, were given in the text and notes and are not repeated here. However, signed articles in the annual *Revista Petén Itzá*, are cited below. Throughout original spelling and use of accents has been retained.

At least since the 1920s, Peteneros have published several magazines, which reproduce colonial and post-colonial documents as well as other material. Except for *Revista Petén Itzá*, they have been short-lived: e.g., *El Impulso*, (circa 1927–1929), *El Amigo del Pueblo* (1928), *Tayazal* (for several years after 1941), and *El Observador Petén* (in the early 1980s). Since the early 1970s, several *municipios* (San Benito, Poptún, and most recently Melchor de Mencos) have published their own annuals.

Adams, R. N.
  1957 *Cultural Surveys of Panama-Nicaragua-Guatemala-El Salvador-Honduras.* Washington, D.C.: Pan American Sanitary Bureau, No.33.
  1970 *Crucifixion by Power: Essays on Guatemalan National Social Structure, 1944–1966.* Austin: University of Texas Press.
Aldana M., F.
  1974 "Censos de Población de El Petén." *Revista Petén Itzá* 15:13.
Anderson, A. J. O. (ed.)
  1950 *Morleyana: A Collection of Writing in Memoriam Sylvanus Griswold Morley— 1883–1948.* Santa Fe: School of American Research and the Museum of New Mexico.
Andrews, A. P.
  1983 *Maya Salt Trade and Production.* Tucson: University of Arizona Press.
Anonymous
  1959 "Life in the Chicle Camps." *Awake* June 22:13–15.
Applebaum, H. A.
  1981 *Royal Blue: The Culture of Construction Workers.* New York: Holt, Rinehart and Winston.

Aybar de Soto, J. M.
  1978 *Dependency and Intervention: The Case of Guatemala in 1954*. Boulder, Colo.: Westview Press.
Azurdia A., T. H.
  1975 *Mordeduras de Serpientes en El Petén*. Guatemala: Universidad de San Carlos.
Balmori, D., S. F. Voss, and M. Wortman
  1984 *Notable Family Networks in Latin America*. Chicago: University of Chicago Press.
Banco de Guatemala
  1981a *Informe Sobre la Producción de Chicle Natural, y Sus Perspectivas*. Guatemala: Banco de Guatemala.
  1981b *Establecimiento de un Empresa Ganadera en El Petén*. Informe Económico (April-June). Guatemala: Banco de Guatemala.
Berendt, C. H.
  1868 "Report of Explorations in Central America." *Annual Report to the Board of Regents of the Smithsonian Institution*, 420–26. Washington, D.C.: Smithsonian Institution.
Black, G., M. Jamail, and N. Stoltz Chinchilla
  1984 *Garrison Guatemala*. London: Zed Books Ltd., in association with North American Congress on Latin America.
Blanton, R., S. Kowalewski, F. Feinman, and J. Appel
  1981 *Ancient Mesoamerica: A Comparison of Changes in Three Regions*. Cambridge: Cambridge University Press.
Blom, F. and O. LaFarge
  1926–27 *Tribes and Temples*. New Orleans: Tulane University, Middle American Research Institute, Publication 1.
Boddam-Whetham, J. W.
  1877 *Across Central America*. London: Hurst and Blackett.
Boix de la Torre, R.
  1936 "Monografía del Municipio de Flores." *Vida Scoutica* 9:28–34.
Bolland, O. N.
  1977 *The Formation of a Colonial Society: Belize, from Conquest to Crown Colony*. Baltimore: Johns Hopkins University Press.
Bricker, V. R.
  1981 *The Indian Christ, the Indian King: The Historical Substrate of Maya Myth and Ritual*. Austin: University of Texas Press.
Brintnall, D. E.
  1979 *Revolt Against the Dead: The Modernization of a Mayan Community in the Highlands of Guatemala*. New York: Gordon and Breach.
Brunhouse, R. L.
  1971 *Sylvanus G. Morley and the World of the Ancient Mayas*. Norman: University of Oklahoma Press.
  1976 *Frans Blom, Maya Explorer*. Albuquerque: University of New Mexico Press.

Bullitt, J. M.
  1966 (1953) *Jonathan Swift and the Anatomy of Satire: A Study of Satiric Technique.*
    Cambridge, Mass.: Harvard University Press.
Bulmer-Thomas, V.
  1987 *The Political Economy of Central America since 1920.* New York: Cambridge
    University Press.
Bunzel, R.
  1952 *Chichicastenango: A Guatemalan Village.* New York: J. J. Augustin Pub-
    lisher.
Cahuiche, C. J.
  1964 "Historical Facts of San José, Petén." Ms.
Calvert, P.
  1985 *Guatemala: A Nation in Turmoil.* Boulder, Colo.: Westview Press.
Camara, F.
  1952 "Religious and Political Organization." In *Heritage of Conquest: The Eth-
    nology of Middle America,* by S. Tax and members of the Viking Fund
    Seminar on Middle American Ethnology, 142–64. Glencoe, Ill.: Free Press.
Cardenas, L. Jr.
  1963 "The Municipality in Northern Mexico." *Southwestern Studies* 1:3–27.
Carmack, R. M.
  1983 "Spanish-Indian Relations in Highland Guatemala, 1800–1944." In *Span-
    iards and Indians in Southeastern Mesoamerica: Essays on the History of Ethnic
    Relations,* edited by M. J. MacLeod and R. Wasserstrom, 215–52. Lincoln:
    University of Nebraska Press.
Carranza F., M. A.
  1973 *Cooperativas de El Petén: Producción y Cuentas Económicas.* Guatemala: Uni-
    versidad de San Carlos.
Casasola, O.
  1968 *Grandezas y Miserias del Petén.* Guatemala: Ediciones Indiana.
Caufield, C.
  1984 *In the Rainforest.* New York: Alfred A. Knopf.
Central American Reports
  1989 "Oil vs. Environment: Round 2." *Central American Reports* (Guatemala,
    Infopress Centroamericana) 16 (37):293–94, 22 September.
Chambers, E. J. and P. D. Young
  1979 "Mesoamerican Community Studies: The Past Decade." *Annual Review of
    Anthropology* 8:45–70.
Chardon, R.
  1961 *Geographic Aspects of Plantation Agriculture in Yucatan.* Washington, D.C.:
    National Academy of Sciences, Publication 876.
Chase, A. F.
  1976 "Topoxte and Tayasal: Ethnohistory in Archaeology." *American Antiquity*
    41:154–67.
  1985 "Postclassic Peten Interaction Spheres: The View from Tayasal." In *The
    Lowland Maya Postclassic,* edited by A. F. Chase and P. M. Rice, 184–205.
    Austin: University of Texas Press.

Clegern, W. M.
　1962 "Pacification of Yucatán." *The Americas* 18:243–55.
Clower, R. W., G. Dalton, M. Harwitz, and A. A. Walters
　1966 *Growth Without Development: An Economic Survey of Liberia*. Evanston, Ill.:
　　Northwestern University Press.
Cohen, G. A.
　1988 *History, Labour, and Freedom: Themes from Marx*. Oxford: Clarendon Press.
Comisión de Limites
　1929 *Cartografía de la América Central*. Guatemala: Tipografía Nacional.
Cordan, W.
　1963 *Secret of the Forest: On the Track of Maya Temples*. Translated by B. Creigh-
　　ton. London: Victor Gollancz Ltd.
Cowgill, U. M.
　1962 "An Agricultural Study of the Southern Maya Lowlands." *American An-
　　thropologist* 64:273–86.
Deevey, E. S. Jr., M. Brenner, M. S. Flannery, and G. Habib
　1980 "Lakes Yaxha and Sacnab, Peten, Guatemala: Limnology and Hydrology."
　　Archives of Hydrobiology (Supplement) 57:419–60.
DeMott, B.
　1987 Review of T. C. Boyle, *World's End* (New York: Viking 1987), 1 and 52. *New
　　York Times Book Review* 27 September.
Dirección General de Estadística
　1972 *Anuario Estadístico*. Guatemala: Dirreción General de Estadística.
Dixon, W. J.
　1987 "Progress in the Provision of Basic Human Needs—Latin America, 1960–
　　1980." *Journal of Developing Areas* 21:129–40.
Duellman, W. E.
　1963 "Amphibians and Reptiles of the Rainforests of Southern El Peten, Gua-
　　temala." *Museum of Natural History* (University of Kansas) 15:205–49.
Early, J. D.
　1982 *The Demographic Structure and Evolution of a Peasant System: The Guatema-
　　lan Population*. Boca Raton: University Presses of Florida.
Edmonson, M.
　1982 *The Ancient Future of the Itza*. Austin: University of Texas Press.
Estrada Monroy, A.
　1977 *Hombres, Fechas y Documentos de la Patria*. Guatemala: José de Pineda Ibarrá.
Europa Yearbook
　1959–1972 "Guatemala." London: Europa Publications, Ltd.
FAO/FYDEP
　1970 *Estudio de Preinversión Sobre Desarrollo Forestal*. Rome and Guatemala: FAO
　　(7 volumes).
Farriss, N. M.
　1983 "Indians in Colonial Yucatan: Three Perspectives." In *Spaniards and Indians
　　in Southeastern Mesoamerica: Essays on the History of Ethnic Relations*, edited
　　by M. J. MacLeod and R. Wasserstrom, 1–39. Lincoln: University of Ne-
　　braska Press.

1984 *Maya Society Under Colonial Rule: The Collective Enterprise of Survival*. Princeton, N.J.: Princeton University Press.

Feldman, L. H.
1982 "Belize and Its Neighbors: A Preliminary Report on the Spanish Colonial Records of the Audiencia of Guatemala." In *Archaeology at Colha, Belize. The 1981 Interim Report*, edited by T. R. Hester, H. J. Sahfer, and J. D. Eaton. San Antonio: Center for Archaeological Research, University of Texas at San Antonio.

Fisher, G. R.
1974 "Frontier Settlement Patterns in Northern Guatemala." Ph. D. dissertation. Gainesville: University Presses of Florida.

Fletcher, L. B., E. Graber, W. C. Merrill, and E. Thorbecke
1970 *Guatemala's Economic Development: The Role of Agriculture*. Ames: Iowa State University Press.

Forman, S. and J. F. Reigelhaupt
1979 "The Political Economy of Patron-Clientship: Brazil and Portugal Compared." In *Brazil: Anthropological Perspectives, Essays in Honor of Charles Wagley*, edited by M. L. Margolis and W. E. Carter, 379–400. New York: Columbia University Press.

Foster, G. M.
1966 *Culture and Conquest: America's Spanish Heritage*. Viking Fund Publications in Anthropology, No. 27. New York: Wenner-Gren Foundation for Anthropological Research.

FYDEP
1977 *Monografías Socio-Económicos de las Municipalidades del Petén. Santa Elena, Flores, Petén: FYDEP*.
1969–1986 "Memorias de Labores de FYDEP." Santa Elena, Flores, Petén: FYDEP.

Gann, T.
1925 *Mystery Cities: Exploration and Adventure in Lubaatun*. London: Duckworth.

García Márquez, G.
1970 *One Hundred Years of Solitude*. Translated by G. Rabassa. New York: Harper & Row.

Gibson, C.
1964 *The Aztecs Under Spanish Rule*. Stanford, Ca.: Stanford University Press.

Gilmore, D. D.
1976 "Class, Culture, and Community Size in Spain: The Relevance of Models." *Anthropological Quarterly* 49:80–106.

Góngora Zetina de Trujillo, M. C.
1984 *La Tenencia de la Tierra en el Departamento de El Petén y Su Legislación*. Guatemala: Universidad de San Carlos.

González, D. M. S.
1867 "Memorias Sobre el Departamento del Petén." *Gaceta de Guatemala* No. 58.

Gonzalez, N. L.
1986 "Indigenismo and Ethnicity as Modernizing Forces." In *Directions in the*

Anthropological Study of Latin America: A Reassessment, edited by J. R. Roll-wagen, 61–78. Albany, N.Y.: Society for Latin American Anthropology Monograph Number 8.

González Salas, Br. J. L.

    1984 "Costumbres del Campesino y Chiclero Petenero." *El Observador Petén* 1:7.

Graham, E. A., G. D. Jones, and R. R. Kautz

    1985 "Archaeology and Ethnohistory on a Spanish Colonial Frontier: An Interim Report on the Macal-Tipu Project in Western Belize." In *The Lowland Maya Postclassic*, edited by A. F. Chase and P. M. Rice, 206–14. Austin: University of Texas Press.

Grieb, K. J.

    1979 *Guatemalan Caudillo: The Regime of Jorge Ubico, Guatemala 1931–1944*. Athens: Ohio University Press.

Griffith, W. J.

    1965 *Empire in the Wilderness: Foreign Colonization and Development in Guatemala, 1834–44*. Chapel Hill: University of North Carolina Press.

Gudeman, S.

    1978 *The Demise of a Rural Economy: From Subsistence to Capitalism in a Latin American Village*. London: Routledge and Kegan Paul.

Guerra, S.

    1871 "Estado Jeneral del Movimiento de Poblacion Habido en este Departamento." *Boletín Official* (Guatemala) 1 (12):5–6.

Guinea, G.

    1970 *Paralelo 17: El Petén*. Guatemala: FYDEP.

Guzmán, O.

    1984 "Municipio de Flores, Petén." *Revista Petén Itzá* 25:7–10.

Halle, L. J., Jr.

    1941 *River of Ruins*. New York: Henry Holt and Company.

Handy, J.

    1984 *Gift of the Devil: A History of Guatemala*. Boston: South End Press.

Harris, A. and M. Sartor (eds.)

    1984 *Gertrude Blom: Bearing Witness*. Chapel Hill: University of North Carolina Press (for Duke University).

Hawkins, J.

    1984 *Inverse Images: The Meaning of Culture, Ethnicity and Family in Postcolonial Guatemala*. Albuquerque: University of New Mexico Press.

Heinzman, R. and C. Reining

    1988 "Sustained Rural Development: Extractive Forest Reserves in the Northern Petén of Guatemala." Guatemala: USAID/Guatemala.

Hellmuth, N. M.

    1970 *Preliminary Bibliography of the Chol, Lacandon, Yucatec Lacandon, Itzá, Mopan, and Quejache of the Southern Maya Lowlands 1524–1969*. Col.: Katunob Occasional Publications in Mesoamerican Anthropology 4.

    1971 "Some notes on the Ytza, Quejache, Verapaz Chol, and Toquegua Maya: A Progress Report on Ethnohistory Conducted in Seville, Spain, June-August

1971." Mimeographed. New Haven, Conn.: Foundation for Latin American Anthropological Research.

1977 "Cholti-Lacandon (Chiapas) and Petén-Ytzá Agricultural Settlement Pattern and Population." In *Social Process in Maya Prehistory: Studies in Honour of Sir J. Eric S. Thompson*, edited by N. Hammond, 421–48. London: Academic Press.

Helms, M. W.

1975 *Middle America: A Culture History of Heartland and Frontiers*. Englewood Cliffs, N.J.: Prentice-Hall, Inc.

Hendrickson, R.

1976 *The Great American Chewing Gum Book*. Radnor, Pa.: Chilton Book Co.

Hirschman, A. O.

1958 *The Strategy of Economic Development*. New Haven, Conn.: Yale University Press.

Hoar, H. M.

1924 "Chicle and Chewing Gum: A Review of Chicle Production and Sources of Supply, and the Chewing Gum Industry and Trade." Washington, D.C.: U.S. Government Printing Office.

Hojman, D. E.

1985 "From Mexican Plantations to Chilean Mines: The Theoretical and Empirical Relevance of Enclave Theories in Contemporary Latin America." *Inter-American Economic Affairs* 39:27–53.

Holdridge, L. R., F. B. Lamb, and B. Mason, Jr.

1950 *The Forests of Guatemala*. Turrialba, Costa Rica: Inter-American Institute of Agricultural Sciences.

Howard, M. C.

1977 *Political Change in a Maya Village in Southern Belize*. Col.: Katunob Occasional Publications in Mesoamerican Anthropology 10.

Joly, L. G.

1981 "One is None and Two is One: Development from Above and Below in North-Central Panama." Ph. D. disseration. Gainesville: University of Florida.

Jones, C. L.

1940 *Guatemala: Past and Present*. Minneapolis: University of Minnesota Press.

Jones, G. D.

1973 "Maya Intergroup Relations in Nineteenth Century Belize and Southern Yucatan." *Journal of Belizean Affairs* 5:3–13.

1977 "Levels of Settlement Alliance Among the San Pedro Maya of Western Belize and Eastern Petén, 1857–1936." In *Anthropology and History in Yucatán*, edited by G. D. Jones, 139–90. Austin: University of Texas Press.

1982 "Agriculture and Trade in the Colonial Period Southern Maya Lowlands." In *Maya Subsistence: Studies in Memory of Dennis E. Puleston*, edited by K. V. Flannery, 275–93. New York: Academic Press.

1983 "The Last Maya Frontiers in Colonial Yucatan." In *Spaniards and Indians in Southeastern Mesoamerica: Essays on the History of Ethnic Relations*, edited by M. J. MacLeod and R. Wasserstrom, 64–91. Lincoln: University of Nebraska Press.

1989 *Maya Resistance to Spanish Rule: Time and History on a Colonial Frontier*. Albuquerque: University of New Mexico Press.

Jones, G. D., D. S. Rice, and P. M. Rice

1981 "The Location of Tayasal: A Reconsideration of Petén Maya Ethnohistory and Archaeology." *American Antiquity* 46:530–47.

Juarros, D.

1823 *A Statistical and Commercial History of the Kingdom of Guatemala in Spanish America*. Translated by J. Baily. London: George Cowie and Co.

Karling, J. S.

1934 "Dendrograph Studies on *Archas zapota* in Relation to the Optimum Conditions for Tapping." *American Journal of Botany* 12:161–93.

Karnes, T. L.

1961 *The Failure of Union: Central America, 1824–1960*. Chapel Hill: University of North Carolina Press.

Kearney, M.

1972 *The Winds of Ixtepeji: World View and Society in a Zapotec Town*. New York: Holt, Rinehart and Winston, Inc.

Keiser, N. F.

1975 *Macroeconomics*, 2nd ed. New York: Random House.

Kendall, C., J. Hawkins, and L. Bossen (eds.)

1983 *Heritage of Conquest Thirty Years Later*. Albuquerque: University of New Mexico Press.

King, A. R.

1974 *Coban and the Verapaz: History and Cultural Process in Northern Guatemala*. New Orleans: Tulane University, Middle American Research Institute, Publication 37.

Kluckhohn, F. R. and F. L. Strodbeck

1961 *Variations in Value Orientations*. Evanston, Ill.: Row, Peterson and Company.

Konrad, H.

1981 "A Chiclero Population: Historical-Economic Context and a Demographic Profile." *Boletín de la Escuela de Ciencias Antropológicas de la Universidad de Yucatán*.

Kristol, I.

1983 *Reflections of a Neoconservative: Looking Back, Looking Ahead*. New York: Basic Books.

Lamb, F. B.

1966 *Mahogany of Tropical America: Its Ecology and Management*. Ann Arbor: University of Michigan Press.

Latinoconsult S. A.

1968 *Programa Ganadero de La Libertad*. Santa Elena, Flores, Petén: FYDEP.

1974 *Estudio de Factibilidad de un Programa de Desarrollo de la Ganadería en el Departamento del Petén.* Guatemala: República de Guatemala.

Leyland, J.

1972 (1866) *Adventures in the Far Interior of South Africa, including a Journey to Lake Nagami and Rambles in Honduras.* Cape Town: C. Struik (Pty.) Ltd.

Lovell, G. W.

1988 "Resisting Conquest: Development and the Guatemalan Indian." In *Central America: Democracy, Development and Change*, edited by J. M. Kirk and G. W. Schuyler, 101–07. New York: Praeger.

Lundell, C. L.

1937 *The Vegetation of Peten.* Washington, D.C.: Carnegie Institution of Washington, Publication 478.

Lutes, S. V.

1987 "Yaqui Indian Enclavement: The Effects of an Experimental Indian Policy in Northwestern Mexico." In *Ejidos and Regions of Refuge in Northwestern Mexico*, edited by N. R. Crumrine and P. C. Weigand, 11–28. Tucson: Anthropological Papers of the University of Arizona, Publication 46.

MacLeod, M. J.

1983 "Ethnic Relations and Indian Society in the Province of Guatemala ca.1620 —ca.1800." In *Spaniards and Indians in Southeastern Mesoamerica: Essays on the History of Ethnic Relations*, edited by M. J. MacLeod and R. Wasserstrom, 189–214. Lincoln: University of Nebraska Press.

1985 "La Situación Legal de los Indios en América Central Durante la Colonia: Teoría y Práctica." *América Indígena* 45:485–504.

MacLeod, M. J. and R. Wasserstrom (eds.)

1983a *Spaniards and Indians in Southeastern Mesoamerica: Essays on the History of Ethnic Relations.* Lincoln: University of Nebraska Press.

1983b "Introduction" In *Spaniards and Indians in Southeastern Mesoamerica: Essays on the History of Ethnic Relations*, edited by M. J. MacLeod and R. Wasserstrom, ix-xvi. Lincoln: University of Nebraska Press.

Maler, T.

1908a *Explorations of the Upper Usumatsinta and Adjacent Region.* Cambridge, Mass.: Memoirs of the Peabody Museum, Harvard University, Vol. 4 (1).

1908b *Explorations in the Department of Petén, Guatemala and Adjacent Region.* Cambridge, Mass.: Memoirs of the Peabody Museum, Harvard University, Vol. 4 (2).

1910 *Explorations in the Department of Petén, Guatemala and Adjacent Region* Cambridge, Mass.: Memoirs of the Peabody Museum, Harvard University, Vol. 4 (3).

1911 *Explorations in the Department of Petén, Guatemala: Tikal.* Cambridge, Mass.: Memoirs of the Peabody Museum, Harvard University, Vol. 5 (1).

Manger-Cats, S.

1966 "Land Tenure and Economic Development in Guatemala." Ph. D. dissertation. Ithaca, N.Y.: Cornell University.

1971 *Tenencia de la Tierra y Desarrollo Socioeconómico del Sector Agrícola en Guatemala*, 2nd. ed. Guatemala: Editorial Universitaria.

Manz, B.

1988 *Refugees of a Hidden War: The Aftermath of Counterinsurgency in Guatemala*. Albany: State University of New York Press.

Martínez Uck, C.

1971 "Acontecimientos Históricos." *Revista Petén Itzá* 12:6–10.

Maudslay, A. C. and A. P. Maudslay

1899 *A Glimpse at Guatemala and Some Notes on the Ancient Monuments of Central America*. London: John Murray.

Mazzarelli, M.

1976a "Continuity and Change: Settlement in the Upper Belize Valley, Belize." Ph. D. dissertation. Urbana-Champaign: University of Illinois.

1976b "Ethnic Composition and Settlement in the Upper Belize Valley During the 19th Century." Mss.

McCreery, D.

1986 "'An Odious Feudalism': *Mandamiento* Labor and Commercial Agriculture in Guatemala, 1858–1920." *Latin American Perspectives* 13:99–117.

McIntosh, T.

1980 "Economic Crisis and Progress in Spatial Integration: The Case of Guatemala." *Caribbean Quarterly* 26:18–23.

McVay, C. and E. Z. Vogt

1988 "Some Contours of Social Class in a Southern Mexican Town." *Ethnology* 27:27–44.

Means, P. A.

1917 *History of the Spanish Conquest of Yucatan and of the Itzas*. Cambridge, Mass.: Papers of the Peabody Museum of American Archaeology and Ethnology, Harvard University. Vol. 7.

Mejía, J. V.

1904 *El Petén: Datos Geográficos e Históricos*. Guatemala: Tipografía Nacional.

Méndez Zetina, M. A.

1985 "Prolegómenos de Nuestra Historia Cercana." *Revista Petén Itzá* 26:7–9.

Millet, A.

1974 "The Agricultural Colonization of West Central Petén, Guatemala: A Case Study of Frontier Settlements by Cooperatives." Ph. D. dissertation. Eugene: University of Oregon.

Mónzon López, C.

1949 *Petén: Estudio Médico-Social, Geográfico-Sanitario de la Región Nor y Sudoccidental del Departamento del Petén*. Guatemala: Universidad de San Carlos.

Morelet, A.

1871 *Travels in Central America Including Some Accounts of Regions Unexplored Since the Conquest*. Translated by M. F. Squier. New York: Laypoldt, Holt and Williams.

Morley, S. G.

1938 *The Inscriptions of Petén*. Washington, D.C. : Carnegie Institution of Washington, Publication 437, Vol. 1–5.

Morley, S. G. and G. W. Brainerd
  1956 *The Ancient Maya*, 3rd ed. Stanford, Ca.: Stanford University Press.
Morley, S. G., G. W. Brainerd, and R. J. Sharer
  1983 *The Ancient Maya*, 4th ed. Stanford, Ca.: Stanford University Press.
Munch, P. A. and C. E. Marske
  1981 "Atomism and Social Integration." *Journal of Anthropological Research* 37:158–71.
Munro, D. G.
  1918 *The Five Republics of Central America*. New York: Oxford University Press.
Narciso, V. A.
  1913 *Album de Recuerdos, Expedición Musical al Petén y Belice, 1910–1913*. Guatemala: Imprenta de Síguere y Cía.
Nations, J. and R. Nigh
  1980 "The Evolutionary Potential of Lacandon Maya Sustained-Yield Tropical Forest Agriculture." *Journal of Anthropological Research* 36:1–30.
Ollo, A. del
  1870 "Población del Departamento del Peten Habido en el Año de 1869." *Gaceta de Guatemala* 16 (77):1–2.
Pan American Union
  1948 *Selected Economic Data on the Latin American Republics*. Washington, D.C.: Pan American Union.
Parker, F. D. (ed.)
  1970 *Travels in Central America, 1821–1840*. Gainesville: University Presses of Florida.
Partridge, W. L.
  1979 "Banana Country in the Wake of United Fruit: Social and Economic Linkages." *American Ethnologist* 6:491–509.
  1984 "The Humid Tropics Cattle Ranching Complex." *Human Organization* 43:165– 75.
Patch, R. W.
  1985 "Agrarian Change in Eighteenth-Century Yucatán." *Hispanic American Historical Review* 65:21–49.
Pendergast, D. M. (ed.)
  1967 *Palenque: The Walker-Caddy Expedition to the Ancient Maya City, 1839– 1840*. Norman: University of Oklahoma Press.
Pinelo, J. A.
  1937 "Monografía del Departamento de El Petén." *Revista Petén Itzá*.
  1941 "El Tratado Menche-Segura." *Revista Petén Itzá* 27:5–6.
Pitt-Rivers, J. A.
  1954 *The People of the Sierra*. London: Weidenfeld and Nicolson.
Pohl, M.
  1977 "Hunting in the Maya Village of San Antonio Rio Hondo, Orange Walk, Belize." *Journal of Belizean Affairs* 5:52–63.
Posey, D. A., J. Frechione, J. Eddins, and L. F. da Silva
  1984 "Ethnoecology as Applied Anthropology in Amazonian Development." *Human Organization* 43:95–107.

Ramírez M., R.

1980 *Monografía de La Libertad, Petén.* Guatemala: Apolo.

Redfield, R. and A. Villa Rojas

1962 *Chan Kom: A Maya Village,* 2nd ed. Chicago: University of Chicago Press.

Reina, R. E.

1962 "The Ritual of the Skull in Peten, Guatemala." *Expedition* 4:25–35.

1964 "The Urban World View of a Tropical Forest Community in the Absence of a City, Peten, Guatemala." *Human Organization* 23:265–77.

1965 "Town, Community and Multicommunity." *Estudios de Cultura Maya* 5:361–90.

1966 "A Peninsula That May Have Been an Island: Tayasal, Petén, Guatemala." *Expedition* 9:16–29.

1967 "Milpas and Milperos: Implications for Prehistoric Times." *American Anthropologist* 69:1–20.

1968 "Reflections on William Haviland's Comments." *American Anthropologist* 70:565–68.

1984 *Shadows: A Mayan Way of Knowing.* New York: Horizon Press.

Reina, R. E. and N. B. Schwartz

1974 "The Structural Context of Religious Conversion in Peten, Guatemala: Status, Community and Multi-Community." *American Ethnologist* 1:157–91.

Rice, D. S.

1978 "Population Growth and Subsistence Alternatives in a Tropical Lacustrine Environment." In *Pre-Hispanic Maya Agriculture,* edited by P. D. Harrison and B. L. Turner II, 35–62. Albuquerque: University of New Mexico Press.

Rice, D. S. and P. M. Rice

1984 "Lessons from the Maya." *Latin American Research Review* 19:7–34.

Richards, M.

1985 "Cosmopolitan World View and Counterinsurgency in Guatemala." *Anthropological Quarterly* 58:90–107.

Rodríguez Macal, V.

1967 *Guayacán,* 2nd ed. Guatemala: Ministerio de Educación.

Ross, J.

1988 "Mexico: Chimalapas Forest Falls to Loggers, Oil Pipelines, Poppy and Marijuana Fields." *Latin American Press* (Lima, Peru) 21 July:5–6.

Rubel, A. J.

1977 "'Limited Good' and 'Social Comparison': Two Theories, One Problem." *Ethos* 5:224–38.

Saa Vidal, R.

1979 *Mapa de Cobertura y Uso Actual de la Tierra.* Guatemala: Secretaría General del Consejo Nacional de Planificación Económica.

Salati, E.

1985 "The Climatology and Hydrology of Amazonia." In *Key Environments: Amazonia,* edited by G. T. Prance and T. E. Lovejoy, 18–24. Oxford: Pergamon Press.

Sanchez, P. A.
1981 "Soils of the Humid Tropics." In *Blowing in the Wind: Deforestation and Long-Range Implications*, edited by V. Sutlive, N. Altshuler, and M. Zamora, 347–410. Williamsburg, Va. Studies in Third World Societies, Publication 14.

Sanders, W. T.
1977 "Environmental Heterogeneity and the Evolution of Lowland Maya Civilization." In *The Origins of Maya Civilization*, edited by R. E. W. Adams, 287–97. Albuquerque: University of New Mexico Press.

Santley, R. S., T. W. Killion, and M. T. Lycett
1986 "On the Maya Collapse." *Journal of Anthropological Research* 43:163–83.

Saul, F. P.
1973 "Disease in the Maya Area: The Pre-Columbian Evidence." In *The Classic Maya Collapse*, edited by T. P. Culbert, 301–24. Albuquerque: University of New Mexico Press.

Scholes, F. V. and R. L. Roys
1968 *The Maya Chontol Indians of Acalan-Tixchel: A Contribution to the History and Ethnography of the Yucatán Peninsula*, 2nd ed. Norman: University of Oklahoma Press.

Schufeldt, P. W.
1950 "Reminiscences of a Chiclero." In *Morleyana: A Collection of Writings in Memorium Sylvanus Griswold Morley—1883–1948*, edited by A. J. O. Anderson, 224–29. Santa Fe: School of American Research and Museum of New Mexico.

Schumann G., O.
1971 "Descripción Estructural del Maya Itzá del Petén, Guatemala, C. A." *Centro de Estudios Mayas* Cuaderno 6. México: Universidad Nacional Autónoma de México.

Schwartz, N. B.
1968 "The Latent Functions of Factionalism in a Northern Guatemalan Town." Ph. D. dissertation. Philadelphia: University of Pennsylvania.
1969 "Conflict Resolution and Impropriety in a Guatemalan Town." *Social Forces* 48:98–106.
1971 "Assimilation and Acculturation: Aspects of Ethnicity in a Guatemalan Town." *Ethnology* 10:291–310.
1974 "Milperos, Chicleros and Rituals of Passage in El Petén, Guatemala." *Cultures et développement* 4:369–95.
1983 "San Simon: Ambiguity and Identity in Petén, Guatemala." *Sociologus* 33:152–73.
1985 "A Note on 'Weights, Measures,' and Swidden". *Culture and Agriculture* 3:9–12.
1987 "Colonization of Northern Guatemala: The Petén." *Journal of Anthropological Research* 43:163–83.

Schwartz, N. B. and K. W. Eckhardt
1979 "Values, Ethnicity and Acculturation in Petén, Guatemala." *Cultures et développement* 11:219–46.

Scott, J. C. and B. J. Kerkvliet
  1973 "How Traditional Rural Patrons Lose Legitimacy: A Theory with Special Reference to Lowland Southeast Asia." *Cultures et développement* 5:501–40.
Sexton, J. D. (ed. and translator)
  1985 *Campesino: The Diary of a Guatemalan Indian*. Tucson: University of Arizona Press.
Shattuck, G. C.
  1933 *The Peninsula of Yucatan, Medical, Biological, Meteorological and Sociological Studies*. Washington, D.C.: Carnegie Institute of Washington, Publication 431.
Shimkin, D. B.
  1973 "Models for the Downfall: Some Ecological and Culture-Historical Considerations." In *The Classic Maya Collapse*, edited by T. P. Culbert, 269–99. Albuquerque: University of New Mexico Press.
Sierro Franco, R.
  1941 "Importancia de la Explotación del Caucho en Guatemala." *Studium* 51–68.
Silvert, K. H.
  1954 *A Study in Government: Guatemala*. New Orleans: Tulane University, Middle American Research Institute, Publication 21.
Simmons, C. S., J. M. Tárano, and J. H. Pinto Z.
  1959 *Clasificación de Reconocimiento de los Suelos de la República de Guatemala*. Guatemala: Ministerio de Educación Pública.
Smith, C. A.
  1988 "Destruction of the Material Bases for Indian Culture: Economic Changes in Totonicapán." In *Harvest of Violence: The Maya Indians and the Guatemalan Crisis*, edited by R. M. Carmack, 206–31. Norman: University of Oklahoma Press.
Soza, J. M.
  1957 *Pequeña Monografía del Petén*. Guatemala: Ministerio de Educación Pública.
  1970 *Monografía del Departamento de El Petén*, 2nd ed. Guatemala: Ministerio de Educación, Vol. 9 and 10.
Stone, D. Z.
  1932 "Some Spanish Entradas, 1524–1695." New Orleans: Tulane University, Middle American Research Series, Publication 4:210–96.
Stravakis, O.
  1979 "The Effect of Agricultural Change upon Social Relations and Diet in a Village in Northern Belize." Ph. D. dissertation. Minneapolis: University of Minnesota.
Swetnam, J.
  1989 "What Else Did Indians Have to Do With Their Time? Alternatives to Labor Migration in Pre-Revolutionary Guatemala." *Economic Development and Cultural Change* 38:89–112.
Tax, S.
  1952 "Economy and Technology." In *Heritage of Conquest: The Ethnology of Middle America*, by S. Tax and members of the Viking Fund Seminar on Middle American Ethnology, 43–75. Glencoe, Ill.: Free Press.

Tedlock, B.
   1987 "An Interpretive Solution to the Problem of Humoral Medicine in Latin America." *Social Science and Medicine* 24:1069–83.
Teracena de la Cerda, E.
   1974 *Cooperativas de El Petén: Recursos Económicos.* Guatemala: Universidad de San Carlos.
Thompson, G. A.
   1829 *Narrative of an Official Visit to Guatemala and Mexico.* London: John Murray.
Thompson, J. E. S.
   1930 *Ethnology of the Mayas of Southern and Central British Honduras.* Chicago: Field Museum of Natural History, Anthropology Series 17(1).
   1938 "Sixteenth and Seventeenth Century Reports on the Chol Mayas." *American Anthropologist* 40:584–604.
   1963 *Maya Archaeologist.* Norman: University of Oklahoma Press.
   1966 *The Rise and Fall of Maya Civilization*, 2nd ed. Norman: University of Oklahoma Press.
   1970 *Maya History and Religion.* Norman: University of Oklahoma Press.
   1977 "A Proposal for Constituting a Maya Subgroup, Cultural and Linguistic, in the Petén and Adjacent Areas." In *Anthropology and History in Yucatán*, edited by G. D. Jones, 3–42. Austin: University of Texas Press.
Todaro, M. P.
   1985 *Economic Development in the Third World*, 3rd ed. New York: Longman.
United Nations
   1953–1960 *Yearbooks of International Trade Statistics.* New York: United Nations Statistical Office.
Urrutia R., V. M.
   1967 "Corn Production and Soil Fertility Changes under Shifting Cultivation in Uaxactún, Guatemala." MA thesis. Gainesville: University of Florida.
Valdavida, F.
   1975 "Notas Tomadas del Archivo Colonial y Otras Notas Varias para Historia del Petén." Mss. San Benito, Petén: Parroquia de San Benito.
Valenzuela, S.
   1879 "Informe Sobre el Departamento del Petén, Dirigido al Ministerio de Fomento." Reprinted in *Revista Petén Itzá* 1980 21:19–56.
Villacorta C., J. A.
   1942 *Historia de la Capitanía General de Guatemala.* Guatemala: Tipografía Nacional.
Villagutierre Soto-Mayor, Juan de, don
   1983 *History of the Conquest of the Province of the Itzá.* Translated by Br. R. D. Wood, S. M. Notes by F. E. Comparato. Culver City, Ca.: Labyrinthos.
Wadell, H.
   1938 "Physical-Geographic Features of Petén, Guatemala." In S. G. Morley, *The Inscriptions of Petén.* Appendix 1, 4:336–48. Washington, D. C.: Carnegie Institution of Washington, Publication 437.

Wauchope, R.

　1965 *They Found the Buried Cities: Exploration and Excavation in the American Tropics*. Chicago: University of Chicago Press.

Webster, B.

　1983 "Forest's Role in Weather Documented in Amazon." *New York Times* 5 July.

Weeks, J.

　1986 "An Interpretation of the Central American Crisis." *Latin American Research Review* 21:31–53.

Weinstein, B.

　1983 *The Amazon Rubber Boom, 1850–1920*. Stanford, Ca.: Stanford University Press.

Weston, J.

　1985 *The Real American Cowboy*. New York: Schocken Books.

Whetton, N. L.

　1961 *Guatemala: The Land and the People*. New Haven, Conn.: Yale University Press.

Wilk, R. R.

　1981 "Agriculture, Ecology and Domestic Organization among the Kekchí Maya." Ph. D. dissertation. Tucson: University of Arizona.

Wilkie, J. W., D. E. Lorey, and E. Ochoa (eds.)

　1988 *Statistical Abstract of Latin America* Vol. 26. Los Angeles: UCLA Latin American Center Publications.

Willey, G. R., A. L. Smith, G. Tourtelot III, and I. Graham

　1975 *Excavations at Seibal: Department of Peten*. Cambridge, Mass.: Memoirs of the Peabody Musuem of Archaeolo and Ethnology, Harvard University, Vol. 13(1).

Williams, R. G.

　1986 *Export Agriculture and the Crisis in Central America*. Chapel Hill: University of North Carolina Press.

Williams, T. D.

　1965 "Wastage Rates and Teacher Quality in Guatemalan Primary Schools." *Comparative Education Review* 9:46–52.

Wiseman, F. M.

　1978 "Agricultural and Historical Ecology of the Maya Lowlands." In *Pre-Hispanic Maya Agriculture*, edited by P. D. Harrison and B. L. Turner II, 63–115. Albuquerque: University of New Mexico Press.

Woodward, R. L.

　1966 *Class Privilege and Economic Development: The Consulado de Comercio of Guatemala, 1793–1871*. Chapel Hill: University of North Carolina Press.

　1985 *Central America: A Nation Divided*, 2nd ed. New York: Oxford University Press.

Worldmark Encyclopedia

　1984 *Worldmark Encyclopedia of the Nations*, 6th ed. 153–60. New York: Worldmark Press and J. Wiley and Sons Vol.3.

Wortman, M. L.
   1982 *Government and Society in Central America, 1680–1840*. New York: Columbia
      University Press.
Wyld Ospina, C.
   1956 "The Honor of His House," In *Spanish Stories and Tales*, edited by H. de
      Onis, 87–93. New York: Pocket Books.
Zetina O., F. E.
   1980 "Petén Misterioso: 3 Alternativas." *Revista Petén Itzá* 21:11.

Index

This book has been set in Linotron Galliard. Galliard was designed for Merganthaler in 1978 by Matthew Carter. Galliard retains many of the features of a sixteenth century typeface cut by Robert Granjon but has some modifications which give it a more contemporary look.

Printed on acid-free paper.